Feliz Cumple, Hugito—
Wishing you an amazing 30-something birthday full of more fun times together! 2016 is going to be wonderful and have us spinning like Liza Minelli.
♡ you and wishing you many more wonderful years, vieja.
♡ Christian.
January 2016.

always go

Happy Birthday, To my Best Friend ever. I can not wait to visit TX with you! I am so happy we are all friends. You are a great addition to mine & Christian's life. We are forever greatful that we met. Heres to another great year together. Happy 40th!
♡ Brandon
Jan 2016

J/K Someday I hope you will let me in on lifes greatest mystery "your age"

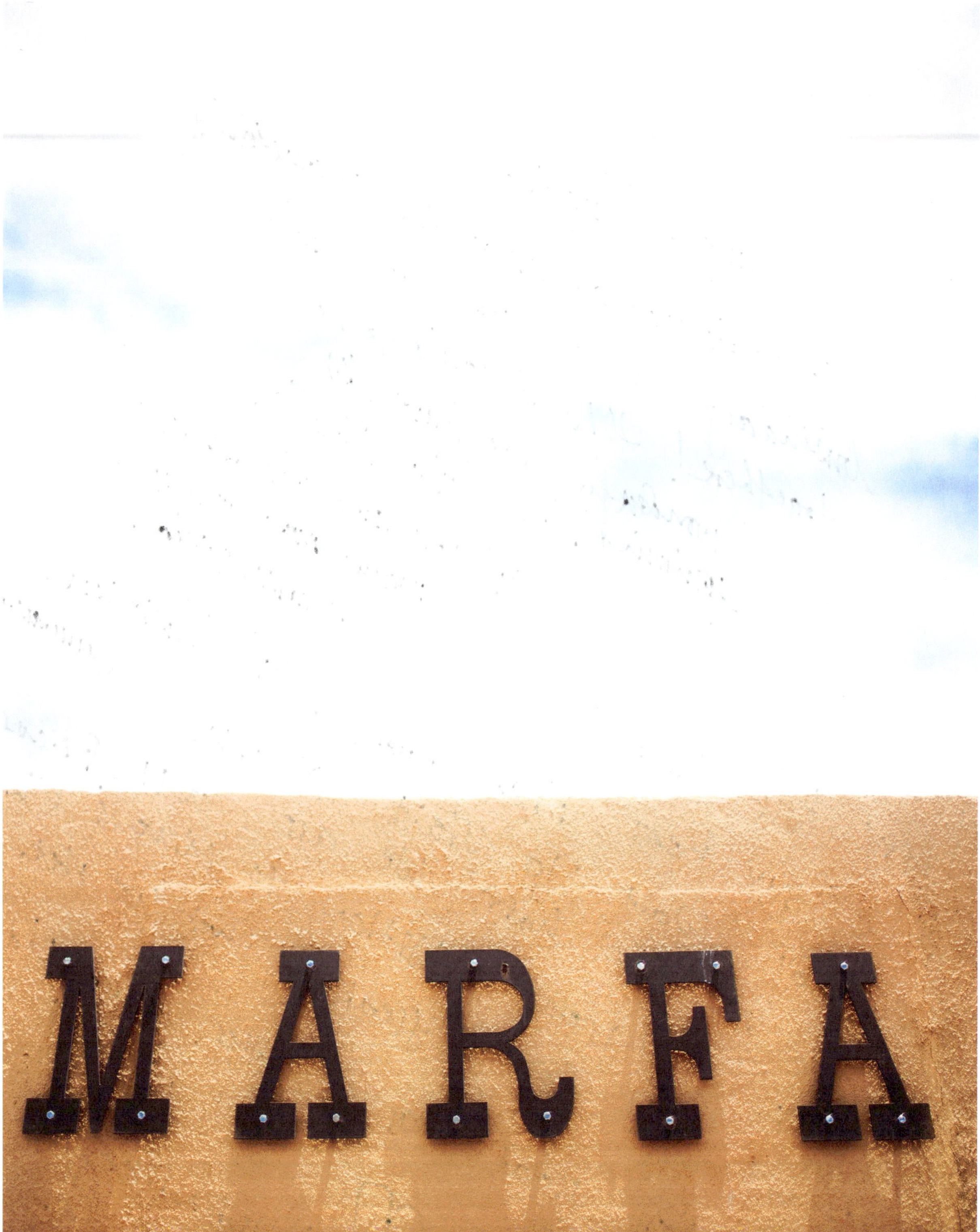
MARFA

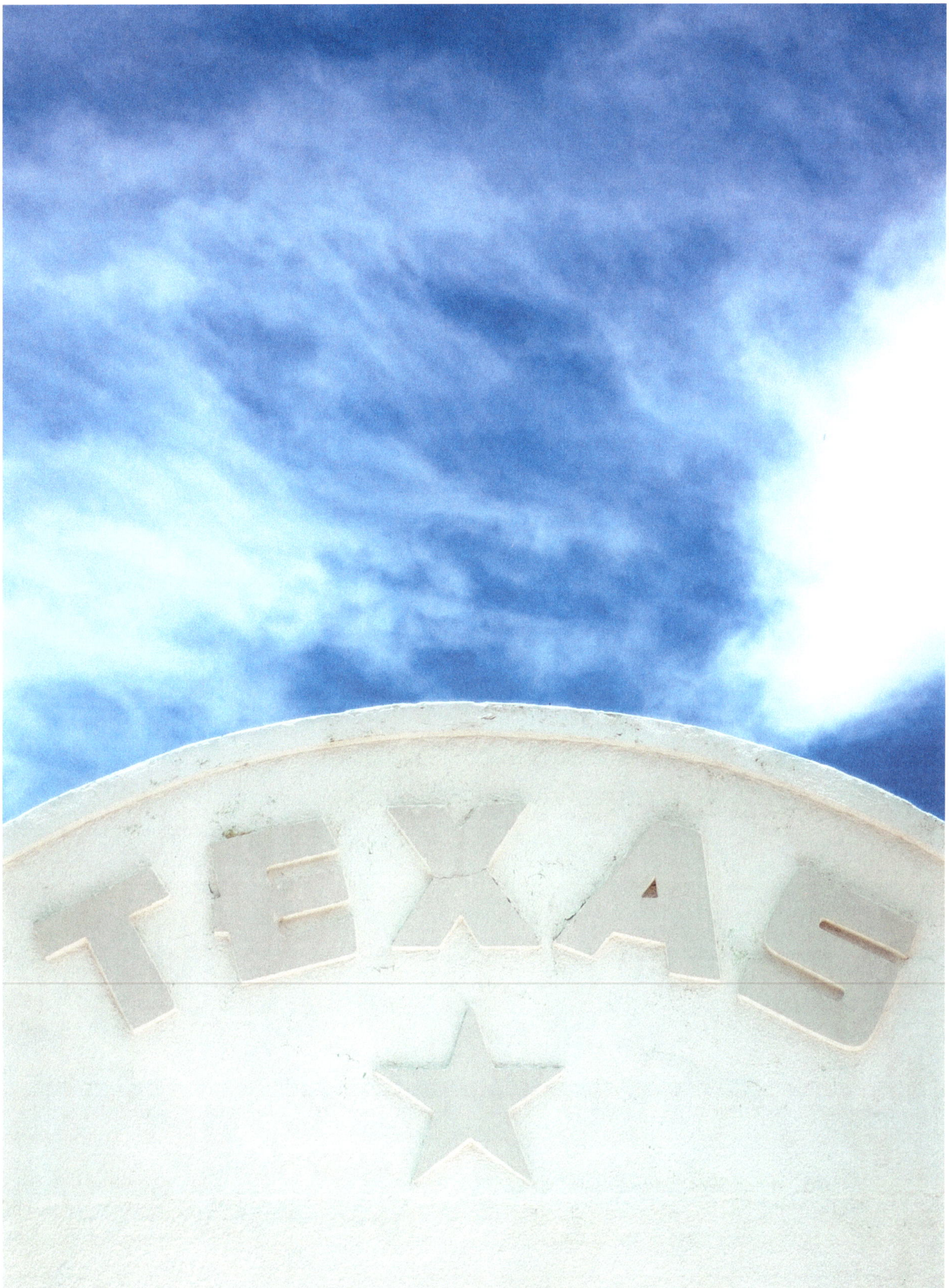
TEXAS

THE

COLLECTIVE

Qtrly

ISSUE Ø MARFA

CREATIVE DIRECTOR
Jesse Lenz

EDITORIAL DIRECTOR
Seth Putnam

DESIGN DIRECTOR
Jesse Southerland

PHOTOGRAPHER Jay Gullion

ILLUSTRATOR Lucy Engelman

CONTRIBUTING EDITOR Adam Risman

COPY EDITORS Carly Dyer, Matt Pollock

CONTRIBUTING WRITERS Emily Ferber, Max Wastler

CONTRIBUTING PHOTOGRAPHERS
Garrett Cornelison, Alex Marks, Kevin Russ, Neal Warren

CHIEF FINANCIAL OFFICER Isaiah Richie

MERCHANDISE DIRECTOR Alexandra Sklar

STOCKISTS
sales@collectivequarterly.com

ADVERTISERS
advertising@collectivequarterly.com

SUBMISSIONS
submit@collectivequarterly.com

SUBSCRIBE
Four Volumes: US $100

Instagram: @collectivequarterly
Facebook: /collectivequarterly
Twitter: @collectiveqtrly

WWW.COLLECTIVEQUARTERLY.COM

The Collective Quarterly
715 Frew Circle
Middlebourne, WV 26149

Content designed proudly in the USA
Printed in Canada by Hemlock Printers Ltd.

HOW TO EXPERIENCE THIS MAGAZINE

See something you like while exploring these pages?
Scan with your phone to find out how to make it yours.

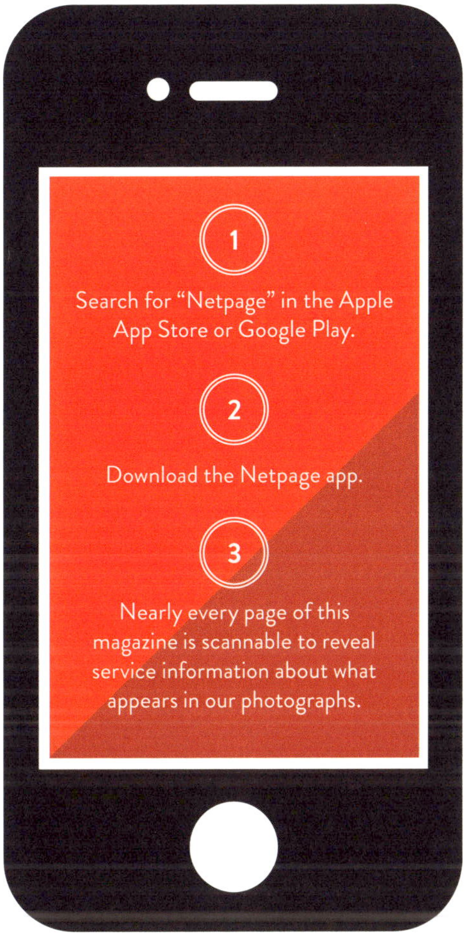

Quality, objective storytelling is this magazine's first commitment. We have decided to move away from the interruption of traditional page ads. Instead, our sponsors outfit and equip us to go tell compelling stories that are unrelated to their companies. We maintain a strong separation between editorial and advertising by not writing features about our advertisers.

Rather than telling you that you need to wear, drink, or use a certain product to be a better version of yourself, we've tried to present a lifestyle—gear we use in our own lives, made by companies we respect.

Ø

CONTENTS

MARFA

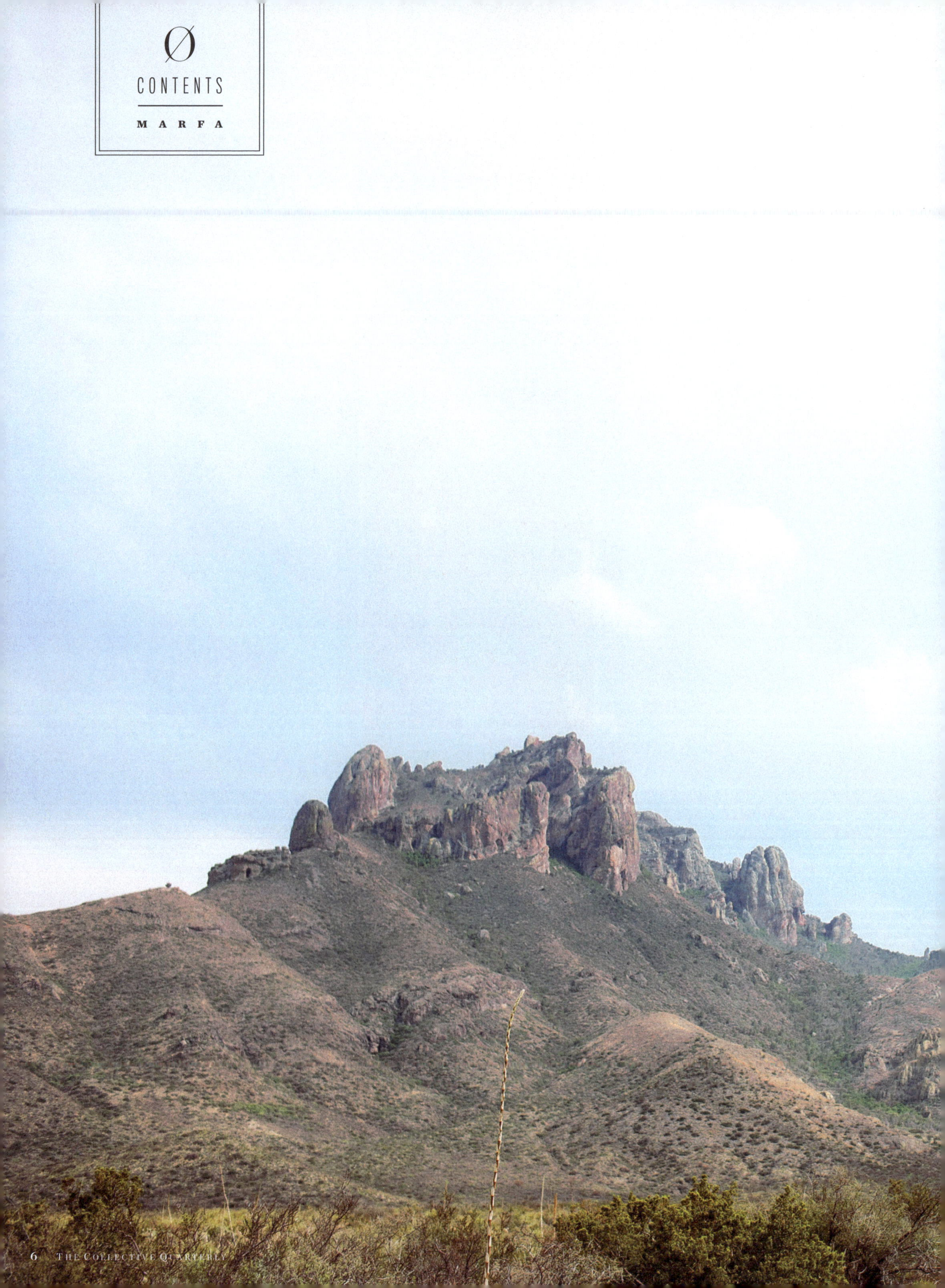

ISSUE Ø

MARFA, TEXAS 20

ON THE ROAD 110

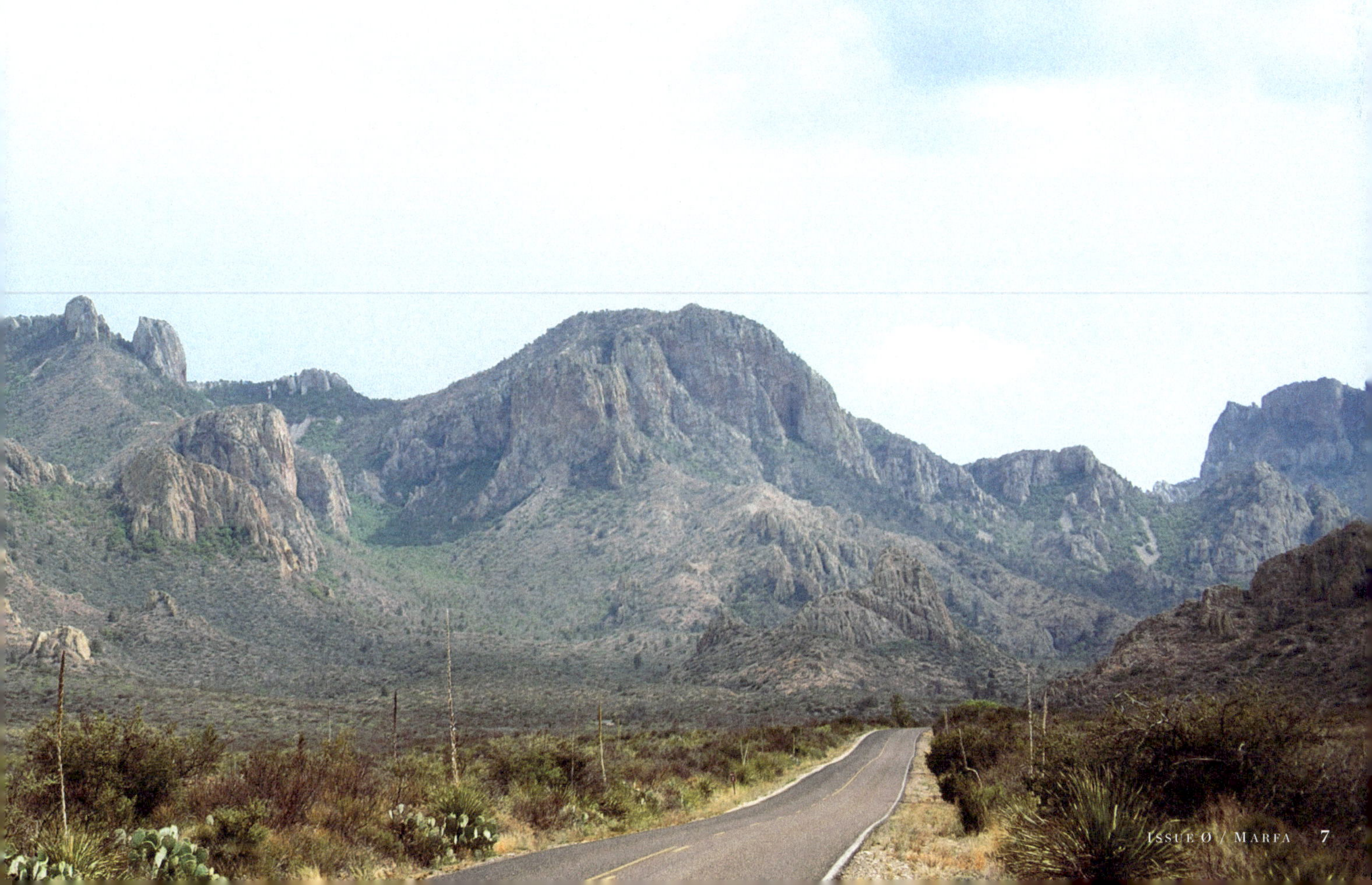

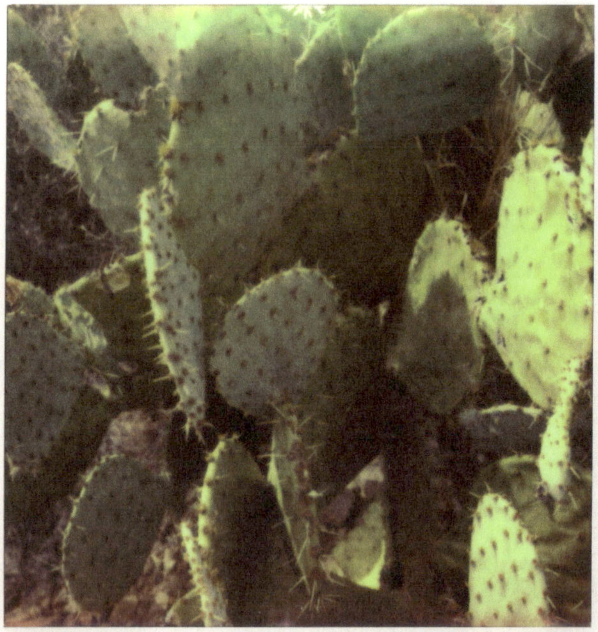

THIS IS A MAGAZINE ABOUT EXPLORING

Each issue follows select craftspeople to an offbeat location. Our camera lens brings into focus the often blurry creative process as they design uncommon objects. In these pages, you'll find a carefully edited selection of dry goods, art, music, food, drink, and stories—all deeply rooted in the land and heritage around us.

Our journeys hinge on assembling a group of compatriots who aim to live well. We are illustrators, photographers, and writers. We are weavers, leather workers, and carpenters. We are chefs, musicians, and bartenders.

We are the Collective.

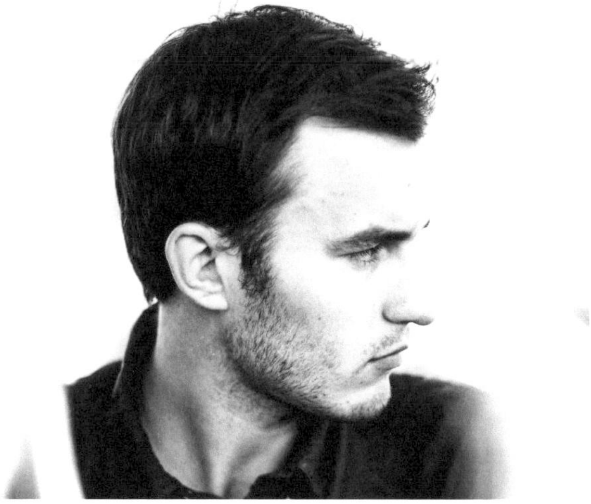

JOHN MOOTY is the creative director at the Faribault Woolen Mill Company. The Minnesota-based purveyor of blankets, scarves, and other dry goods is storied for its devoted craftspeople and 148-year-old heritage. In this issue, John discovers a string of vivid southwestern dyes and textures that inspire a unique departure from Faribault's classic northern lineup.

FARIBAULTMILL.COM

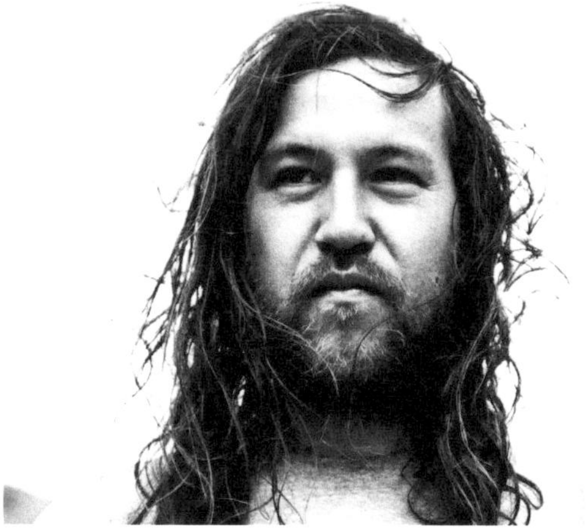

KEVIN RUSS is a landscape photographer currently roving North and Central America. His keen eye for the natural world and his iPhone-only approach form a modern embodiment of a photographic style with roots in the early 1900s. In this issue, Kevin disappears into Big Bend National Park and small-town Mexico, only to re-emerge with a stunning collection of rare vistas.

KEVINRUSS.TUMBLR.COM

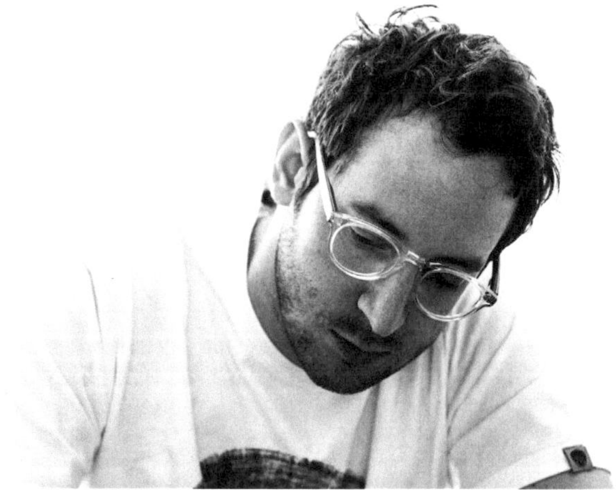

CHRIS MANTZ is the owner of Drift Eyewear, which makes glasses from reclaimed hardwood by hand in Chicago. Their minimalistic cases are made from leather tanned at the legendary Horween Company. In this issue, Chris calls upon his visit to the Chinati Foundation, juxtaposed against the scorched West Texas landscape, to create a limited-edition pair of sunglasses.

DRIFTEYEWEAR.COM

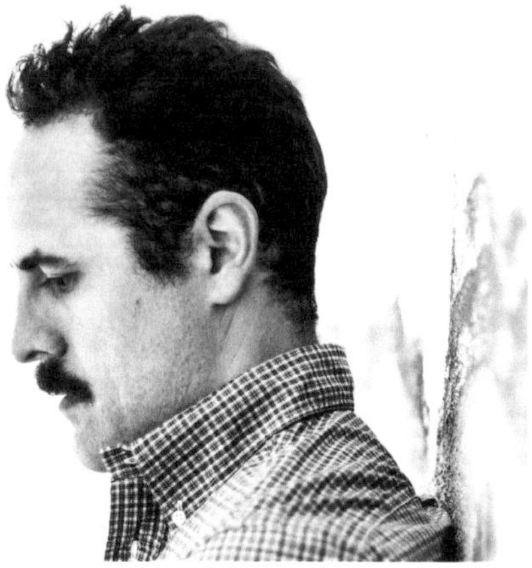

MAX WASTLER is a traveling storyteller whose popular website All Plaidout documents the intricate stories behind heritage goods and icons of American life. He's also an ambassador for Basil Hayden's bourbon. In this issue, Max makes friends with the saloonkeepers, hatters, saddle makers, cobblers, and raspa vendors of Presidio County to find out what drives them.

ALLPLAIDOUT.COM

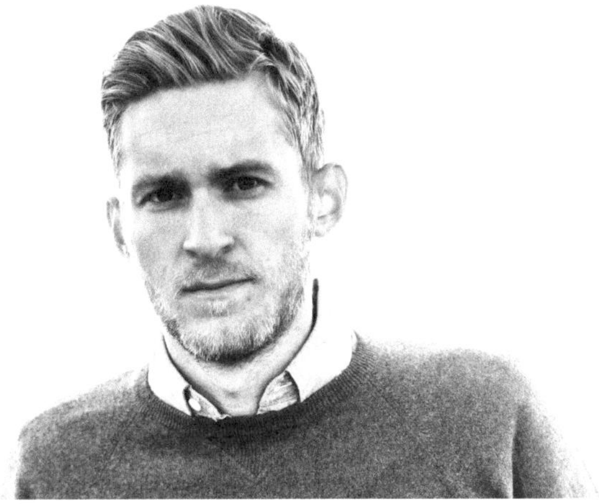

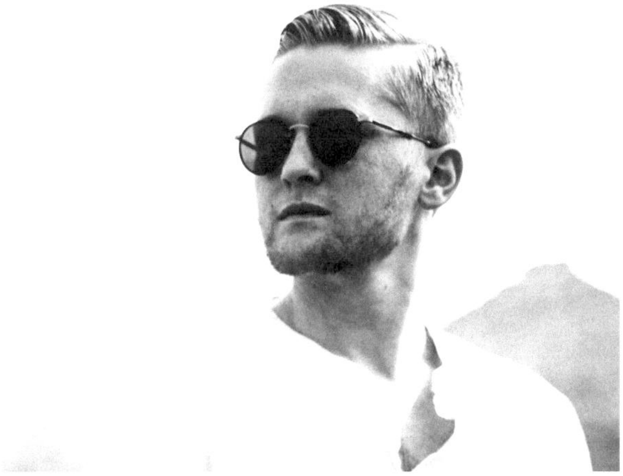

JESSE LENZ is the magazine's creative director. His vision has driven the entire concept of the magazine, from idea to execution. He shot and edited a large portion of the photographs and oversaw the design of the Marfa issue. He lives in the quiet hills of West Virginia with his wife, two sons, and Bull Terrier, Tiberius.

SETH PUTNAM is the magazine's editor. He developed the written voice of the Collective Quarterly. In this issue, he explores a lost Mexican pueblo and dissects creative processes of Mantz, Mooty, Russ, and Wastler. He lives in the City of Big Shoulders, where he writes about living well and coaches high school soccer.

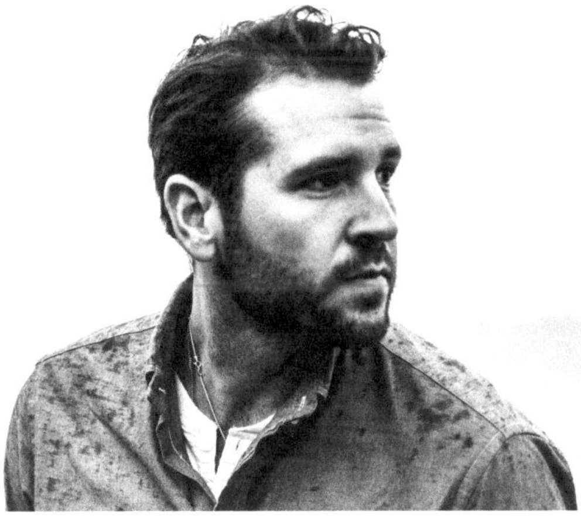

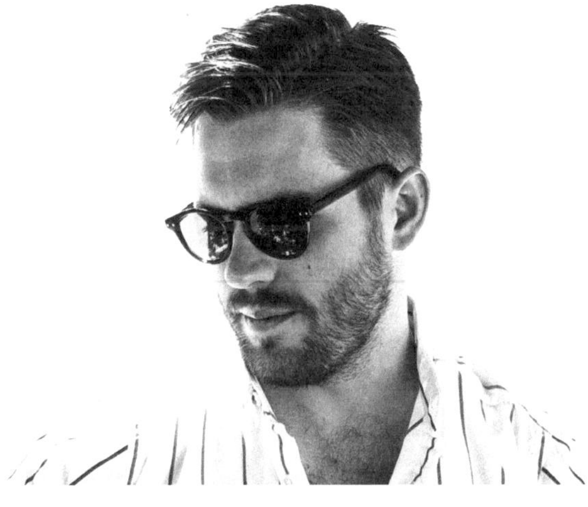

JAY GULLION is the magazine's head photographer. His pictorial eye has influenced the visual storyline of the Marfa issue, and his talent for organizational culture has inspired the very development of the company. Jay is a leader at an online media company and lives in Ohio with his wife and two extraordinary daughters.

DUNCAN WOLFE is the magazine's videographer. He uses Chicago as his home base for jet-setting abroad to record everything from secret weddings in Paris to Nike commercials in Istanbul. In this issue, Duncan sallies forth across the Rio Grande, roams the desolate highways that wind through Big Bend, and captures Marfa in motion.

MUCH OBLIGED

The **VISUAL SUPPLY CO.** makes film effects for digital photo editing. These products, more than any other, have influenced the aesthetic of this magazine from surface to core. The creative team behind **VSCO** has been a consistent source of inspiration, and they repeatedly demonstrate a lifestyle worth emulating. www.vsco.co

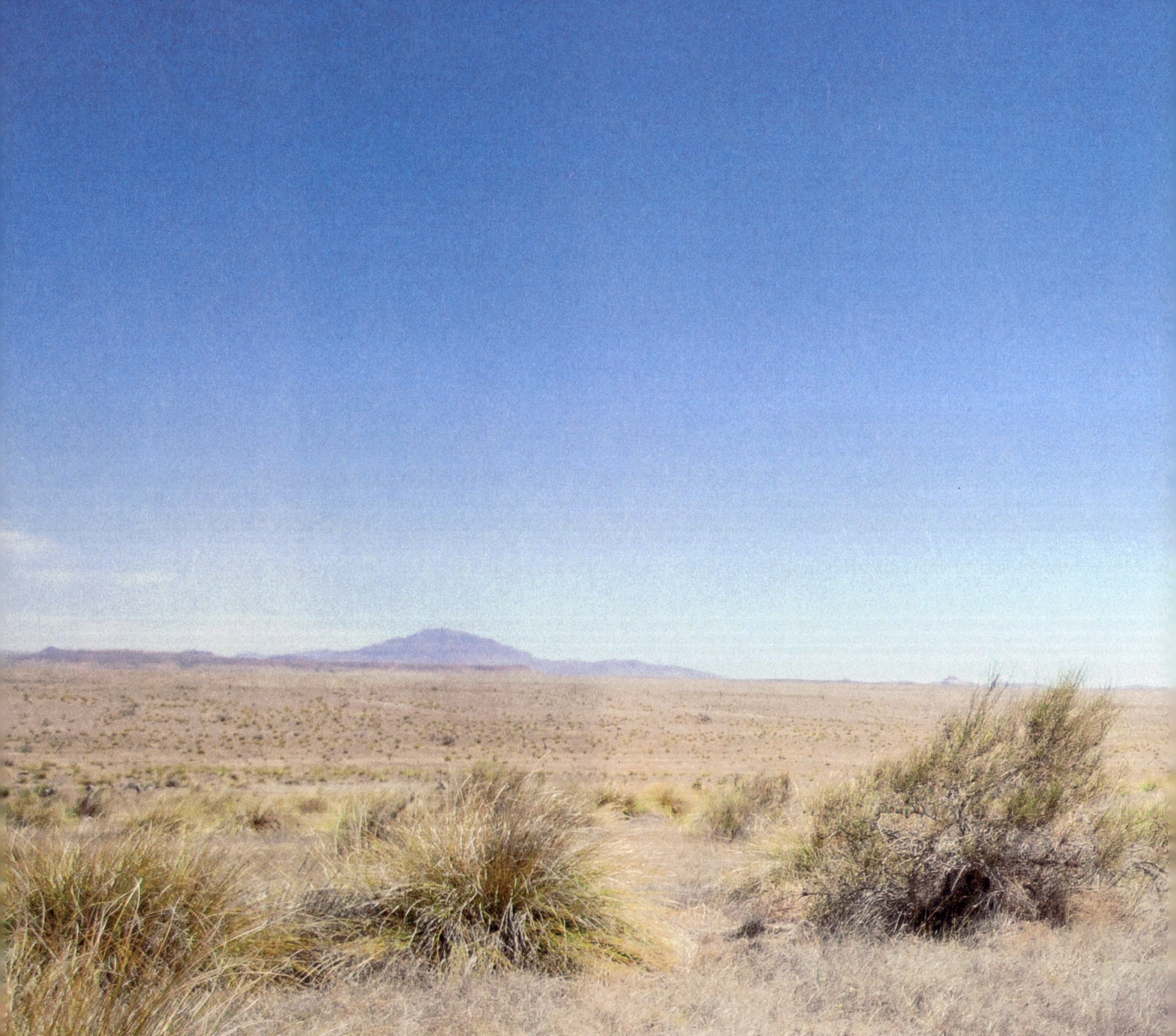

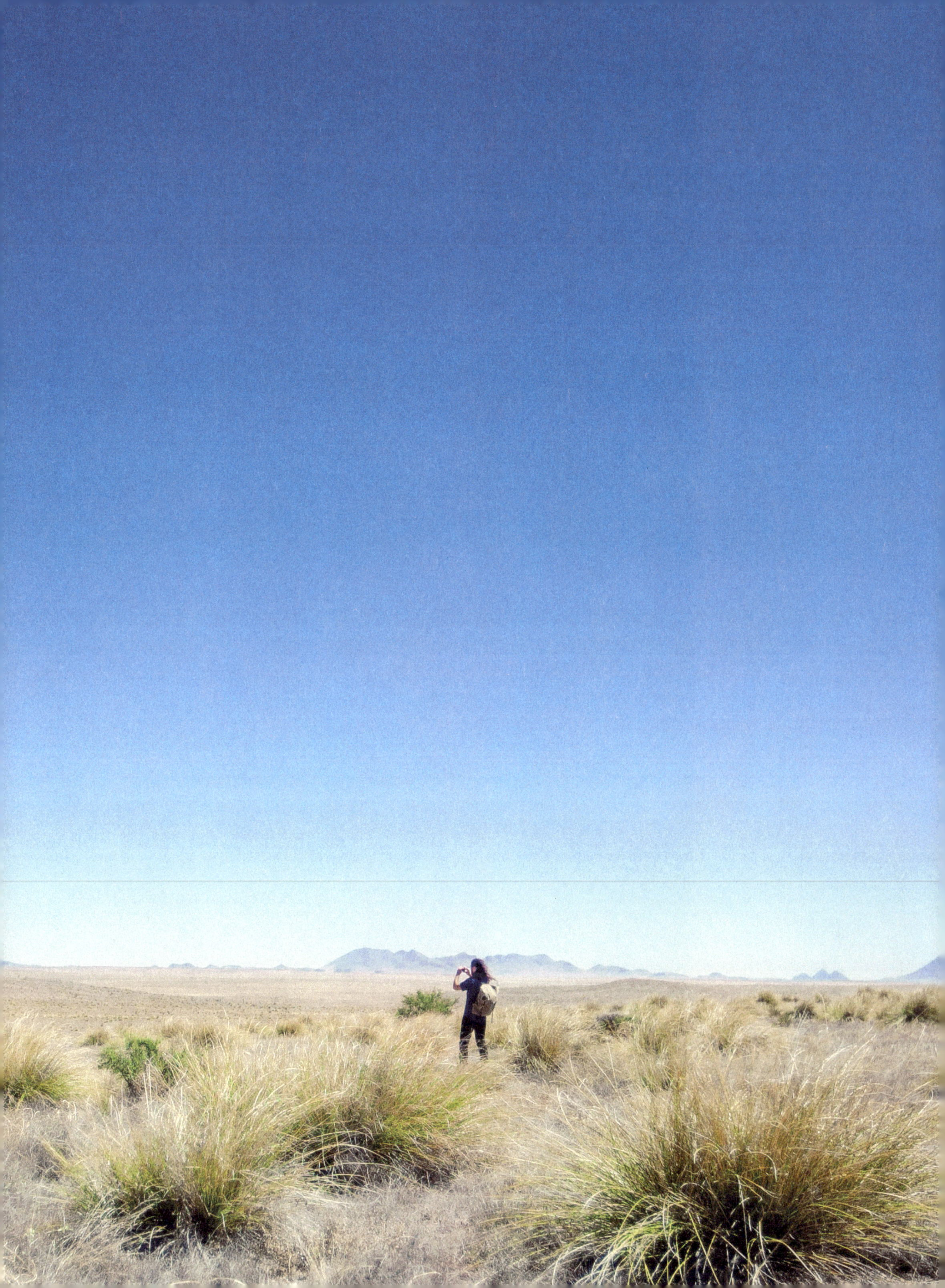

MUCH OBLIGED

Because of the **IMPOSSIBLE PROJECT**, the magic of instant photography is alive, healthy, and available to enthusiasts everywhere. The company picked up where Polaroid left off by refurbishing analog cameras and producing film that's compatible with them. It's a project that has revived a declining medium, making what was previously thought impossible quite the opposite. Our thanks.
www.the-impossible-project.com

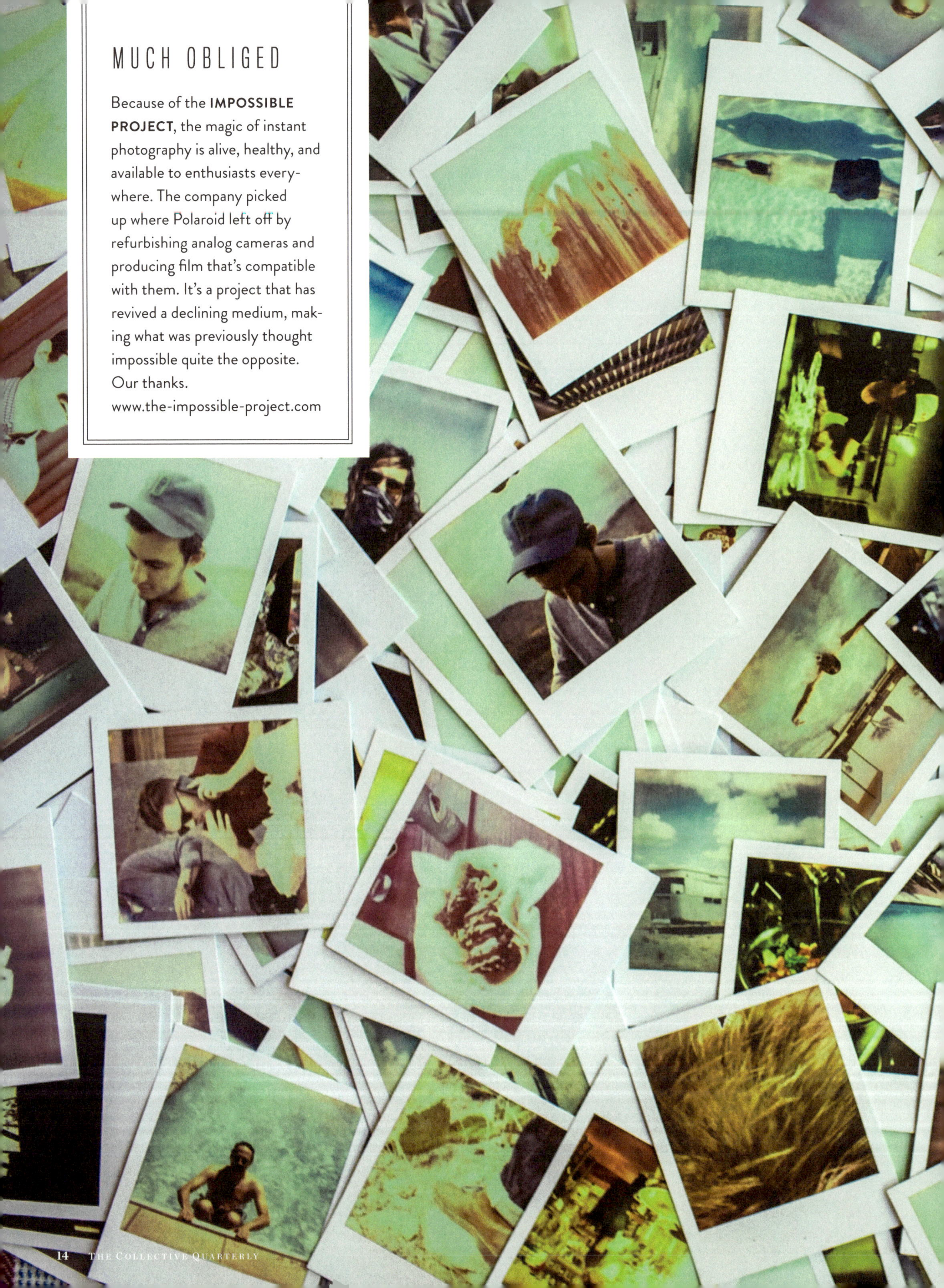

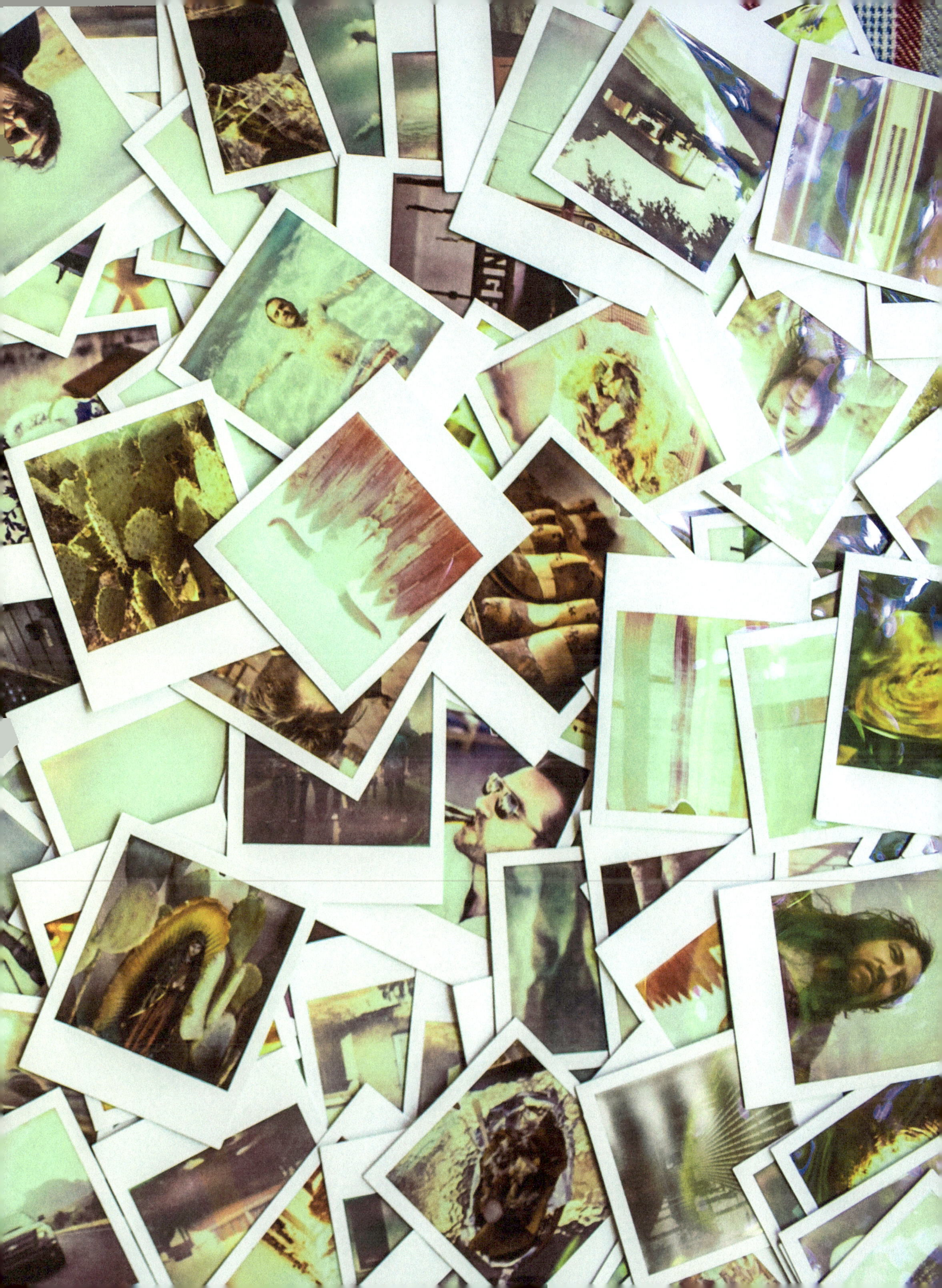

MUCH OBLIGED

Out in the desolate network of Texas roadways, reliable transportation becomes a necessity—right up there with food, water, and shelter. We're grateful to **FORD MOTOR COMPANY** for providing the brand-new Explorer Sport that carried us to Marfa, Mexico, Big Bend National Park, and beyond. Without it, we would have been well and truly lost. www.ford.com

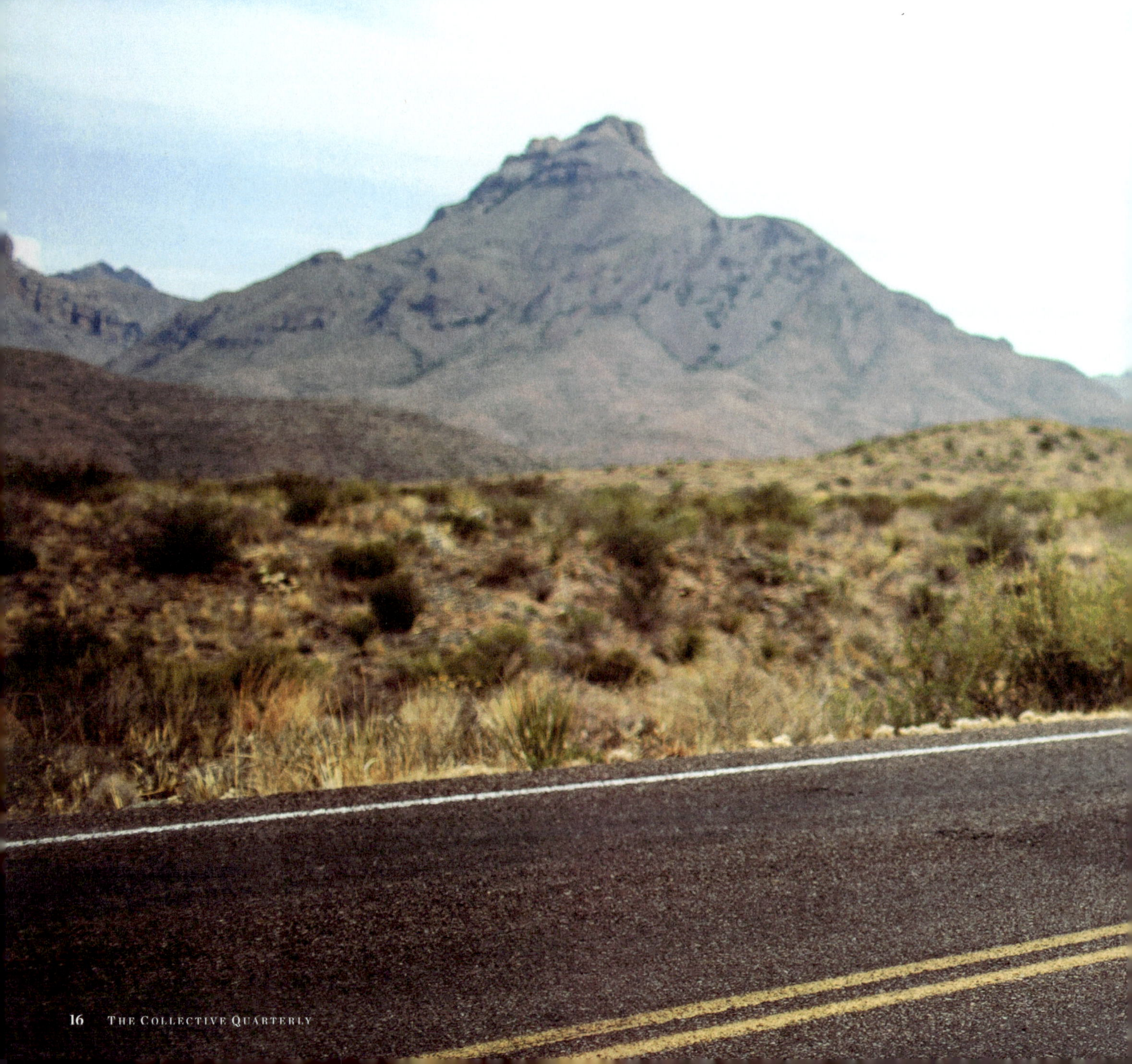

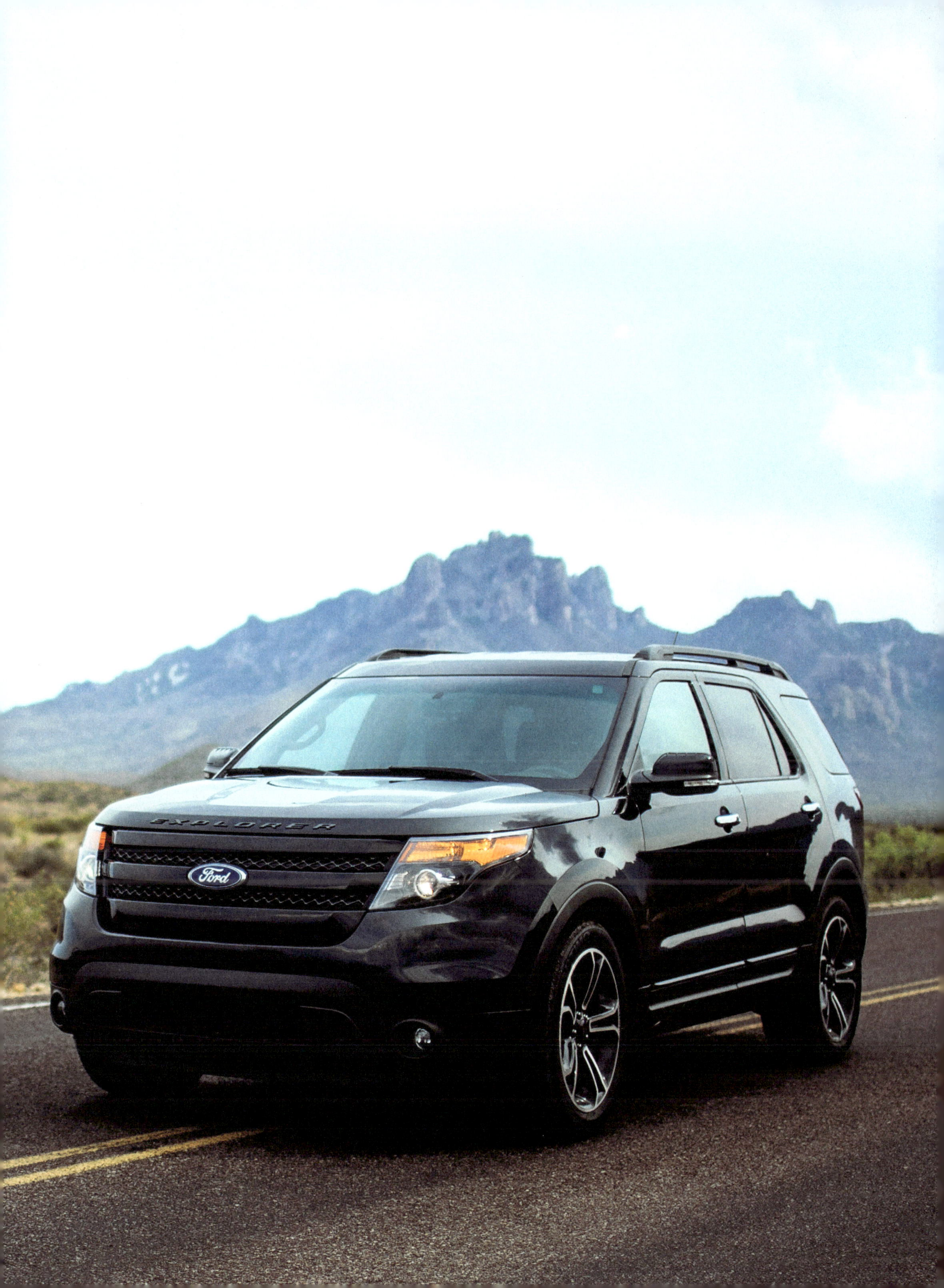
EXPLORER
Ford

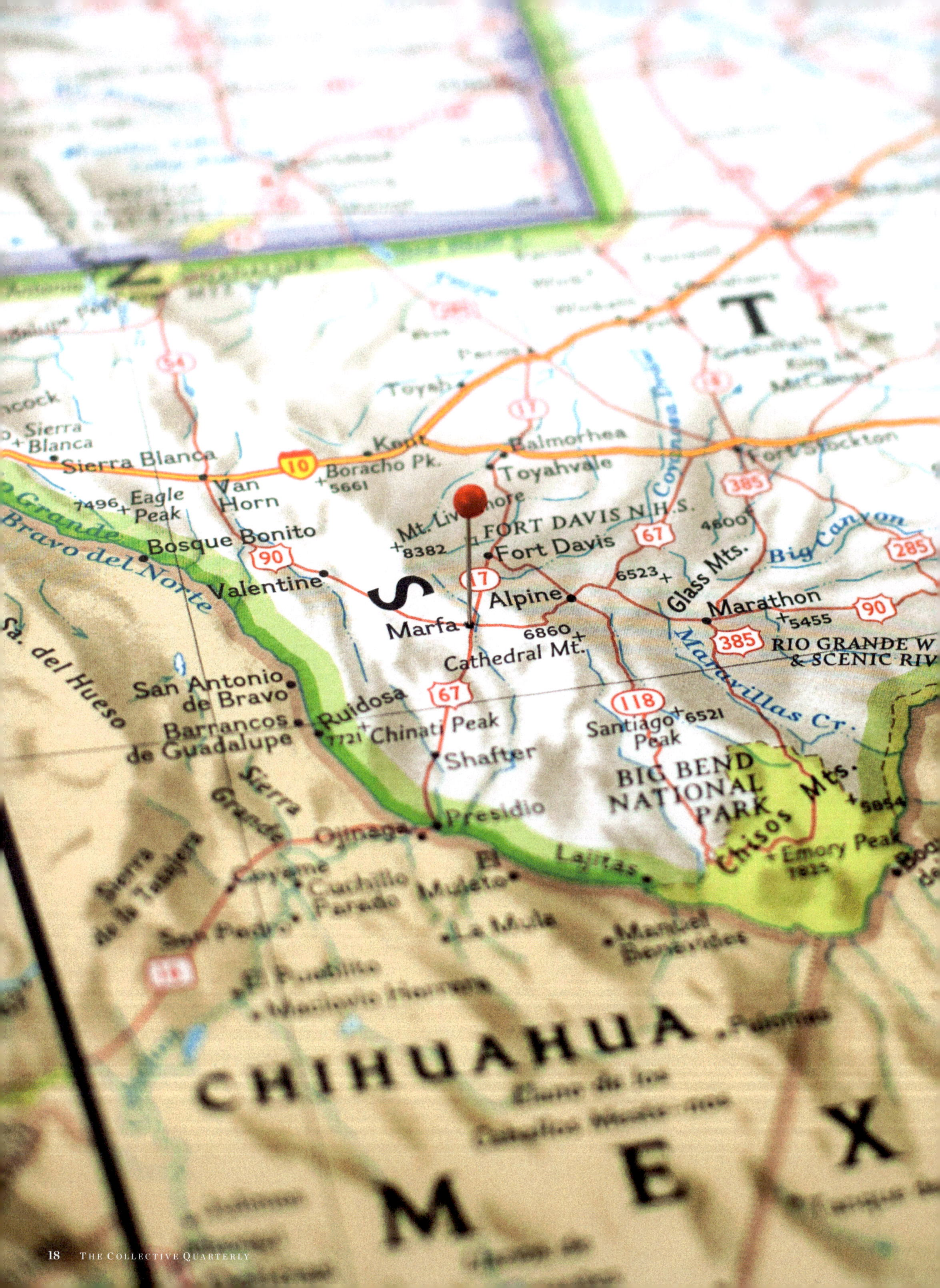
T
S
Sierra Blanca
Van Horn
Eagle Peak
7496
Kent
Boracho Pk.
5661
Balmorhea
Toyahvale
Fort Stockton
10
385
Bosque Bonito
Mt. Livermore
8382
FORT DAVIS N.H.S.
Fort Davis
67
4600
Big Canyon
285
90
Valentine
Bravo del Norte
17
Alpine
6523
Glass Mts.
Marathon
90
5455
Marfa
6860
Cathedral Mt.
385
RIO GRANDE W
& SCENIC RIV
Maravillas Cr.
Sa. del Hueso
San Antonio de Bravo
Barrancos de Guadalupe
Ruidosa
67
7721
Chinati Peak
118
Santiago Peak
6521
Shafter
BIG BEND NATIONAL PARK
Chisos Mts.
Sierra Grande
Presidio
Ojinaga
Lajitas
El Muleto
Emory Peak
CHIHUAHUA
M E X

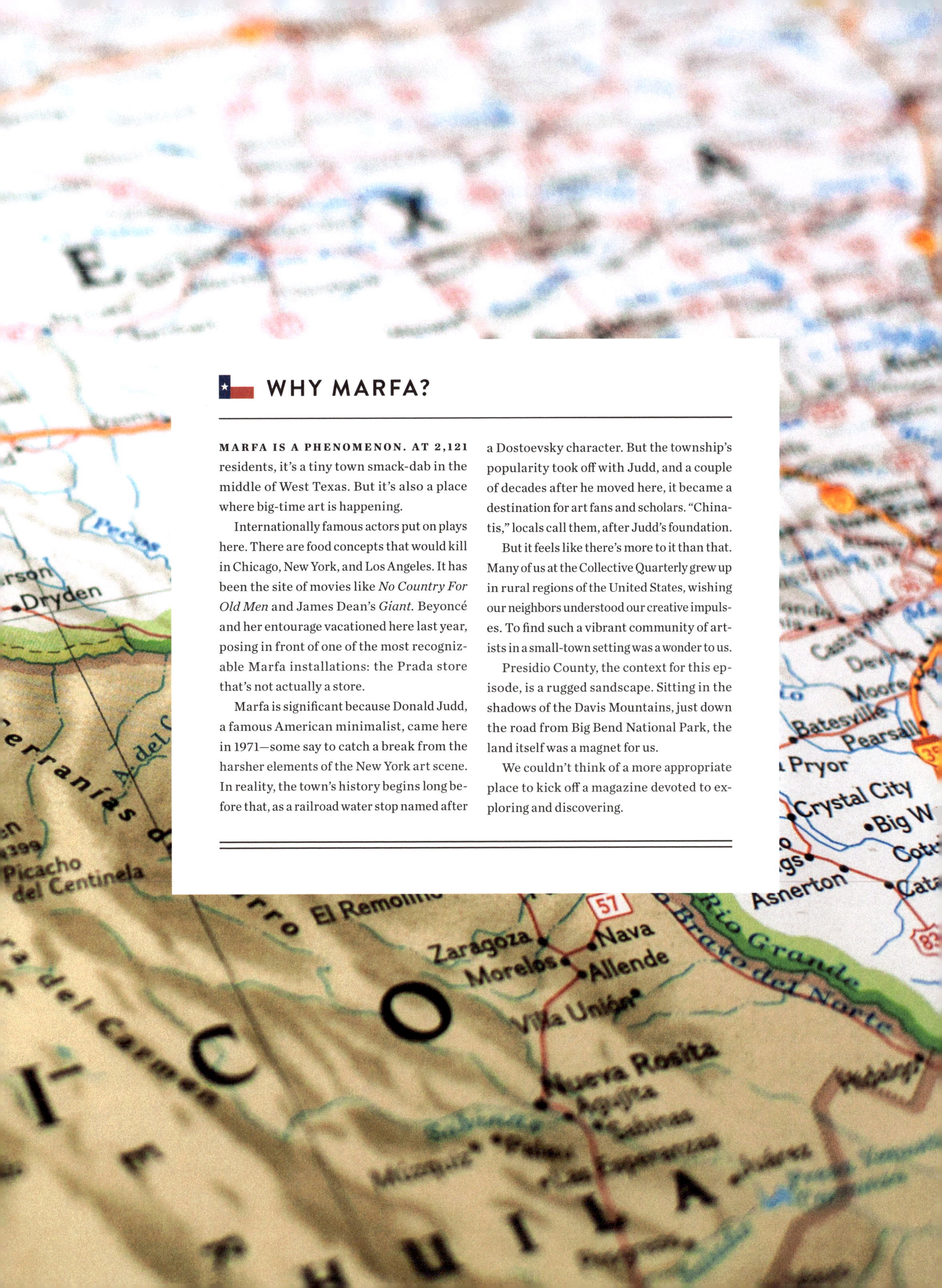

WHY MARFA?

MARFA IS A PHENOMENON. AT 2,121 residents, it's a tiny town smack-dab in the middle of West Texas. But it's also a place where big-time art is happening.

Internationally famous actors put on plays here. There are food concepts that would kill in Chicago, New York, and Los Angeles. It has been the site of movies like *No Country For Old Men* and James Dean's *Giant*. Beyoncé and her entourage vacationed here last year, posing in front of one of the most recognizable Marfa installations: the Prada store that's not actually a store.

Marfa is significant because Donald Judd, a famous American minimalist, came here in 1971—some say to catch a break from the harsher elements of the New York art scene. In reality, the town's history begins long before that, as a railroad water stop named after a Dostoevsky character. But the township's popularity took off with Judd, and a couple of decades after he moved here, it became a destination for art fans and scholars. "Chinatis," locals call them, after Judd's foundation.

But it feels like there's more to it than that. Many of us at the Collective Quarterly grew up in rural regions of the United States, wishing our neighbors understood our creative impulses. To find such a vibrant community of artists in a small-town setting was a wonder to us.

Presidio County, the context for this episode, is a rugged sandscape. Sitting in the shadows of the Davis Mountains, just down the road from Big Bend National Park, the land itself was a magnet for us.

We couldn't think of a more appropriate place to kick off a magazine devoted to exploring and discovering.

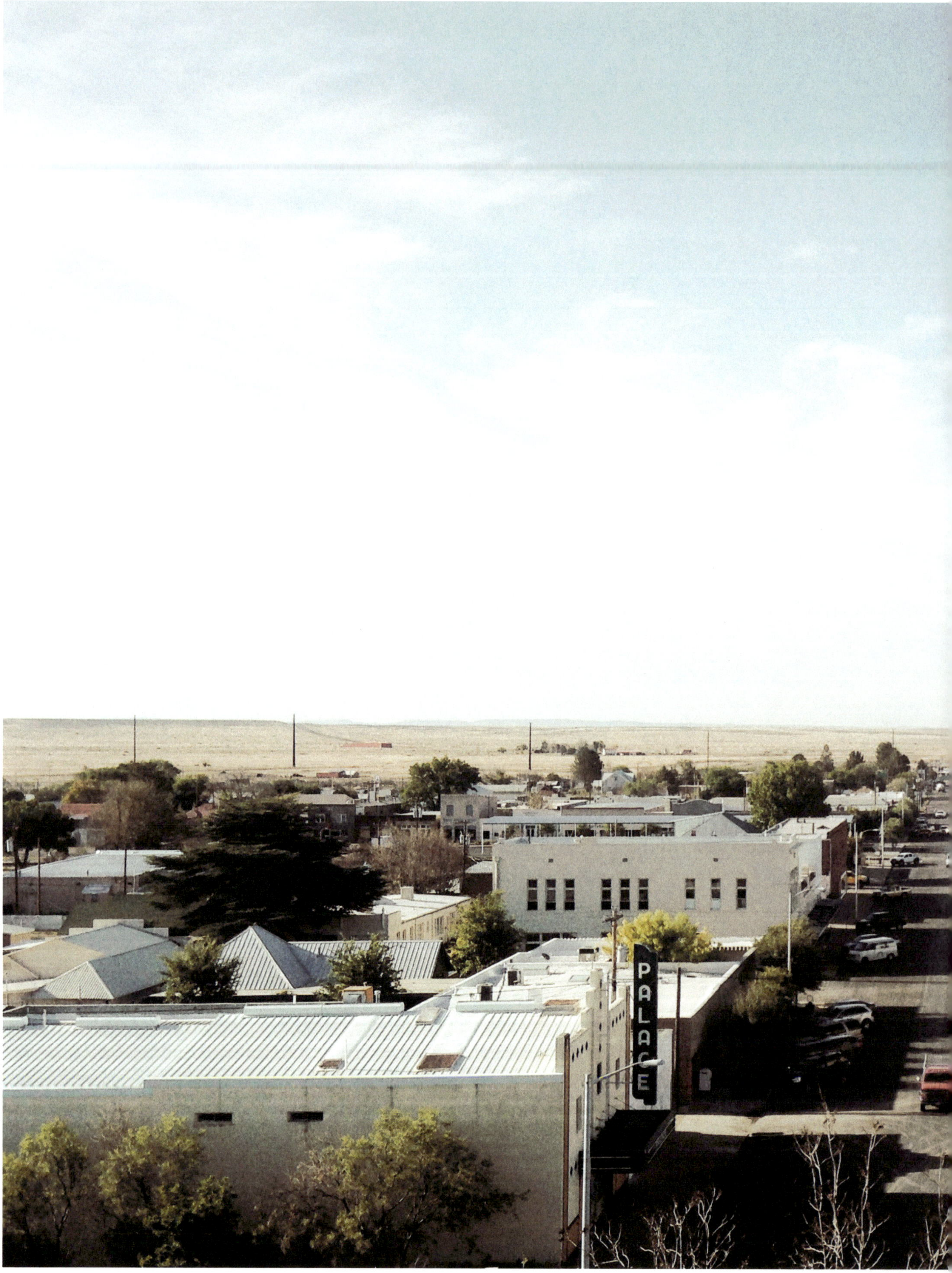
PALACE

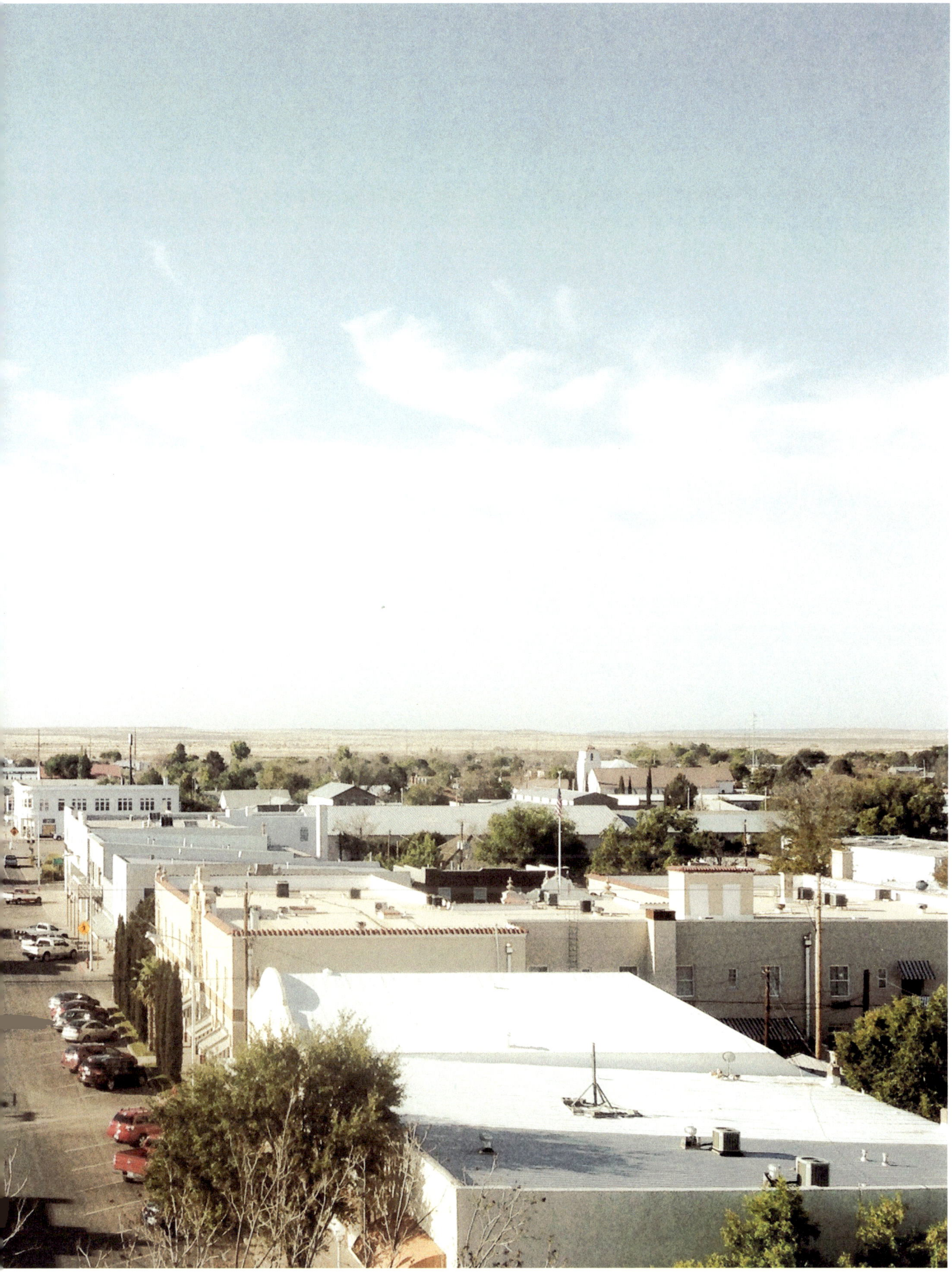

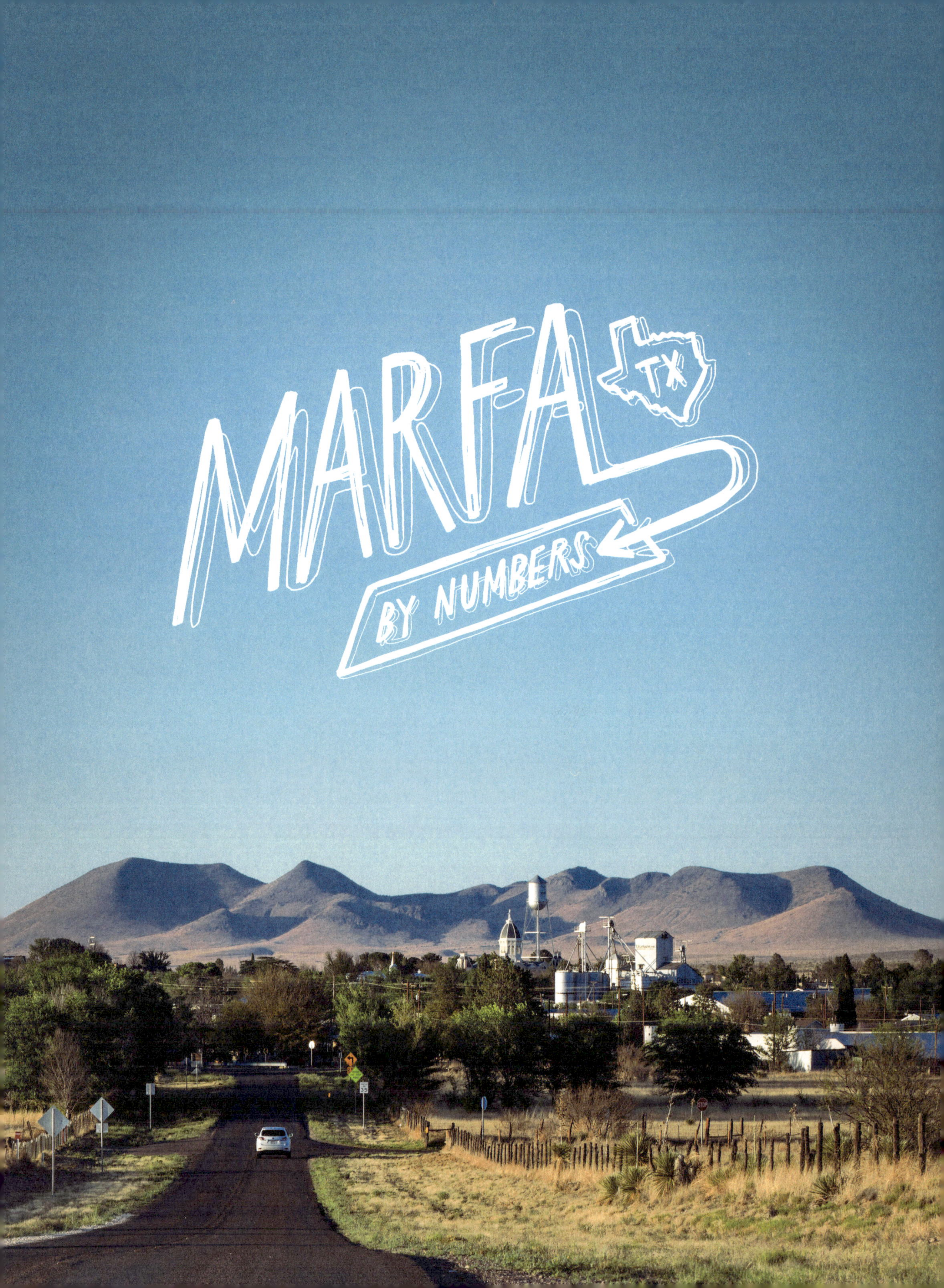
MARFA
TX
BY NUMBERS

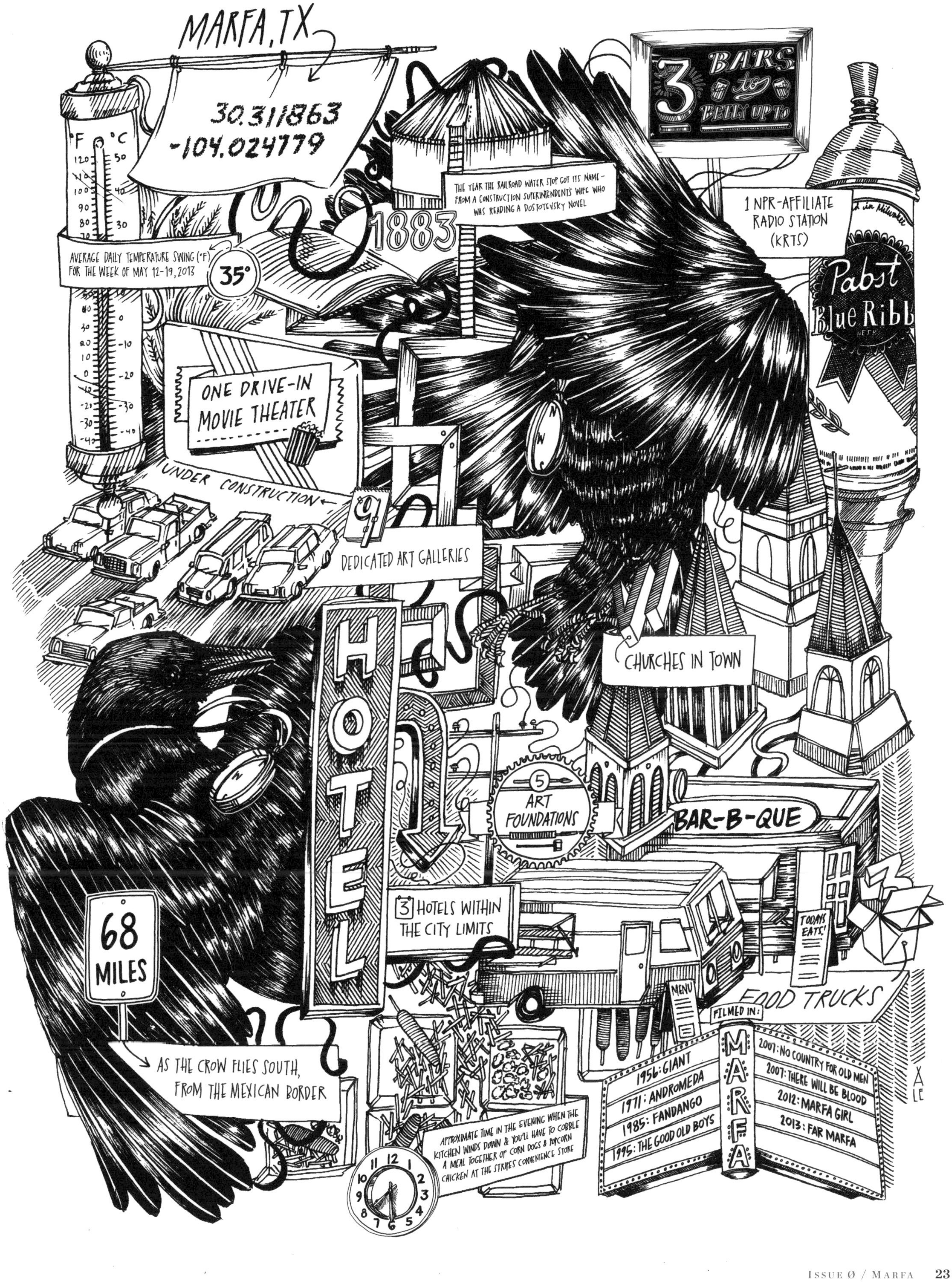

MARFA, TX
30.311863
-104.024779
3 BARS to BELLY UP TO
THE YEAR THE RAILROAD WATER STOP GOT ITS NAME – FROM A CONSTRUCTION SUPERINTENDENT'S WIFE WHO WAS READING A DOSTOYEVSKY NOVEL
1883
1 NPR-AFFILIATE RADIO STATION (KRTS)
AVERAGE DAILY TEMPERATURE SWING (°F) FOR THE WEEK OF MAY 12-19, 2013
35°
Pabst Blue Ribb
ONE DRIVE-IN MOVIE THEATER
UNDER CONSTRUCTION
9
DEDICATED ART GALLERIES
HOTEL
CHURCHES IN TOWN
5 ART FOUNDATIONS
BAR-B-QUE
3 HOTELS WITHIN THE CITY LIMITS
68 MILES
TODAYS EATS!
MENU
FOOD TRUCKS
FILMED IN:
MARFA
1956: GIANT
1971: ANDROMEDA
1985: FANDANGO
1995: THE GOOD OLD BOYS
2007: NO COUNTRY FOR OLD MEN
2007: THERE WILL BE BLOOD
2012: MARFA GIRL
2013: FAR MARFA
AS THE CROW FLIES SOUTH, FROM THE MEXICAN BORDER
APPROXIMATE TIME IN THE EVENING WHEN THE KITCHEN WINDS DOWN & YOU'LL HAVE TO COBBLE A MEAL TOGETHER OF CORN DOGS & POPCORN CHICKEN AT THE STRIPES CONVENIENCE STORE

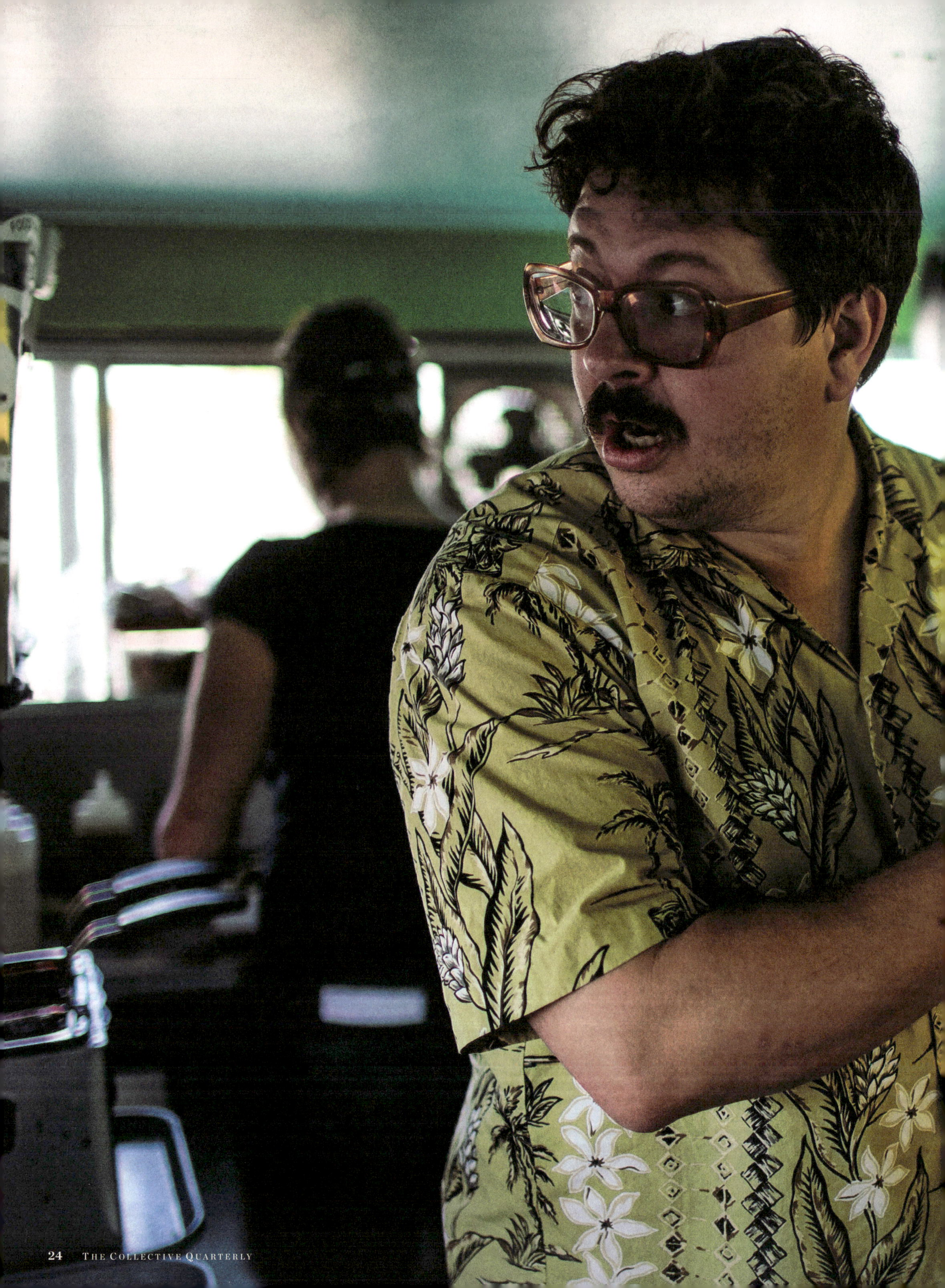

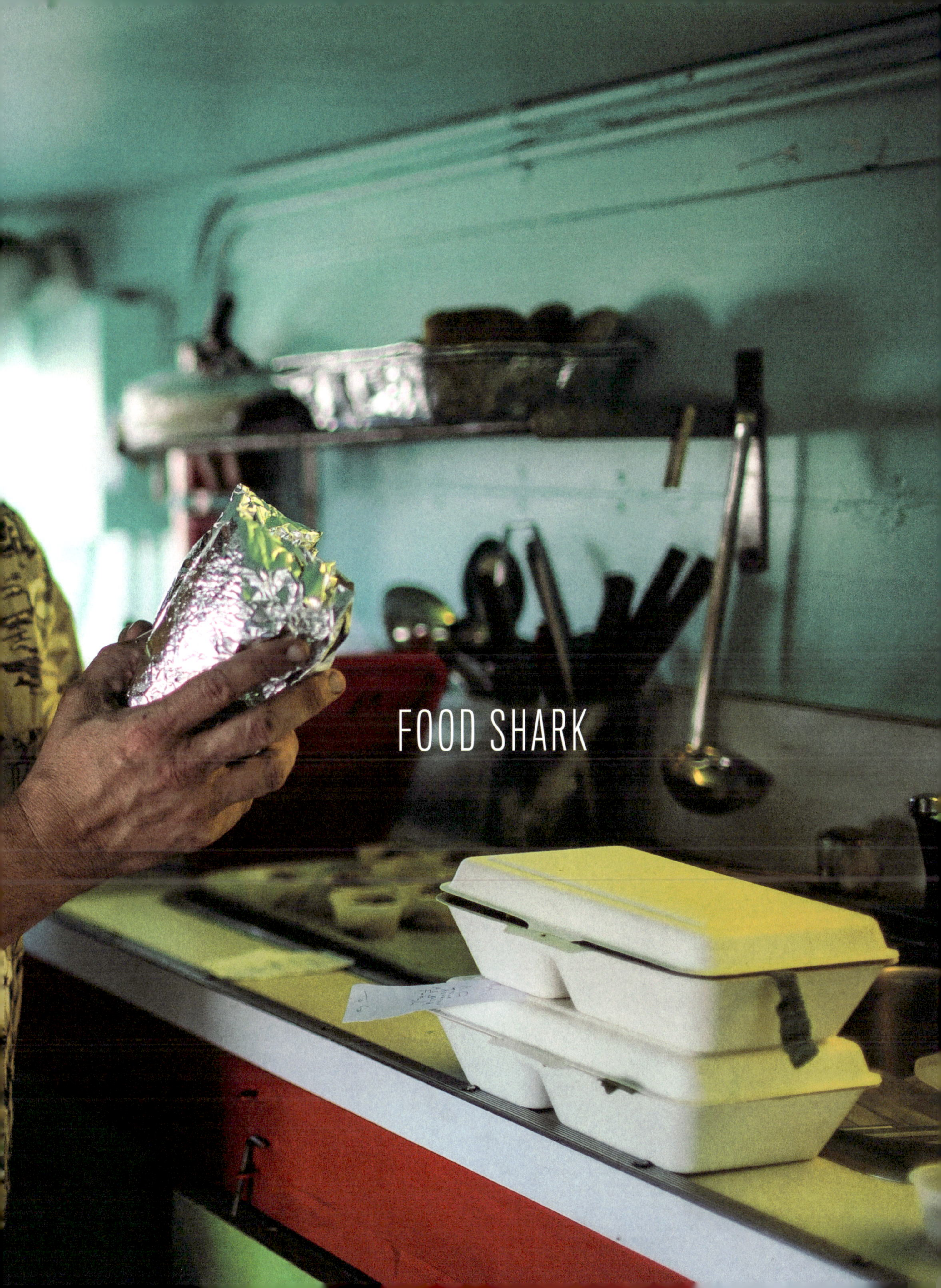

FOOD SHARK

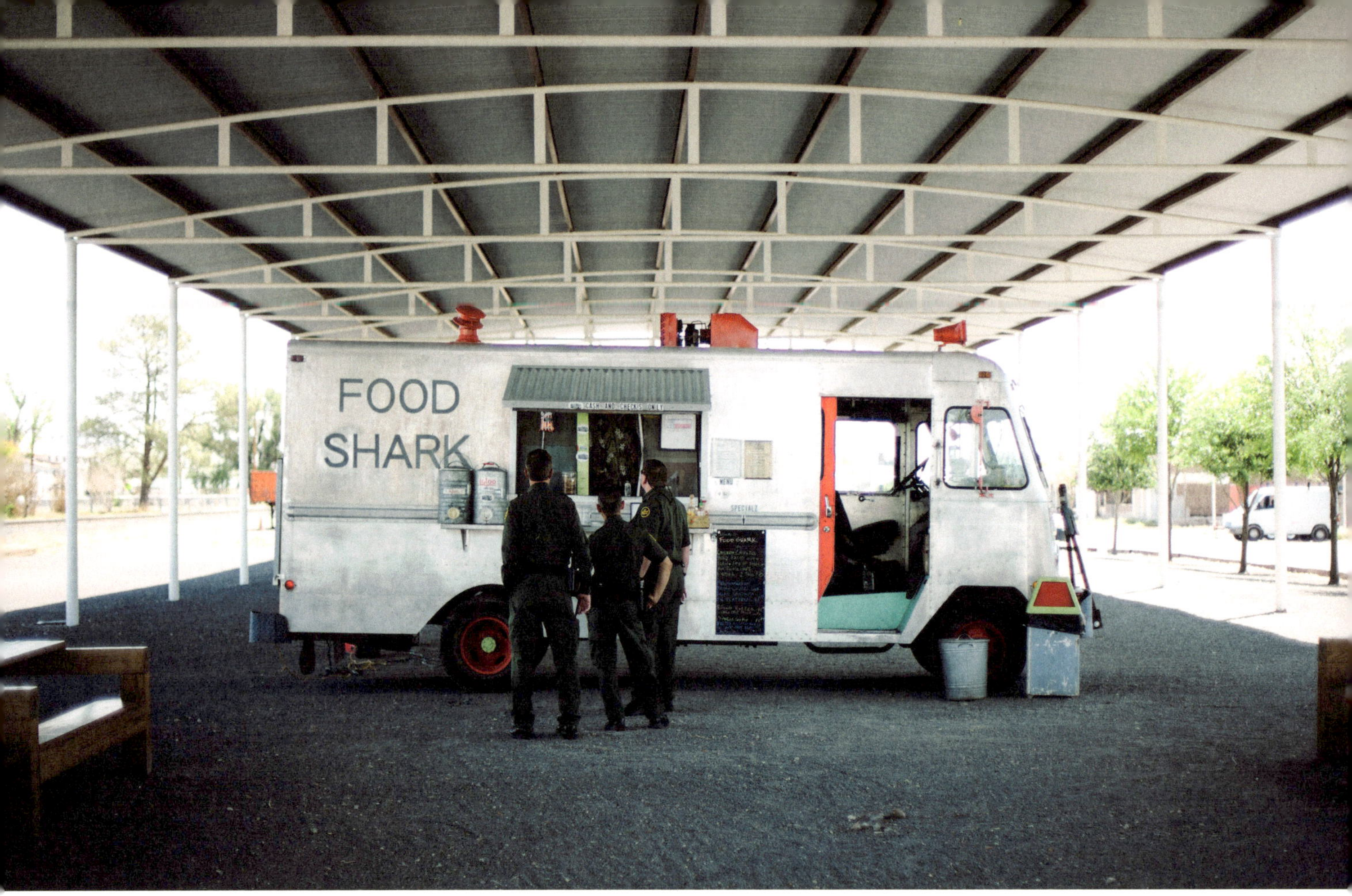

OF ALL THE OUT-OF-STATE-AND-MIND CONCEPTS THAT have wound their way to Marfa, the Mediterranean street snack of deep-fried chickpea balls may have come the farthest. Here, scribbled on a chalkboard menu under a rustic railroad pavilion, they call it the "Marfalafel." The dish is served in a manner deviated from its heritage, ditching the pita for a local-approved flower tortilla wrap.

This is the flagship item of Food Shark, a converted 1974 Butter-Krust bread delivery truck turned small-town lunch haven that sits by itself under a rustic metal awning across El Paso Street from Marfa Book Co.

"It's desert food for a desert town," says co-owner Adam Bork, who opened the 'Shark in 2006 with his wife, Krista Steinhauer. "You can find green chile chicken, red chile beef, or shrimp Veracruz tacos, but the core menu is Mediterranean."

Locals and tourists can pull up to the Food Shark truck and dine on one of five Donald Judd-designed outdoor tables Wednesday through Friday from noon to 3 p.m. The brand's flavor, however, isn't limited to daylight hours.

After throwing back a few Shiner beers at the iconic Lost Horse Saloon on Friday and Saturday nights, those in search of a savory late-night snack can stumble a few blocks west on San Antonio Street to the Museum of Electronic Wonders & Late Night Grilled Cheese Parlour. Vintage cars stamped with the Food Shark name are often parked around the building's exterior. Inside, patrons will find a dimly lit room packed with television sets from the late '50s to the early '70s, music playing exclusively from eight-track cartridges, Plexiglas trays lined with AstroTurf, and of course, grilled cheese.

"It's the '60s and '70s vision of what the future might have held," says Bork, who credits Steinhauer with the concept. "There's not just the Chinati Foundation and Judd, but there's also food tourism [in Marfa]. It's not easy to get here, so you have to really attract people. With the cars, old TVs, and food, I think we're doing that." –*ADAM RISMAN*

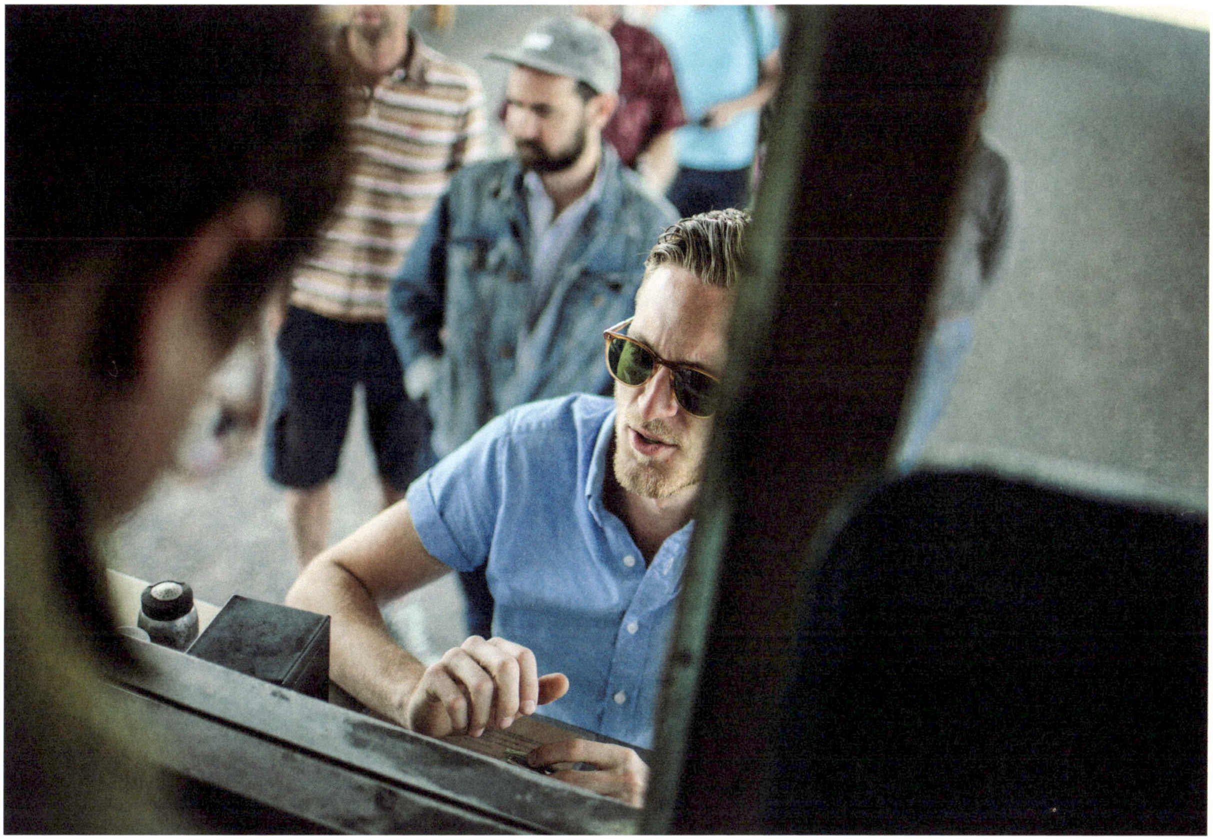

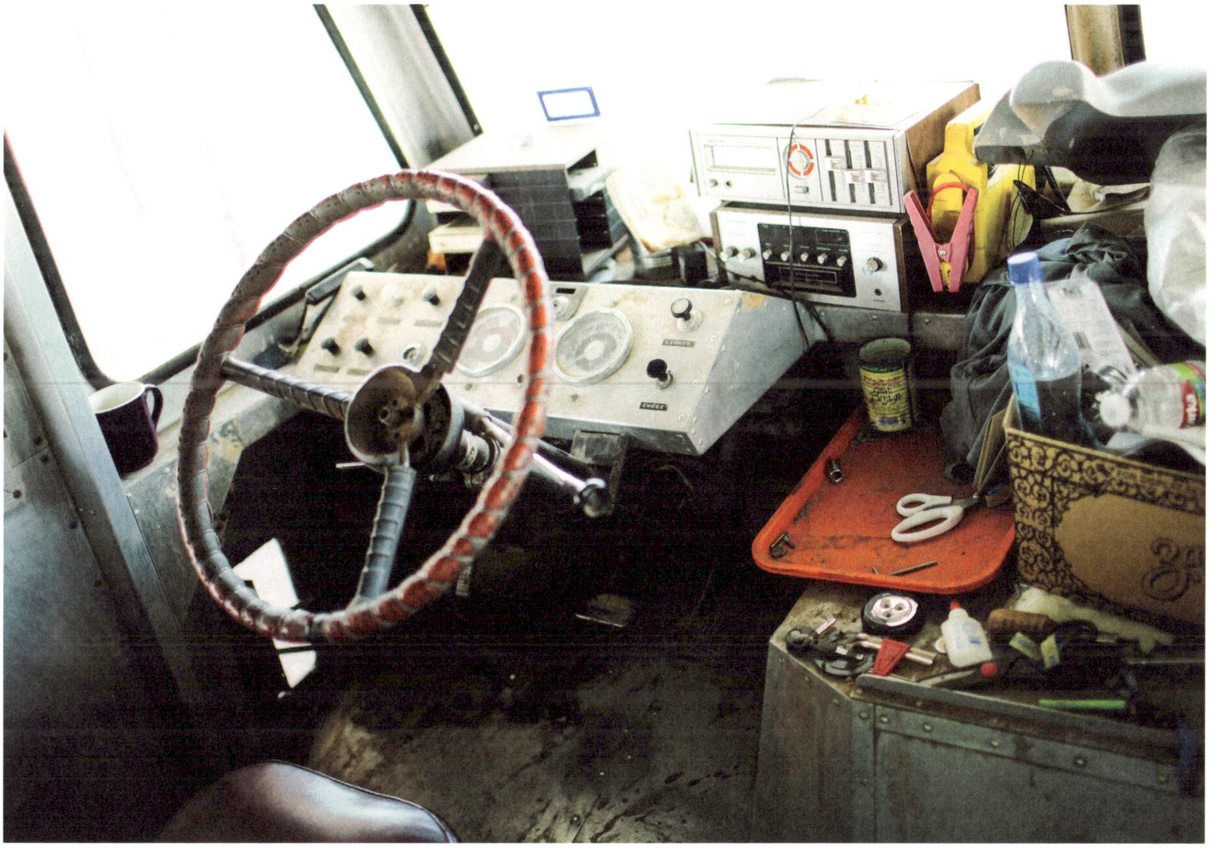

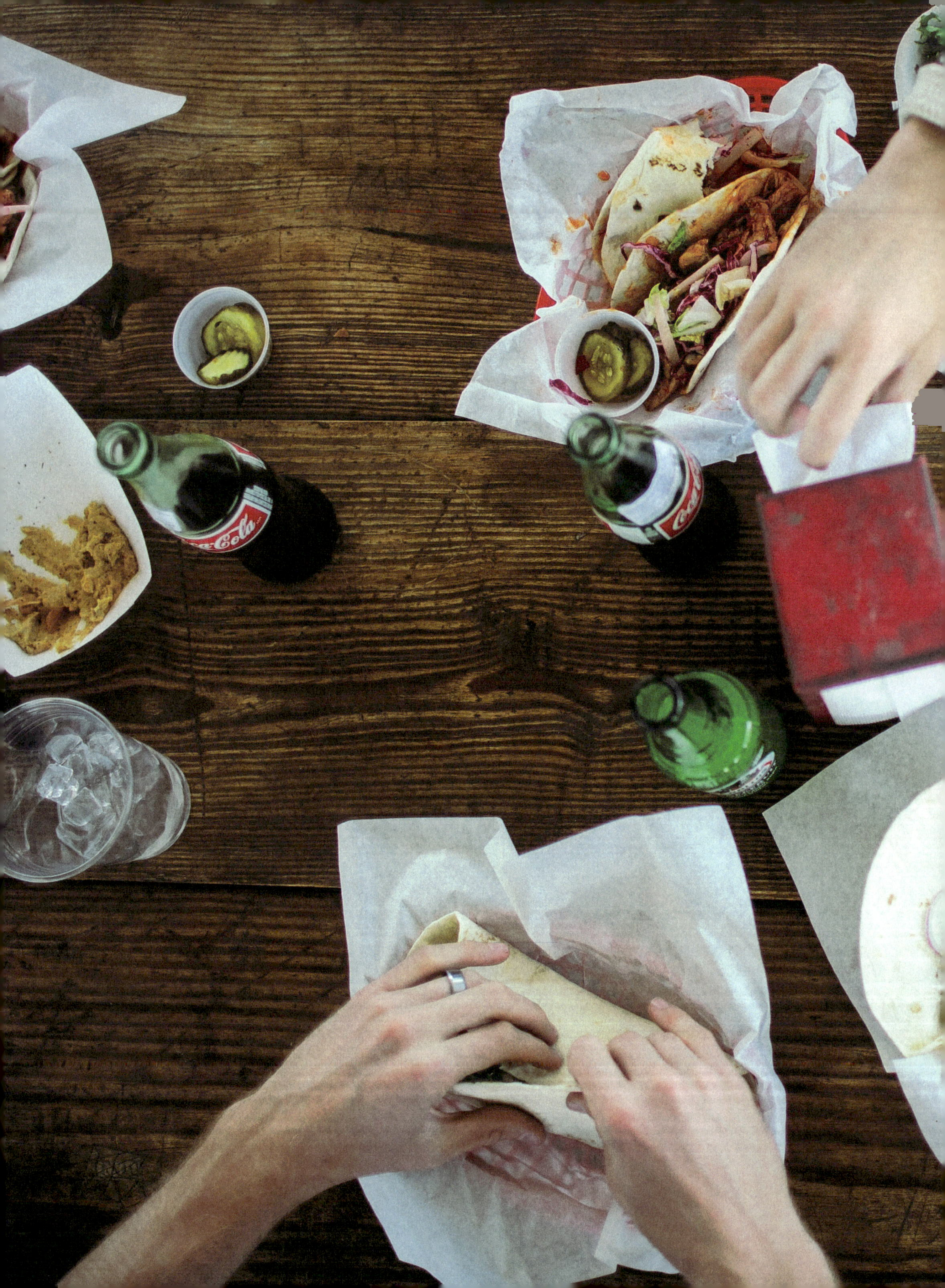

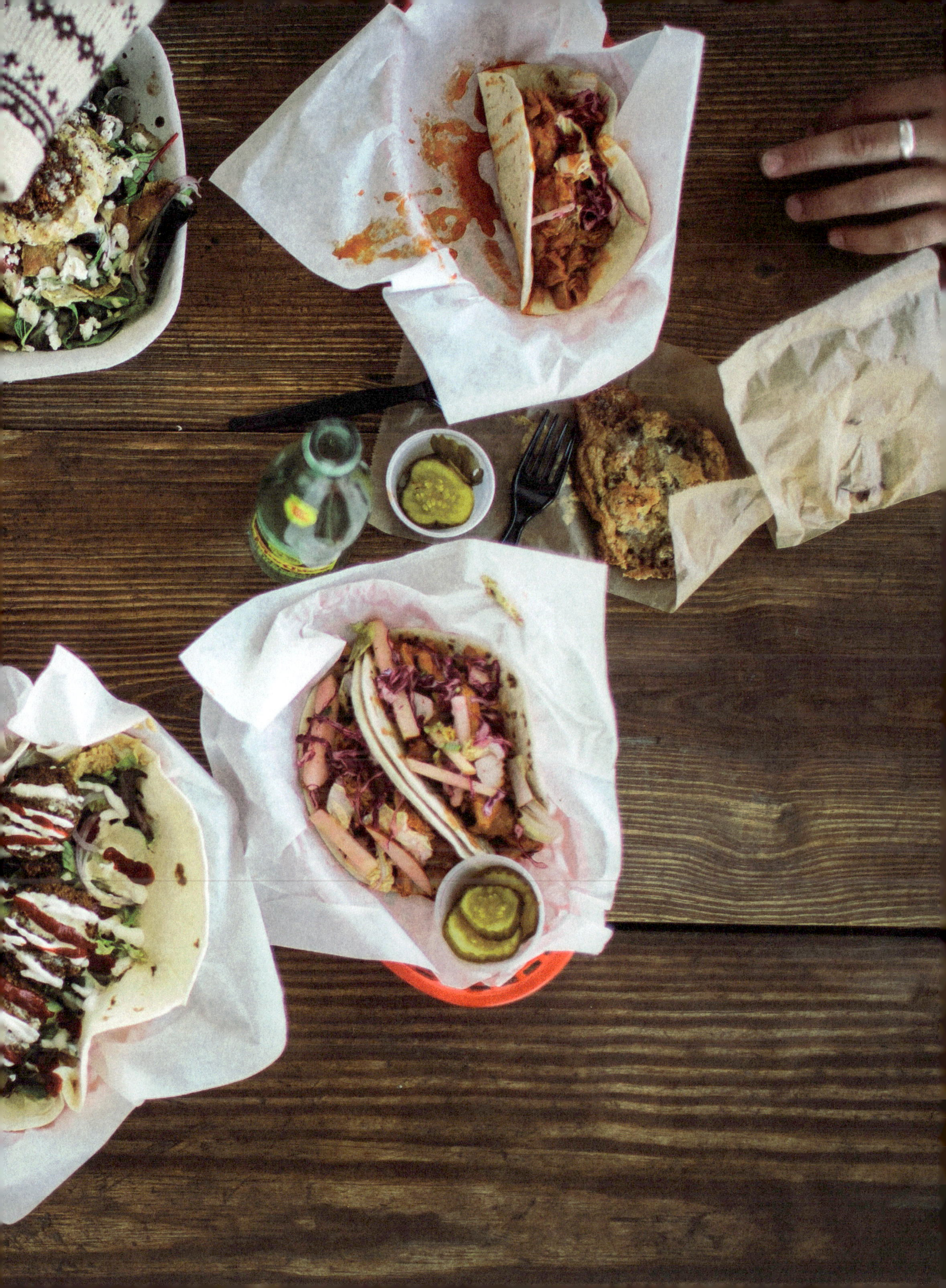

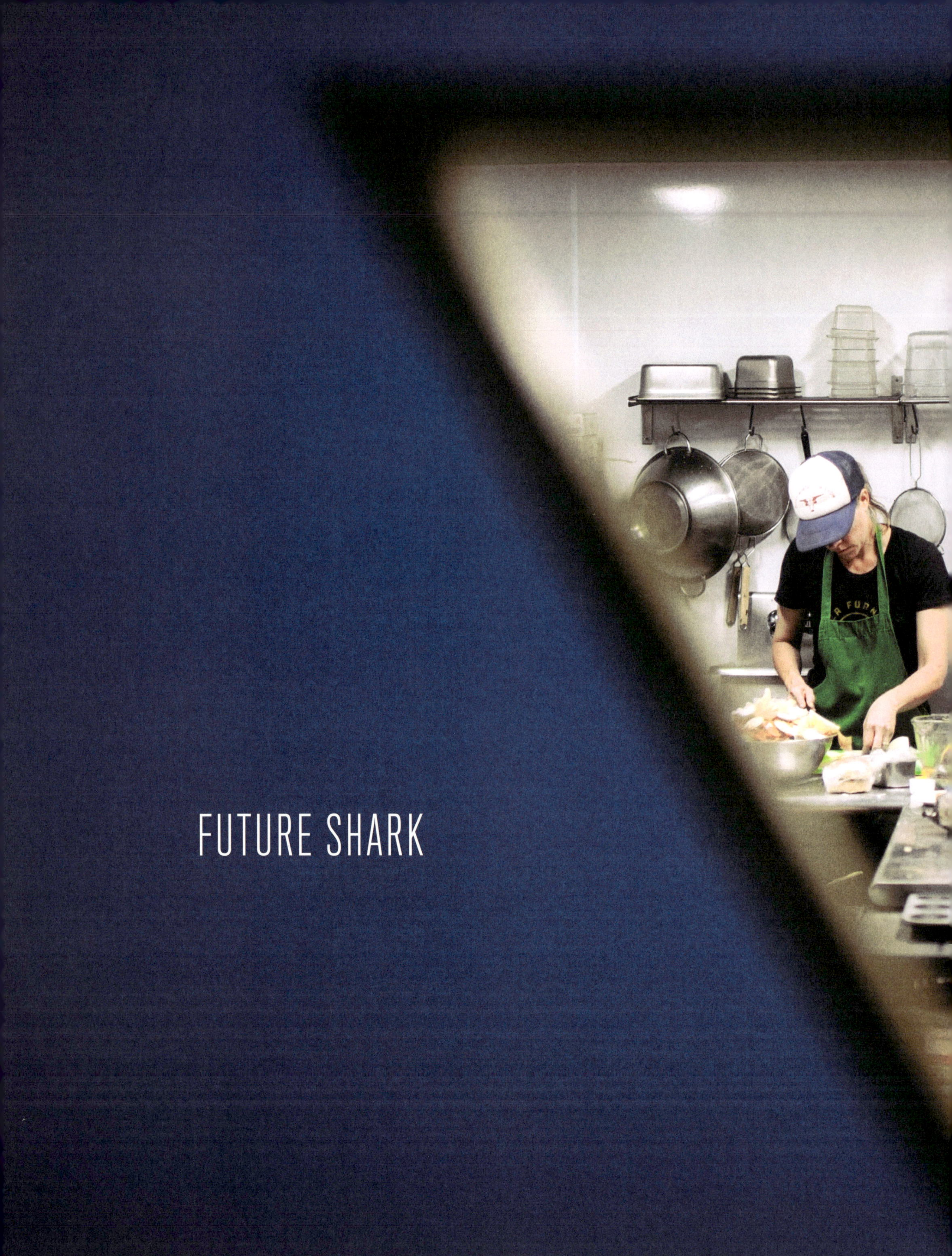

FUTURE SHARK

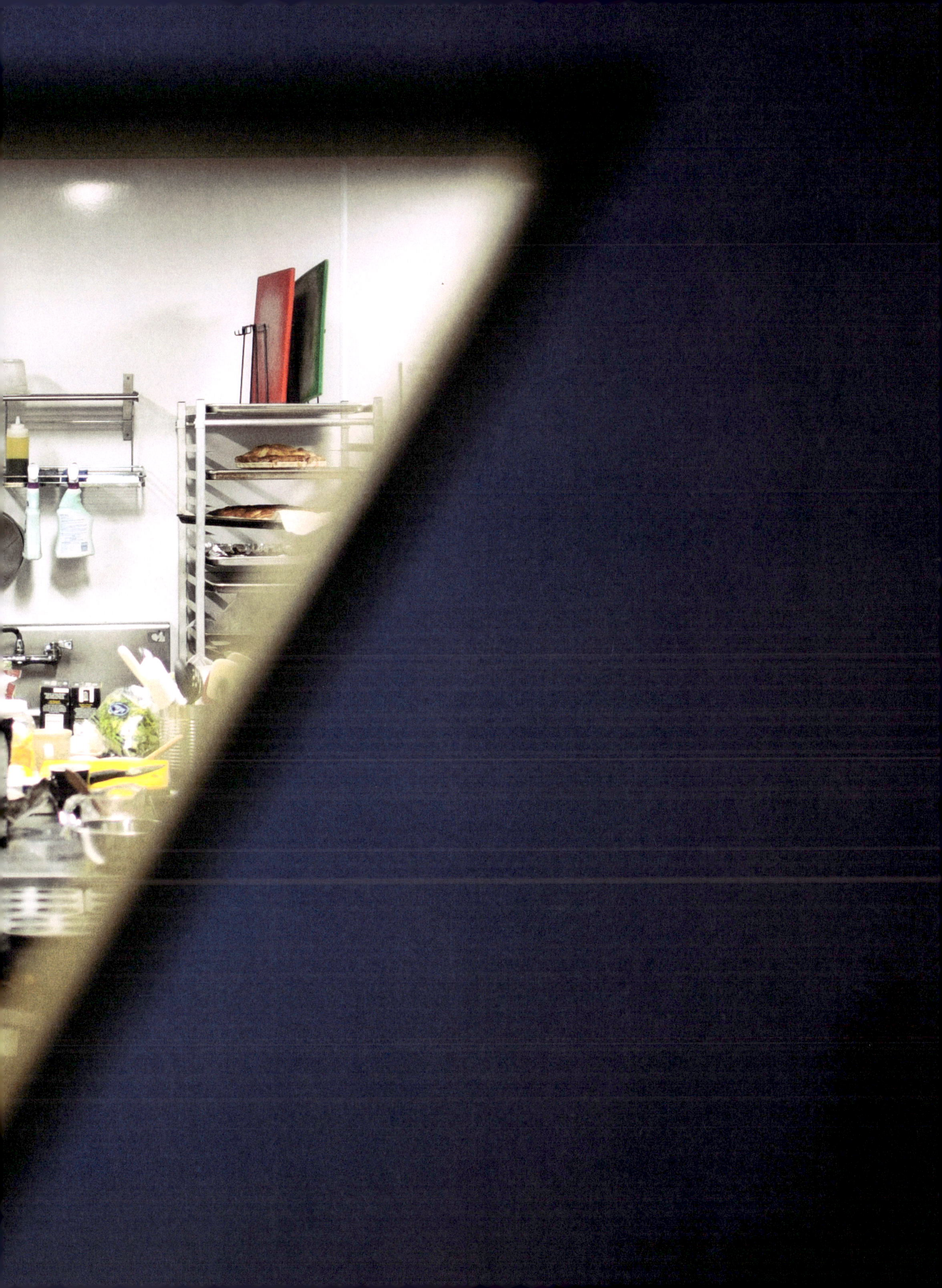

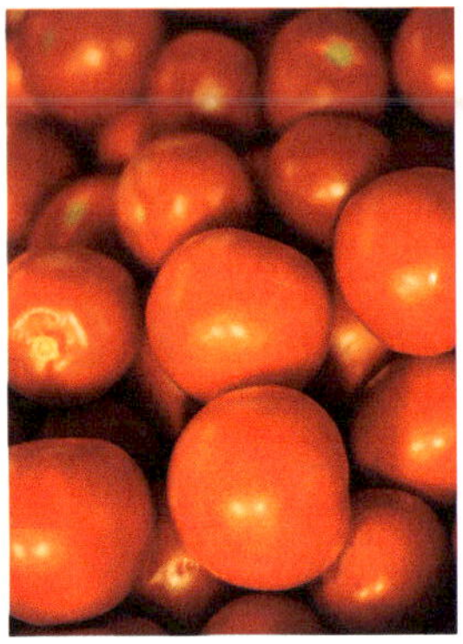
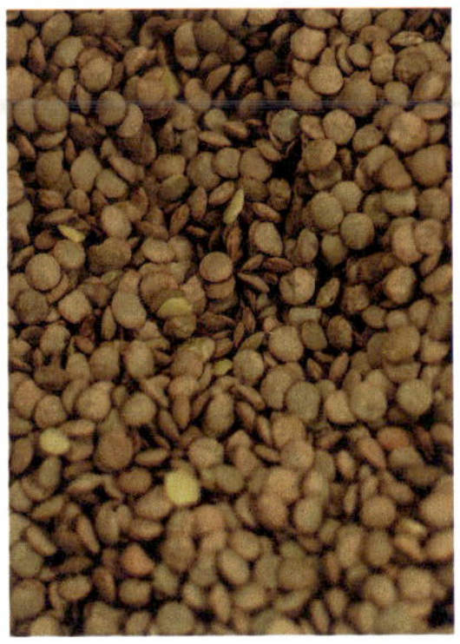
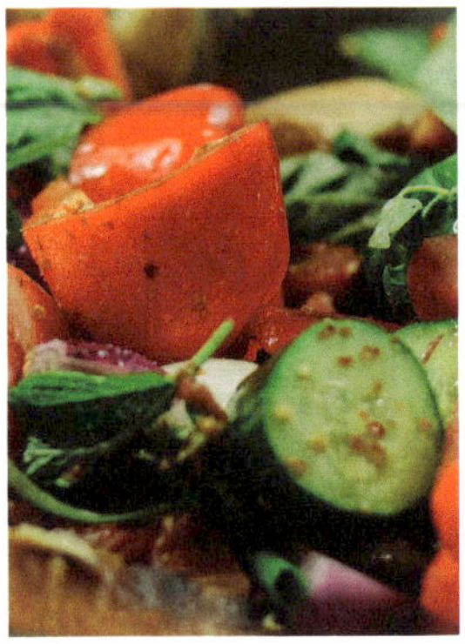
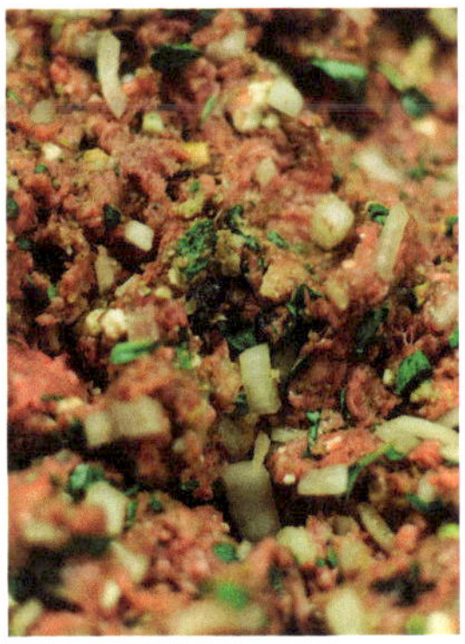

THERE'S A STOREFRONT ON HIGHLAND AVENUE, Marfa's main drag, with 11 antique TVs in the window. They blink, cascade, and pop. Each screen displays one letter from the name of the restaurant: Future Shark.

Inside you'll find funky décor, such as the plastic army soldiers climbing the decorative geodes in the bathroom. In the kitchen, there's a walk-in freezer named "Christopher Walken." On opposite walls in the dining area, there are two light boxes designed to host a rotating gallery of art. On this particular day, there are giant cinematic photographs, one of which depicts a man in a bicycle cap shooting pool at the nearby Lost Horse Saloon. If you were to show up around lunchtime a couple days later, you might be surprised to see the subject himself in the very same bicycle cap, eating at the community-style lunch table beneath his own photo. This sort of star sighting is no oddity around here; the man from the photo is an employee at the Marfa Public Radio down the street.

Restaurants in Marfa are funny. Several open only once a month, while others serve only on the weekends. Most close no later than 9 p.m.—early by city standards, but typical for a small town. There was no place for people to come during the day to meet or work. Future Shark was the answer.

It's 8 a.m., and Krista Steinhauer is hard at work in the back, preparing to open in three and a half hours. On the menu today? Gazpacho, stewed lentils, meatballs, and strawberry rhubarb pie—the ingredients for the latter having come from her recent trip to El Paso. "I was so happy to find rhubarb," she says. "You can't get that here."

It's a window into the way she cooks—like a game—with only what fresh, mostly local ingredients she can find; the recipes simply provide a place from which to leap.

She points to today's cookbook, *Jerusalem* by Yotam Ottolenghi and Sami Tamimi. Steinhauer lived in Italy for a time, and has been playing around with Mediterranean flavors lately. "I don't really follow the recipes, but they're good points of departure."

She follows her instincts to fill the ever-changing lineup on the counter. Nothing is ever certain, except that she'll fill four slots: a meat main, a vegetarian main, a salad, and sweets.

Part of the charm is that, because Steinhauer plays fast and loose with the ingredients, you'll never end up with the same taste twice, even if it's the same conceptual dish. Of course, that's also part of the frustration. "One time you'll do it, and it'll be like, 'Yes. That's what I want!' But I can't reproduce it."

Born in Lubbock, Texas, Steinhauer left after college in 1995: "[I] swore I'd never come back to Texas. Here, you have to make it up. There's nothing just waiting for you." But after more than a few years abroad, Texas got her back. She found herself working at the Hotel San Jose in Austin in 2003 with a guy named Adam Bork. The following year, they pulled up stakes and moved to Marfa—"Just far enough away from family," Steinhauer says. They were married in 2010.

The pair was working at the Thunderbird Hotel, when they came up with the idea for Food Shark. Future Shark followed, along with their grilled cheese emporium (open Friday and Saturday nights, offering leftovers from the restaurant and truck). Bork is the "art director" of the operation, masterminding the groove. Steinhauer executes.

To hear Steinhauer tell it, Texas has a way of pulling you back in—even when you think you're out. And just like in the wrangling days, making a life here takes initiative. (Especially one that rewards creative inclinations.) You want a path? You have to blaze it. Through their zany culinary experiments, Steinhauer and Bork seem to be personifying just that: two funky sharks making a future. —*SETH PUTNAM*

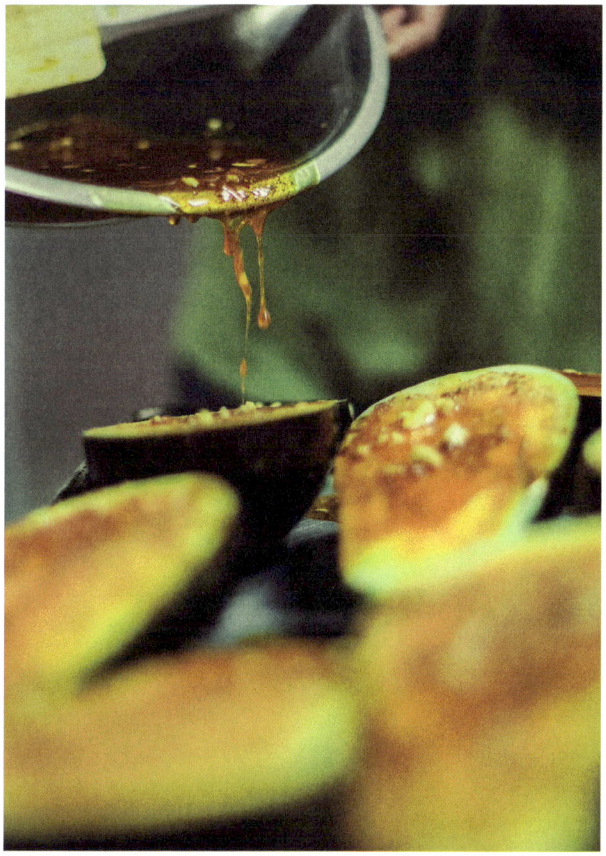

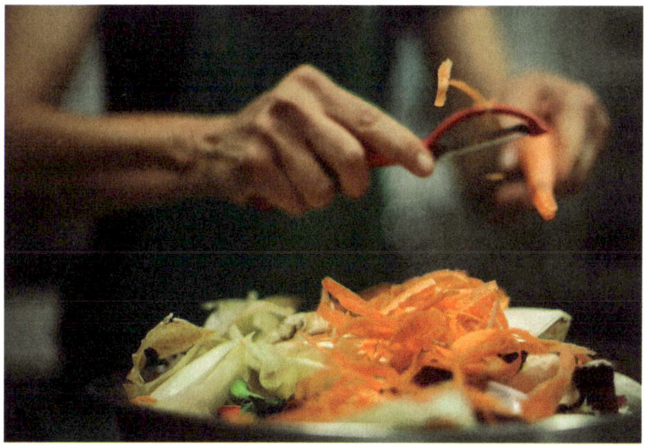

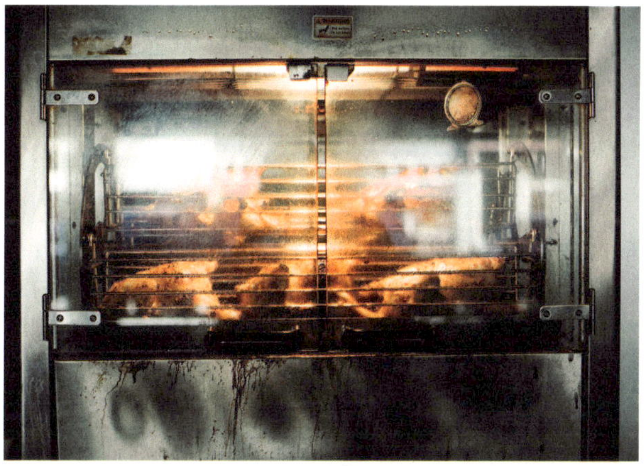

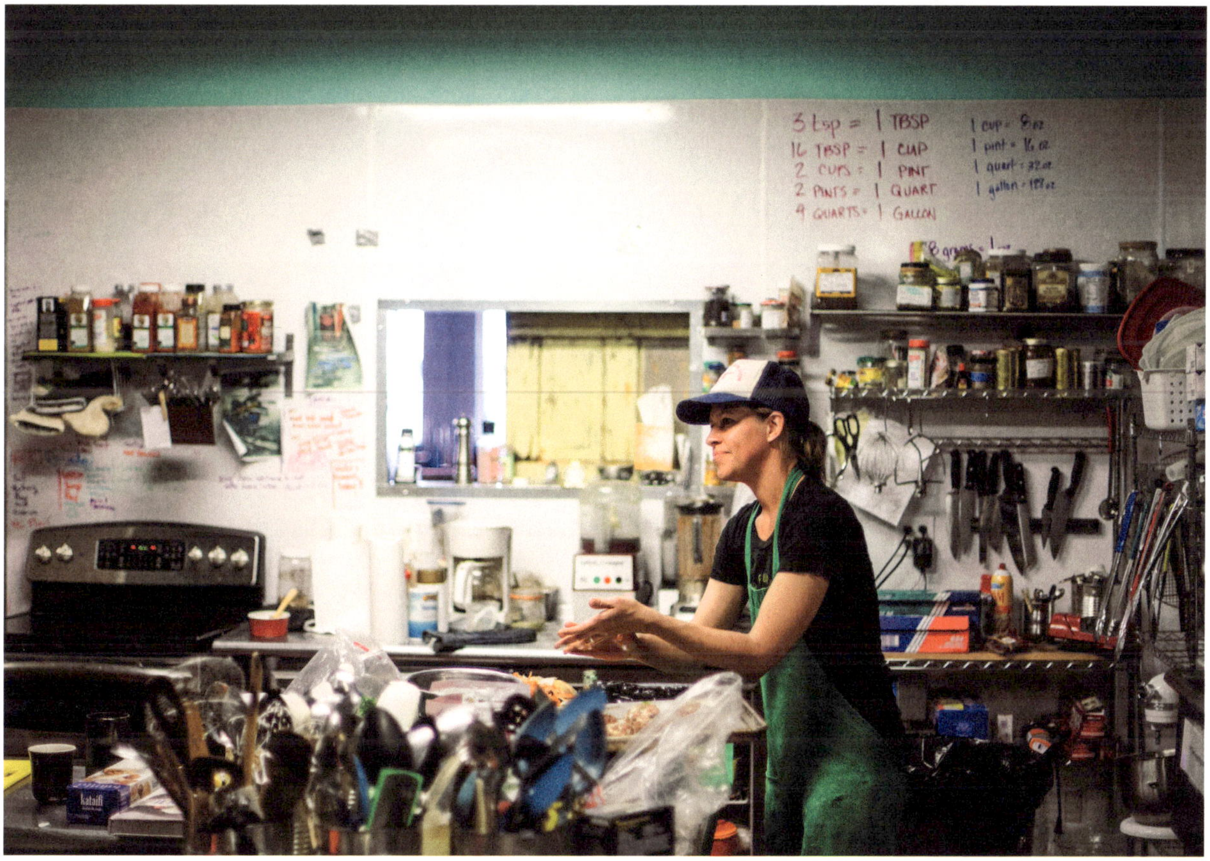
3 tsp = 1 TBSP
16 TBSP = 1 CUP
2 CUPS = 1 PINT
2 PINTS = 1 QUART
4 QUARTS = 1 GALLON
1 cup = 8 oz
1 pint = 16 oz
kataifi

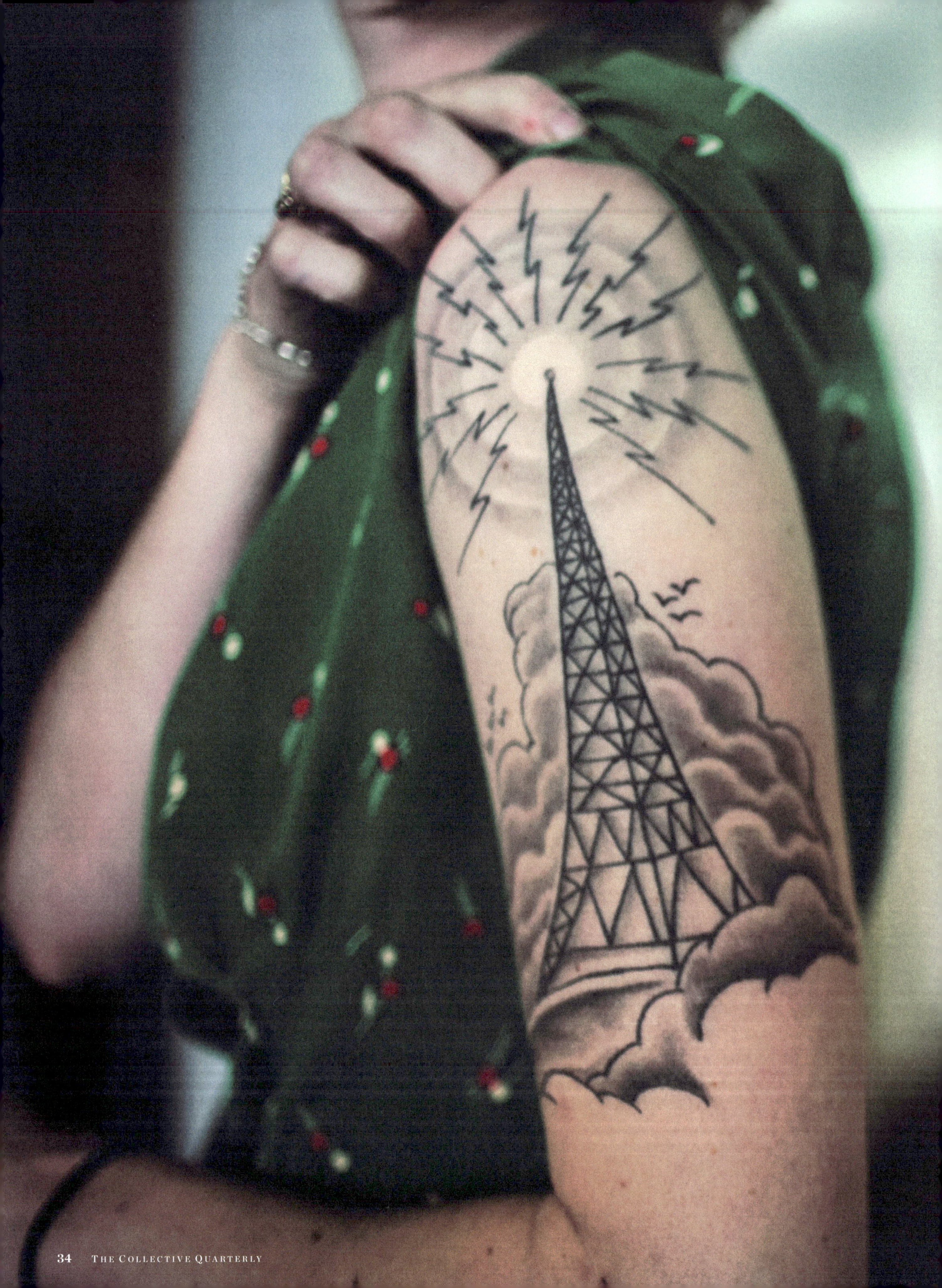

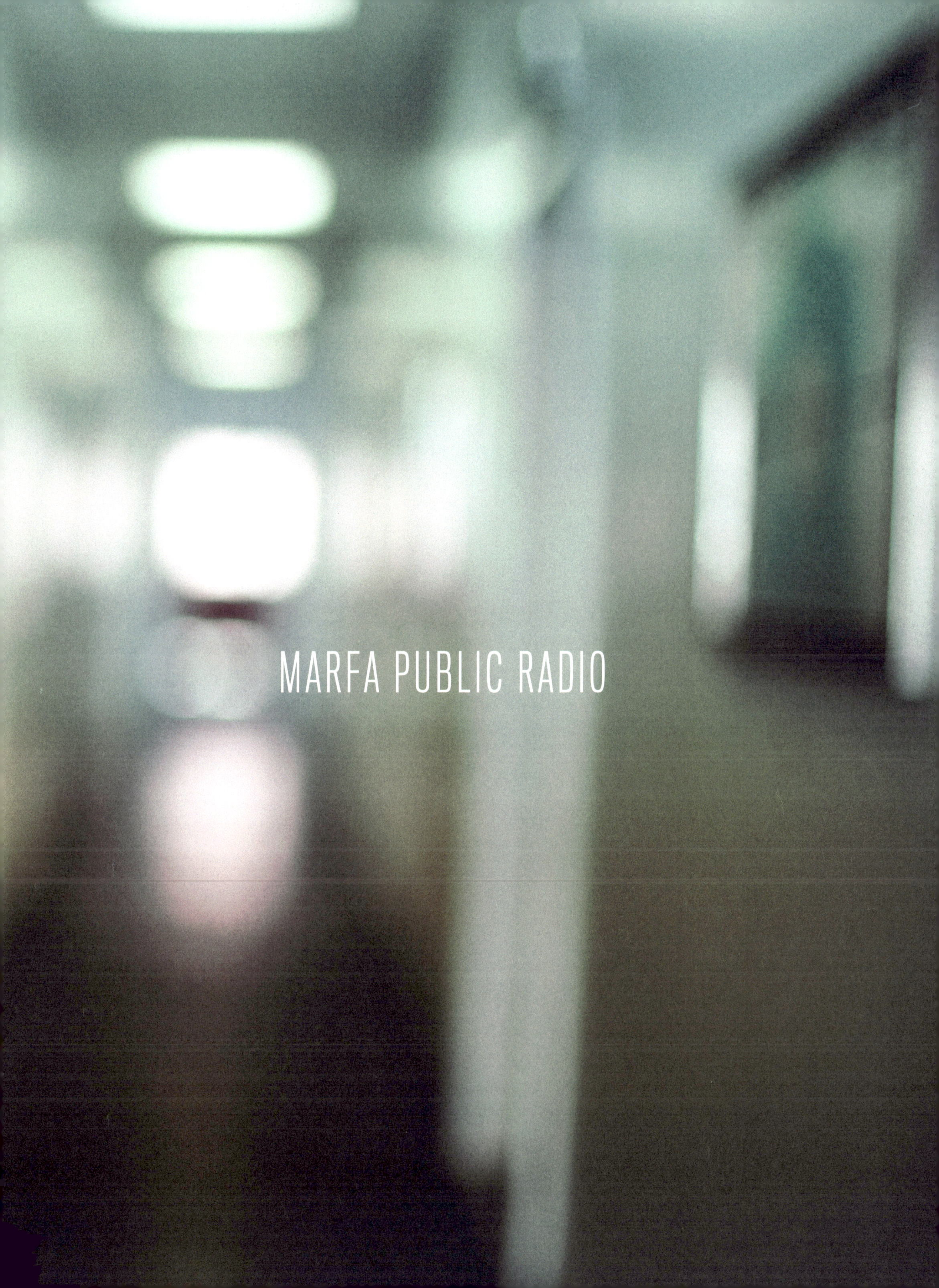

MARFA PUBLIC RADIO

To run a member-funded NPR affiliate is no small task for a town of Marfa's size. The reach of this place is amazing; one of the technicians reveals that a few ranchers have reported picking up Marfa Public Radio's signal (and nothing else) on some of the dusty, lonely roads across the Mexican border. Overseeing it all is station manager Tom Michael, a northern transplant who has become one of the most recognizable voices in Presidio County. MAX WASTLER sits down with Tom to find out what lured him from the big city to this desert hamlet.

How did you make your way from editing encyclopedias in Chicago to managing a radio station in Marfa?

I was an editor at Encyclopædia Britannica in Chicago for a decade and I always worked as a freelance journalist. I began hosting an interview show on radio on the side. I once asked a public radio consultant about going into radio full-time. Working in educational publishing, I was on the low end of the publishing salary scale. The consultant asked me, "How much do you make?" I told him the amount. He responded, "Well then don't go into public radio!" In 2002 I sold everything in Chicago, got into a camper van, and headed out. In 2005, I founded Marfa Public Radio. In 2006, I built the studio. In 2007, we began broadcasting continuously.

How does a town of 2,000 people fund a public radio station?

Well, it doesn't. I imagine this will come out in your reporting: Marfa is just a single town within the vibrant Big Bend region of West Texas. So then the question might be, "How does a region of about 12,000 people fund a public radio station?" Well, if we received $10 from absolutely every man, woman, and child, we still wouldn't have a station. In the NPR world, we're considered an economic miracle. There's no business underwriting to speak of, so it's just membership and grants. I write grants and used to be a professional grant writer. The CPB, the Corporation for Public Broadcasting, provides the greatest level of grant support. We also have a very generous listener base, such as a large number of major donors for our size. Plus there are many folks who don't live in the region, but consider themselves "spiritual residents" of far West Texas, and they are our members, too.

What percentage of your content is homemade?

For a long time, it was the majority—60-something percent. We added a syndicated overnight show, so it appears to be just under 50 percent now.

Who are your most popular radio personalities?

I'm the general manager of a public radio station. I love all my children equally.

Your favorite memory from the past five years with MPR?

Our greatest moment of community service—though a tragic event for our region—was providing emergency information in the face of the raging Rock House fire in April 2011. During that episode, as we became the community hub for safety information, I thought: "This is why we were put on God's green Earth." We won a regional Murrow Award for reporting, but it was our level of public service that made me most proud.

What are your big plans for the future?

We just held a staff retreat. We have a full-time staff of three, and we'll double that to six in the coming months. We will continue to expand our news reporting. We joined the Fronteras consortium of public radio stations across the southwest. We have begun contributing more on the national level.

Who are your heroes of radio journalism?

The late Studs Terkel of Chicago.

Can you talk a bit about the ethic of MPR and how it differs from say, KCRW, WBEZ or WNYC?

Well, I believe we all begin with similar public radio ethics. There are many medium and large stations that are under-performing, but not those great stations. As a smaller station in a rural area, though, we're much easier to touch. Localism is the mantra of public radio, and due to our small size and large ambition, we can make a big impact in the community. We can react so much faster than a large station. We can take risks, be more fun, be more intimate, be more lively, and interact with the community on a person-to-person level. Also, I hire good people. We live and breathe this stuff. Marfa also demands you be talented, to rise above, no matter what you do here.

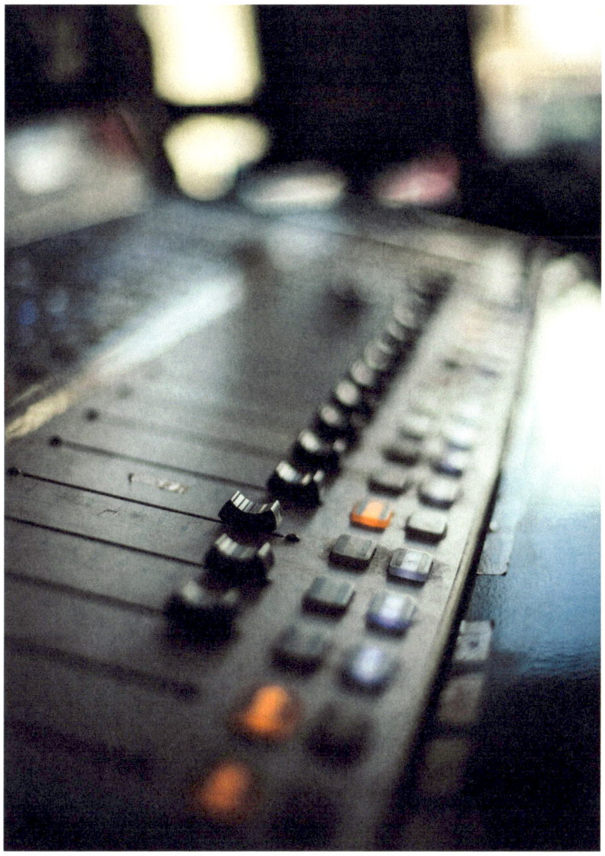

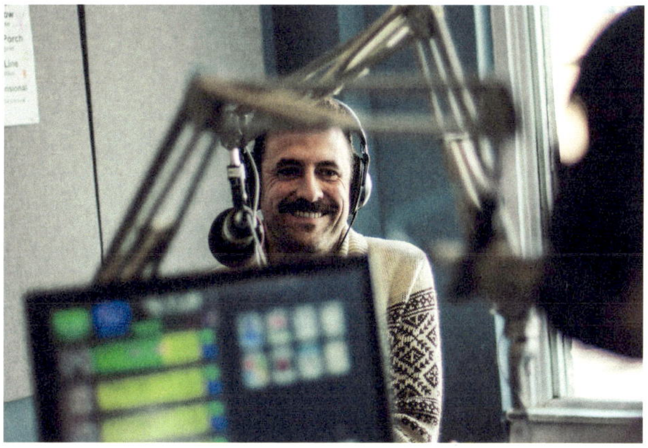

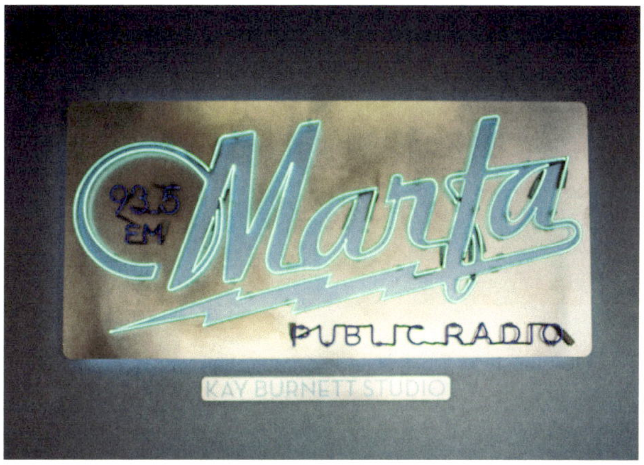
Marfa
PUBLIC RADIO
KAY BURNETT STUDIO

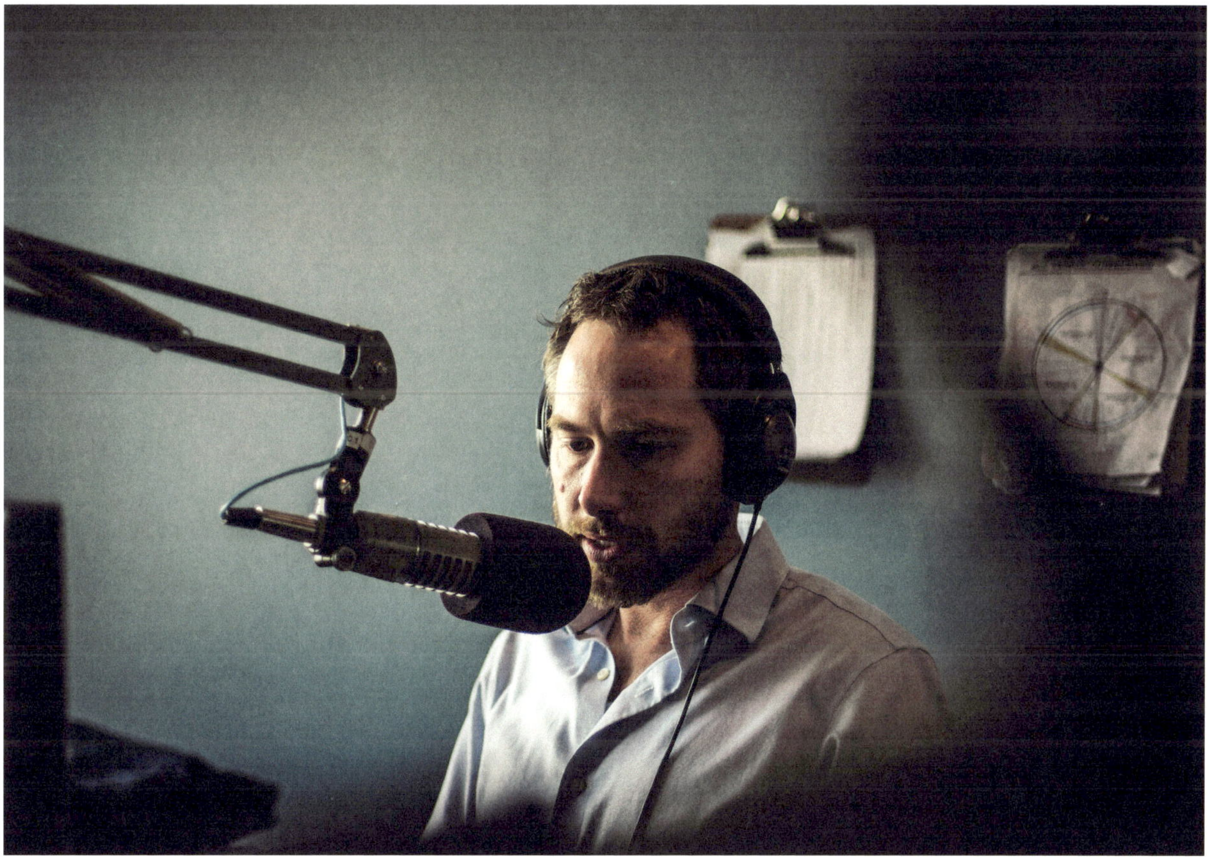

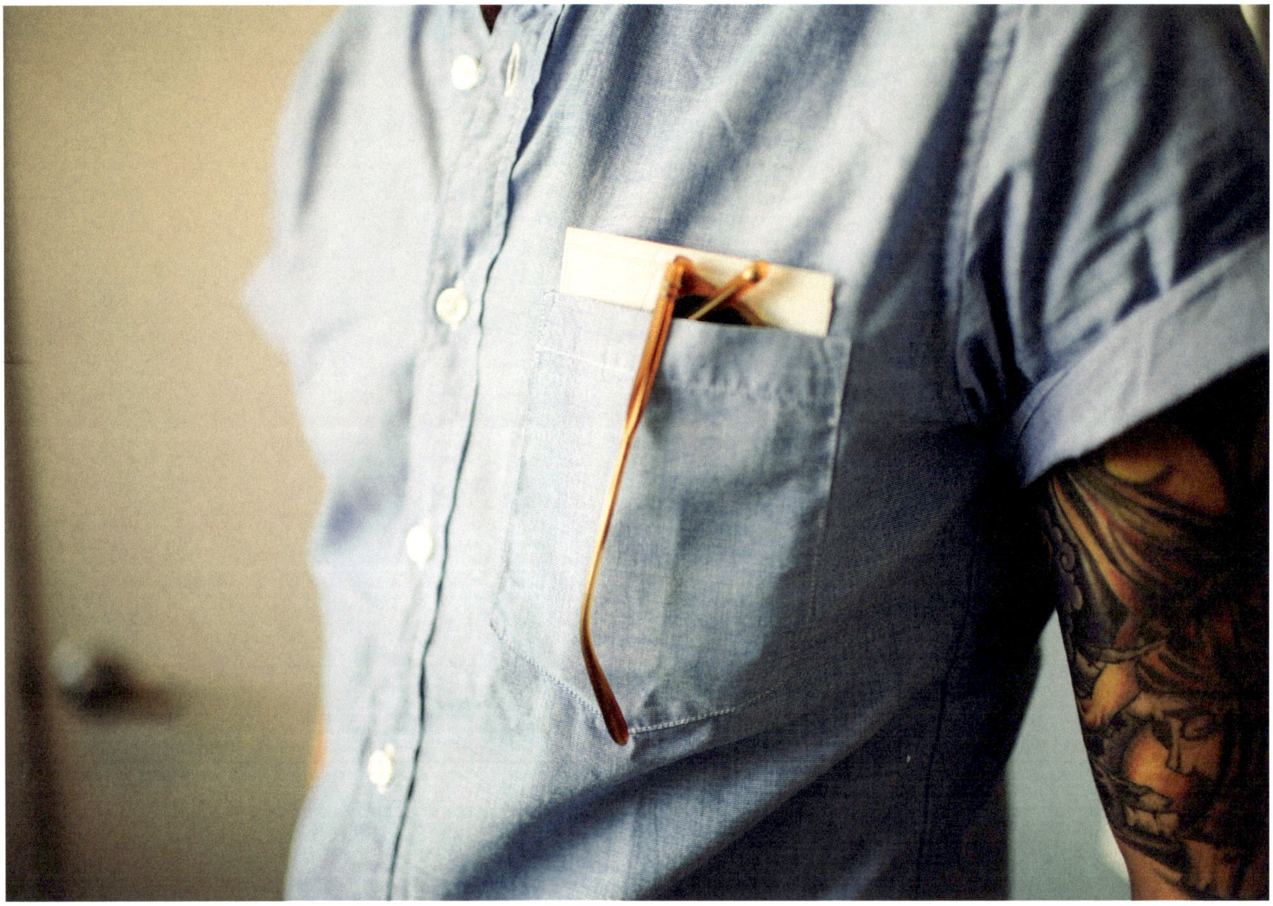

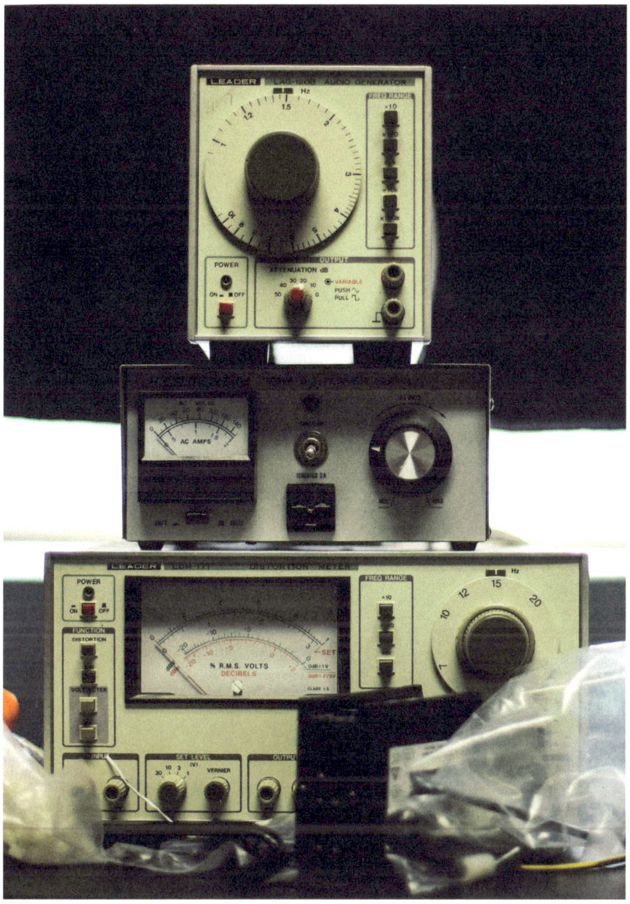
LEADER
AUDIO GENERATOR
FREQ RANGE
POWER
OUTPUT
ATTENUATION dB
AC AMPS
R.M.S. VOLTS
DECIBELS
FUNCTION
DISTORTION
SET LEVEL
VERNIER

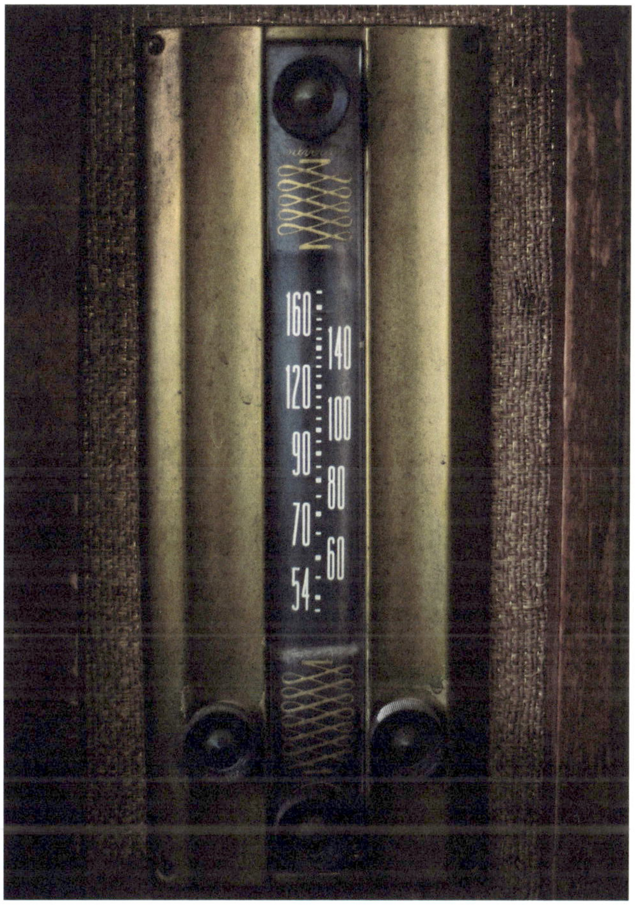
160
140
120
100
90
80
70
60
54

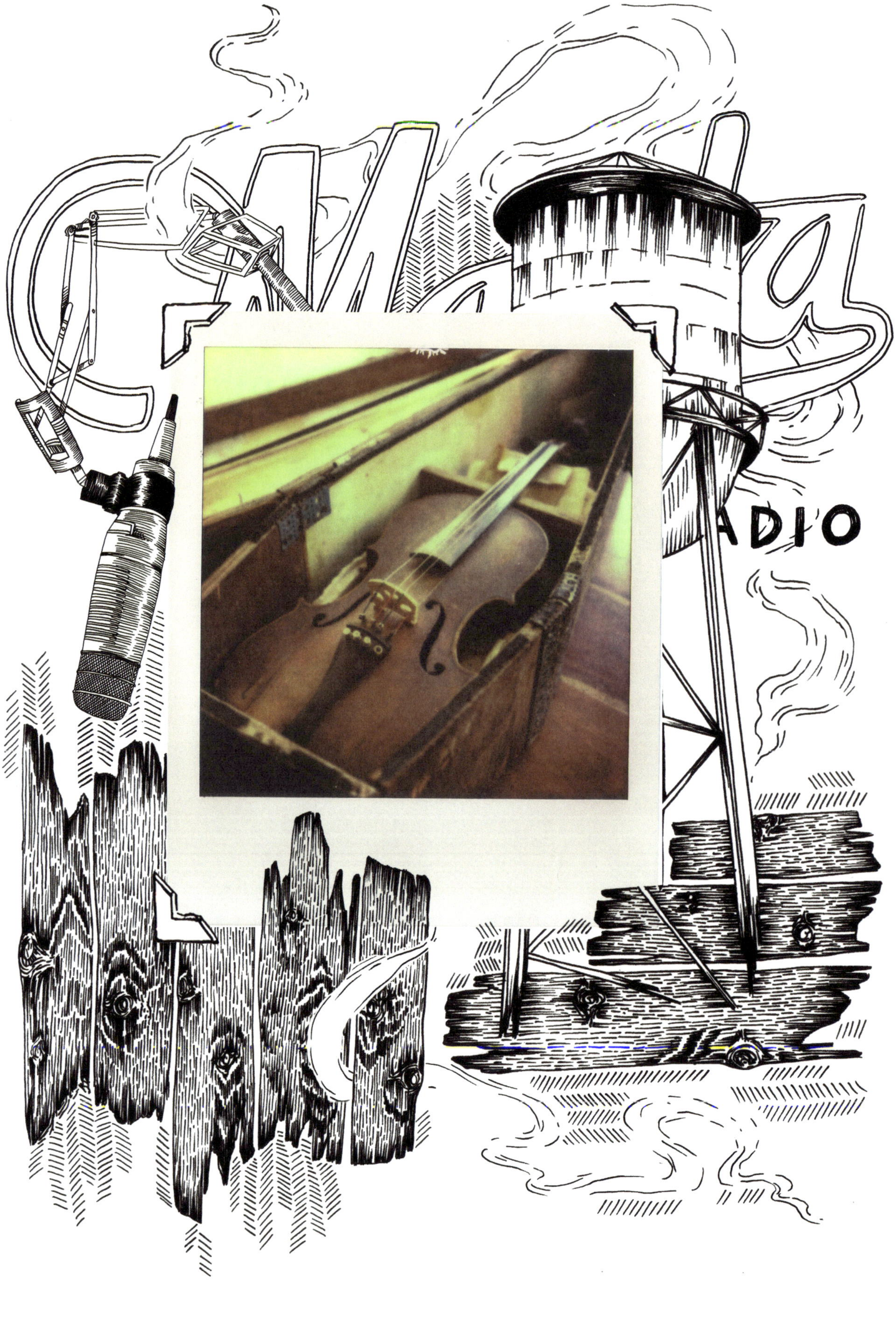
ADIO

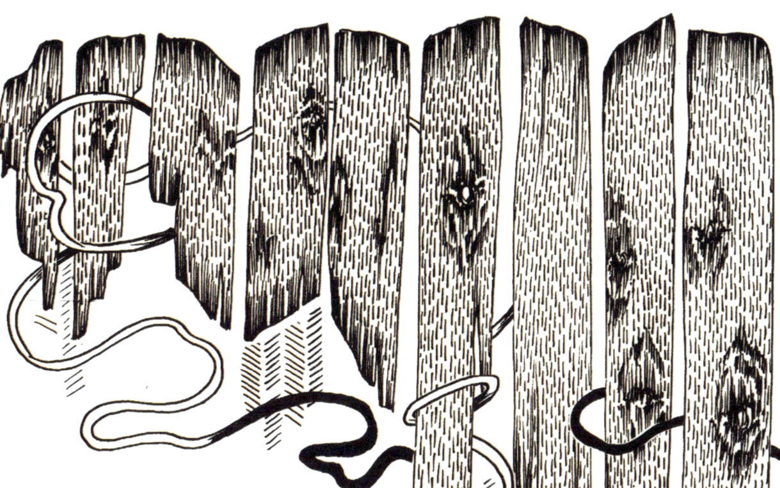

AFTER MEETING WITH TOM MICHAEL, THE TACK-SHARP STATION MANAGER WHO'S BEEN HOLDING DOWN THE FORT HERE FOR THE LAST SEVERAL YEARS, HE INVITES US INTO HIS OFFICE TO SHOW US SOMETHING. HE PRODUCES A WEATHERED WOODEN BOX & BEGINS TO TELL US ABOUT THE WEATHERED, OLD WEST TEXAS MAN WHO TOTED IT TO THE STATION AROUND THE TIME OF WILLIE NELSON'S 80TH BIRTHDAY. HERE'S TOM, WITH THE STORY:

WE WERE DOING A BIRTHDAY TRIBUTE FOR WILLIE NELSON. AND THIS OLD GUY COMES IN HERE CARRYING THIS CASE & A NOTE THAT SAYS, "HAPPY 80TH, WILLIE. GERALD." AND HE'S SIGNED HIS NAME. AND HE WANTS WILLIE TO HAVE THIS.

I'M THINKING:
GOD, IS THIS AN INFANT COFFIN OR SOMETHING?
OR A FIDDLE?

(AND IN THE HANDS OF A BLUEGRASS MUSICIAN, THEY'RE BOTH JUST AS TRAGIC, RIGHT?)

IT TURNS OUT TO BE A FIDDLE. AND IT'S SIGNED BY ERNEST TUBB! THAT'S INCREDIBLE ON ITS OWN, BECAUSE TUBB WAS SUCH A LEGEND.

GERALD SAYS, "LISTEN: MAYBE WILLIE WILL JUST LEAVE IT IN SOME HOTEL ROOM. I WANT YOU TO HAVE IT INSTEAD."

THEN, RIGHT AS HE'S WALKING OUT, HE DANGLES THIS ONE FINAL CRYPTIC COMMENT.

"YOU KNOW, IT WAS WILLIE'S BIRTHDAY, SO I LIT ONE UP & I WAS DRIVING AROUND. I THOUGHT, 'I'M GOING TO GIVE HIM THE VIOLIN.' SO, JUST MAKE SURE WILLIE SEES IT SOMEDAY. AND TELL HIM..... IT'S A WRAPPER."

TOM HOLDS UP THE FIDDLE, EYEBROWS RAISED AS IF HE'S LETTING US IN ON A SECRET. SOMETHING INSIDE — PERHAPS A SMALL BAGGIE? — SLIDES FROM TOP TO BOTTOM WITH A RASPY THUD.

*1 THE "TEXAS TROUBADOUR," FAMOUS AMONG OTHER THINGS FOR SIGNALING THE RISE OF HONKY TONK WITH HIS SINGLE "WALKING THE FLOOR OVER YOU" (1941). HE DIED 30 YEARS AGO NEXT SEPTEMBER.

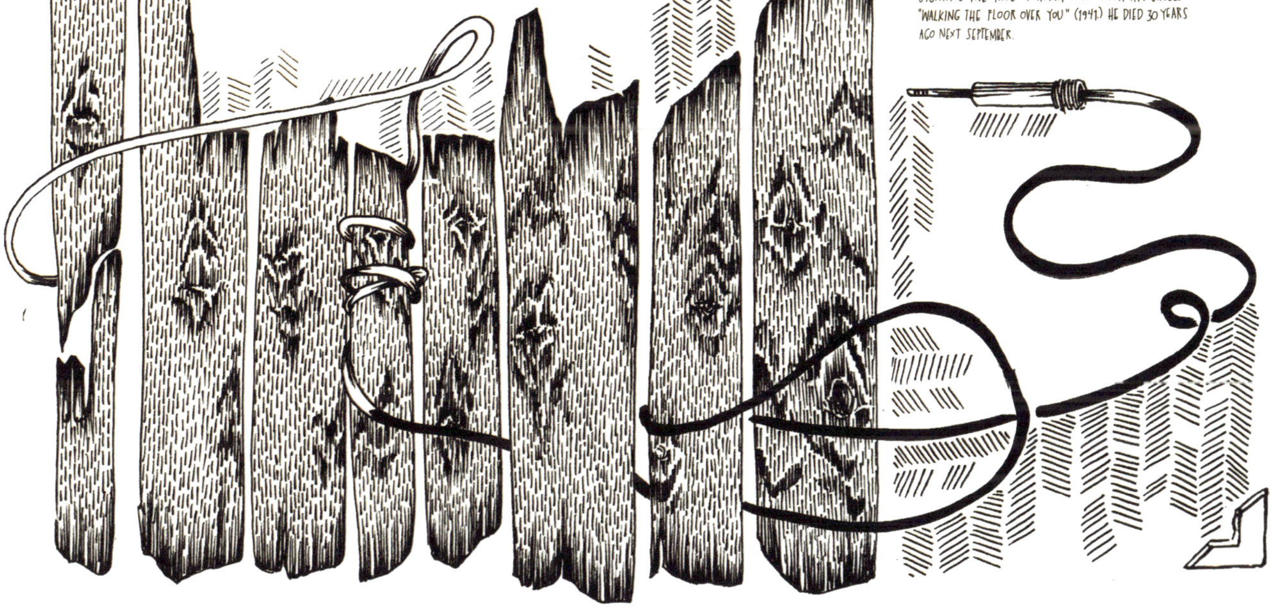

COBRA ROCK BOOT CO.

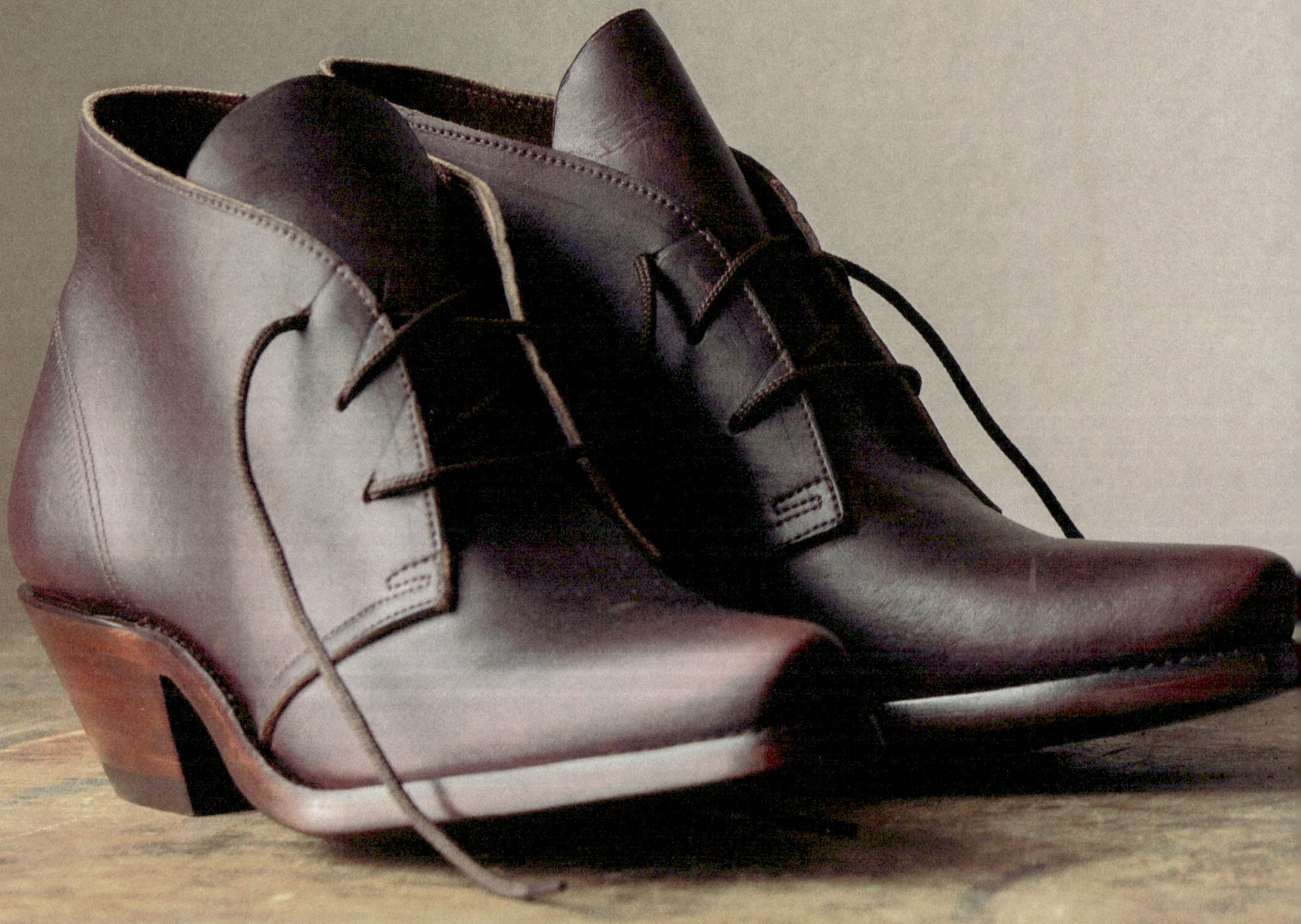

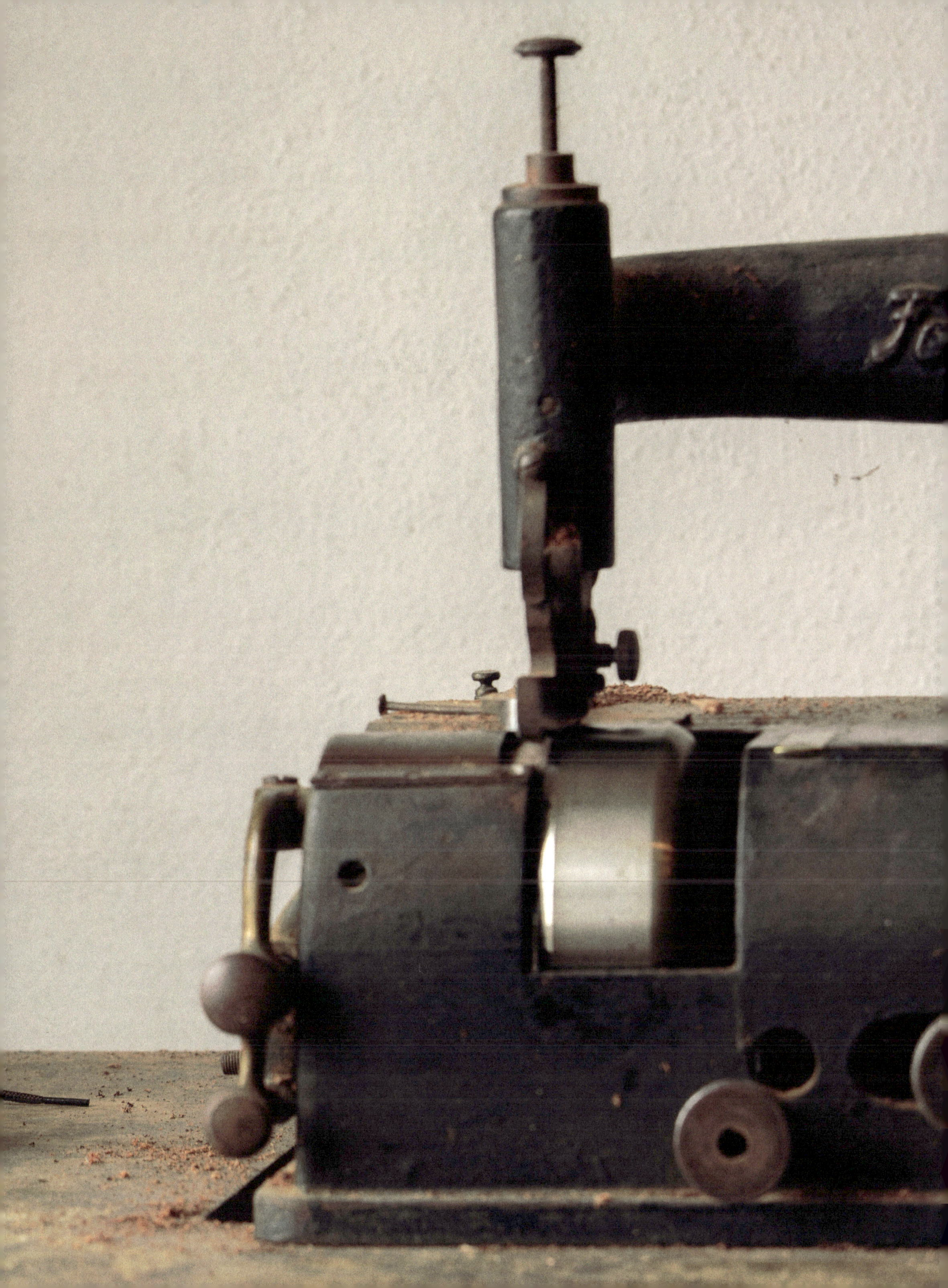

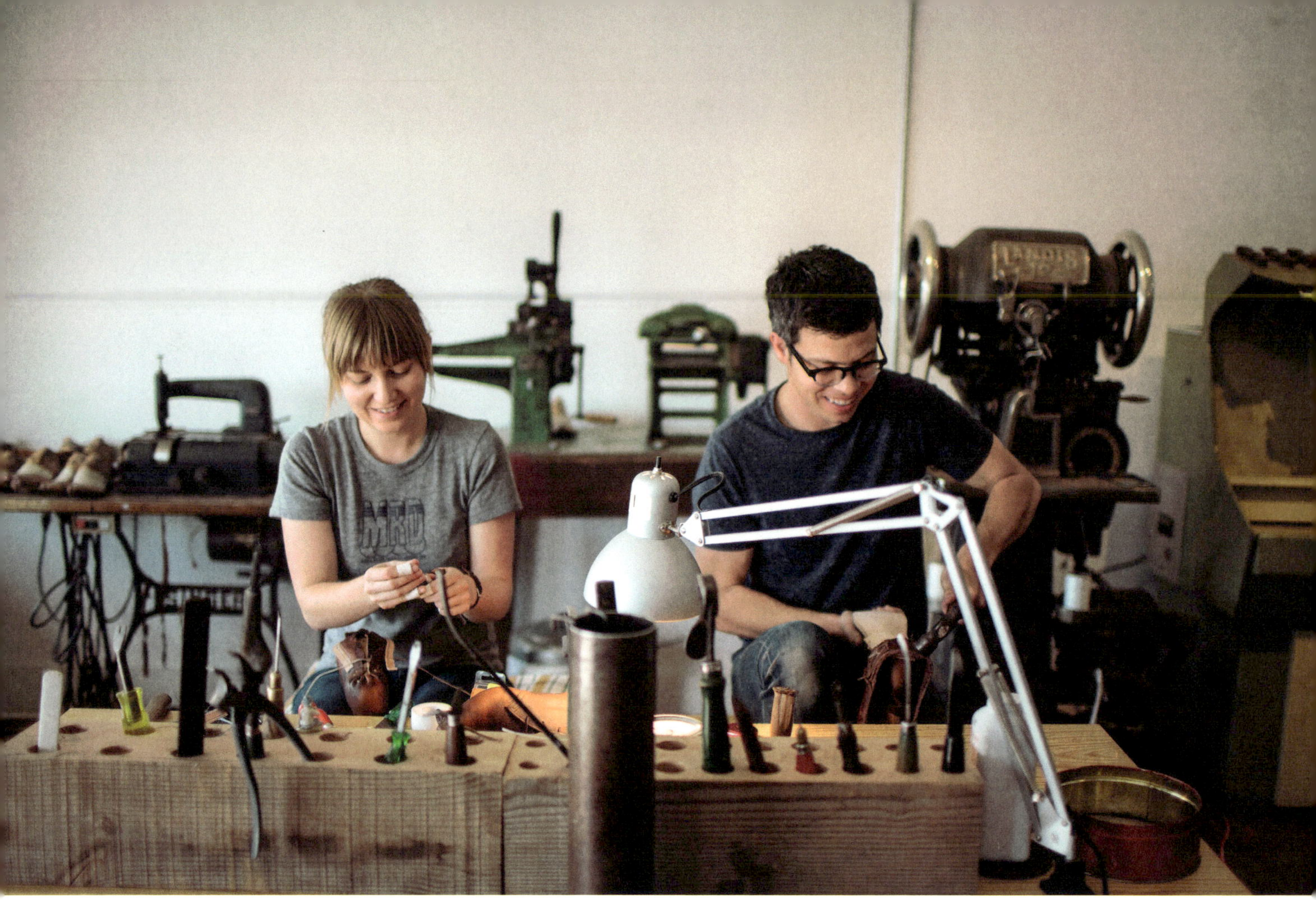

IT WOULD FIGURE THAT "BENEATH THE SHOES," a tune about a man who falls off his horse while crossing a river, is the most popular song by the band Thrift Store Cowboys.

Colt Miller, their one-time guitarist and the son of a rancher, used to trade guitar lessons for bootmaking lessons in his hometown of Lubbock, Texas. In 2010, he would move to Marfa for his muse, a Canadian woman named Logan Caldbeck who was an artist and photographer.

"Seven years ago, we were living in a log cabin on my family's ranch, tying fence in the morning, and in the afternoon riding my dirt bike up to an old airplane hangar where I was keeping my equipment," he says, noting that Caldbeck would help out with the tops and vamps of custom cowboy boots he was making. It was through finding her that he also found Cobra Rock Boot Company. "She was a quick learner with great ideas and attention to detail. Logan got a job at the Chinati Foundation, and after living in Marfa for a while, we knew it was the right place to start Cobra Rock with our own line of boots."

And what a founding. Since establishing their South Highland boot—a cross between a lace-up desert boot and a cowboy boot—in 2011, they've gained a loyal following that stretches from California to New York. When we spoke with them last, they had accrued a nine month waiting list.

To date, Miller and Caldbeck have focused on a female style, producing boots at a rate of about one pair a week, though they have been developing new designs that will debut later this year. They use materials sourced in the US, including full grain oil-tanned cowhides, leather soles, and metal shanks held in place with lemon-wood pegs. They work with antique tools and equipment, including a Landis K sole stitcher built in 1921, a Singer topstitcher built in 1939, and vintage lasts they found in a couple defunct shoe shops in the Texas panhandle.

"It was like a history lesson because I got to see the different lines and shapes that were popular when those lasts were made from about 1939 to 1951," Miller recalls. "Logan and I really loved this one shape with a great square toe, and that's what we built our South Highlands on. Later, we were able to have resin lasts made from that shape, with adjustments made so they better fit modern feet and have a lace-up fit, rather than a cowboy slip-on fit."

Refusing to hand off any element of production to an outside source "because [they] like to do it all," Miller and Caldbeck continue to make each pair of boots one at a time, all by hand, and all by themselves.

This is all to say: There's a lot beneath their shoes. – *M.W.*

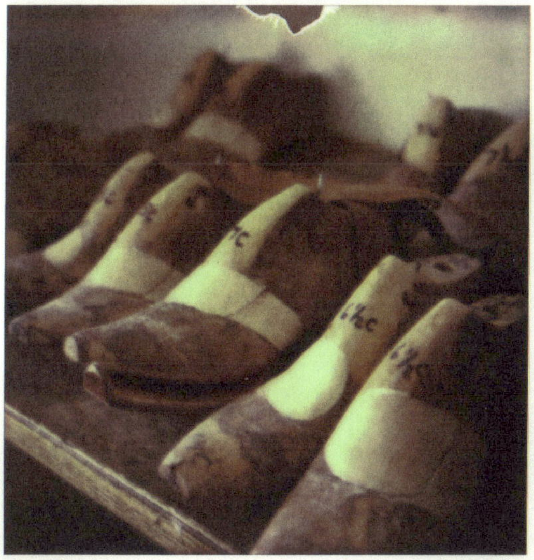

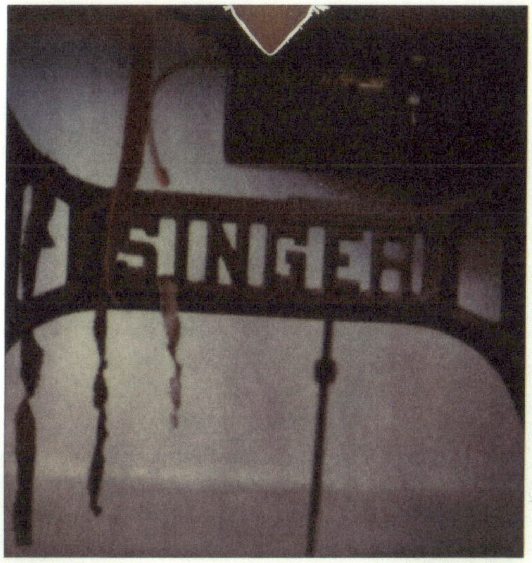
SINGER

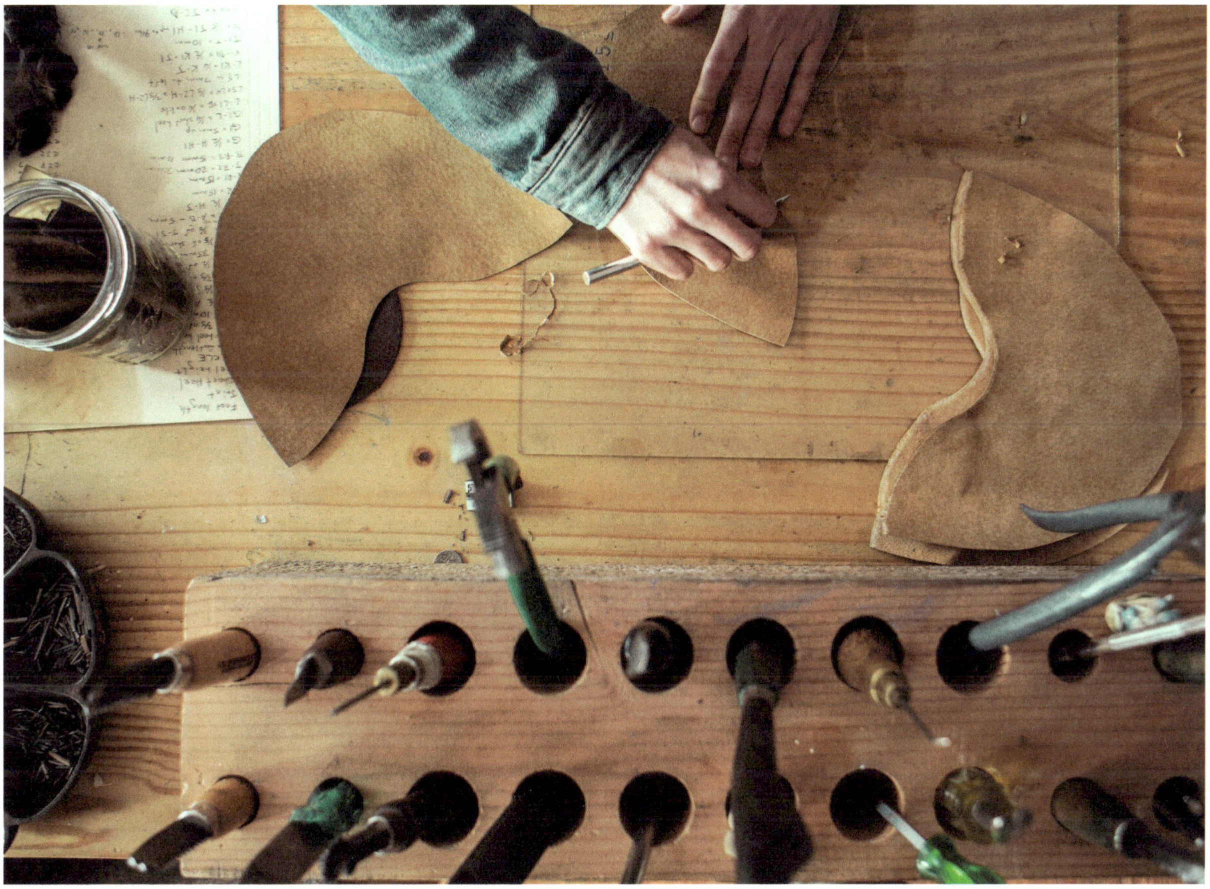

THE UNLIKELY STORY OF PRADA, PLAYBOY & THE TEXAS DEPARTMENT OF TRANSPORTATION

BY EMILY FERBER

IT GOES AS FOLLOWS: ON THE SIDE OF U.S. ROUTE 90, THERE IS A FAKE PRADA STORE. ARCHITECTURAL ARTISTS MICHAEL ELMGREEN & INGAR DRAGSET BUILT IT IN 2005 AS AN EXTENSION OF A PROJECT THEY STARTED AT THEIR NEW YORK CITY GALLERY IN 2001. WITH PERMISSION FROM THE BRAND, THEY CONSTRUCTED A REPLICA OF A STANDALONE PRADA STORE JUST OUTSIDE MARFA, FILLED IT WITH THE BRAND'S LEATHER GOODS, AND LOCKED THE DOORS. NO ONE CAN GET INTO THE STORE, AND IT DOESN'T SELL ANYTHING. AFTER THE INSTALLATION WAS VANDALIZED & SUBSEQUENTLY PATCHED UP, ELMGREEN & DRAGSET DECIDED THAT THE STORE WOULD STAND THERE, UNFIXED & LEFT TO DECOMPOSE NATURALLY.

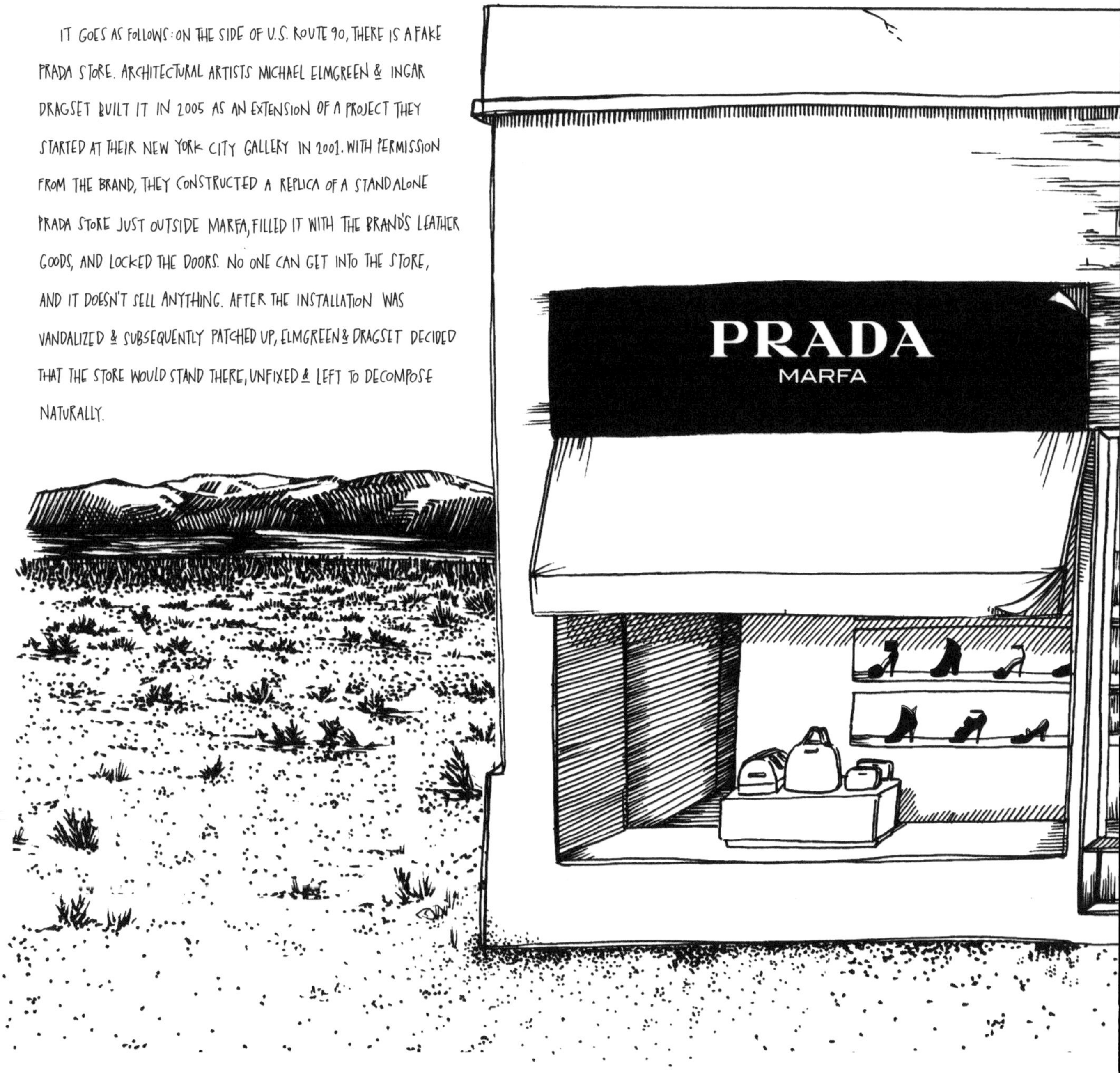

ALL WAS GOING ALONG SWIMMINGLY—SO SWIMMINGLY THAT *PLAYBOY* DECIDED TO BUILD THEIR OWN INSTALLATION JUST UP THE ROAD, IN THE FORM OF A LARGE, NEON PINK BUNNY FLANKED BY A 1972 DODGE CHARGER.

ENTER: THE TEXAS DEPARTMENT OF TRANSPORTATION. OFFICALS ARE NOW QUESTIONING WHETHER THE INSTALLATIONS ARE ART OR ADVERTISING, WHICH COULD POSE A PROBLEM SINCE NEITHER *PLAYBOY* NOR ELMGREEN AND DRAGSET APPLIED FOR THE PERMITS REQUIRED FOR ADVERTISERS TO LAWFULLY ADORN THE HIGHWAY. THE DIFFERENCE IS THAT WHILE THE *PLAYBOY* FIXTURE WAS COMISSIONED BY A BRAND, PRADA MARFA WAS AN INDEPENDENT ENDEAVOR. NOW ONLY TIME (AND LEGAL PROCEEDINGS) WILL TELL WHICH COUNTS FOR ART AND WHICH FOR AD.

BUT IF ELMGREEN & DRAGSET INTENDED FOR PRADA MARFA TO DISAPPEAR EVENTUALLY ANYWAY, THIS FATE MIGHT NOT BE SO INORGANIC AFTER ALL.

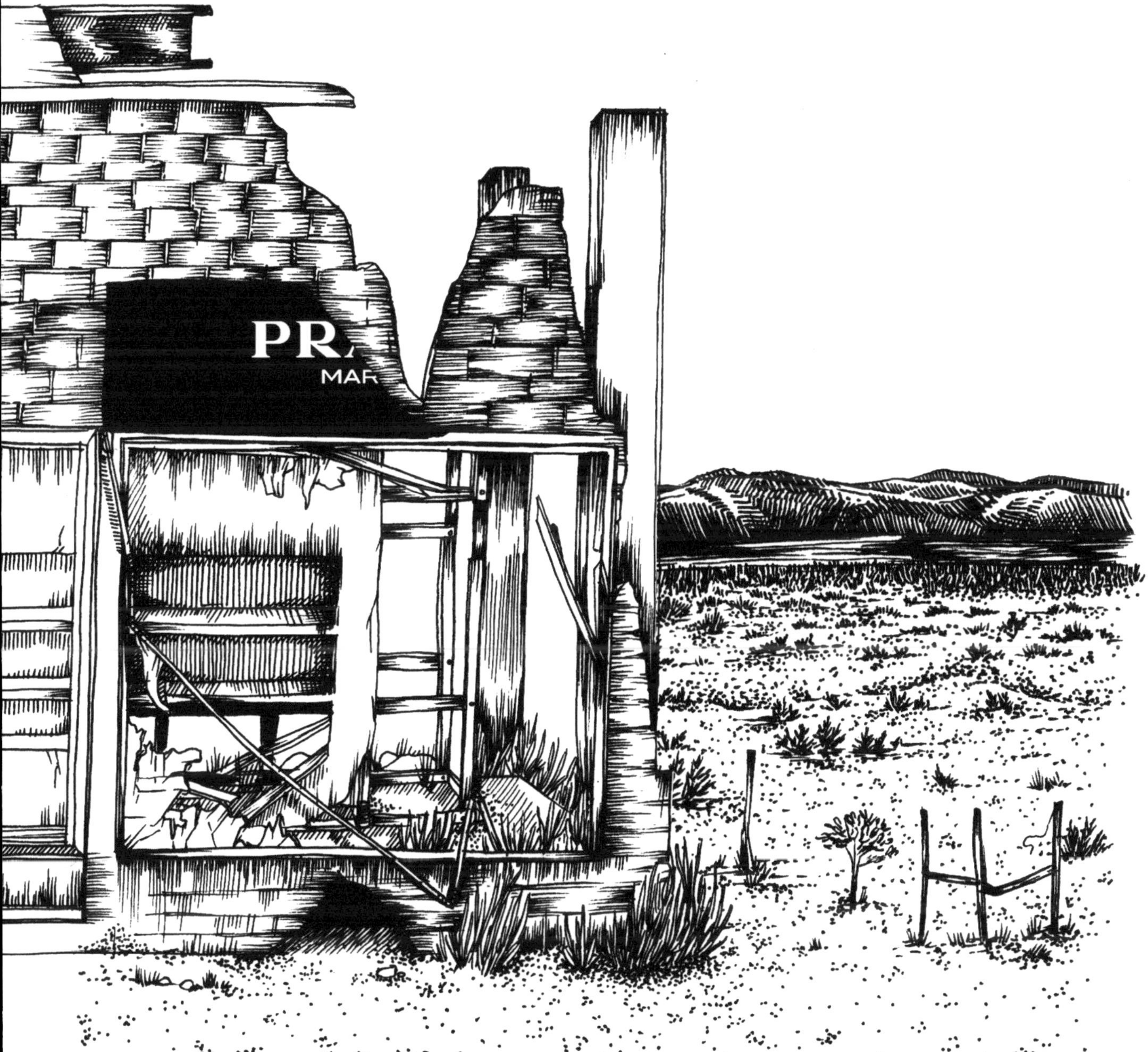

EL COSMICO

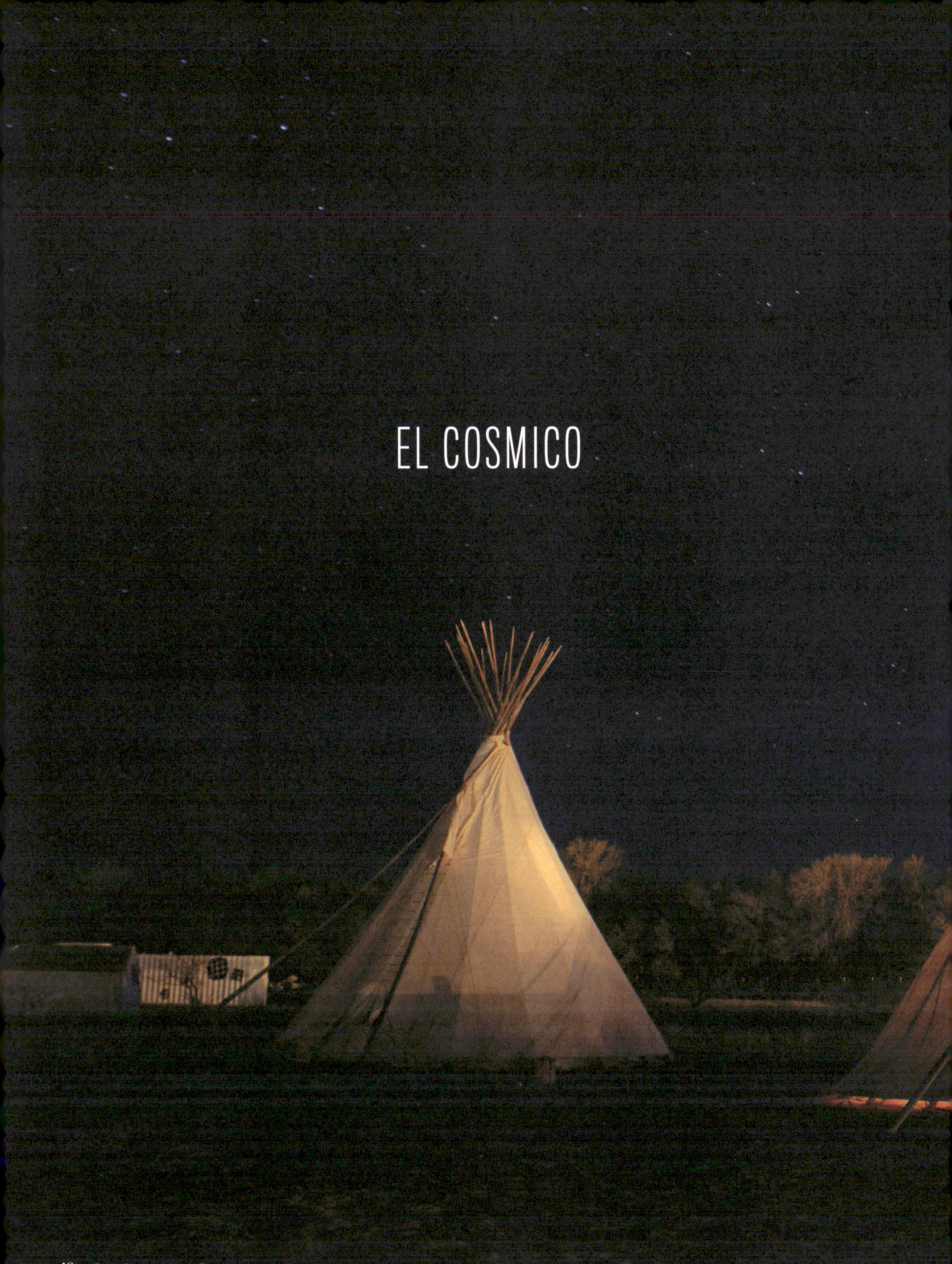

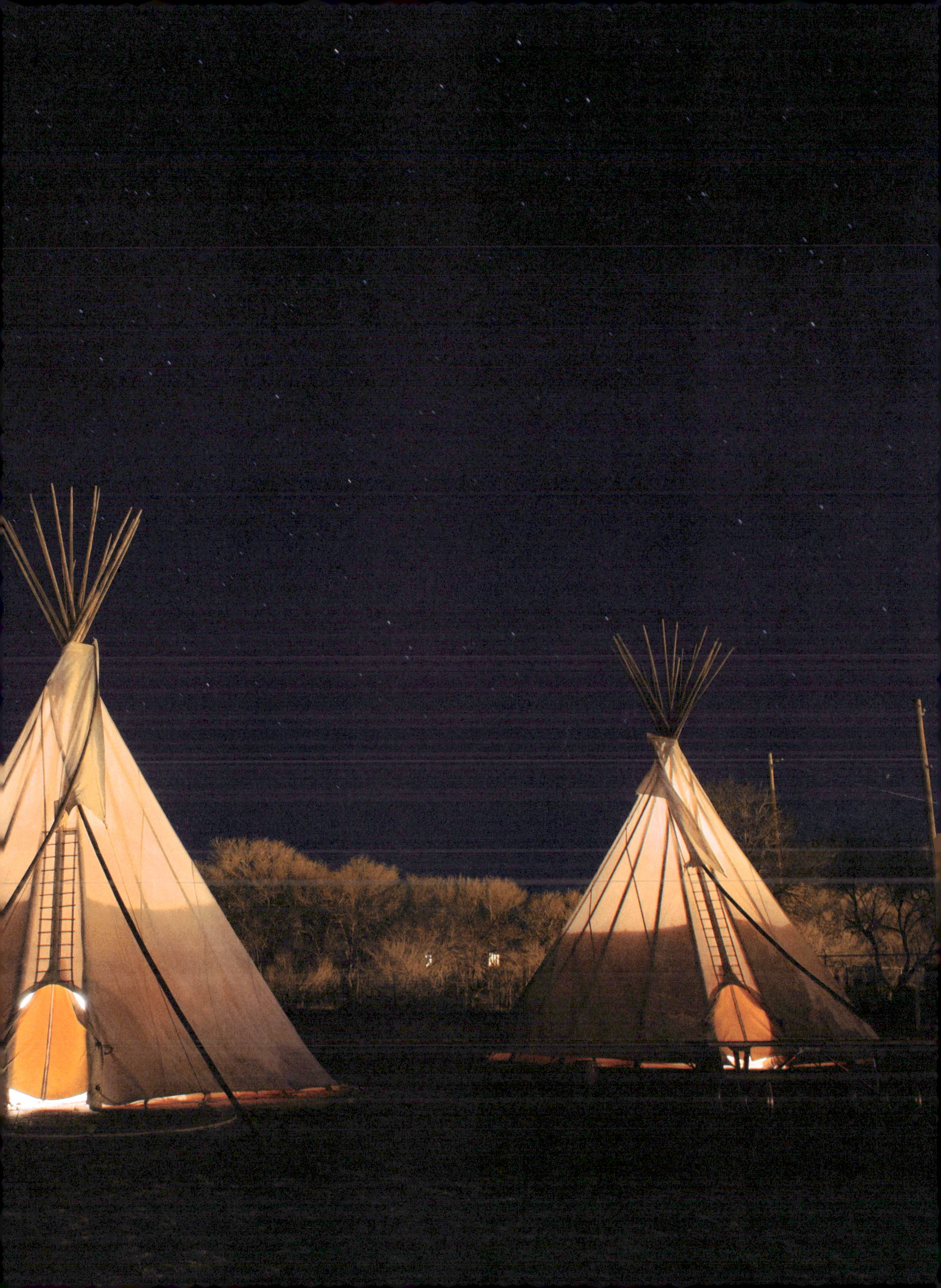

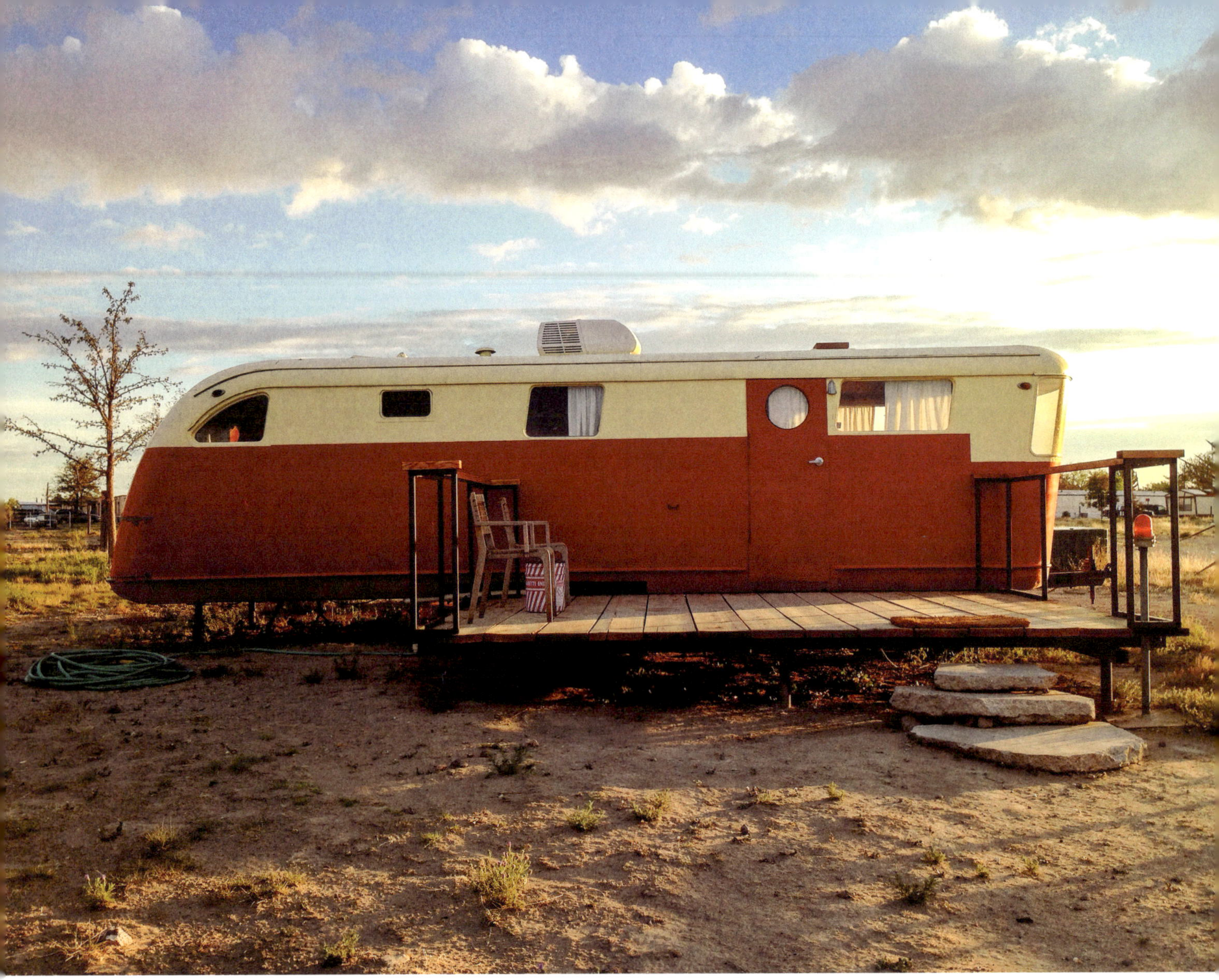

IT'S HARD NOT TO BE CHARMED BY EL COSMICO'S assorted accommodations. Like the pricier end of Marfa's lodging spectrum, Ranch 2810 (p. 88), El Cosmico isn't exactly a hotel in the traditional sense.

Owner Liz Lambert bought the property in 2006—then, just an 18-acre expanse of desert—but it wasn't until three years later that she opened it as a continually evolving arrangement of alternative dwellings. Lambert, whose Bunkhouse Group includes similarly unorthodox hotel offerings in Austin and San Antonio, scattered the plot with campsites, safari and scout tents, Sioux-style tepees, and renovated vintage trailers.

Among the offerings is a 1950 Branstrator Trailer with full bed and indoor plumbing for $90 a night and a roomier 1956 Imperial Mansion with a king and twin bed for $125 a night. Dwellers tight on cash can opt for more rustic yurts or tepees, furnished with futons and lanterns, starting at $80 a night. Visit at the end of summer to catch the Trans-Pecos Festival of Music and Love, an annual three-day music festival, workshop, and marketplace hosted on the property.

Intel: Prices vary by accommodation:, from safari tents ($65-75/night) to teepees ($80-85/night) to trailers ($110-170/night). The campground has a bath house, dutch tubs, a hammock grove, a shared outdoor kitchen, picnic tables, and public bikes. WiFi is purposely restricted to the main office, but you're never too far off the grid. For more information, visit *elcosmico.com*. —E.F.

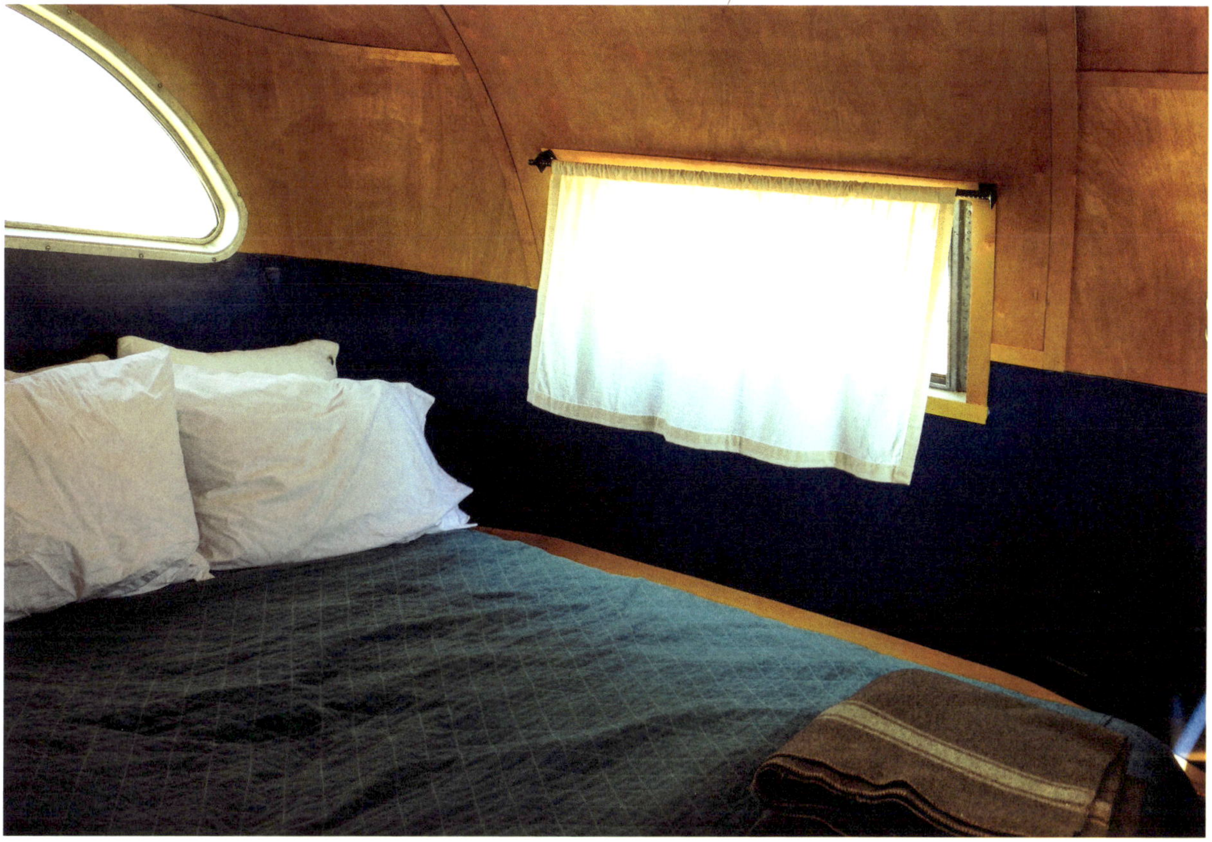

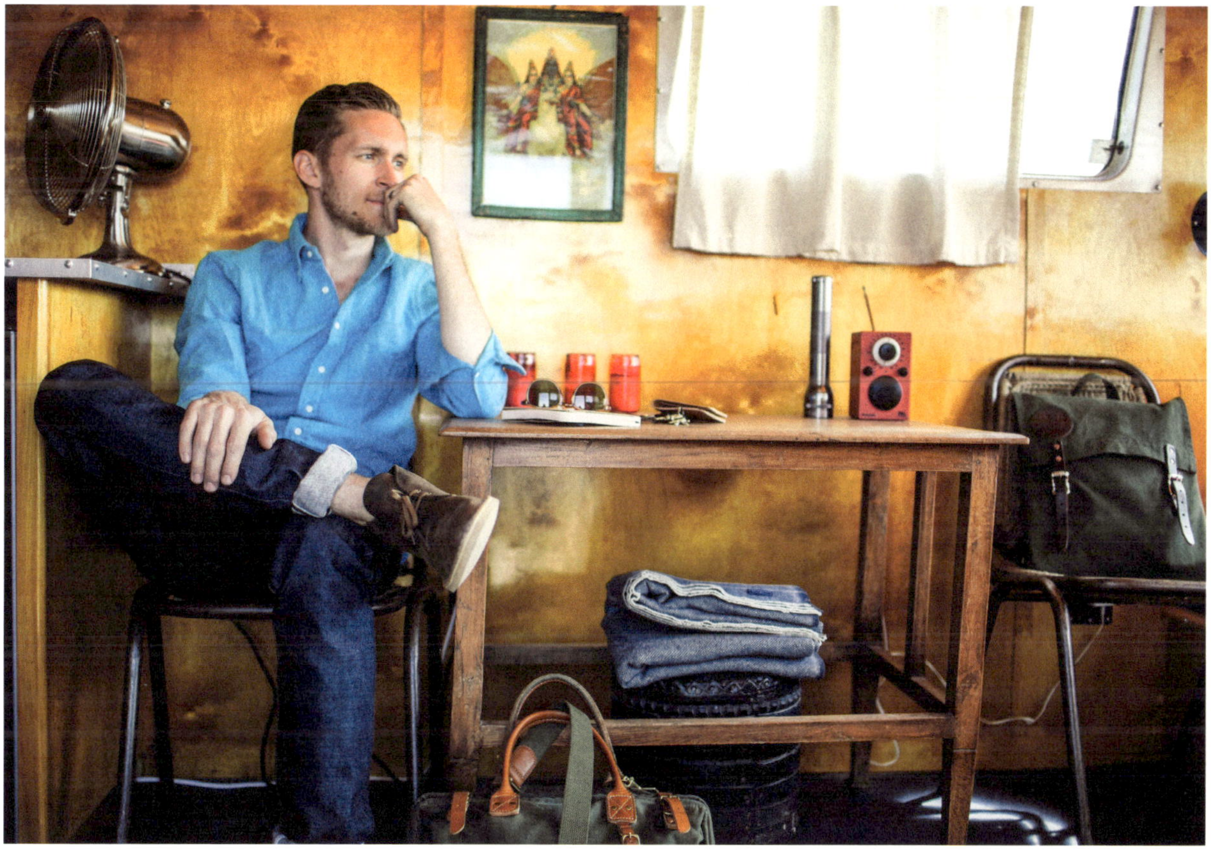

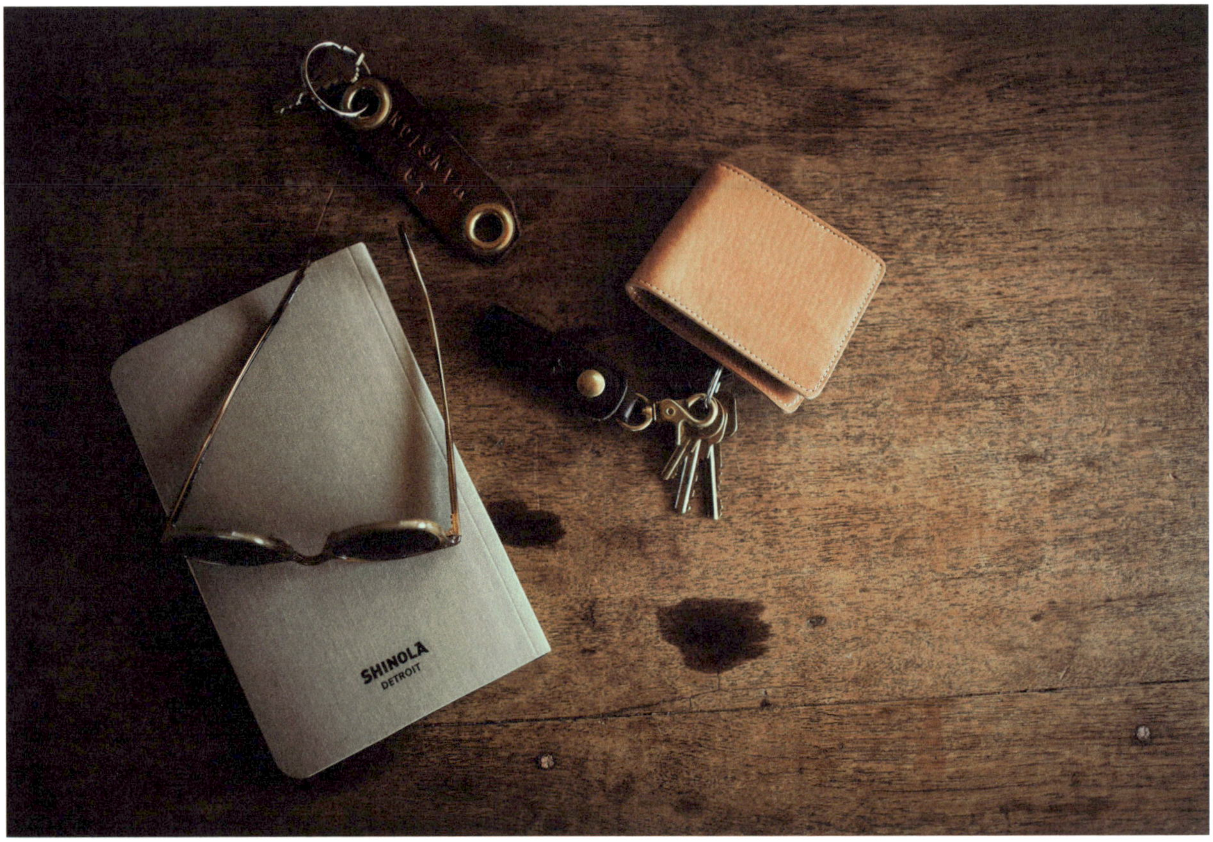
SHINOLA
DETROIT

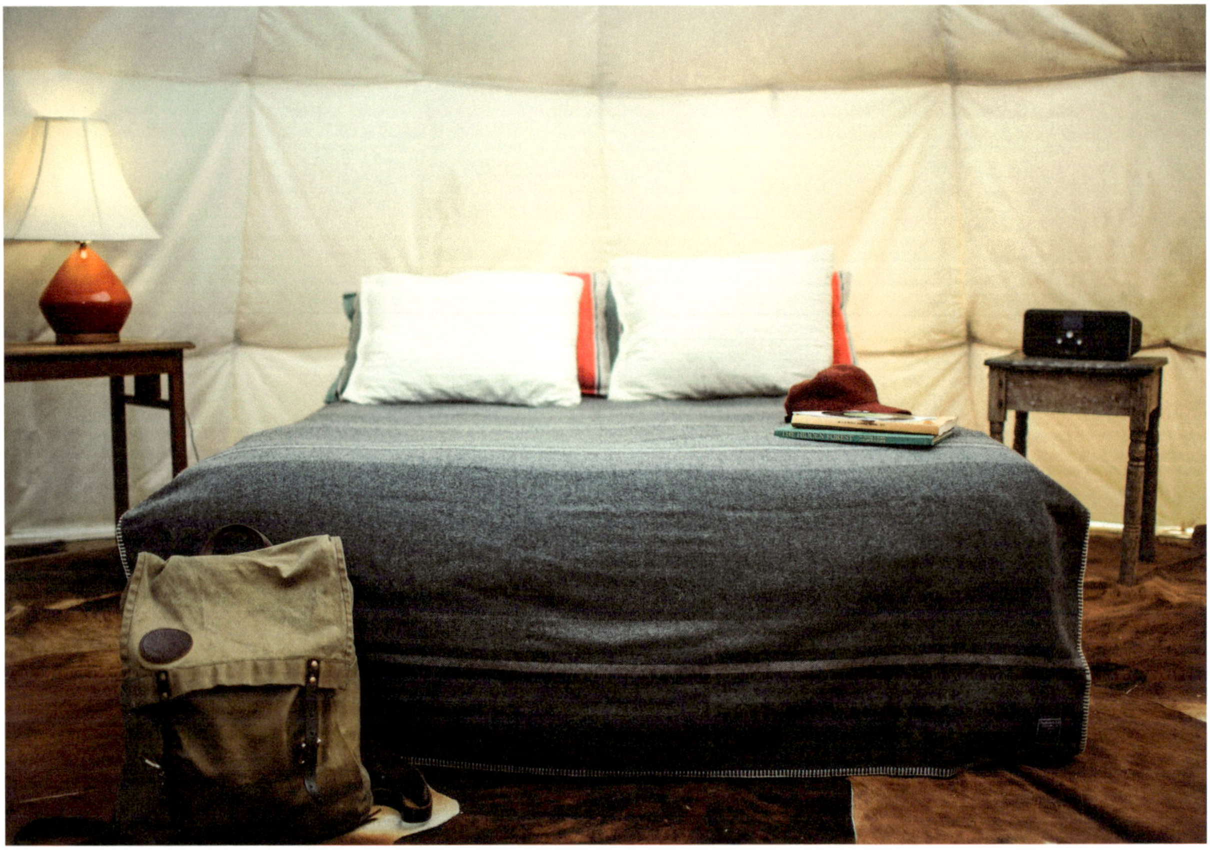

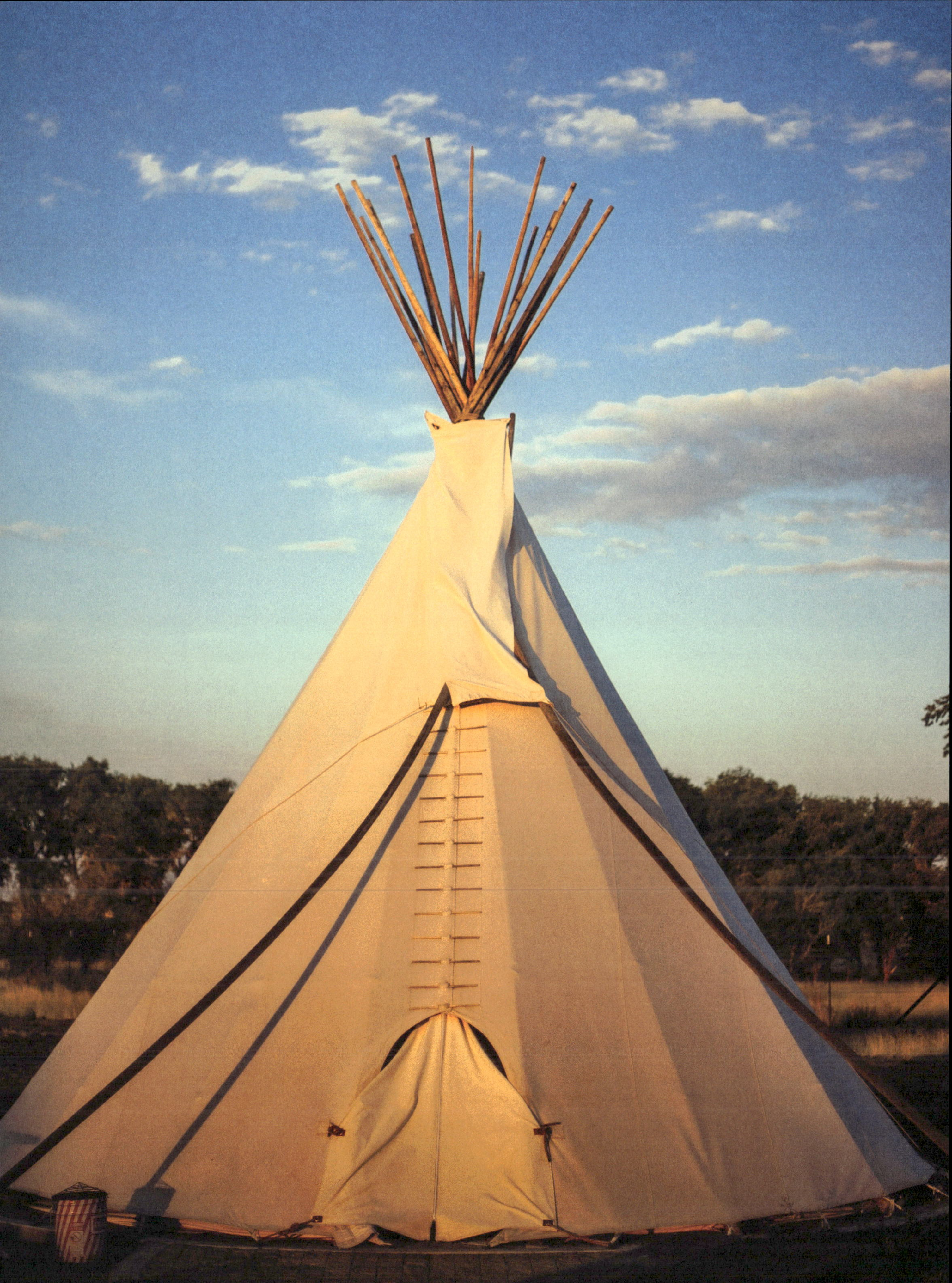

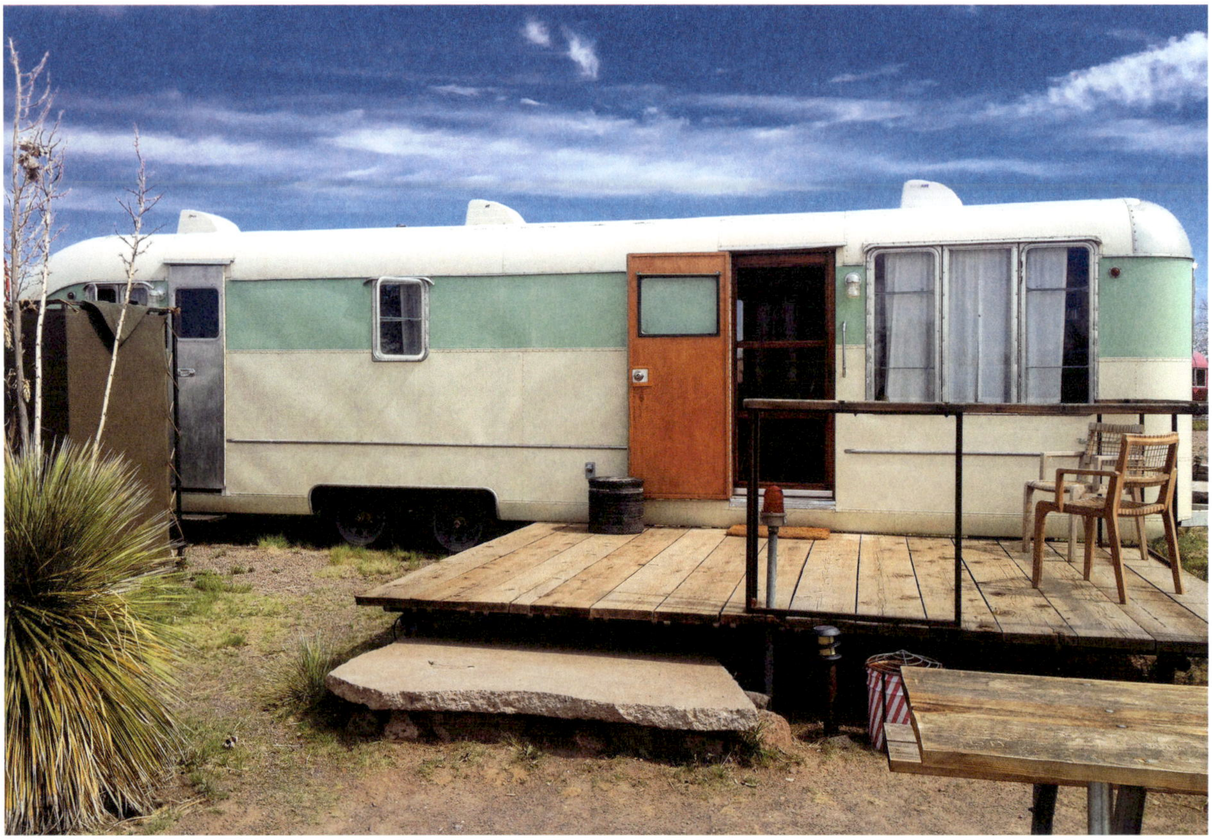

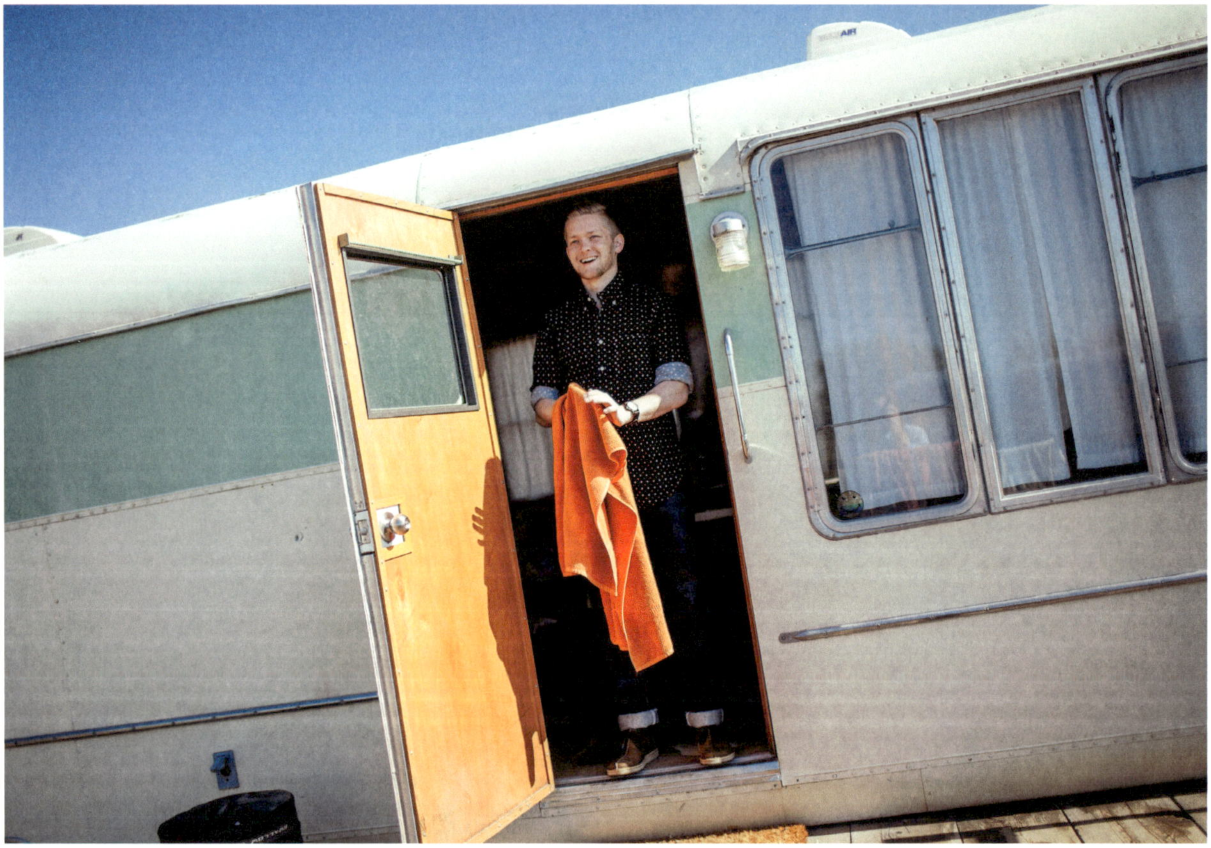

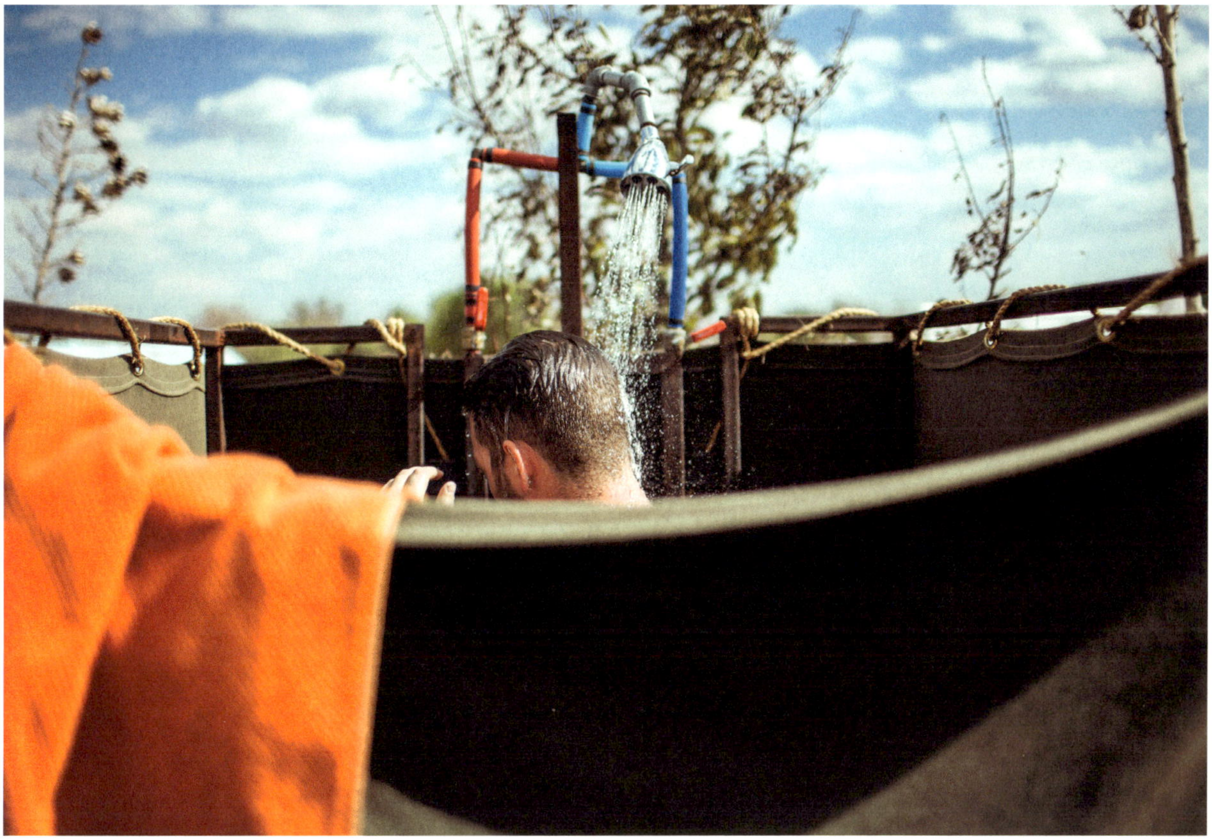

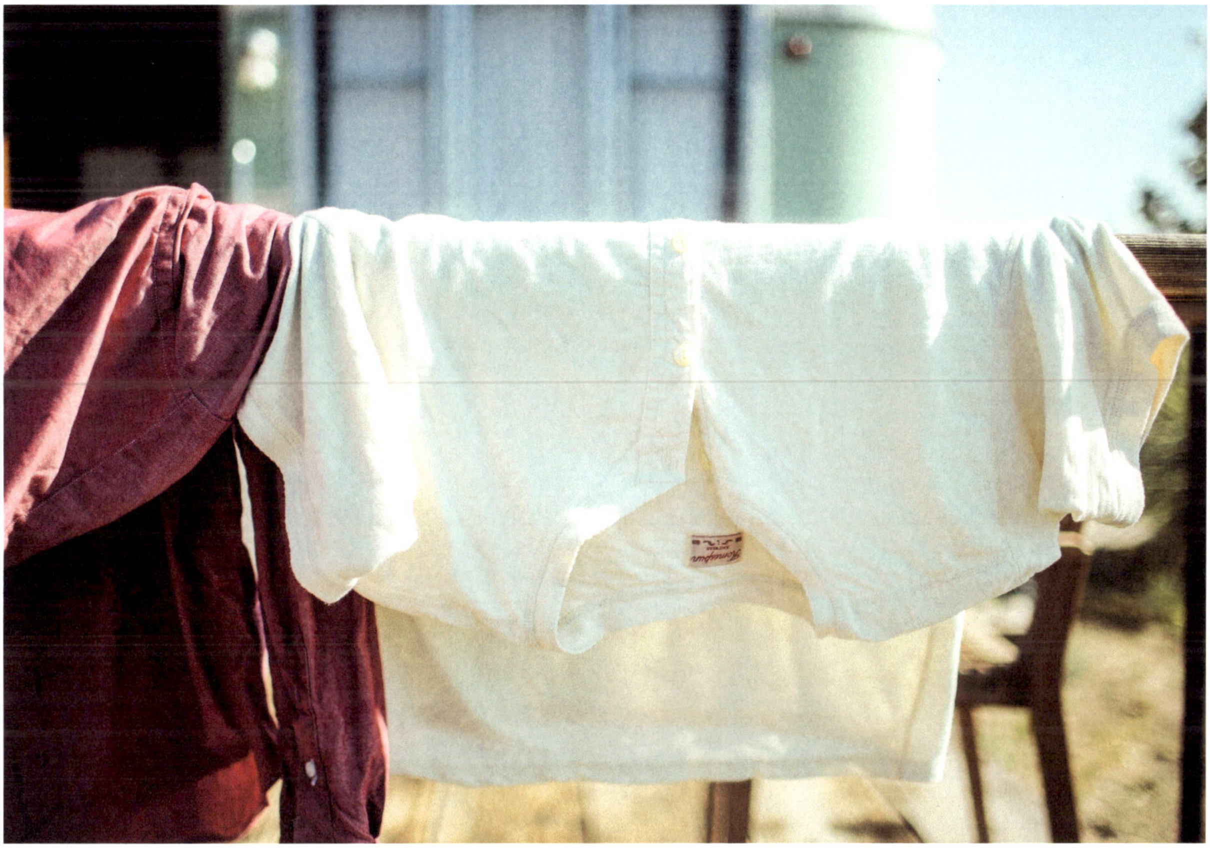

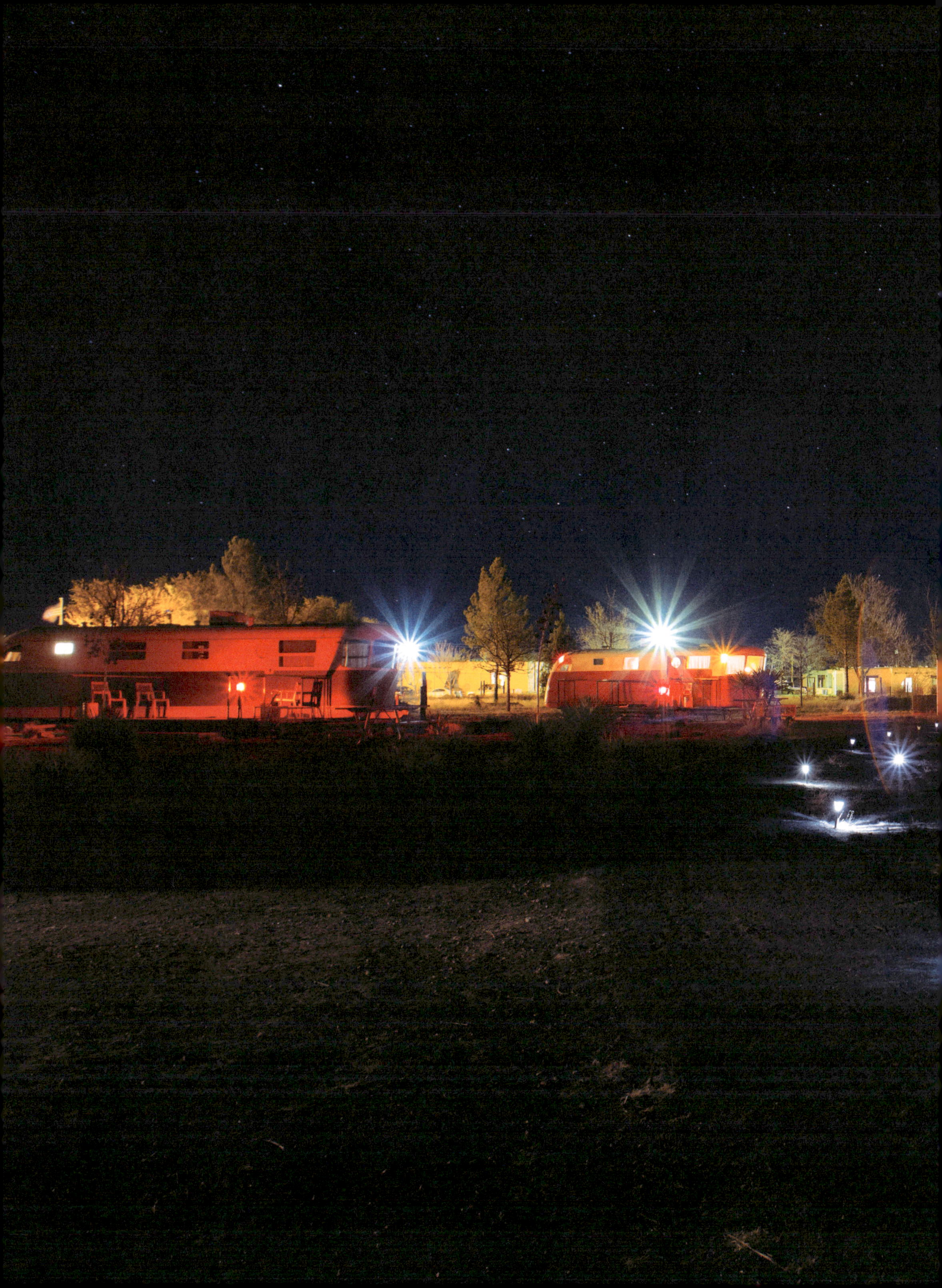

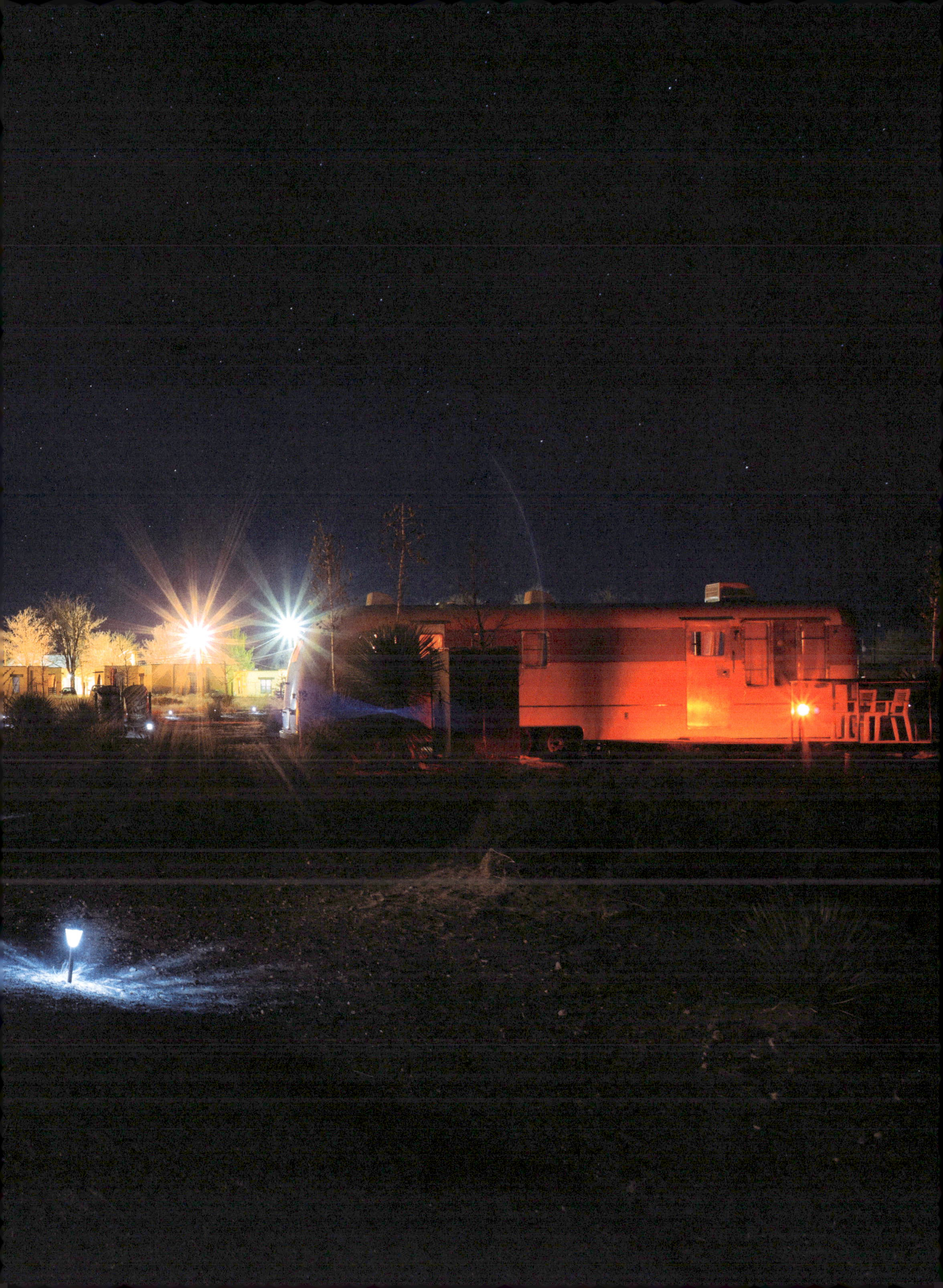

GARZA MARFA

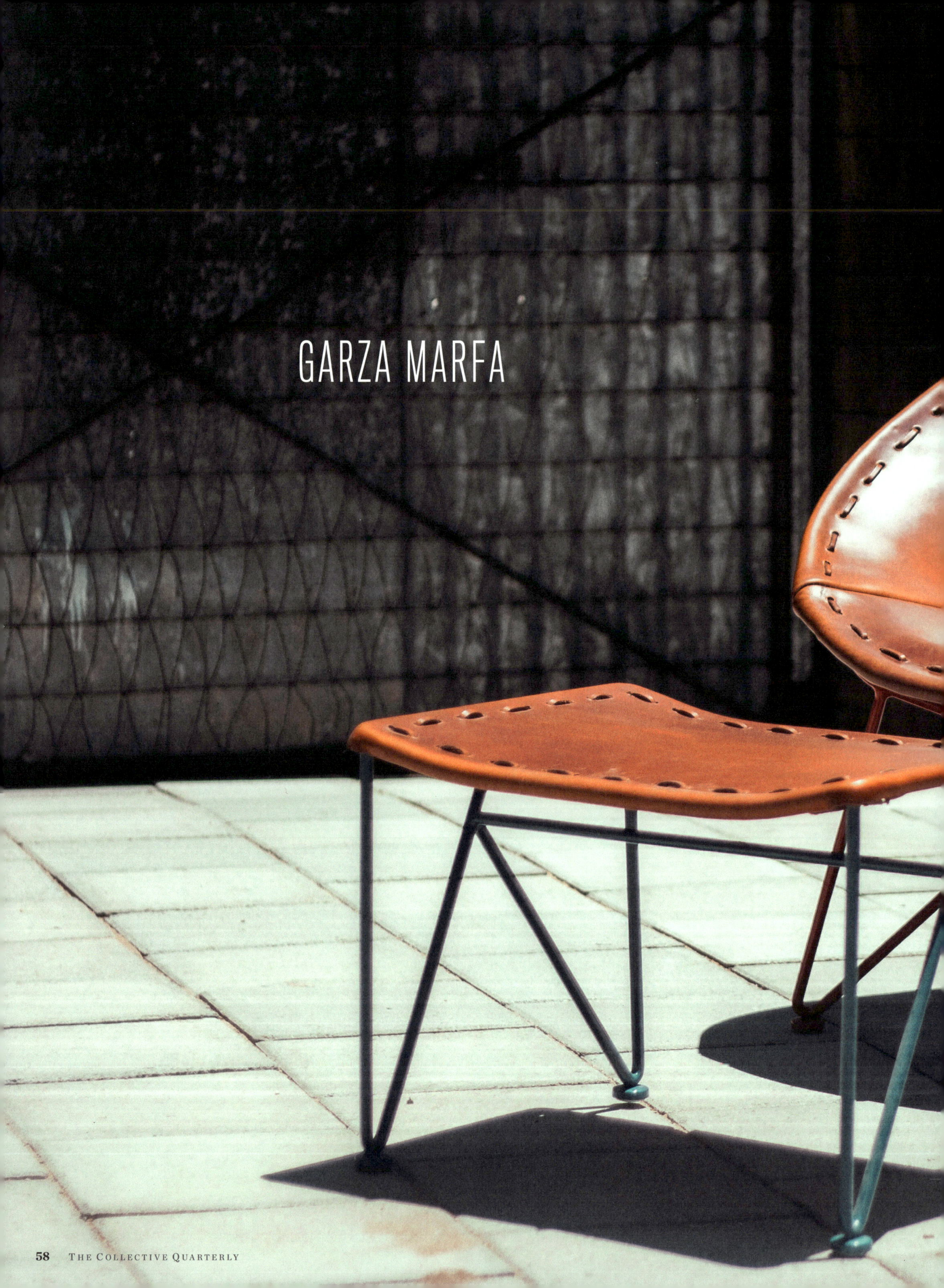

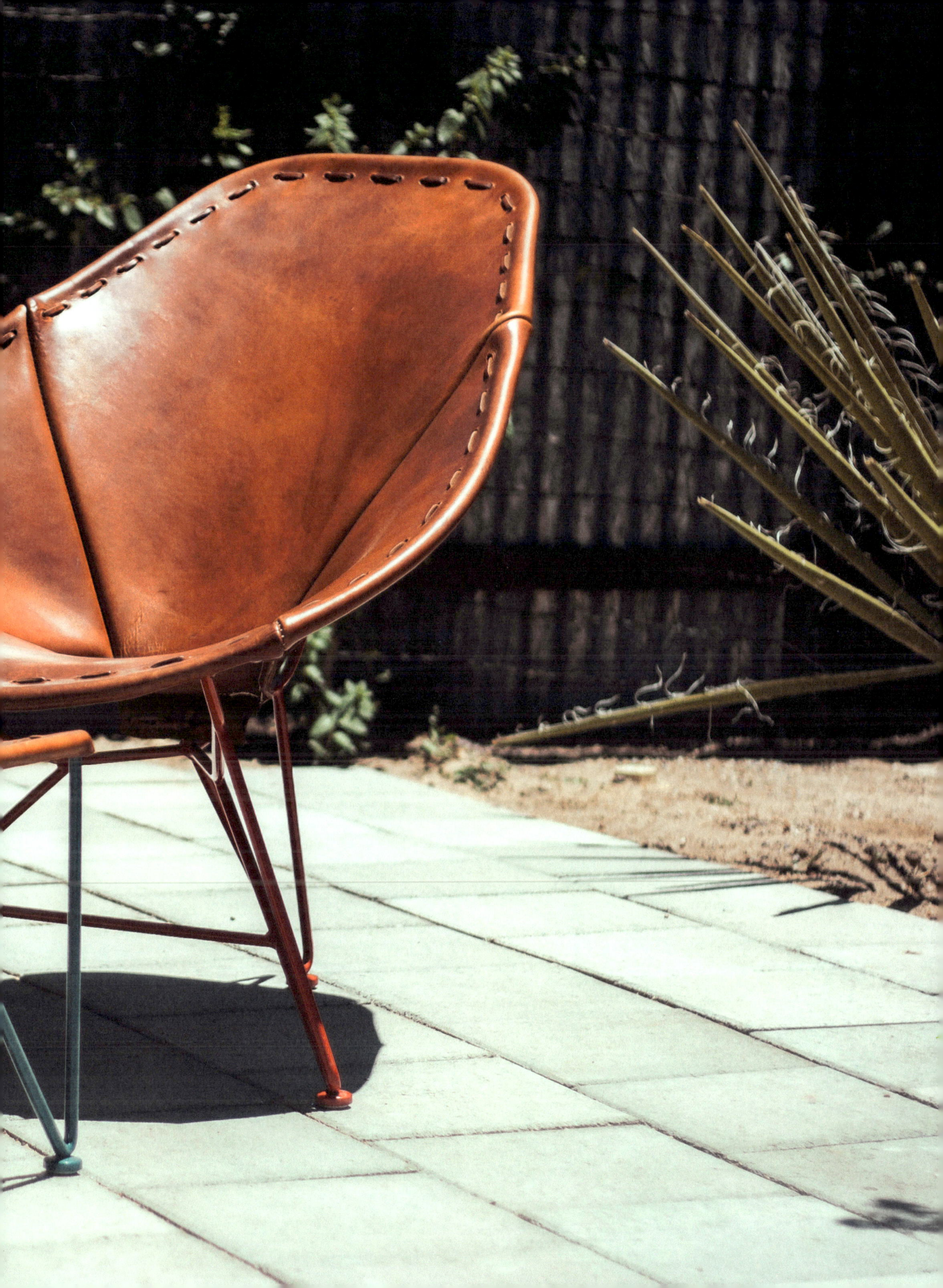

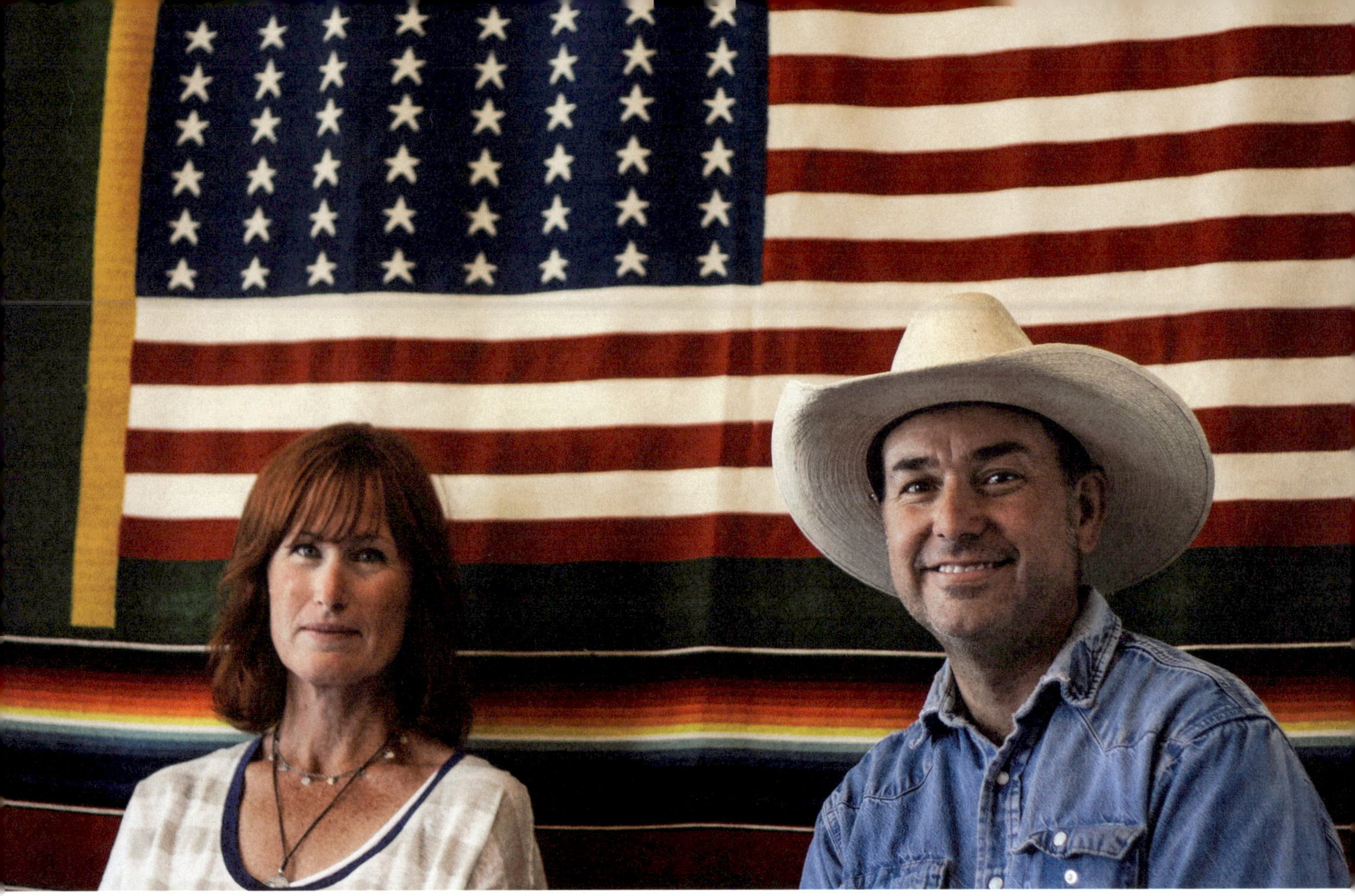

INSPIRED BY THE SIMPLE BEAUTIES OF WEST TEXAS— the colorful sunsets, the armadillo, the yucca, the agave, and the tumbleweed—the Garzas epitomize Southwestern Minimalism.

For nearly a decade, Jamey Garza has made custom furniture. The showroom he shares with his wife, Constance Holt-Garza, is situated on a corner lot across from their home, not far from one of the four-way stops in downtown Marfa. The 900 square-foot space is filled with Jamey's powder-coated steel, wood, and saddle leather furniture; Constance's rugs, table linens, and throw pillows; and drawings and paintings from local artists Leslie Wilkes and Meghan Gerety.

Jamey studied studio art at the University of Texas. As an Austin native, dare he be considered a country boy, he met his city girl when he moved to San Francisco to earn an MFA in painting at the San Francisco Art Institute and fell for Constance, a Bay Area native, who owned a clothing boutique at the time called Salon de Thé.

Though he learned to weld as a boy, it didn't find its way into his work until he began building furniture. He created a business centered on the Southwestern influences of his youth and the simplicity of clean, modern design he'd grown to appreciate in grad school. Using raw saddle leather typically found on the back of a cowboy's mustang, paired with an industrial material like steel or wrought iron, Jamey's furniture speaks to his life as both a country mouse and a city mouse. He sits perfectly in both worlds.

After living in Los Angeles for some time, Jamey and Constance were tapped in 2003 by their longtime friend Liz Lambert to build furniture for Marfa's Thunderbird Hotel.

"Before we'd moved, we purchased an old adobe house in Marfa," Jamey says. "After we arrived, we had this idea that we would complete the furniture for the hotel, make our adobe house 'livable,' and then make our way to Austin."

"But we quickly realized Marfa was home," Constance adds.

Jamey sums up the little town's pull on their process: "For us, the physical open space of Marfa absolutely inspires our individual creative mind spaces. It's great. We can turn totally inward in the studio or the workshop, and then we can walk outside and see an endless landscape, and that big, big sky." –*M.W.*

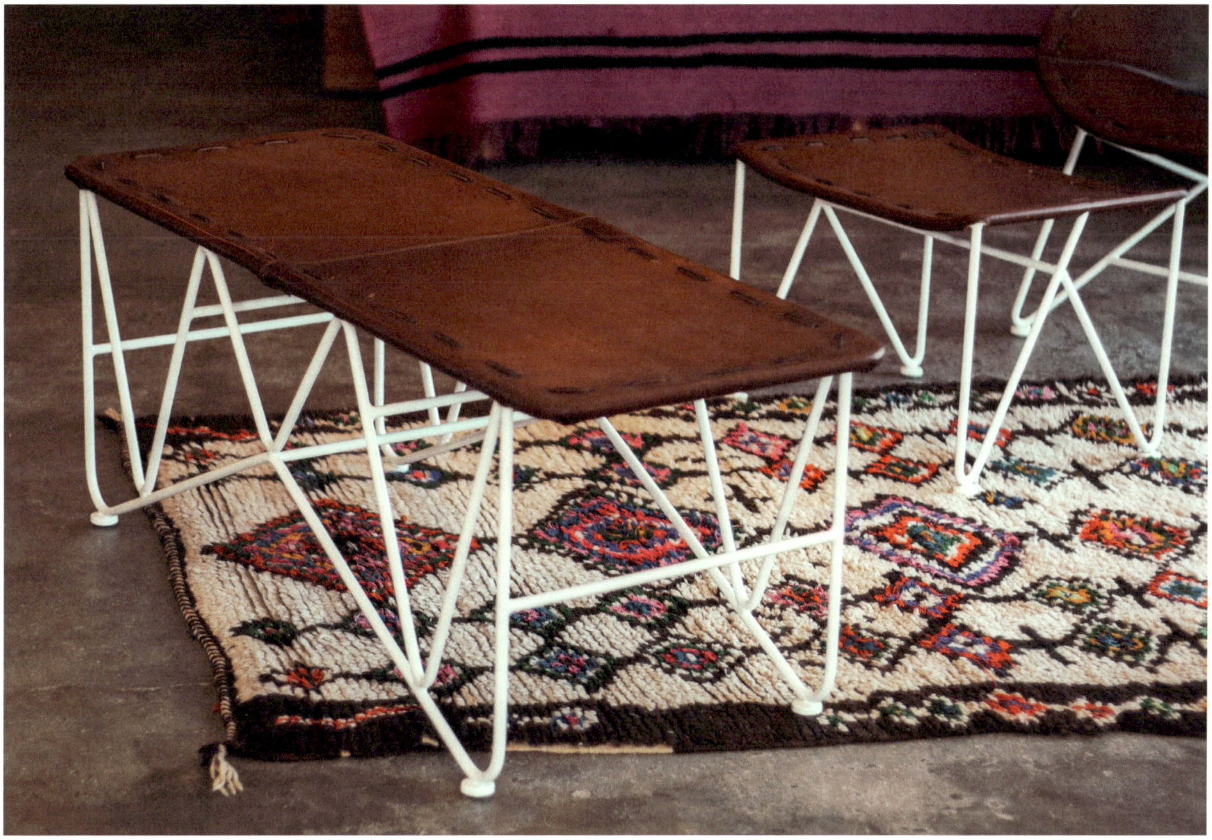

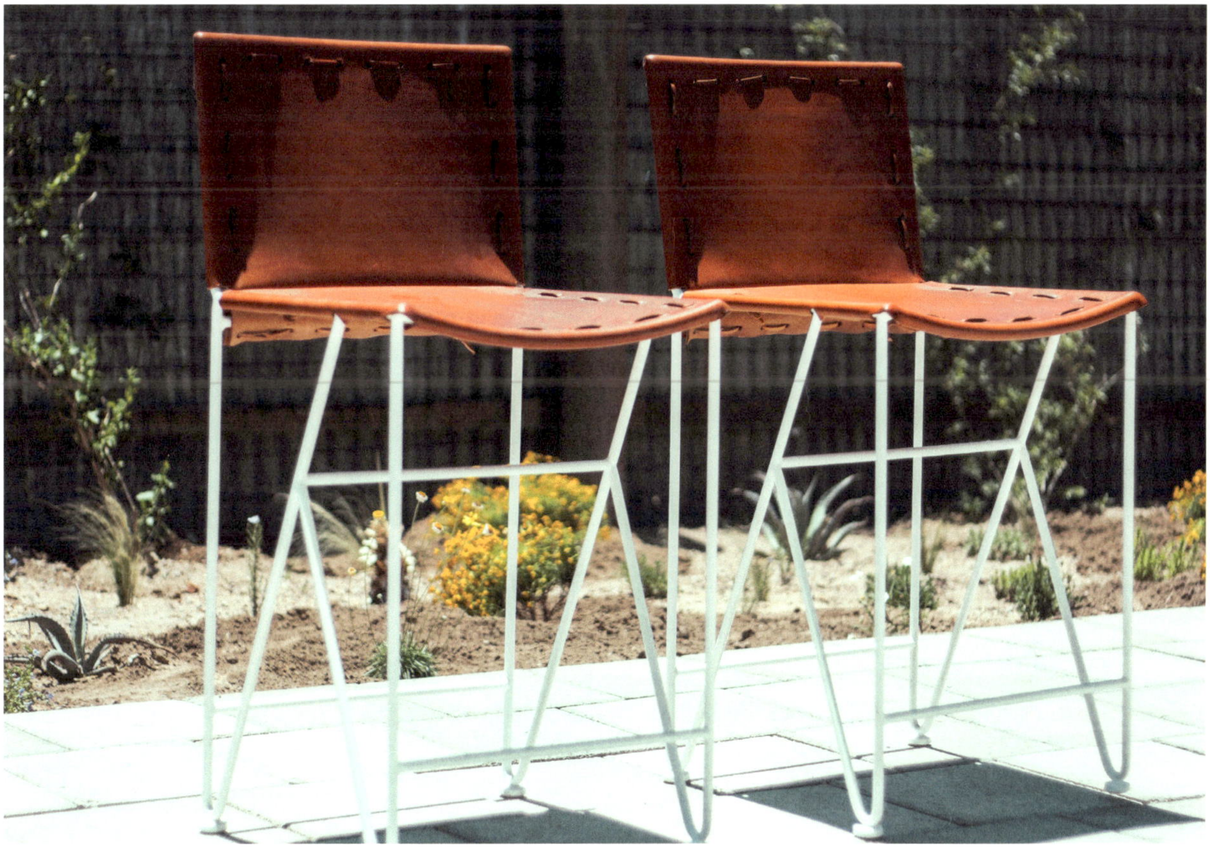

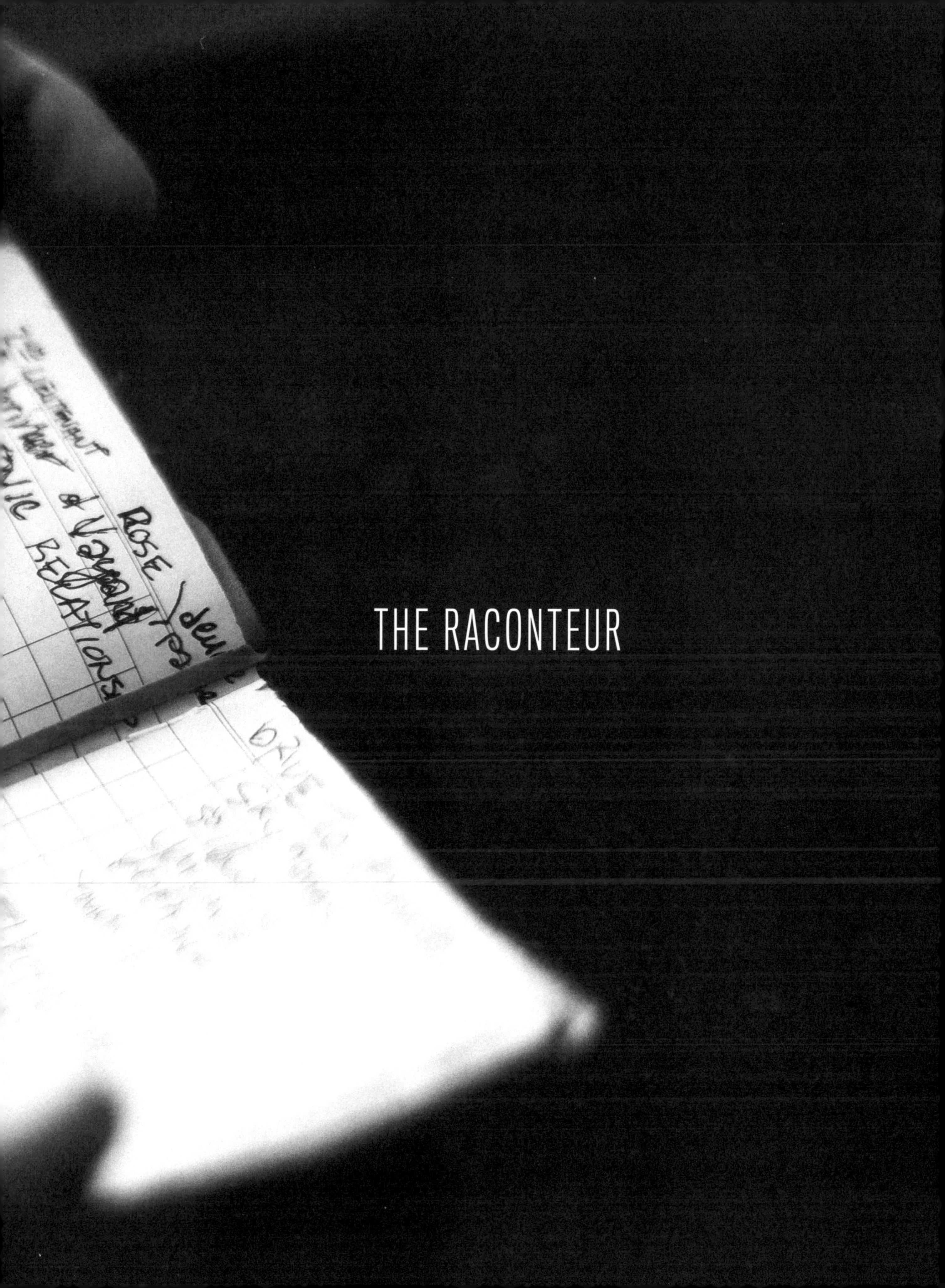

THE RACONTEUR

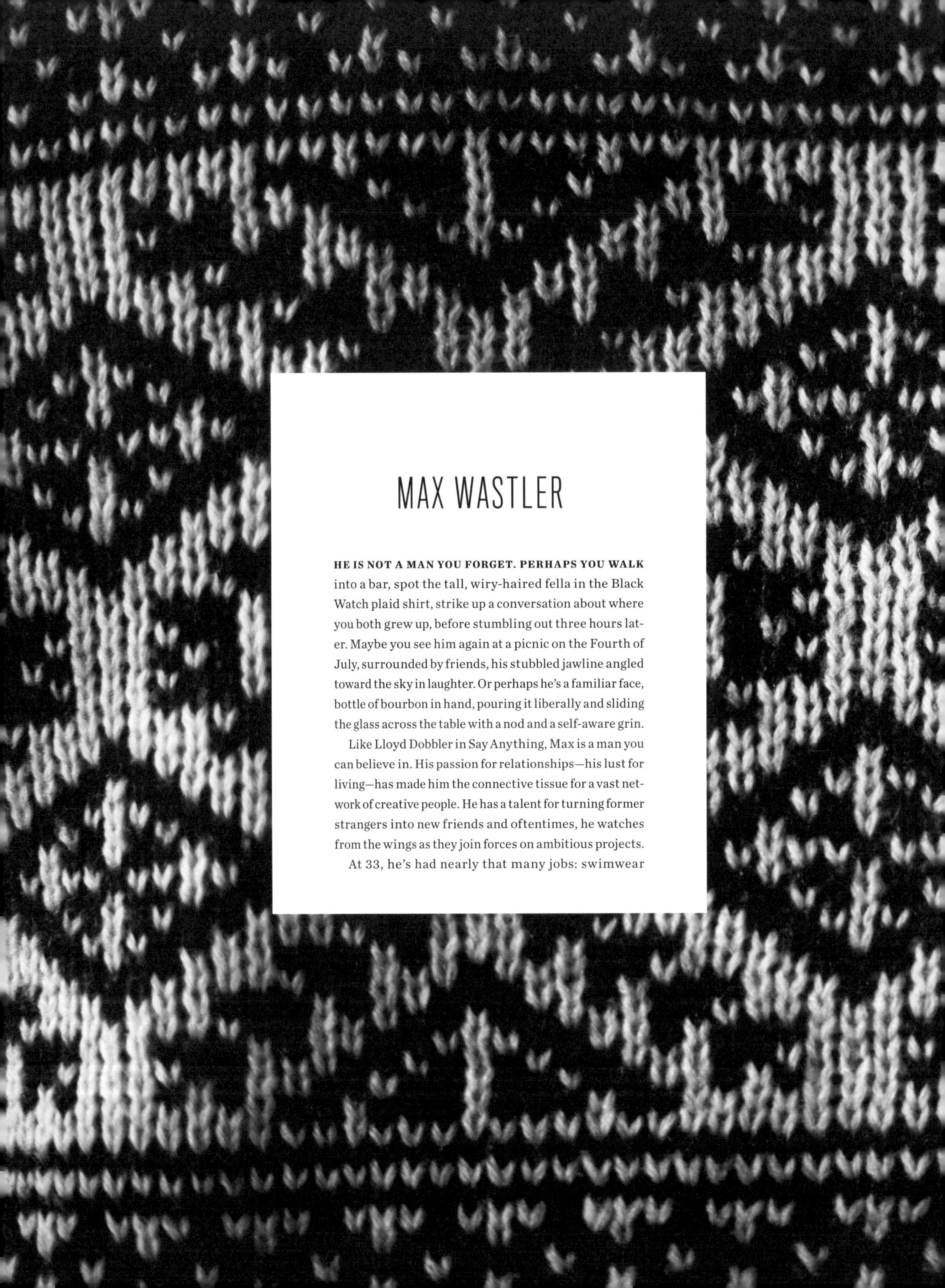

MAX WASTLER

HE IS NOT A MAN YOU FORGET. PERHAPS YOU WALK into a bar, spot the tall, wiry-haired fella in the Black Watch plaid shirt, strike up a conversation about where you both grew up, before stumbling out three hours later. Maybe you see him again at a picnic on the Fourth of July, surrounded by friends, his stubbled jawline angled toward the sky in laughter. Or perhaps he's a familiar face, bottle of bourbon in hand, pouring it liberally and sliding the glass across the table with a nod and a self-aware grin.

Like Lloyd Dobbler in Say Anything, Max is a man you can believe in. His passion for relationships—his lust for living—has made him the connective tissue for a vast network of creative people. He has a talent for turning former strangers into new friends and oftentimes, he watches from the wings as they join forces on ambitious projects.

At 33, he's had nearly that many jobs: swimwear

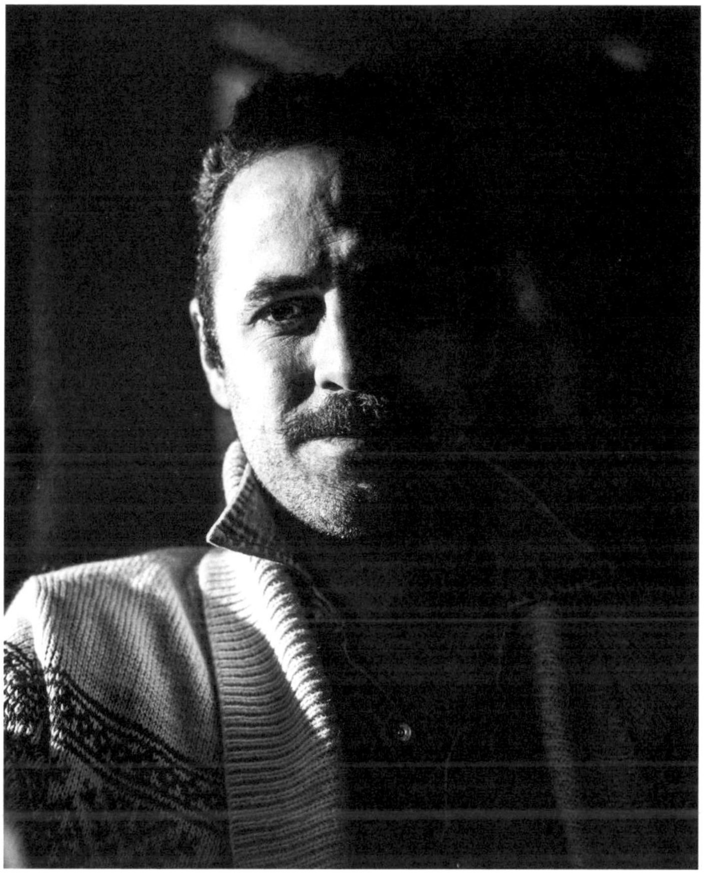

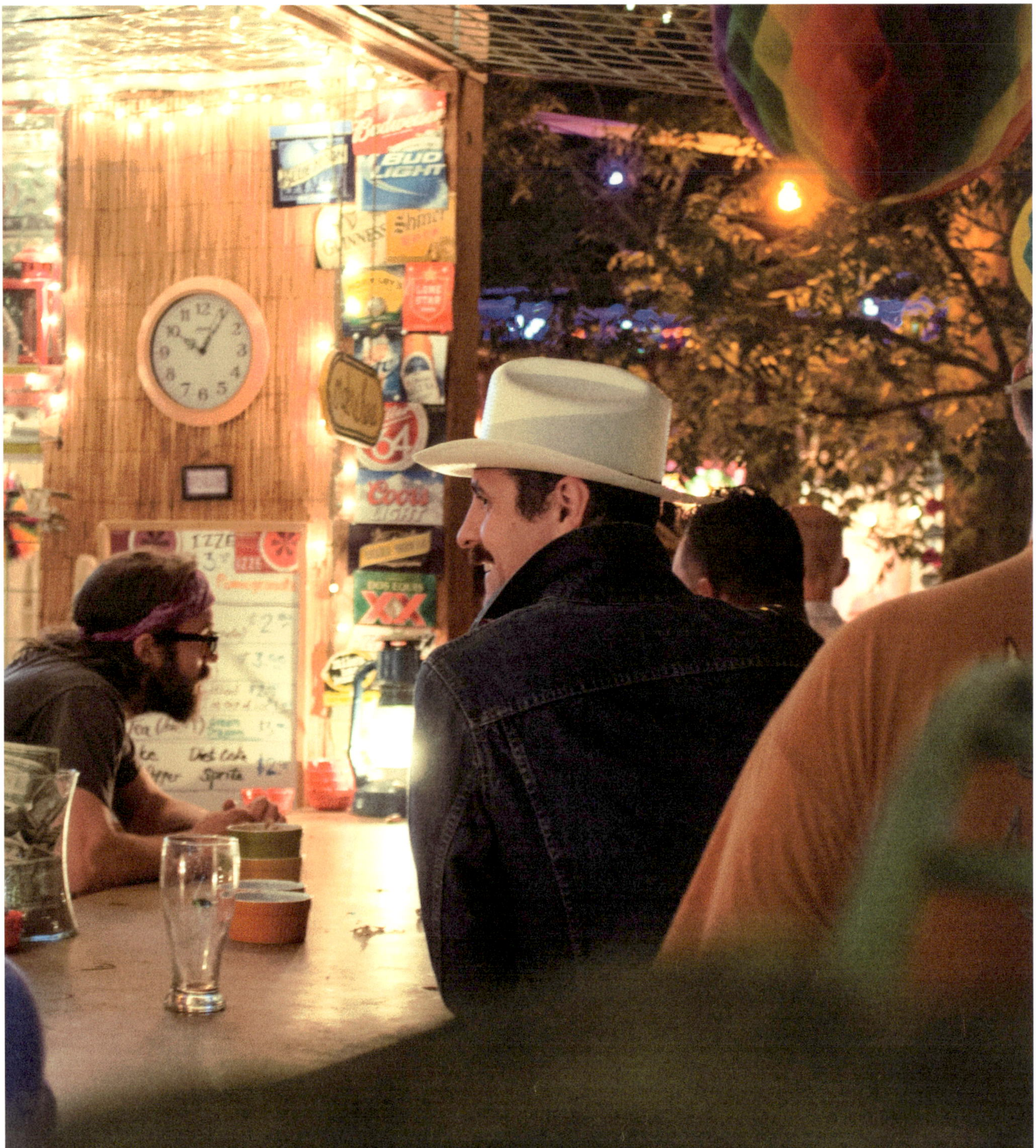

designer, bartender, shirt salesman, advertiser, store owner. The list goes on. Recently, he's found himself in a career that seems tailor-made for him. His business card says "bloodhound," which is fancy for "storyteller," and his task is to sniff out the stories of American towns, through the eyes of artists and craftsmen who drink Basil Hayden's bourbon.

For his biggest contribution to this issue, Max employs his talent as a raconteur to spin the yarn of Ty Mitchell, who as you'll soon discover, seems like the kind of hombre many would be too timid to approach. Writing in the second person, Max lends his fearlessness to the rest of us and hands the reader the reins to reveal the man behind the eyepatch. *–S.P.*

THE COWBOY OUT OF THE BOX

BY MAX WASTLER

BEFORE YOU MEET TY MITCHELL, YOU'VE ALREADY ENCOUNTERED him. His aura covers Marfa, but nowhere is it stronger than the Lost Horse Saloon.

You approach the long, low, sloped roof, where you hope to hang your hat for the next few hours. As you pass beneath a small sign out front, you notice that the neon red has a particularly sharp, ruby flicker and cries out "BEER, BEER, BEER." That's it: a lone lit sign, promising an all-caps experience.

As you enter, you train your eye on the fetching young woman behind the bar, her braided ponytail pulled tight to reveal a neck tattoo of a Texas state flag. Obliging the cliché, you order a Lone Star Light and scan the room. You crack a wry smile as you notice a band of bearded college students setting up a drum kit in the corner. Just then, a loud cheer comes from the bar's side yard, where a collection of local men has corralled around a widescreen TV to hoot and holler over the San Antonio Spurs. In the crowd of men, you spot him tipping his longneck bottle toward a blonde woman with a serious tan.

Ty Mitchell fits right in at the Lost Horse Saloon: a 6-foot-4 cowboy, with an improbable 28-inch waist, clad in a black hat and an eyepatch.

Lost in your daydream, you snap to it when you realize the two of you have locked eyes. He grins at you. You return the smile. The craggiest face you've ever seen seems to be inviting and blackballing you all at once. His face is the personification of a "Welcome to Marfa" sign and perhaps, at the same time, the best iteration this side of an Alamo gift-shop coffee mug that says, "Don't Mess with Texas."

The next day, you ask folks around town, "What's the deal with Ty Mitchell?"

You get the same response from everyone you talk to.

"A true Texan," some say.

"A real cowboy," others echo.

A pair of women you meet declare, "He's so sweet!"

Tom Michael at Marfa Public Radio wonders aloud, "When'd he start wearing an eye patch?"

Returning that afternoon, the sun spills into the bar from a set of windows on either side of the front door. The tattooed bartender is back. You ask if Ty's around. He's outside having a smoke.

Heading in that direction, you see his back is turned. He's balancing on the back two legs of a ratty chair, pencil-thin legs crossed and resting on a tree stump. Petting his Blue Heeler, he pulls from a pale blue-and-white can of beer that he rests on the scorched grass.

You hesitate to introduce yourself, wondering if he'll be sour to you—an outsider, a Northerner. Turning around to buy a shot of courage, you tell yourself you'll assimilate by simply ordering whatever he's drinking. You flash your cash at the bartender, and she cracks open a can for you. You order two whiskies, hoping to smooth over the introduction with the offering of your favorite bourbon.

You tip your brand new straw "Open Road" classic cowboy hat, the one LBJ wore (and as you'll later discover, so do all the suits in Texas), in his direction. He touches a long, finger to the brim of his dusty, old Spradley black beaver as he takes a prolonged drag from the last nub of a hand-rolled cigarette.

"Hot day," you swallow.

"Yep," he grins, as he deadens the butt of the cigarette and pulls a pack from his shirt pocket. As he rolls another, you recognize the red Prince Albert label.

"Pipe tobacco? My grandpa smoked Prince Albert," you say.

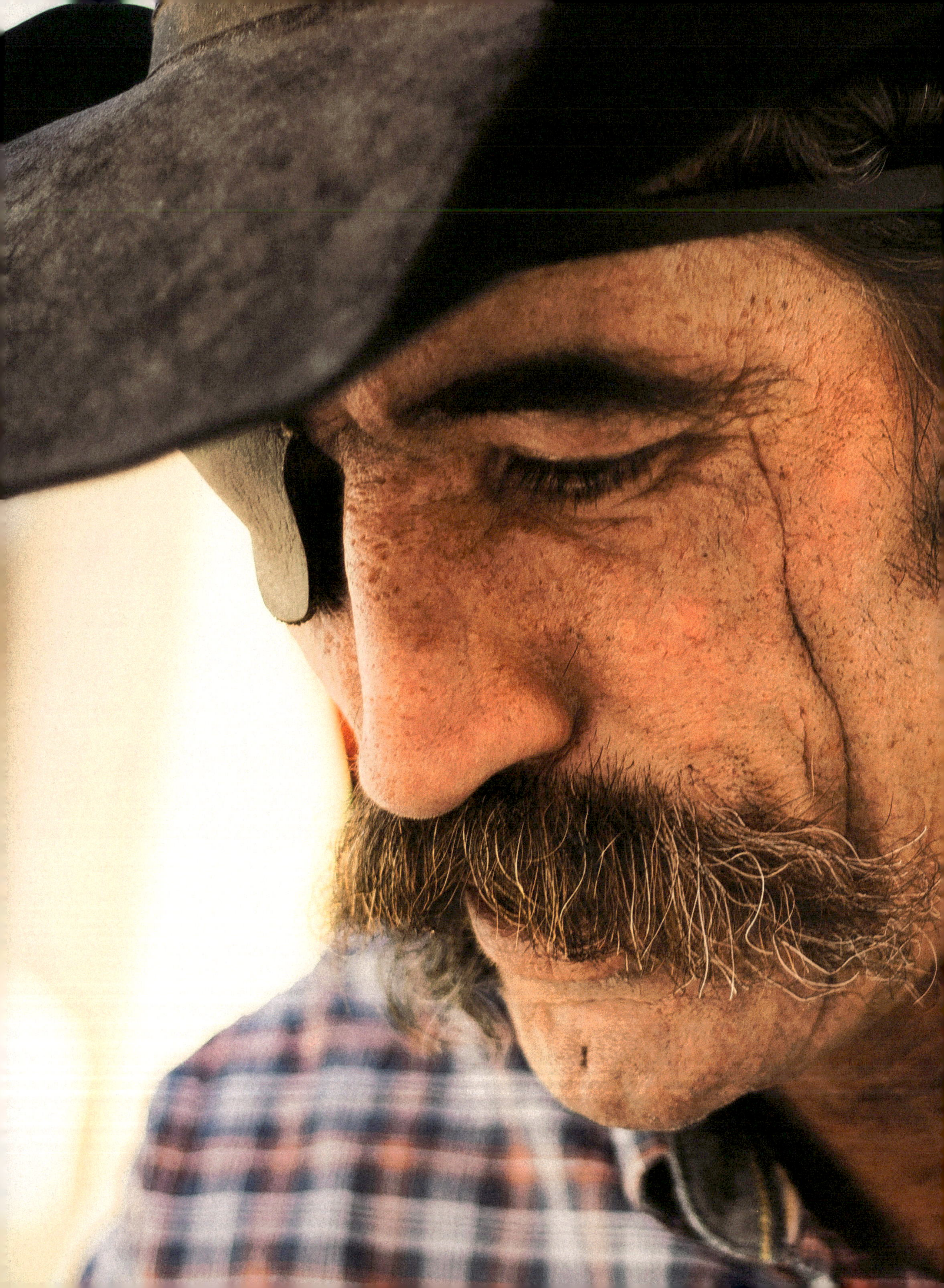

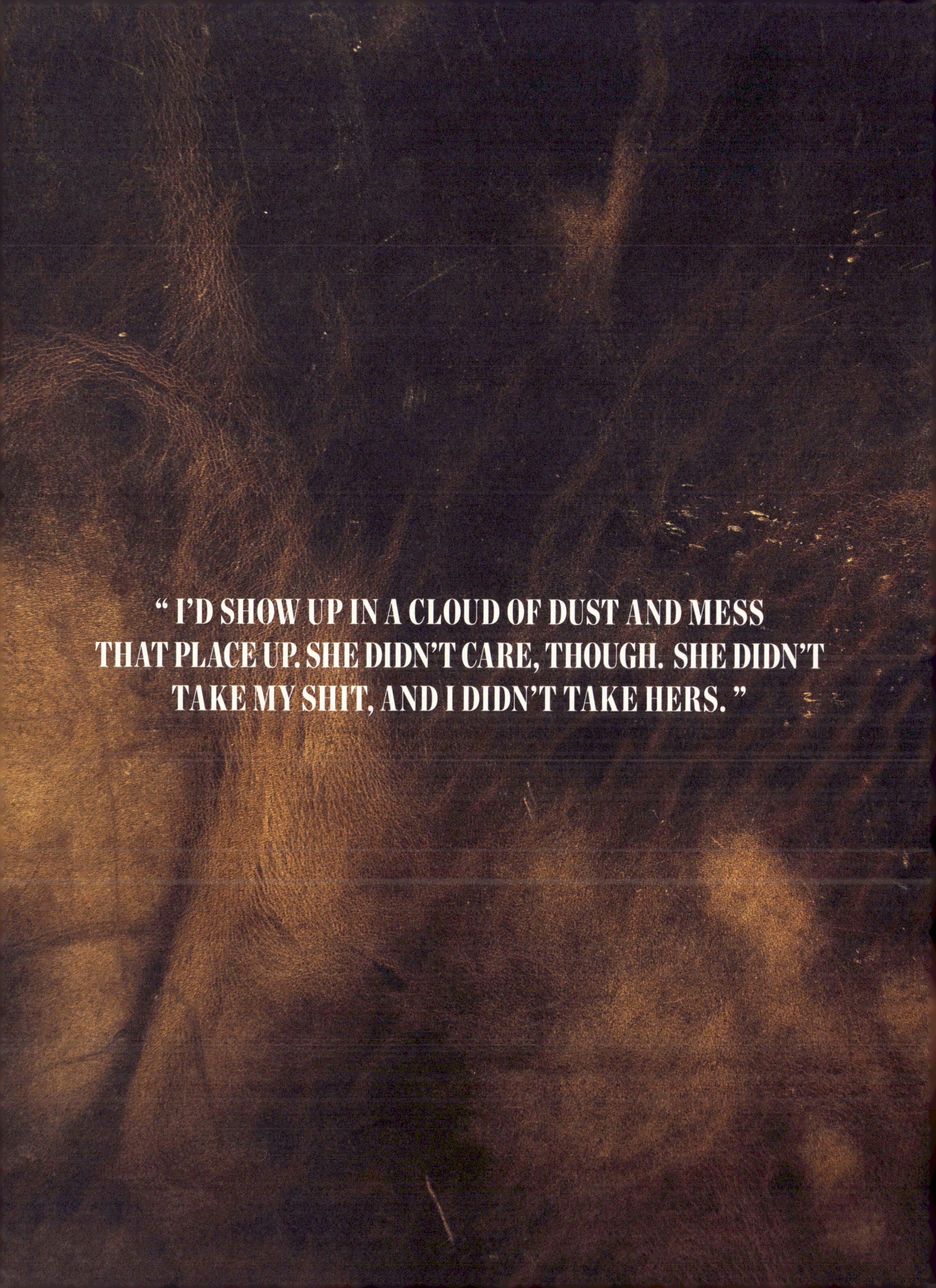

"I'D SHOW UP IN A CLOUD OF DUST AND MESS THAT PLACE UP. SHE DIDN'T CARE, THOUGH. SHE DIDN'T TAKE MY SHIT, AND I DIDN'T TAKE HERS."

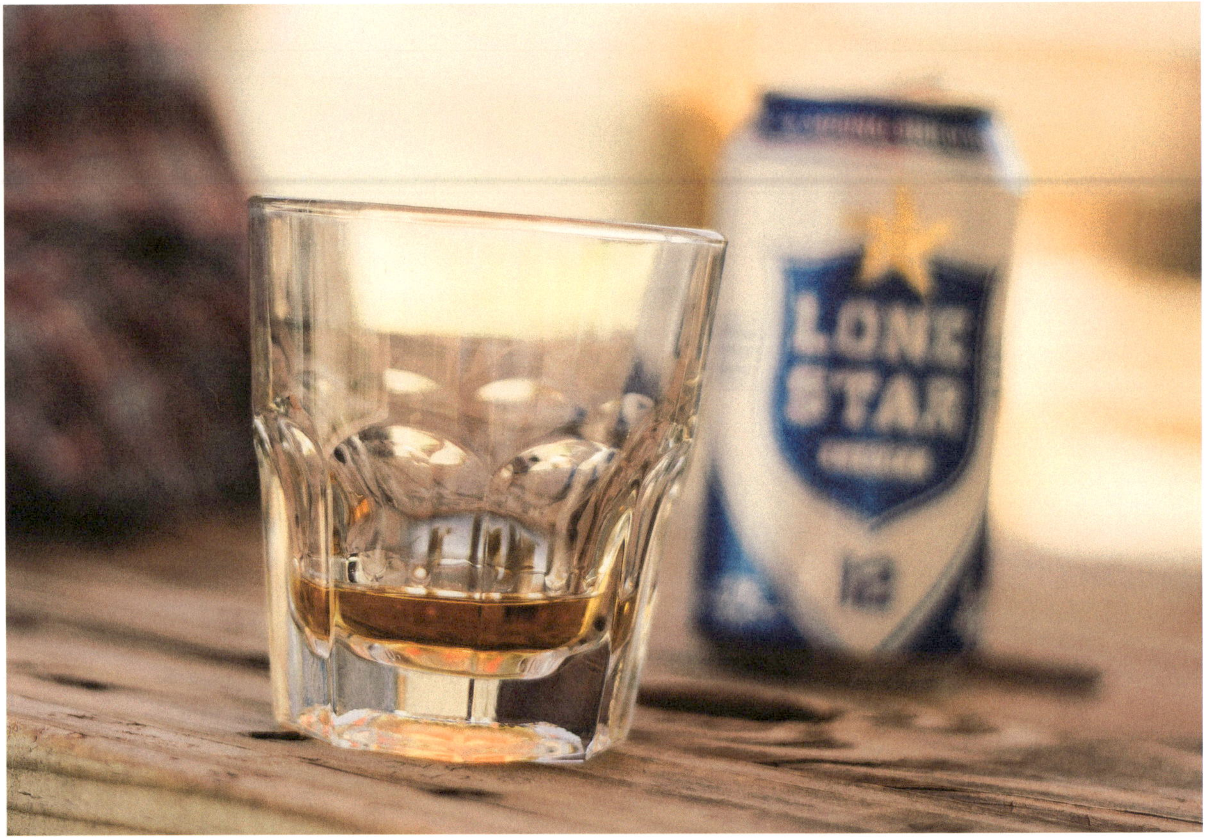
LONE
STAR

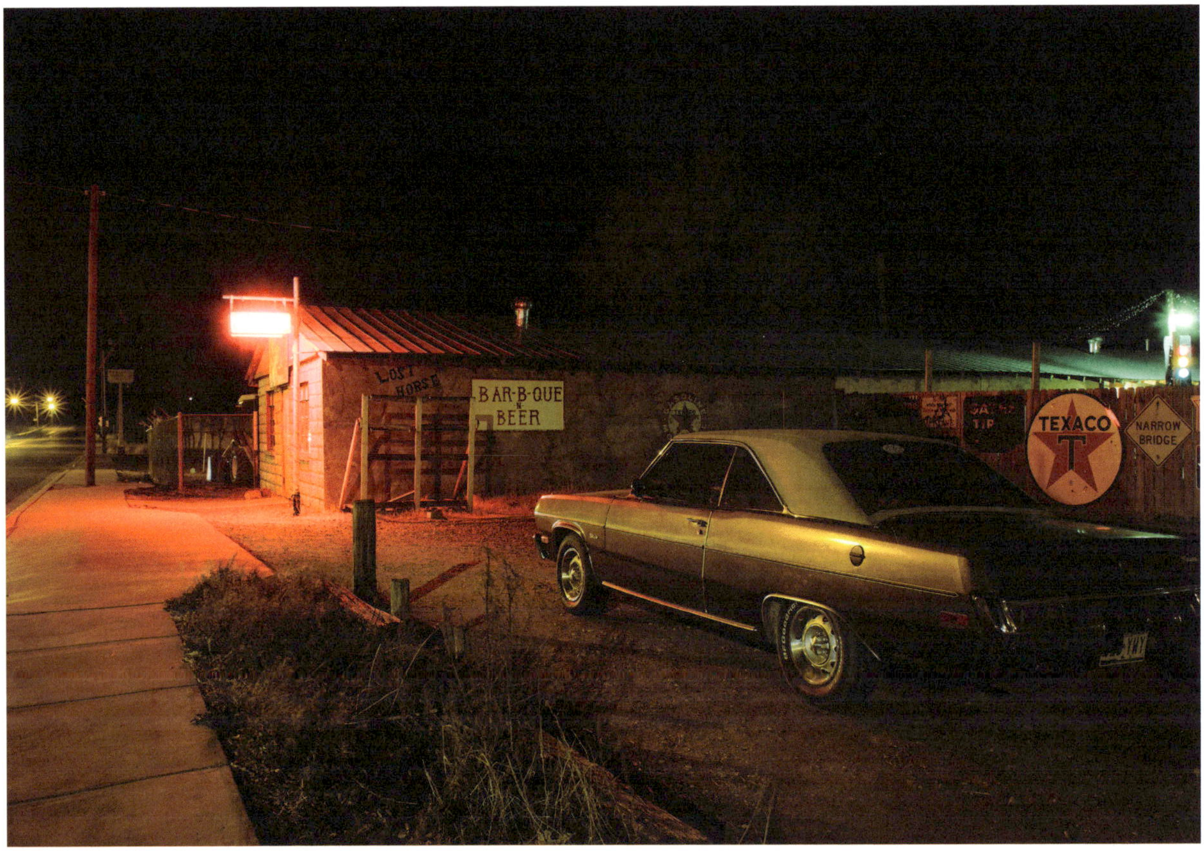
LOST HORSE
BAR-B-QUE
BEER
TEXACO
NARROW BRIDGE

"Mine too." His smile widens into an introduction. "Ty Mitchell. I own this place."

As he looks up at you from under his brim, his one good eye scans the bar. You shake his hand firmly. His palms are tough, but not as tough as you'd expect for the man you had pictured hopping off a tired American Paint Horse, lasso in a gloved hand, tying down a stray calf. He's kind, you realize, handing him a glass of bourbon, which he immediately raises in a toast to you.

That's when you start to pepper him with questions. He takes each one, considers it, and offers a mountain's worth of information, whatever the subject. That Lone Star Light can you're enjoying? Purchased to serve at the local roller derby. He figured cans were better than glass bottles to serve at a roller rink, and when the derby girls no longer neededthe abundance of leftovers, he put them behind the bar.

Though he spent all but the first year of his life in Texas, he refuses to refer to himself as a Texan. "Born in New Mexico," he reveals. "Actually, I have a certificate from the governor declaring me an honorary Texan."

You pry into the story. You learn that while she was the governor, the legendary politician Ann Richards (the tart-tongued Texan who once quipped, "Ginger Rogers did everything Fred Astaire did, she just did it backwards and in high heels") befriended Ty while campaigning, and she invited him to the governor's mansion more than once.

"I'd show up in a cloud of dust and mess that place up," he recalls. "She didn't care, though. We really got along well. She didn't take my shit, and I didn't take hers."

You find out he's more than just a bar owner and a rancher. He is also a seasoned professional actor. "Can't tell you how many times I get somebody that comes in here [saying], 'I seen you a mile high in Times Square.' Or, 'That was you, weren't it, in that one movie that shot here?'"

Ty explains that a few movies have featured his mangy mug, a face that so typifies this one-stoplight town in West Texas. He goes on to tell you that Marfa was founded on the quality of the ranches tucked into the surrounding hillsides that make their way toward Big Bend. And it blossomed from the magnificent light that drew filmmakers to take advantage of its wide, impressive sunrises and sunsets.

Much like Ty, for several decades the smartest Marfa residents have capitalized on these two defining features of this incomparable place for decades. When Hollywood and Madison Avenue come calling, Ty and his Blue Heeler, Quatro, are often first on the casting directors' call sheets.

"One year, that dog made more money than I did," he says. "But some girl came in here and took too many pictures of her. Now she don't sit still."

The conversation turns serious when you ask about his eye. "Shrapnel," he says. He probably wants to leave it at that, but he chooses to explain a bit further. "I was in Libya, in the merchant marines. We were doing some work and some shrapnel hit my eye, and I wasn't able to take care of it properly. It's been a problem on-and-off for a long time, and I think, as of a few weeks ago, I'll be wearing this eye patch for good."

The dry air West Texas air, mixed with windy days on the ranch, doesn't help and causes his eye to flare up. "It's the iron in the soil. It gets up in my eye socket, and it gets really irritated."

He asks if you've got a girlfriend. You nod and answer with the same question. "Yep, German," he says. "She's a novelist."

And at that, his face lights up. The wrinkles—well, most of them—disappear. He says she moved to Marfa from Germany to focus on her latest project. The two had an instant kinship. She, a fish out of water, and he, who couldn't be more in his element, found themselves spending more and more time together. A long-distance relationship was born.

"I'm trying to get her to move here," he says as he smiles wide and takes a drag from his umpteenth cig.

"I think I have her convinced." (You'll learn after leaving Marfa that he did convince her, and the two were married by the end of the year.)

As he continues to speak highly of his lady, you take a glance around the yard. Several projects in various stages of completion strewn around. Beyond the fence, the clouds have gathered, and the sun is about to set. Ty notices you've locked in with the sky, and he motions toward the pink and yellow streaks: "That is a masterpiece. Hard to argue with something like that, right?"

Walking away from the Lost Horse Saloon, you recall another of Governor Richards' one-liners: "I thought I knew Texas pretty well, but I had no notion of its size until I campaigned it." And you realize: She may as well have been talking about Ty. ★

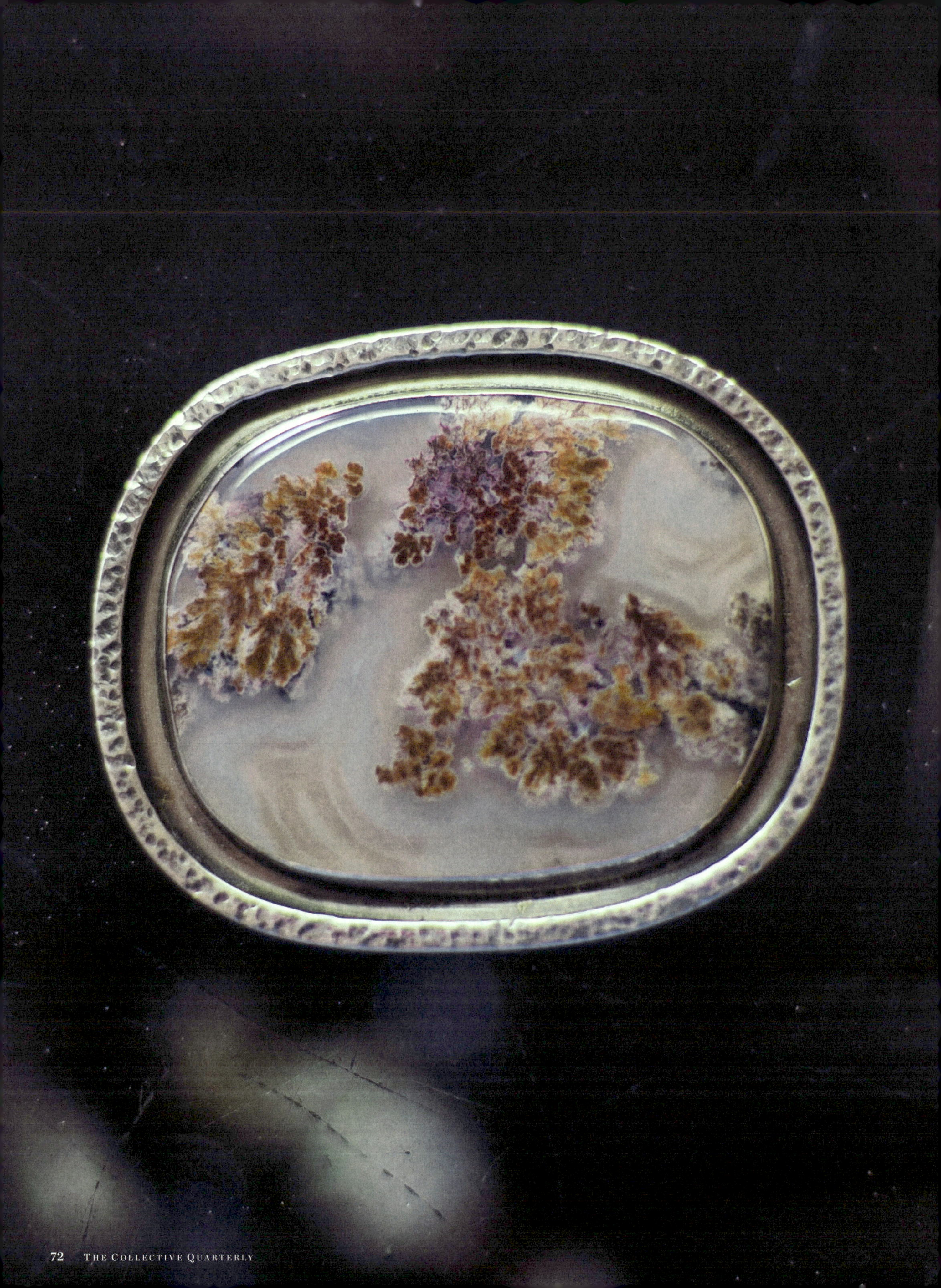

MOONLIGHT GEMSTONES

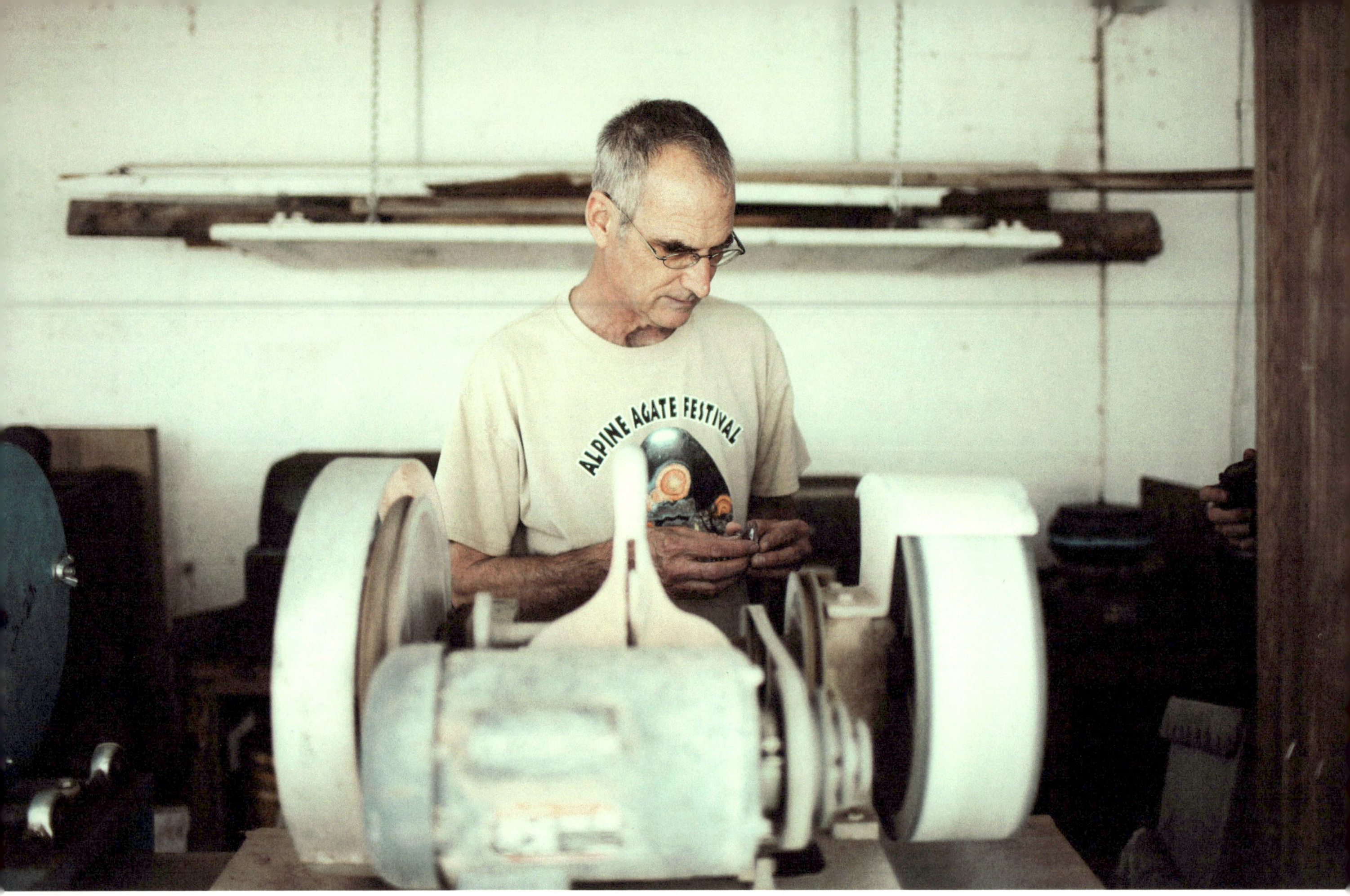

"They call me the wanderer. Yeah, the wanderer. I roam around, around, around."

DION AND THE BELMONTS' "THE WANDERER" PLAYS ON A SMALL radio caked in dust and drips of dried paint: "Oh well, I roam from town to town. I go through life without a care, and I'm as happy as a clown. A-with my two fists of iron, but I'm going nowhere."

The hair on the back of Paul Graybeal's neck is standing on end as he hunches over the wheel of a pumice grinder. Sparks fly. His face lights up with a big, gap-toothed smile. "Look at that." His grin widens as he points to a white striation in the rock. "See the way it just creeps in there. That's when you know you got it."

The proprietor of Moonlight Gemstones settles back in at his workstation, surrounded by colorful rocks. "Gemstones," he says as a means of correction.

"That's called a Marfa Bouquet," he continues. "Picked that out of one of my favorite spots not too far from here." He winds his way around the shelves of his shop, which clearly have an organizational code that only Graybeal knows.

"Apache, Blue Lapis Lazuli, Plume, Moss, and that?" he says, pointing to a ruddy, bubbling Fire Agate. "That's the result of this beautiful, iron-colored lava."

Ask him to divulge some of his favorite spaces to hunt for the dusty rocks he polishes, and he becomes the slightest bit cagey—cagier still when prodded about his involvement in the film *No Country for Old Men*, which was filmed in Marfa.

"Oh, that?" Graybeal shrugs. "Yeah, I had a couple belt buckles in there. Can't remember which ones, but you'll watch it now and you'll see them."

Though he trained as an electrician and worked for a number of years at the nearby McDonald Observatory, he focused on teaching his eye to find literal gems on the rock formations of Big Bend and began to develop a serious agate collection. Eventually, he took a class in silversmithing at Sul Ross State University, and a new profession was born.

Graybeal says hunting for rocks is his favorite thing in the world. To him, a life of isolation, hunting rocks in the desert, is a life well-spent.

After he runs some water over his newly polished gem, a colorful stone that has become the purest shade of greenish-blue, he hands it over. "That's a Sleeping Beauty Turquoise, which has been shaped and polished in the cabochon shape," he explains. "'Cabochon' is French for 'dome'."

Walking out of Graybeal's shop, strolling down the sidewalk back to one of downtown Marfa's fourway stops, you can hear another agate screeching as it hit the pumice. Suddenly, Dion and the Belmonts are coaxing the wheel "around, around, around." Yet the man, much like the wanderer in the tune, isn't really going anywhere. –*M.W.*

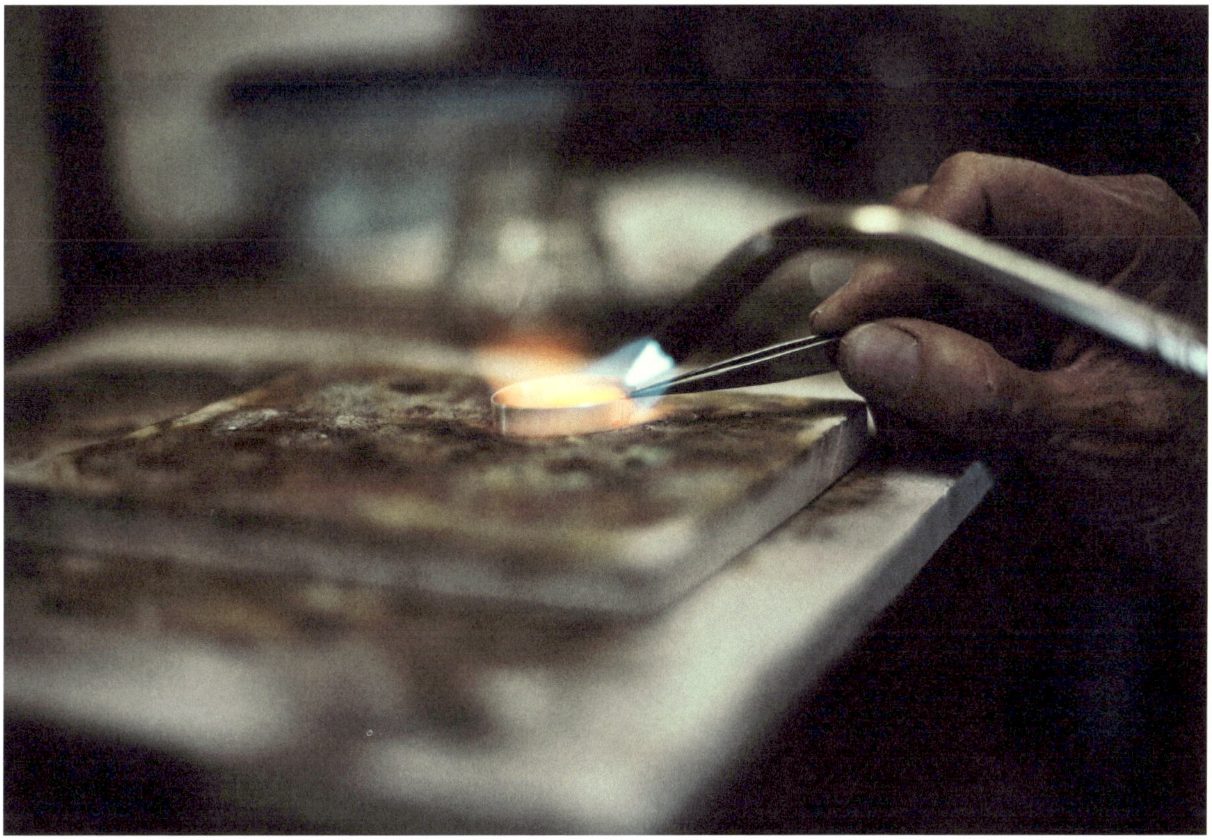

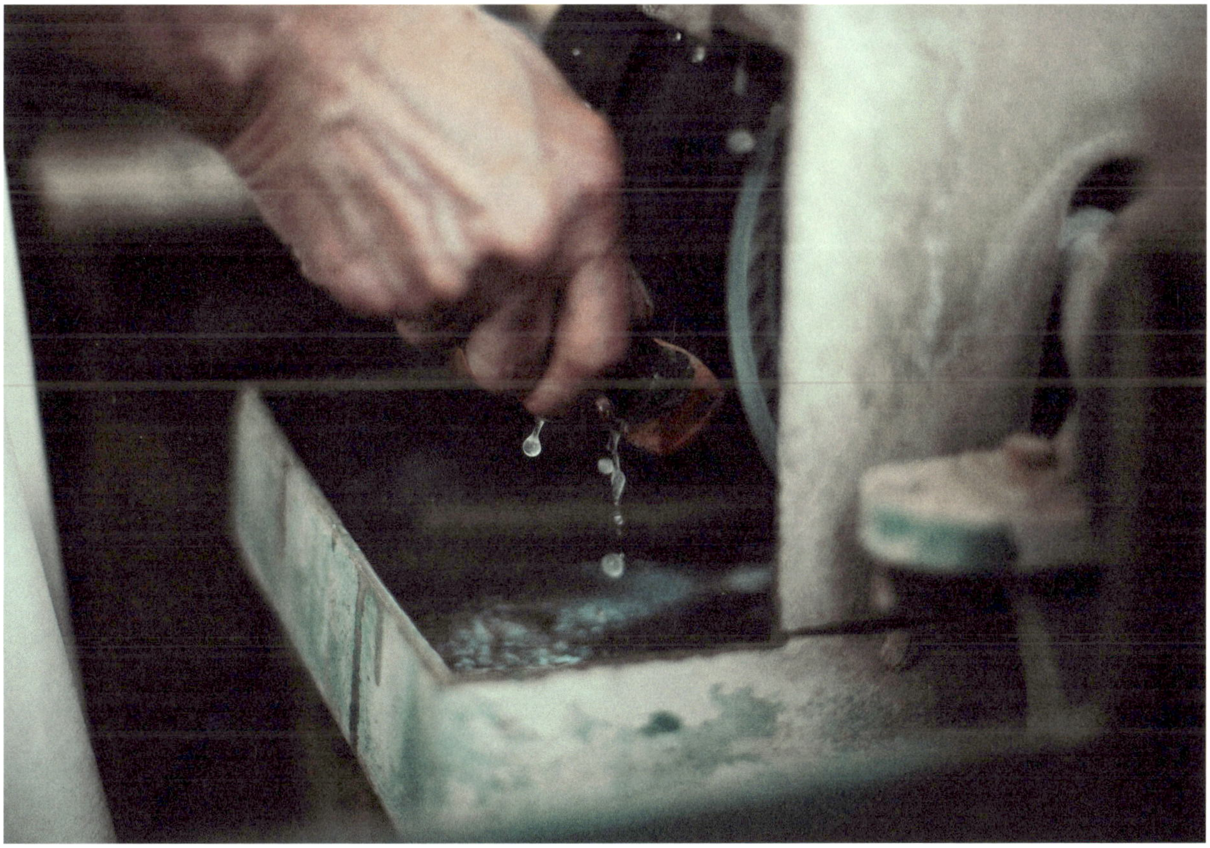

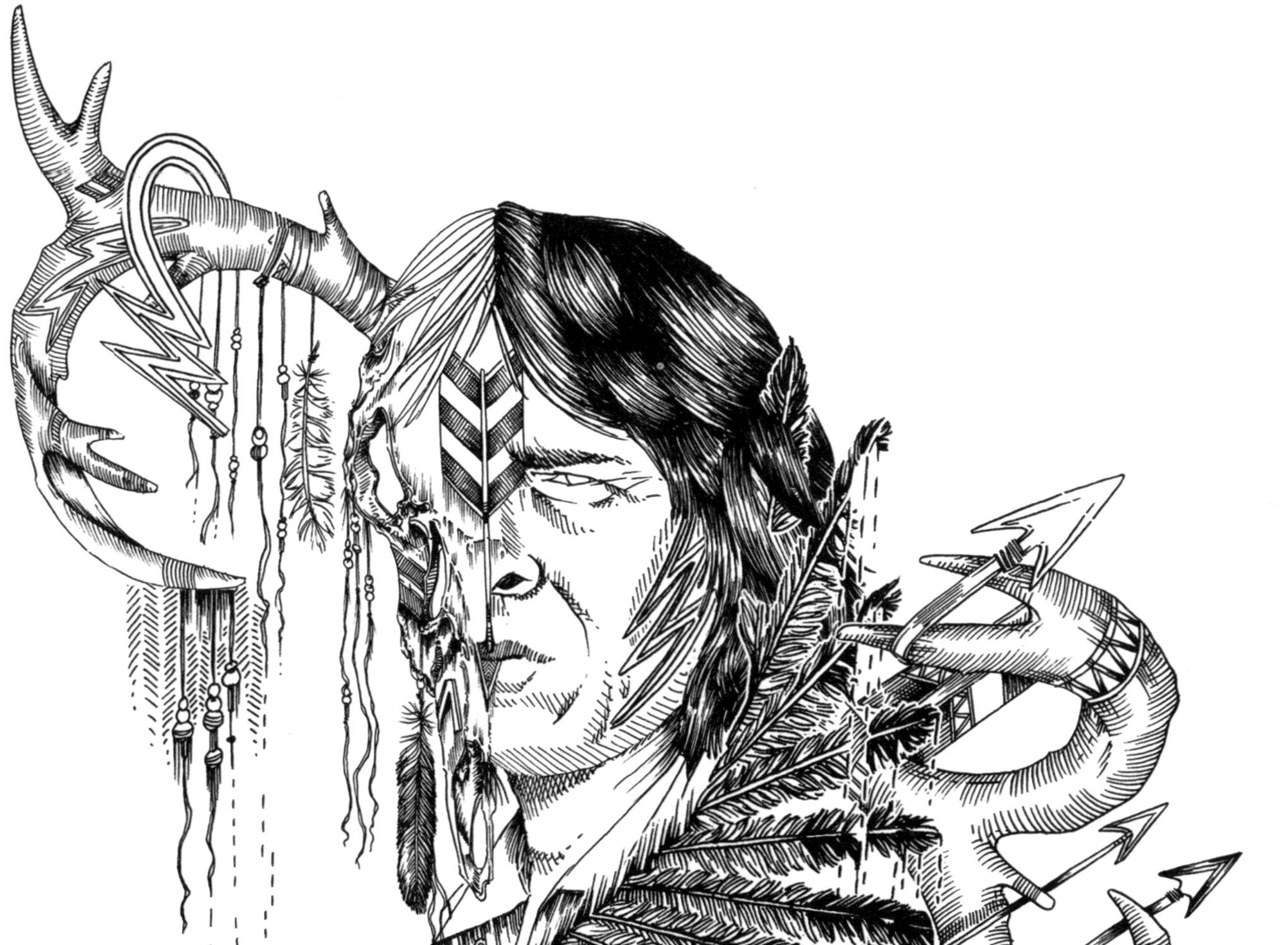

"EL CHINGADERO"

IN VALENTINE, TEXAS— HALF AN HOUR FROM MARFA IF YOU DRIVE FAST— LIVES A MAN NAMED

BOYD ELDER.

BOYD WAS PALS WITH DAN FLAVIN & DONALD JUDD WHEN MARFA WAS THEIR STOMPING GROUND, BUT UNLIKE MANY OF THE ARTISTS WHO HAVE ADOPTED THIS TEXAS TOWN, THE MAN KNOWN TO HIS FRIENDS AS "EL CHINGADERO" HAS ALWAYS BEEN HERE.

HE'S THE ARTIST BEHIND THE ICONIC, PAINTED, FEATHERED BOVINE SKULL THAT APPEARS ON THE EAGLES' 1975 ALBUM, "ONE OF THESE NIGHTS." HE DID THE ARTWORK FOR THEIR GREATEST HITS ALBUM, TOO. AND OVER IN MARFA, HIS SAME UNMISTAKABLE STYLE HANGS ABOVE ONE OF THE POOL TABLES AT THE LOST HORSE SALOON.

RECENTLY, HE'S BEEN REPORTING THE WEATHER FOR TOM MICHAEL, STATION MANAGER AT MARFA PUBLIC RADIO. ONE DAY, NOT TOO LONG AGO, A FIBER LINE GOT CUT, KNOCKING OUT MOST COMMUNICATION.

"ALL INTERNET WAS DOWN IN THE TRI-COUNTY AREA," TOM REMEMBERS. "9-1-1 DIDN'T WORK. NO ONE WAS ONLINE. IT WAS A WEIRD MOMENT."

BOYD'S SCHEDULED TO DO HIS WEATHER REPORT. SO TOM SAYS: "OKAY, BOYD. WITHOUT THE INTERNET, YOU'VE GOT TO DO IT

WEST TEXAS STYLE.

I WANT YOU TO LOOK AT THE SKY AND TELL ME WHAT YOU THINK IT'S GOING TO BE LIKE."

BOYD LOOKS UP AT THE CLOUDS HE'S LIVED UNDER ALL HIS LIFE, SQUINTS THROUGH HIS BLACK, THICK-FRAMED GLASSES, AND SAYS,

"MIGHT BE SOME RAIN."

"THAT WAS GREAT, BOYD," TOM SAYS.

"NO PROBLEM, MIKE," BOYD SAYS TO TOM. "HAVE A GREAT WEEKEND."

IT WAS MONDAY. LATER, IT BEGAN TO RAIN.

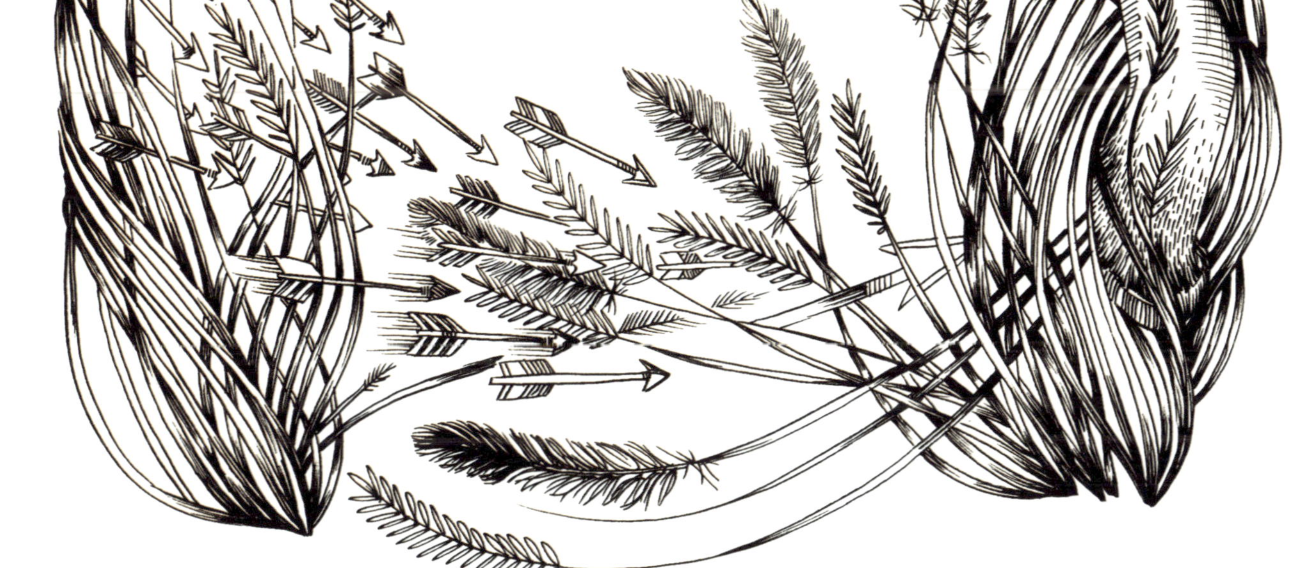

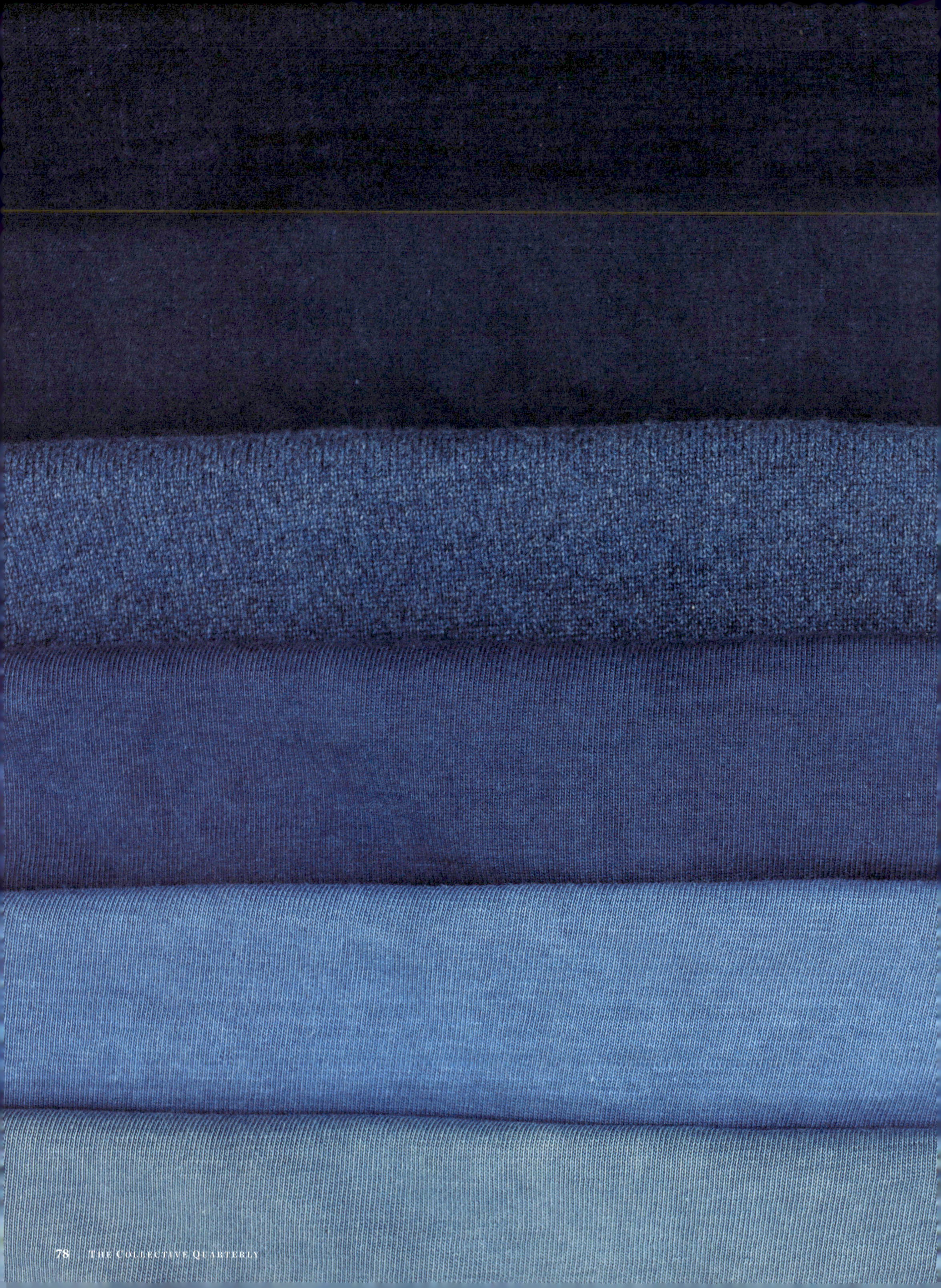

PARALLEL PATTERNS

A PHOTOGRAPHIC EXPLORATION OF TEXTILE DESIGNS IN THE REAL WORLD.

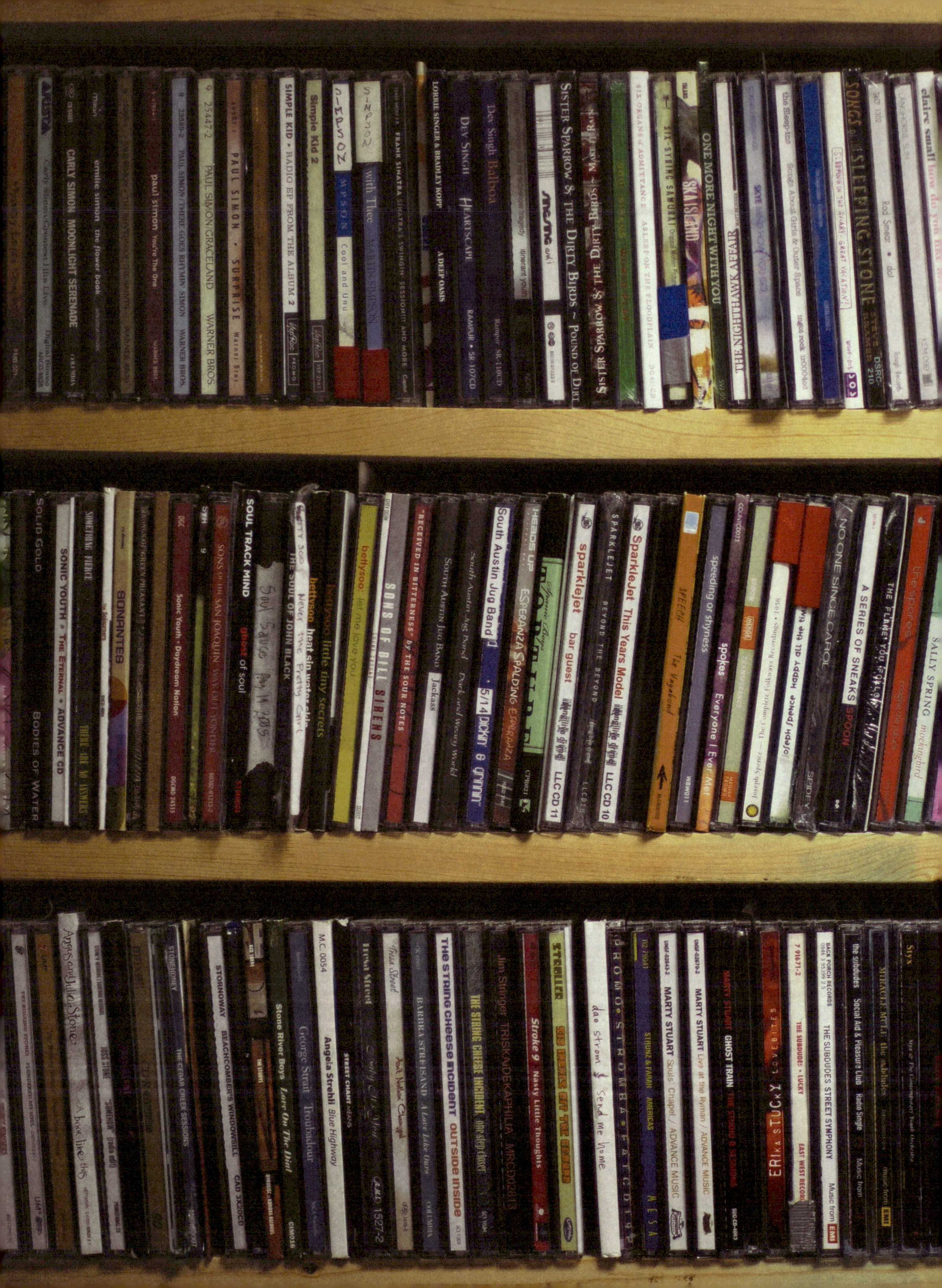

CARLY SIMON MOONLIGHT SERENADE
emilie simon the flower book
paul simon You're The One
PAUL SIMON THERE GOES RHYMIN SIMON WARNER BROS.
PAUL SIMON GRACELAND WARNER BROS
PAUL SIMON • SURPRISE Warner Bros.
SIMPLE KID • RADIO EP FROM THE ALBUM 2
Simple Kid 2
SIMPSON Cool and Unu
with Thee MARTIN SIMPSON
FRANK SINATRA SINATRA'S SWINGIN' SESSION!!! AND MORE
LORRIE SINGER & BRADLEY KOPP A DEEP OASIS
DEV SINGH HEARTSCAPE
Dev Singh Balboa
SISTER SPARROW & THE DIRTY BIRDS ~ POUND OF DIRT
SIX ORGANS OF ADMITTANCE ASLEEP ON THE FLOODPLAIN
SIX-STRING SAMURAI
ONE MORE NIGHT WITH YOU
THE NIGHTHAWK AFFAIR
the Sleep-ins Songs About Girls & Outer Space
SONGS OF THE SLEEPING STONE
Rod Smart • dol
claire small
SOLID GOLD BODIES OF WATER
SONIC YOUTH • THE ETERNAL • ADVANCE CD
SONANTES
Sonic Youth • Daydream Nation
SONS OF THE SAN JOAQUIN
SOUL TRACK MIND ghost of soul
THE SOUL OF JOHN BLACK
bettysoo heat sin waterfalls
bettysoo little tiny secrets
bettysoo let me love you
SONS OF BILL SIRENS
"RECEIVED IN BITTERNESS" by THE SOUR NOTES
SOUTH AUSTIN JUG BAND Jackass
South Austin Jug Band Dark and Weary World
South Austin Jug Band
ESPERANZA SPALDING ESPERANZA
sparklejet bar guest
SPARKLEJET BEYOND THE BEYOND
SparkleJet This Years Model
speeding or shyness
spokes Everyone I Ever Met
Joseph Spence — The Complete Folkways Recordings • 1958
NO ONE SINCE CAROL
A SERIES OF SNEAKS SPOON
the spores
SALLY SPRING mockingbird
Angus and Julia Stone A book like this
JOSS STONE
THE CEDAR CREEK SESSIONS
STORNOWAY BEACHCOMBER'S WINDOWSILL
Stone River Boys Love On The Dial
George Strait Troubadour
Angela Strehli Blue Highway
STREET CHANT
BARBRA STREISAND A Love Like Ours
THE STRING CHEESE INCIDENT OUTSIDE INSIDE
Jim Stringer TRISKAIDEKAPHILIA
Stroke 9 Nasty Little Thoughts
STROLLER
dao strom send me home
MARTY STUART Souls' Chapel ADVANCE MUSIC
MARTY STUART Live at the Ryman ADVANCE MUSIC
MARTY STUART GHOST TRAIN THE STUDIO B SESSIONS
ERIKA STUCKY LOVEBITES
THE SUBDUDES • LUCKY
THE SUBDUDES STREET SYMPHONY
the subdudes Social Aid & Pleasure Club
Styx

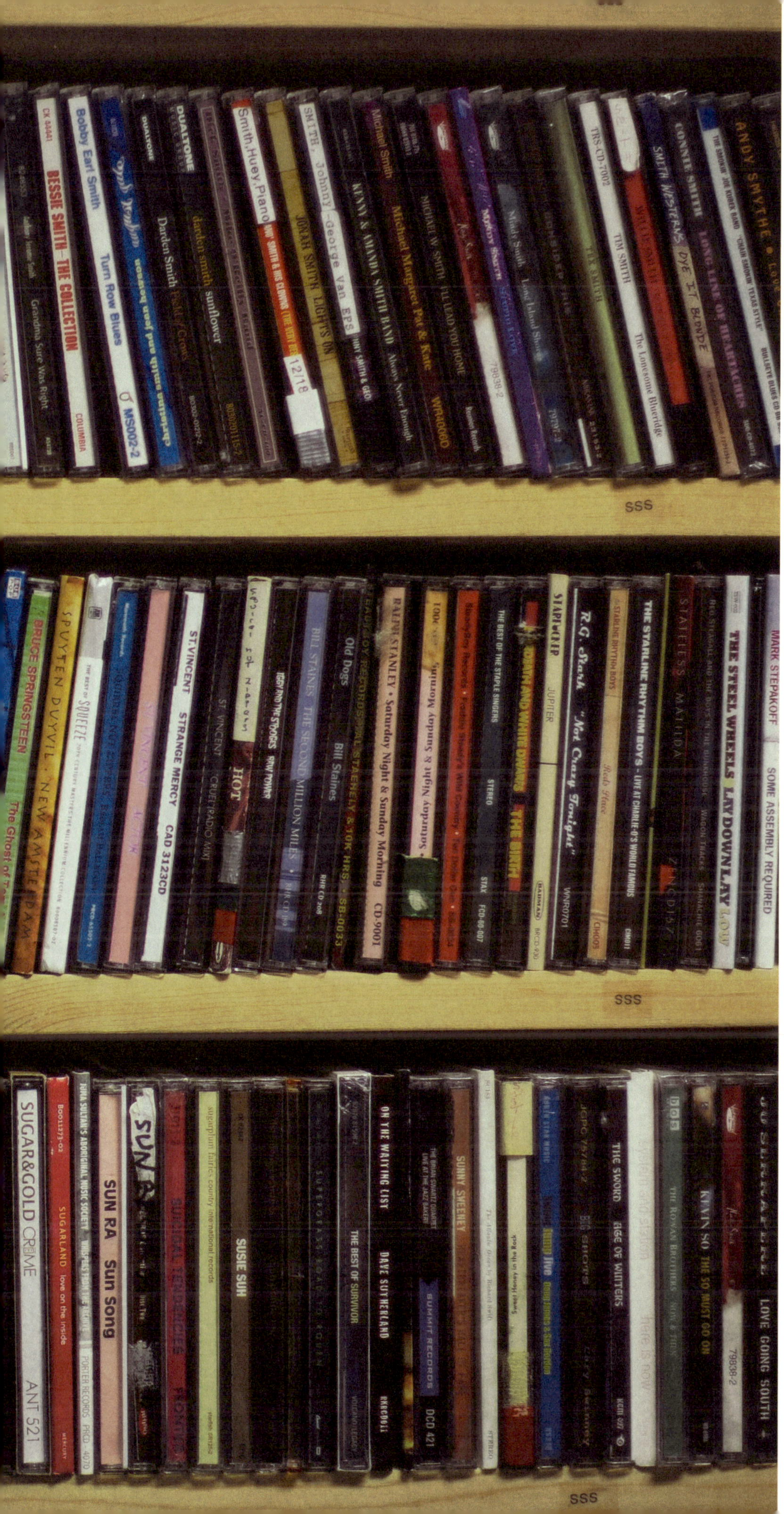
BESSIE SMITH - THE COLLECTION
Bobby Earl Smith
Turn Row Blues
Darden Smith
sunflower
Smith,Huey,Piano
JONAH SMITH LIGHTS ON
KENNY & AMANDA SMITH BAND
Michael Smith
TIM SMITH
The Lonesome Bluerridge
SMITH WESTERNS DYE IT BLONDE
CONNIE SMITH
ANDY SMYTHE
sss
BRUCE SPRINGSTEEN
SPUYTEN DUYVIL NEW AMSTERDAM
ST.VINCENT STRANGE MERCY
BILL STAINES THE SECOND MILLION MILES
Old Dogs
RALPH STANLEY • Saturday Night & Sunday Morning
THE BEST OF THE STAPLE SINGERS
JUPITER
R.G. Stark "Not Crazy Tonight"
THE STARLINE RHYTHM BOYS - LIVE AT CHARLIE-O'S WORLD FAMOUS
STATELESS MATILDA
THE STEEL WHEELS LAY DOWN LAY LOW
MARK STEPAKOFF SOME ASSEMBLY REQUIRED
sss
SUGAR&GOLD CRÈME
SUGARLAND love on the inside
SUN RA Sun Song
SUSIE SUH
ON THE WAITING LIST
THE BEST OF SURVIVOR
DAVE SUTHERLAND
SUNNY SWEENEY
THE SWORD AGE OF WINTERS
KEVIN SO THE SO MUST GO ON
LOVE GOING SOUTH
sss

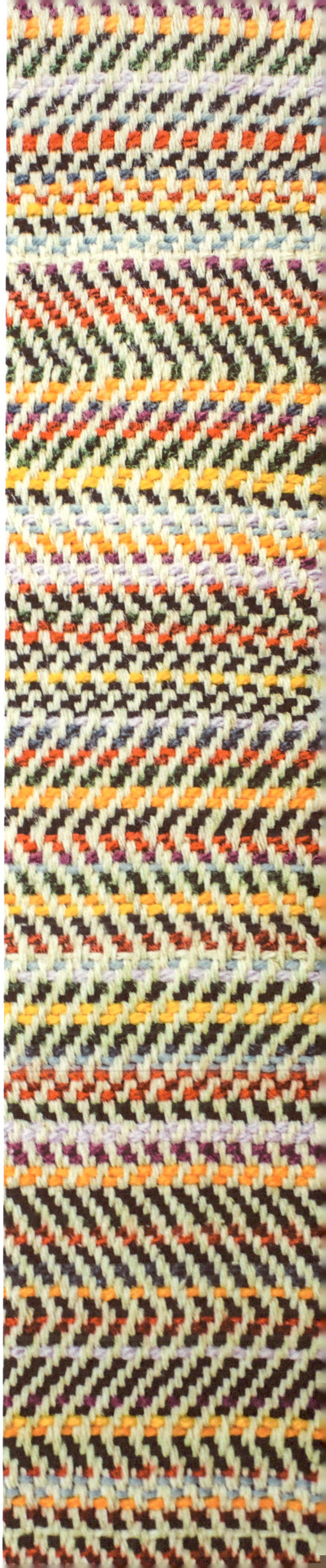

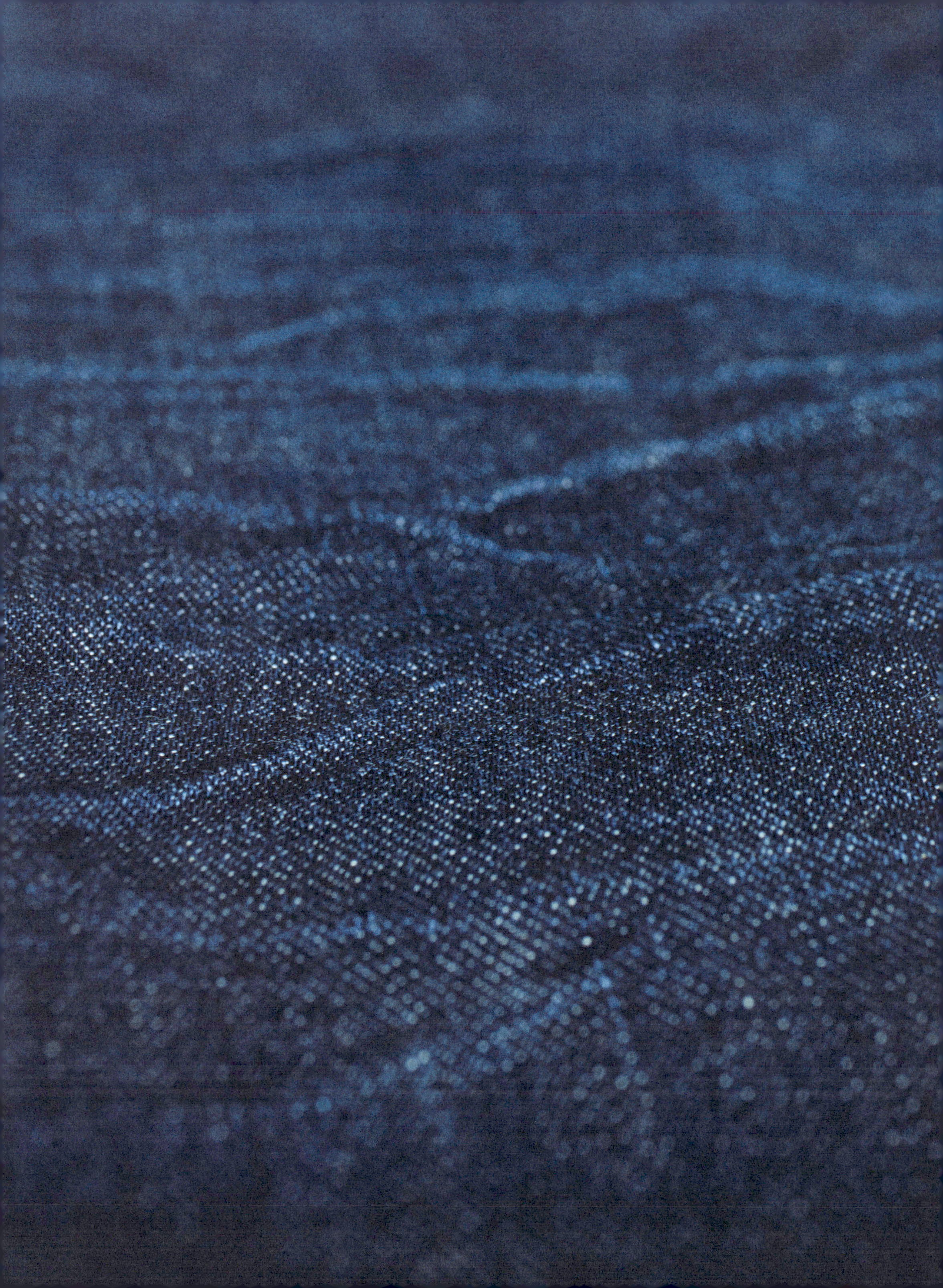

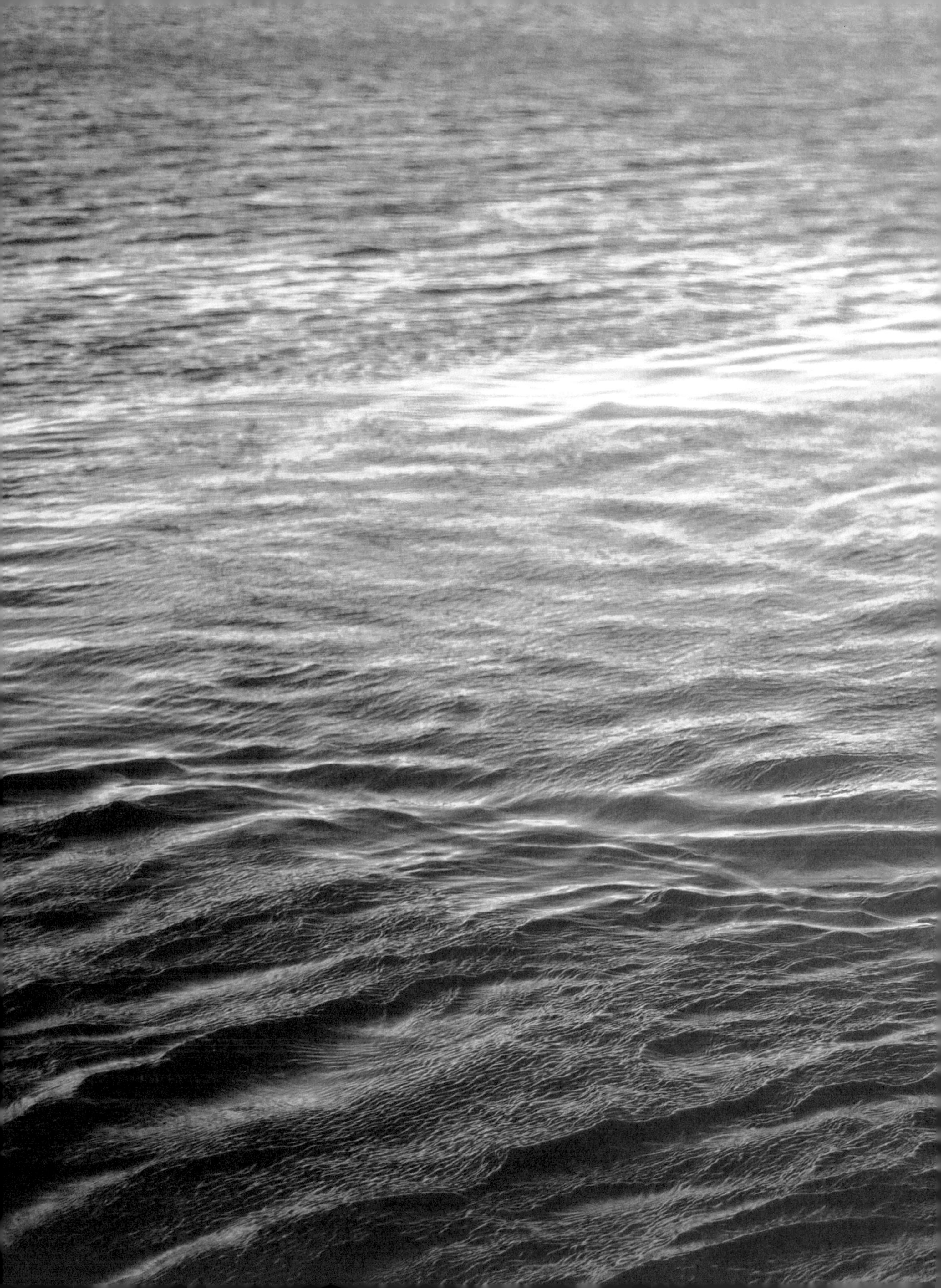

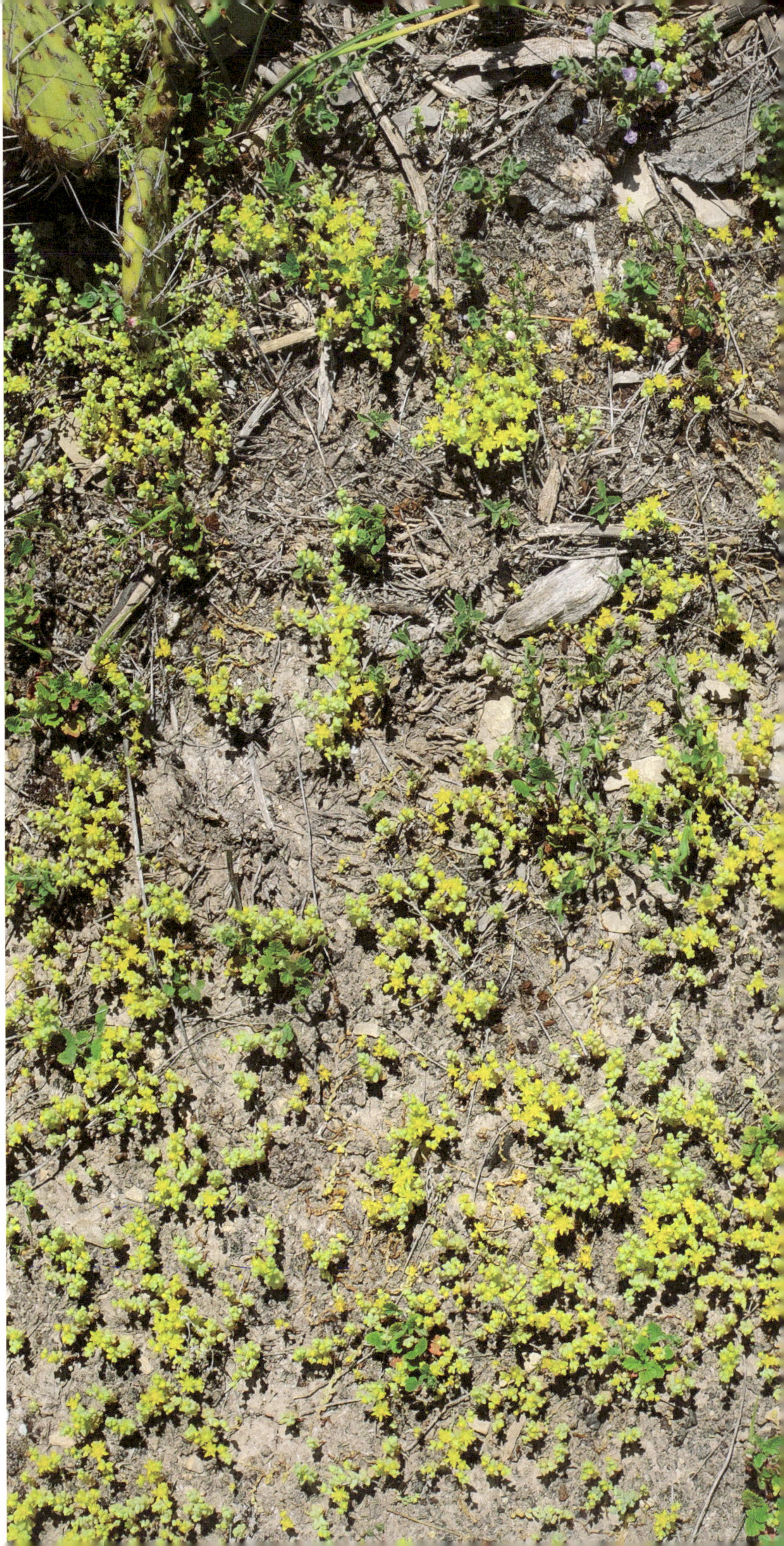

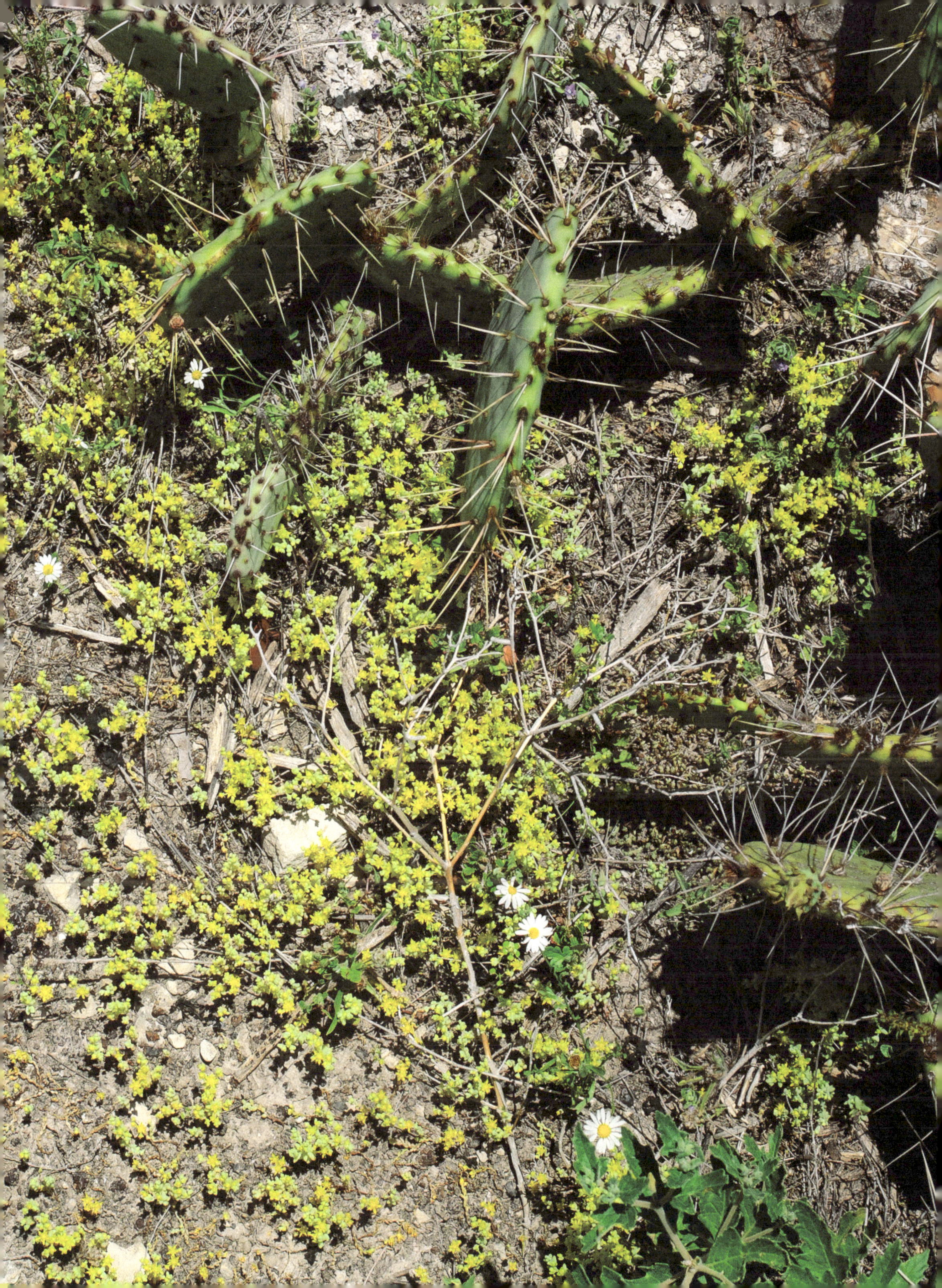

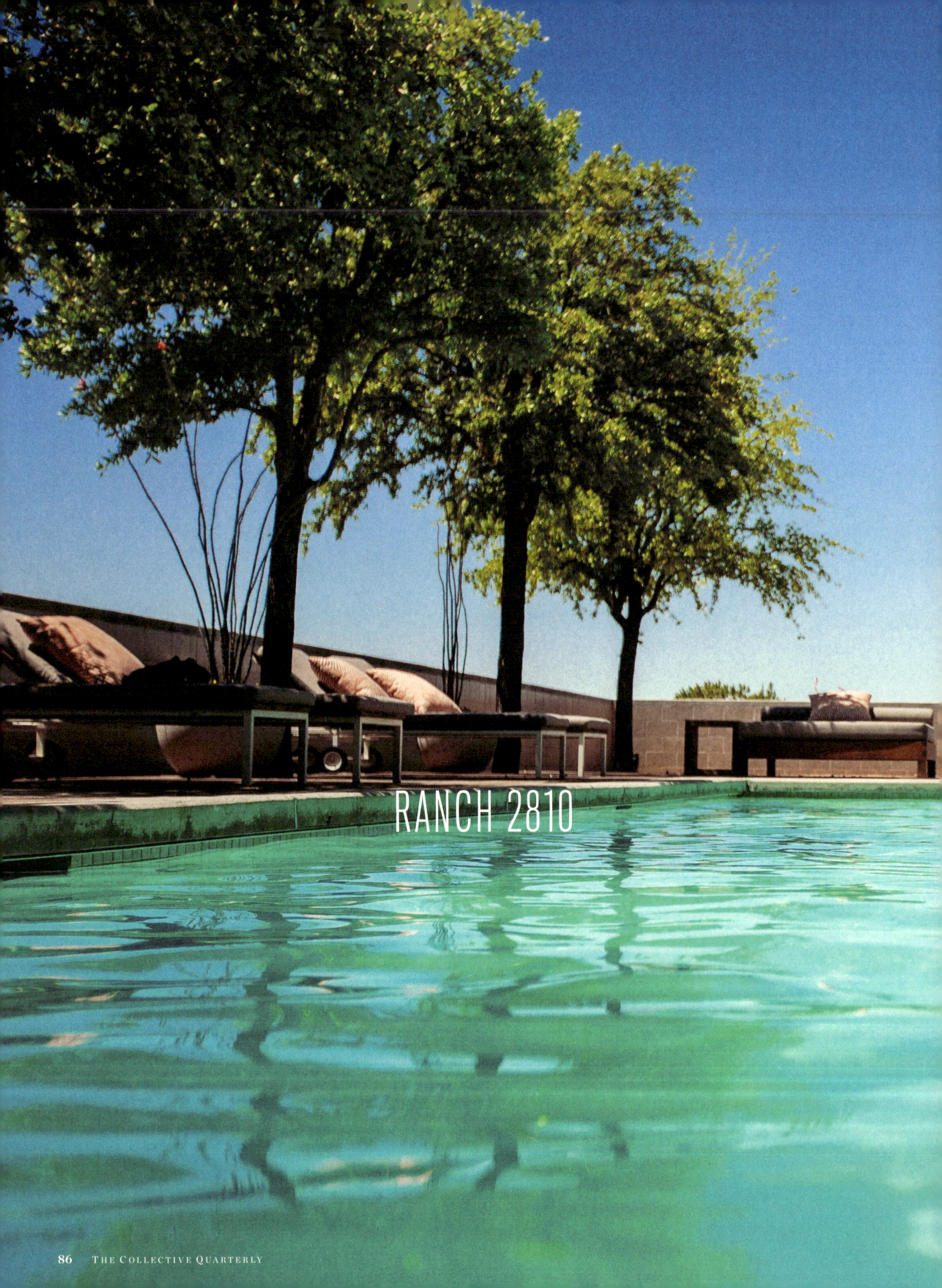

RANCH 2810

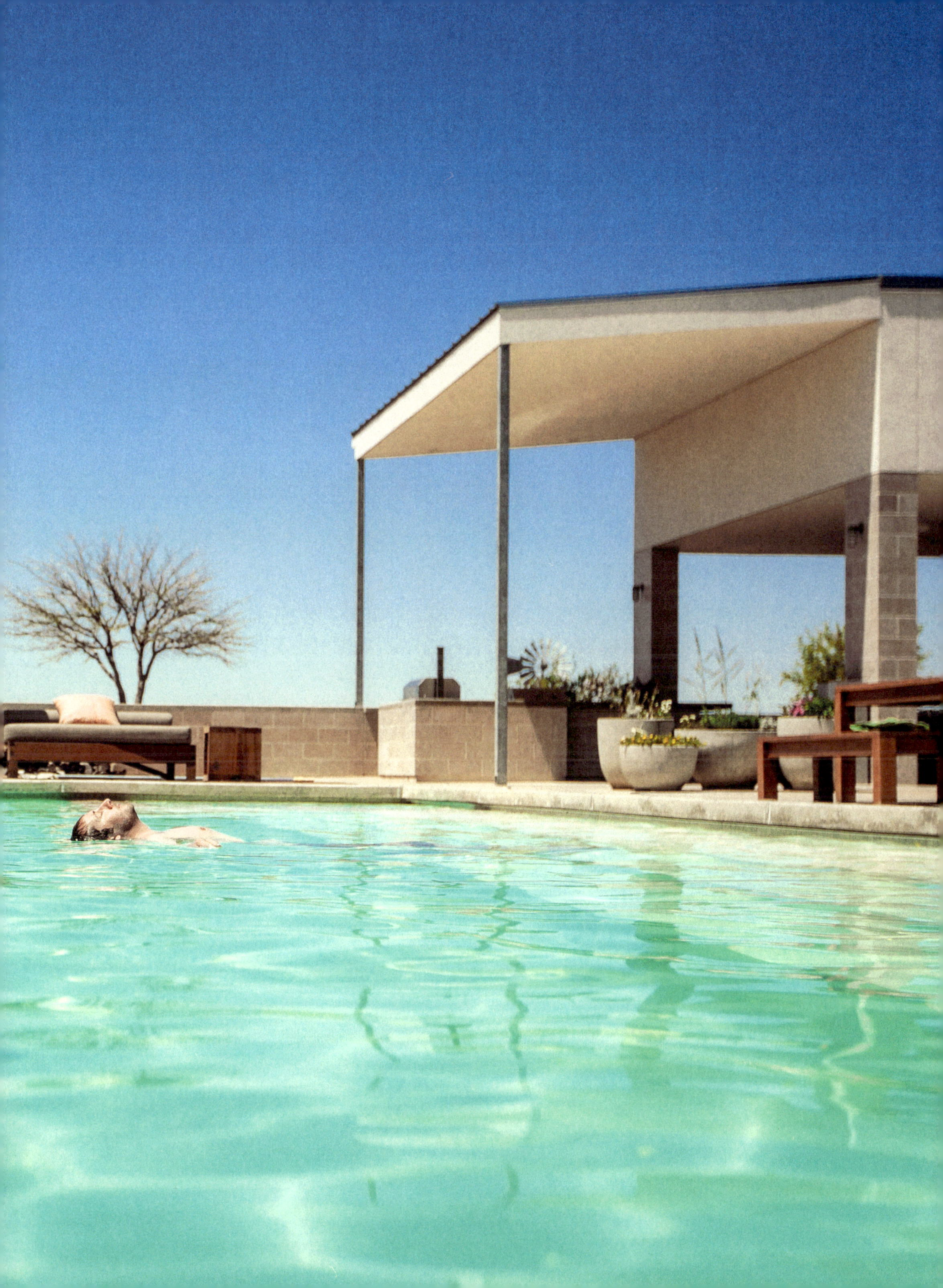

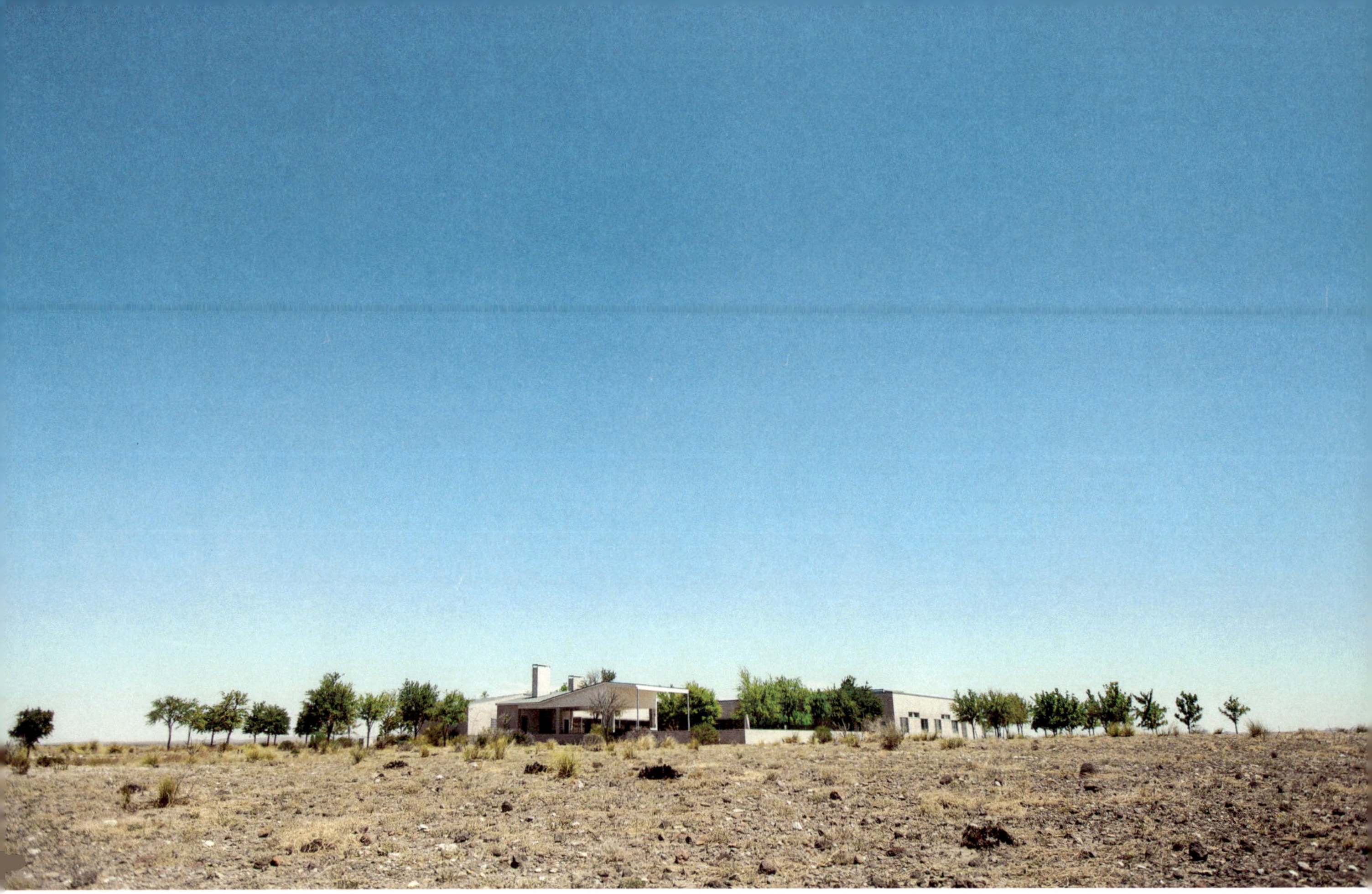

RANCH 2810 ISN'T SO MUCH A MANSION AS IT IS A a vanishing act. A sleek expanse of steel, wood, and windows, at times it becomes hard to tell where the house ends and the natural environment begins.

The abstract, Modernist mansion is the last thing you'd expect in a ranch house. It's as if a Brobdingnagian hand had uprooted it from Palm Springs and deposited it unceremoniously in the wilderness. The crisp white walls, rich wood floors, and chrome fixtures form a stark juxtaposition to the barren desert. It's at once cool during the blazing day and somehow cozy when the frigid night sets in. A giant picture window in the living room gazes upon the Davis Mountains, 30 miles away, as if they were a painting on the wall. An organic orchard of fruit trees, vegetables, and herbs anchors the architecture on its vast 2,700 acres. The walls, adorned with prints of sweeping landscape by Argentine Marcos Furer, seem to disappear into the watercolored world beyond.

Perhaps it's this external locus of control that drives the peace and quiet. Separated from the general buzz of town by six miles, past a mechanical gate and down two miles of gravel driveway, the 8,000 square-foot ranch house stands alone in the midst of the endless, arid landscape of the Chihuahuan Desert. As much as the house disappears into the landscape, so too do your obligations. Time here expands to fill the space.

That was architect Carlos Jiménez's goal when he originally designed the house for Tim Crowley and Lynn Goode, two of Marfa's patron saints of development. The couple, now divorced, were some of the initial forces behind Marfa's quickfire rise to art world fame. In 2011, they sold the house to Lindsay and Ford Smith, Jr., a couple from Austin, Texas, for whom it was something of an impulse buy. After visiting a number of West Texas ranches that didn't move them, their realtor brought them to the Crowley house. "As we were driving away, my husband looked at me and said he thought we should do it," Lindsay says.

"We didn't sit down and say, 'Let's create a destination resort,'" she continues. But later that year, Beyoncé called. Looking for a getaway for her posse, they wondered if they might rent the ranch. "We figured out a price and hired caterers. They had a blast."

And with that, a resort was born. The couple created a website and hired a permanent staff of three to look after the property and guests. They host about eight groups per year. The five stylishly appointed bedrooms are lush with tonal upholstery and fur accents. But even the well-stocked media room, library, and home gym seem extraneous compared to the effortless ease found in outdoor living area—complete with kitchen and fire pit—best enjoyed with ice cold El Guapo cocktails, good friends, and Marfa's lights twinkling faintly in the distance.

Intel: Ranch 2810 sleeps up to 10 people, starting at $2,000 a night. There is a three-night minimum stay. For more information, visit *ranch2810marfa.com*. – E.F.

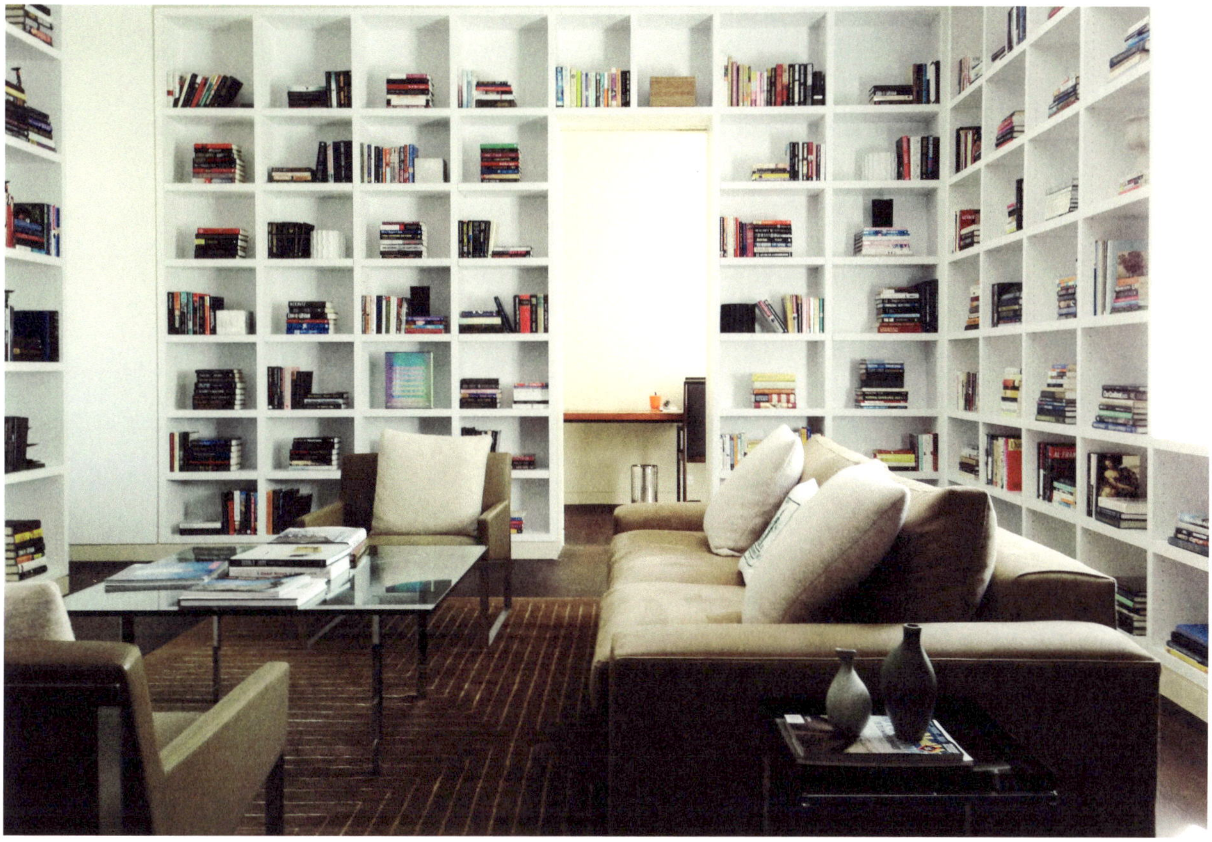

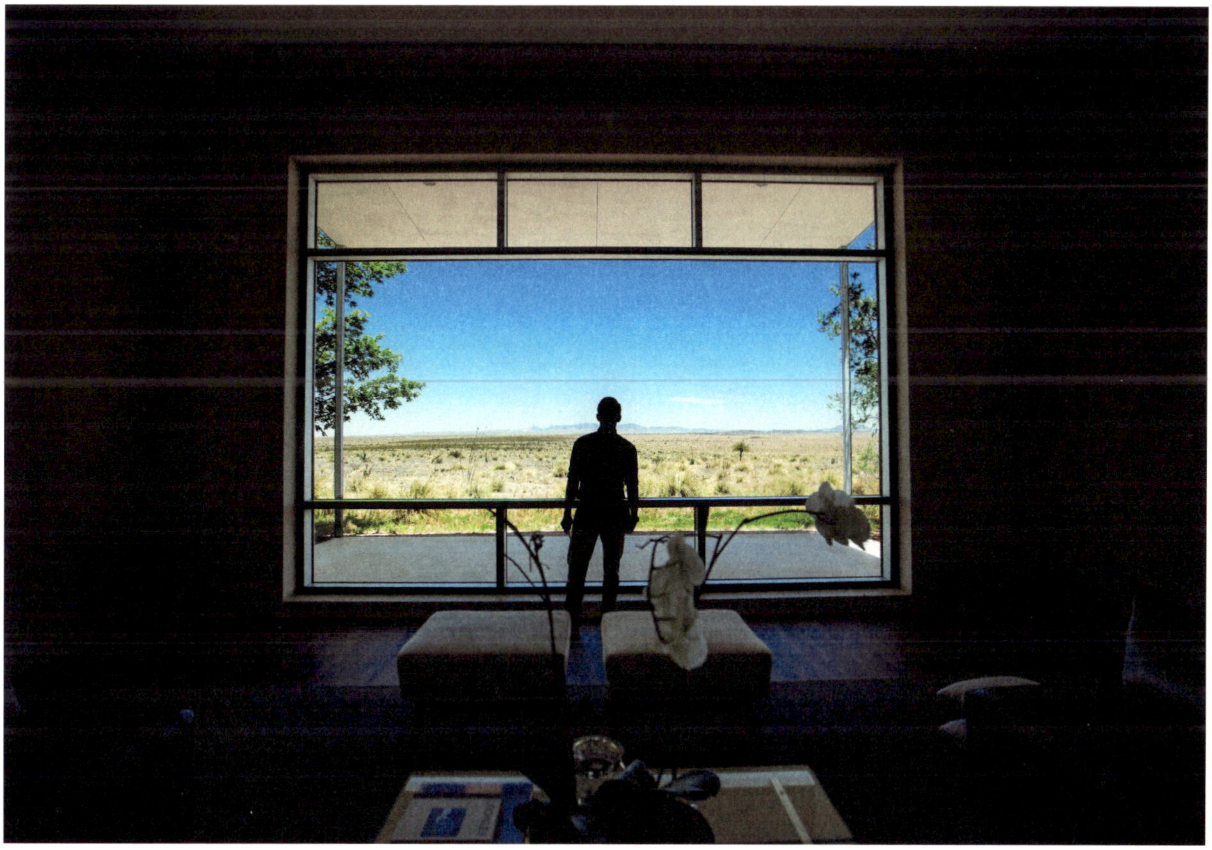

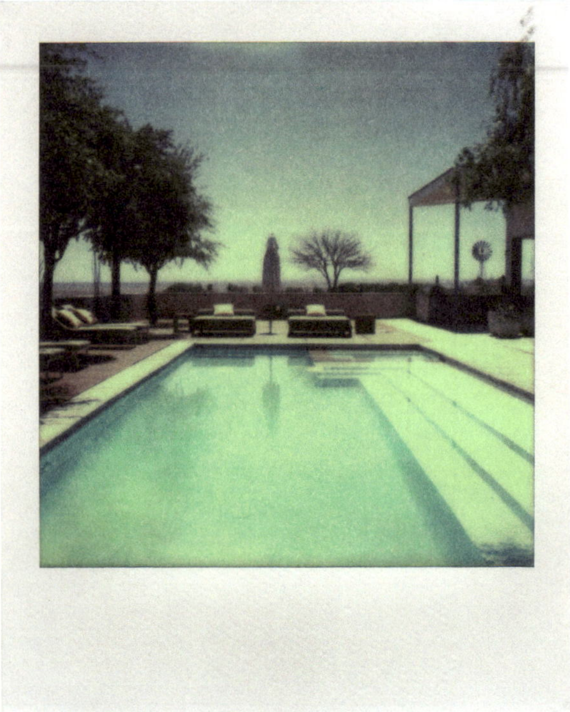

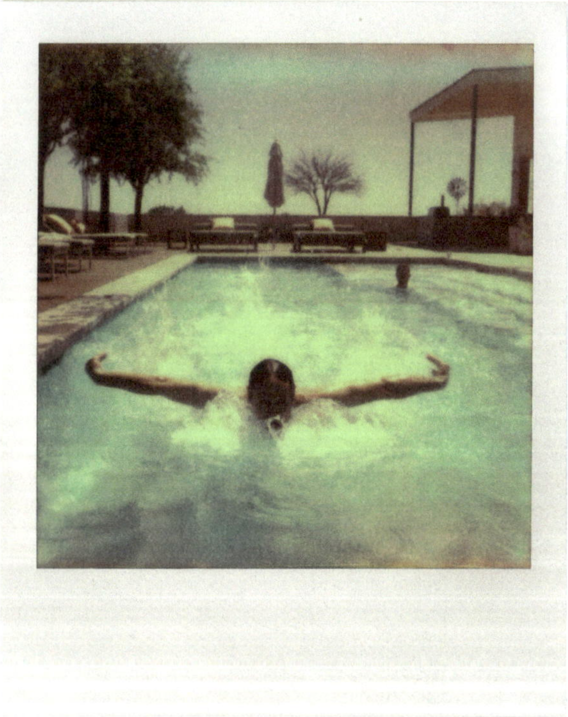

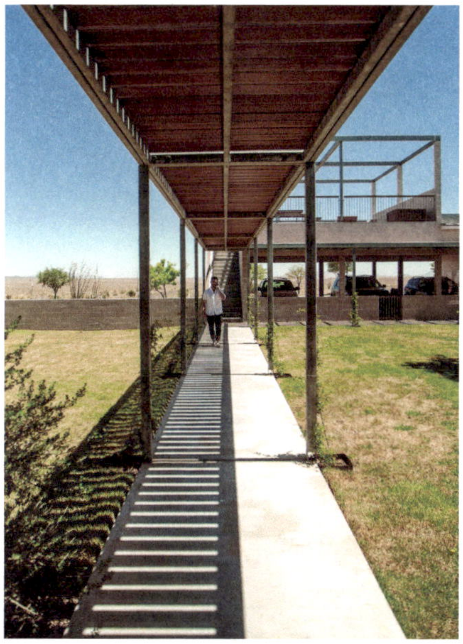

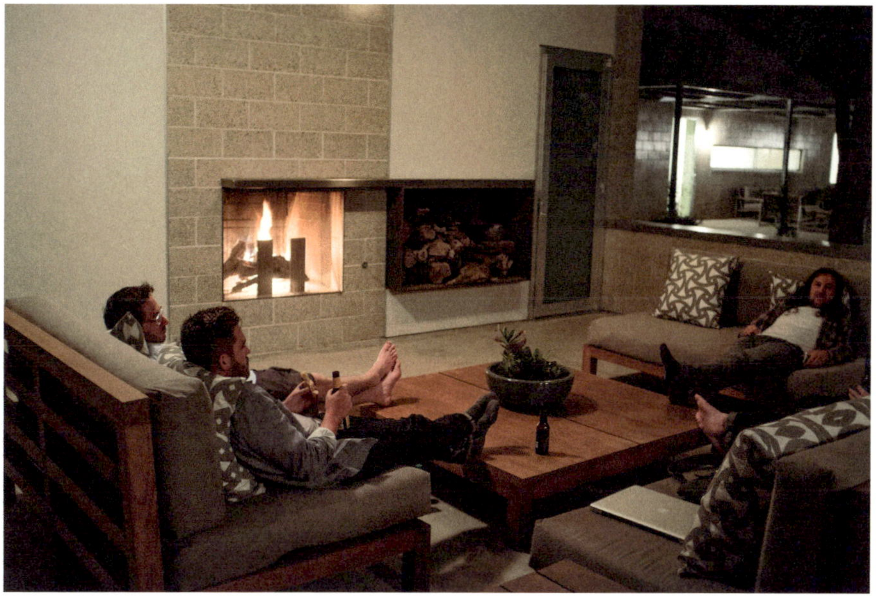

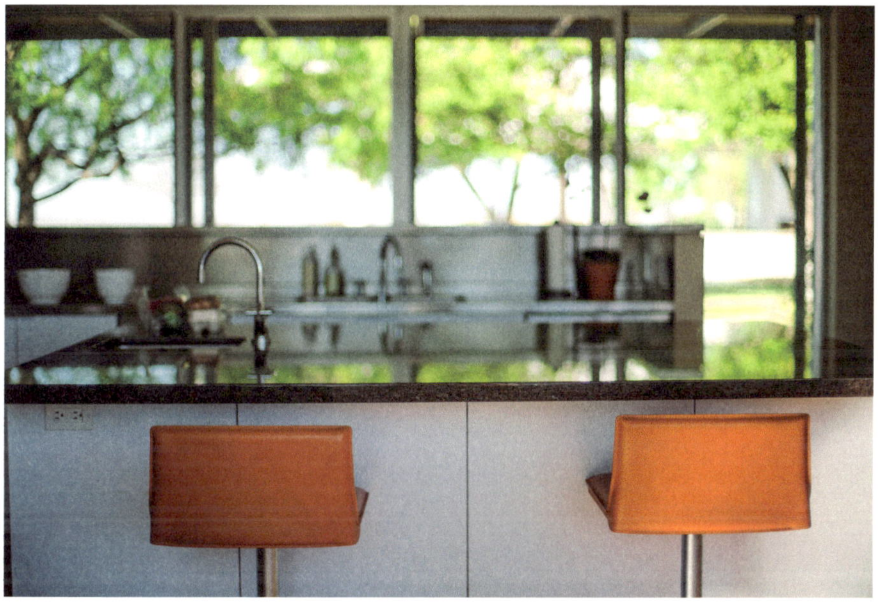

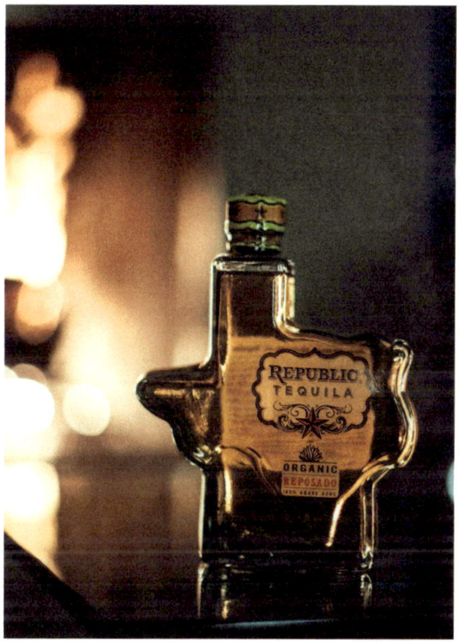
REPUBLIC
TEQUILA
ORGANIC
REPOSADO

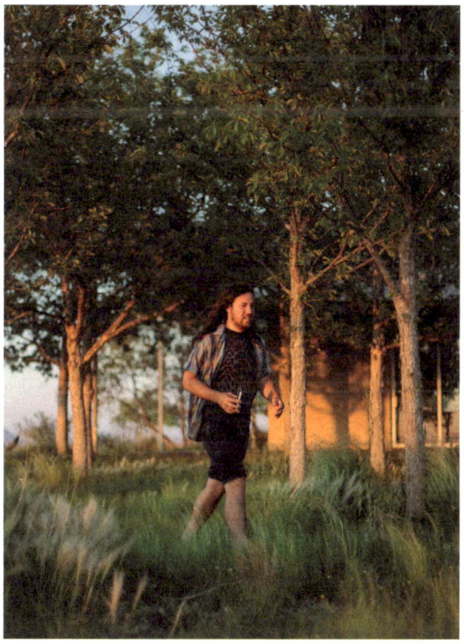

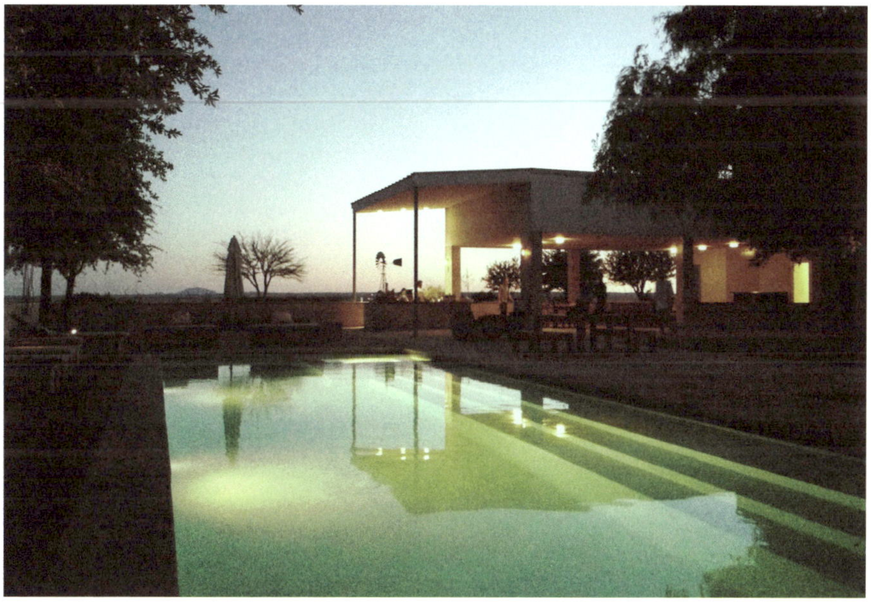

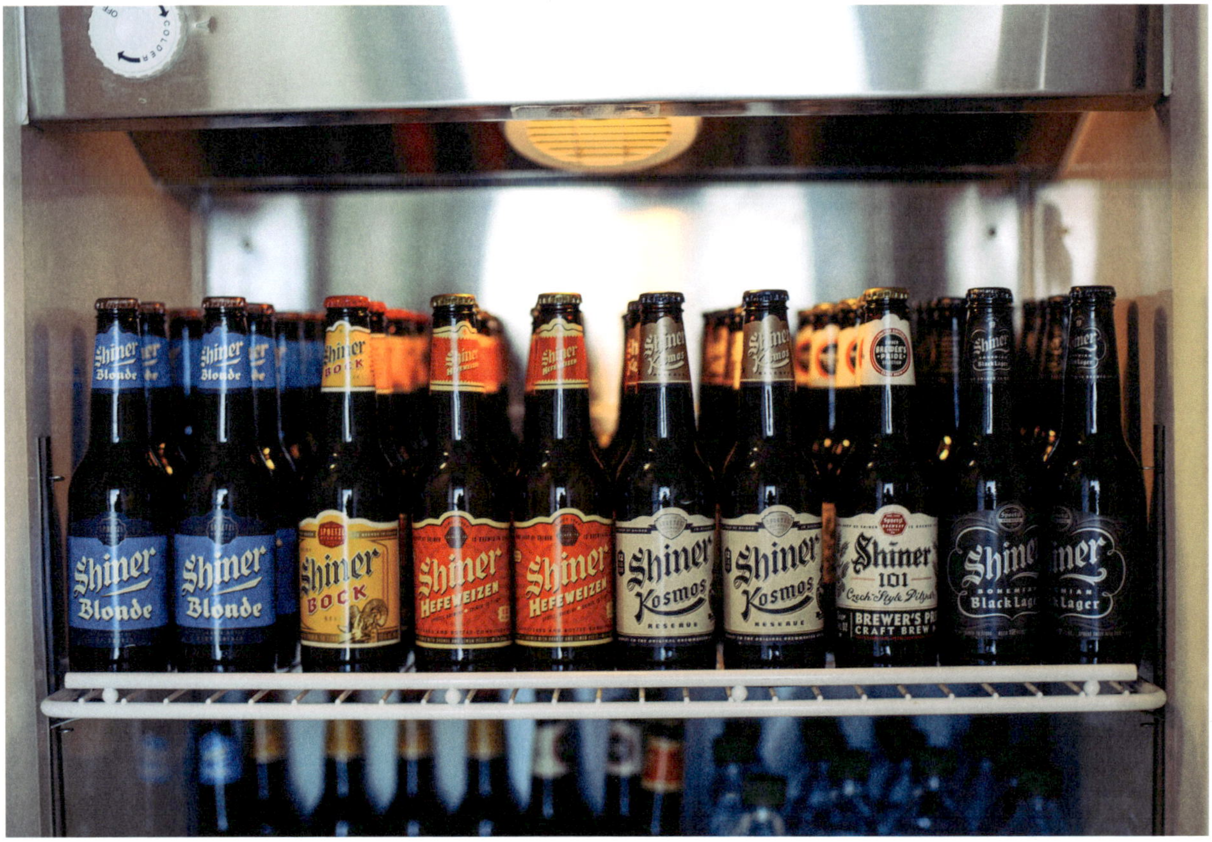
Shiner Blonde
Shiner Bock
Shiner Hefeweizen
Shiner Kosmos Reserve
Shiner 101 Czech-Style Pilsner
Shiner Bohemian Black Lager

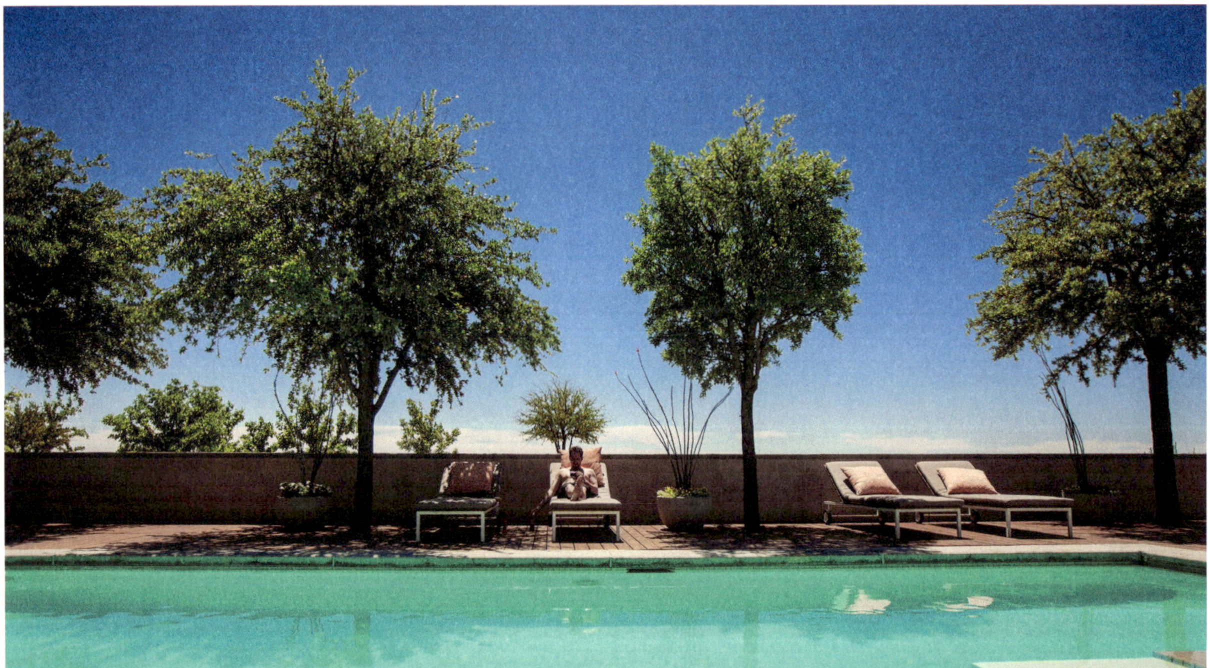

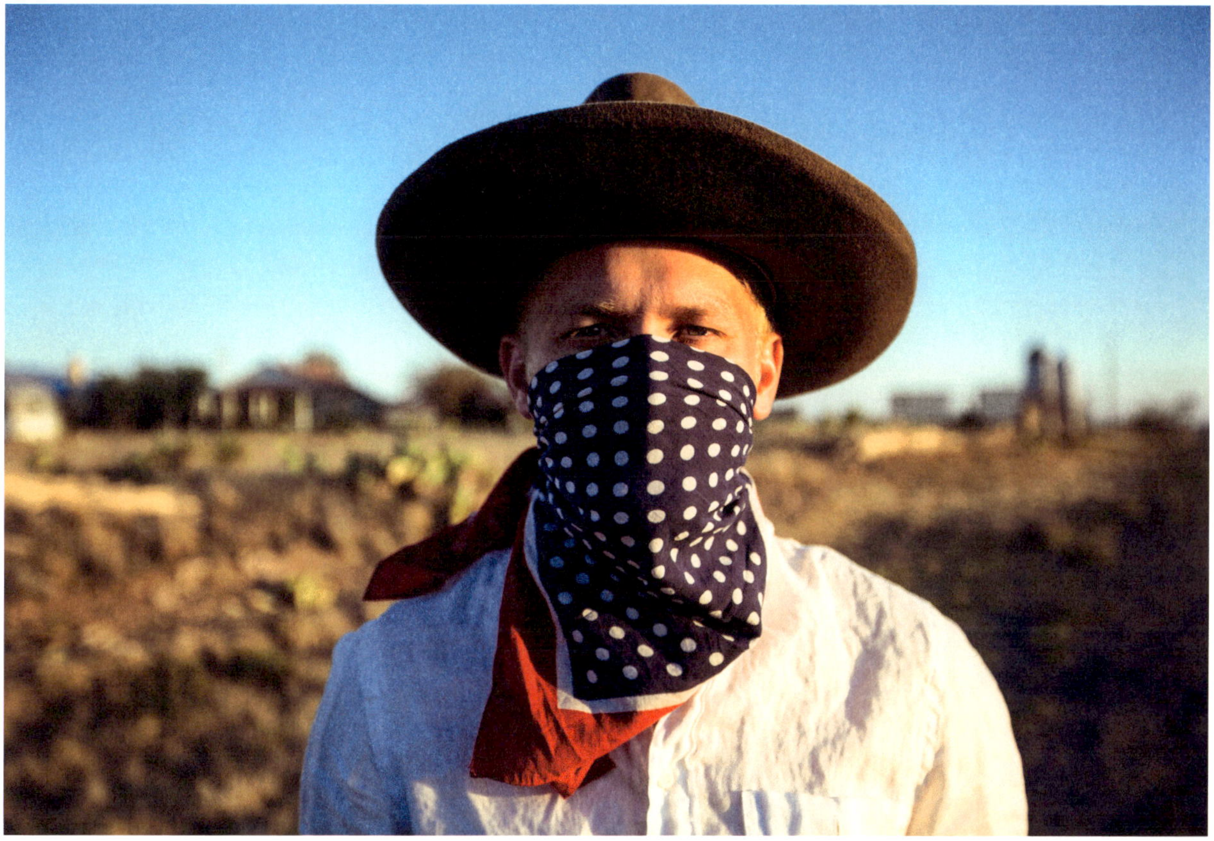

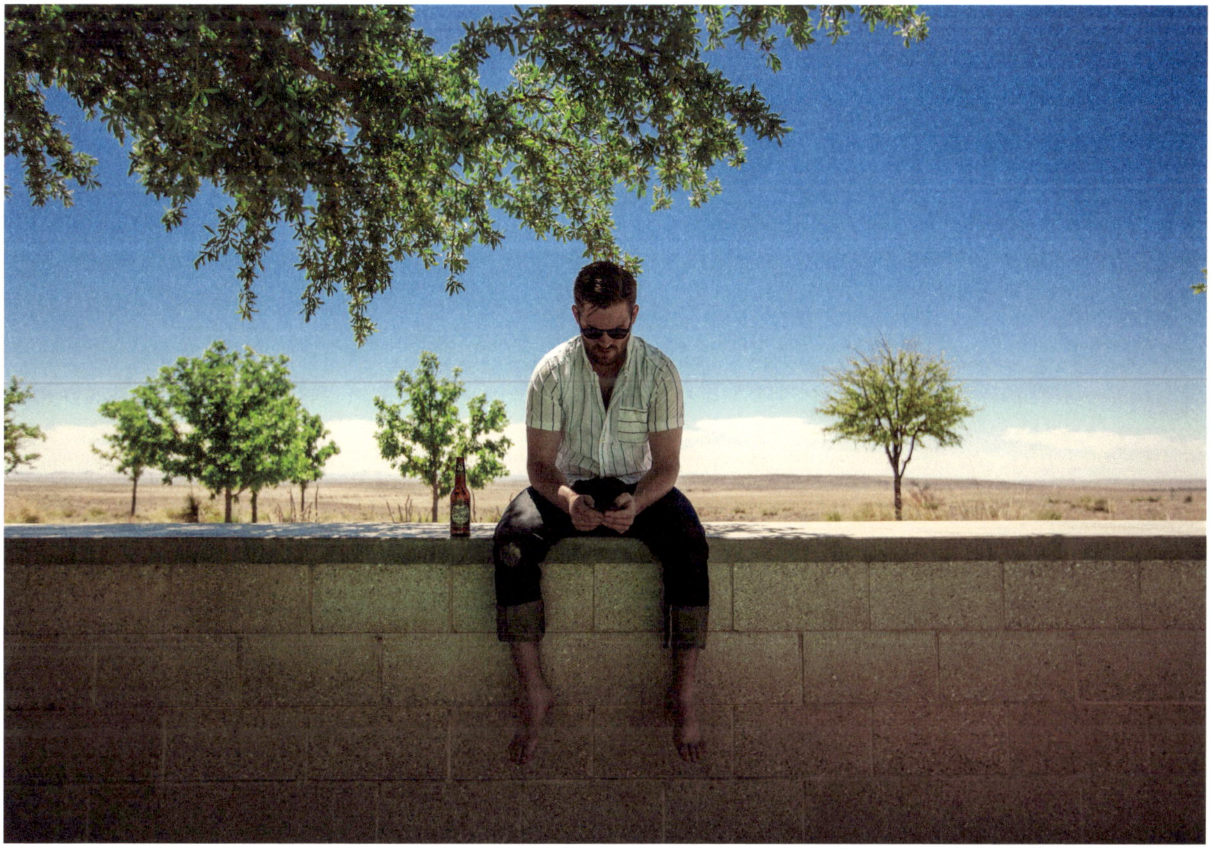

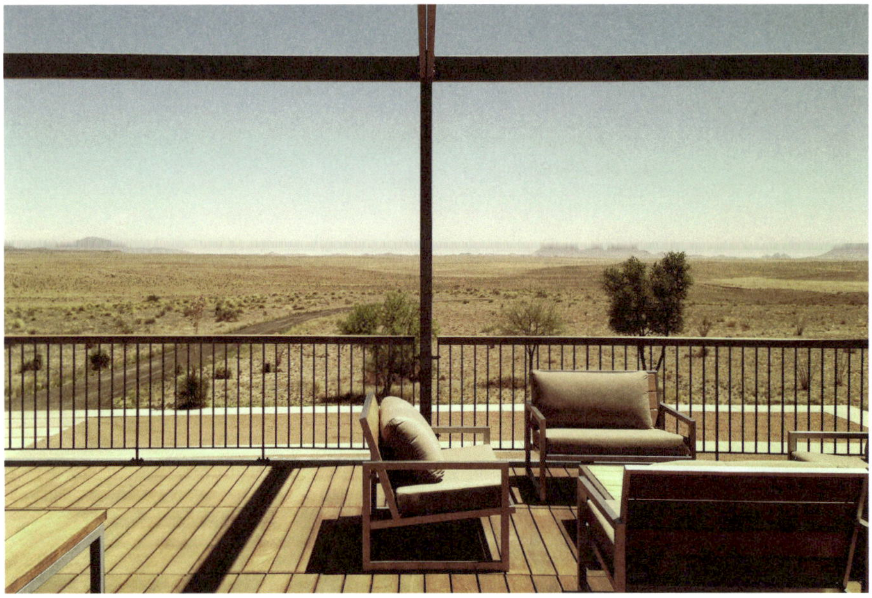

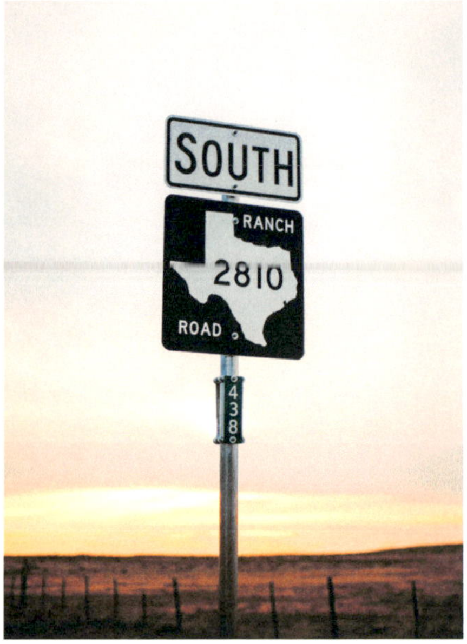
SOUTH
RANCH
2810
ROAD

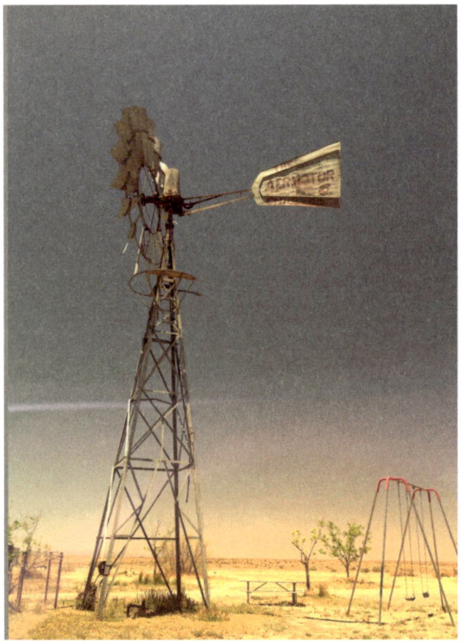

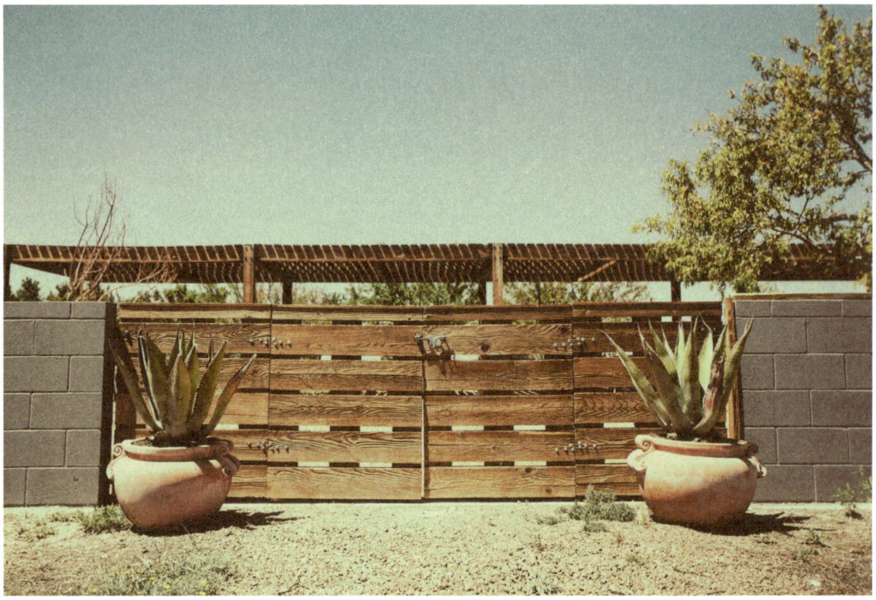

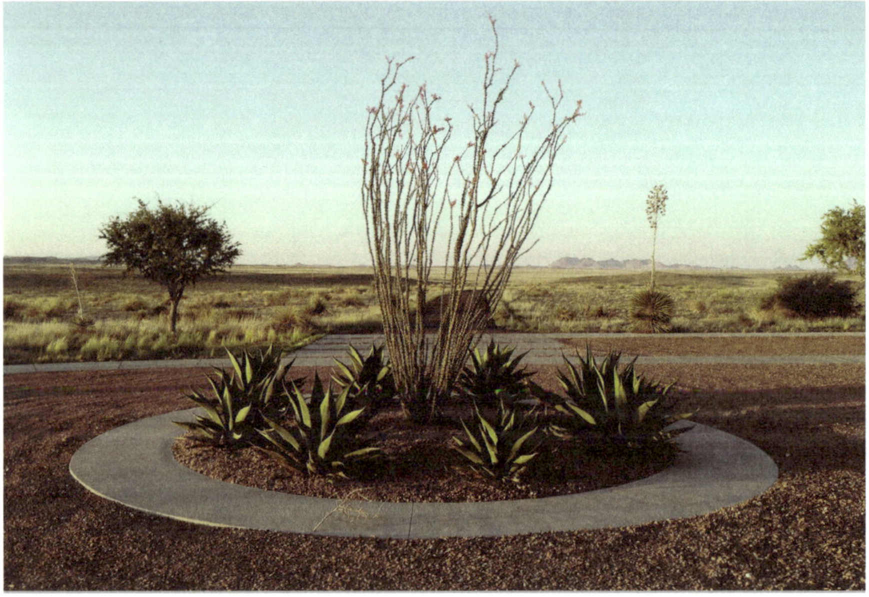

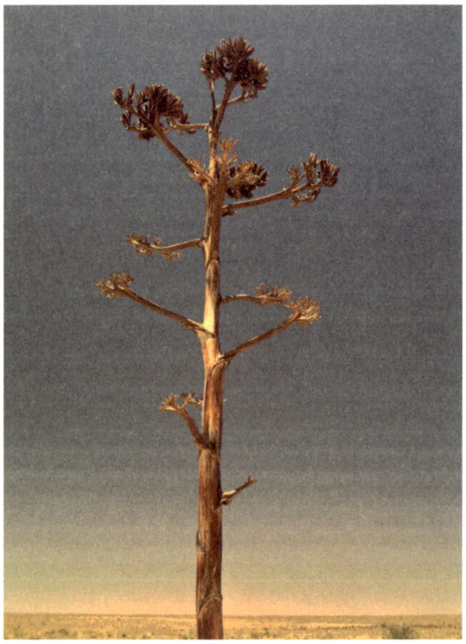

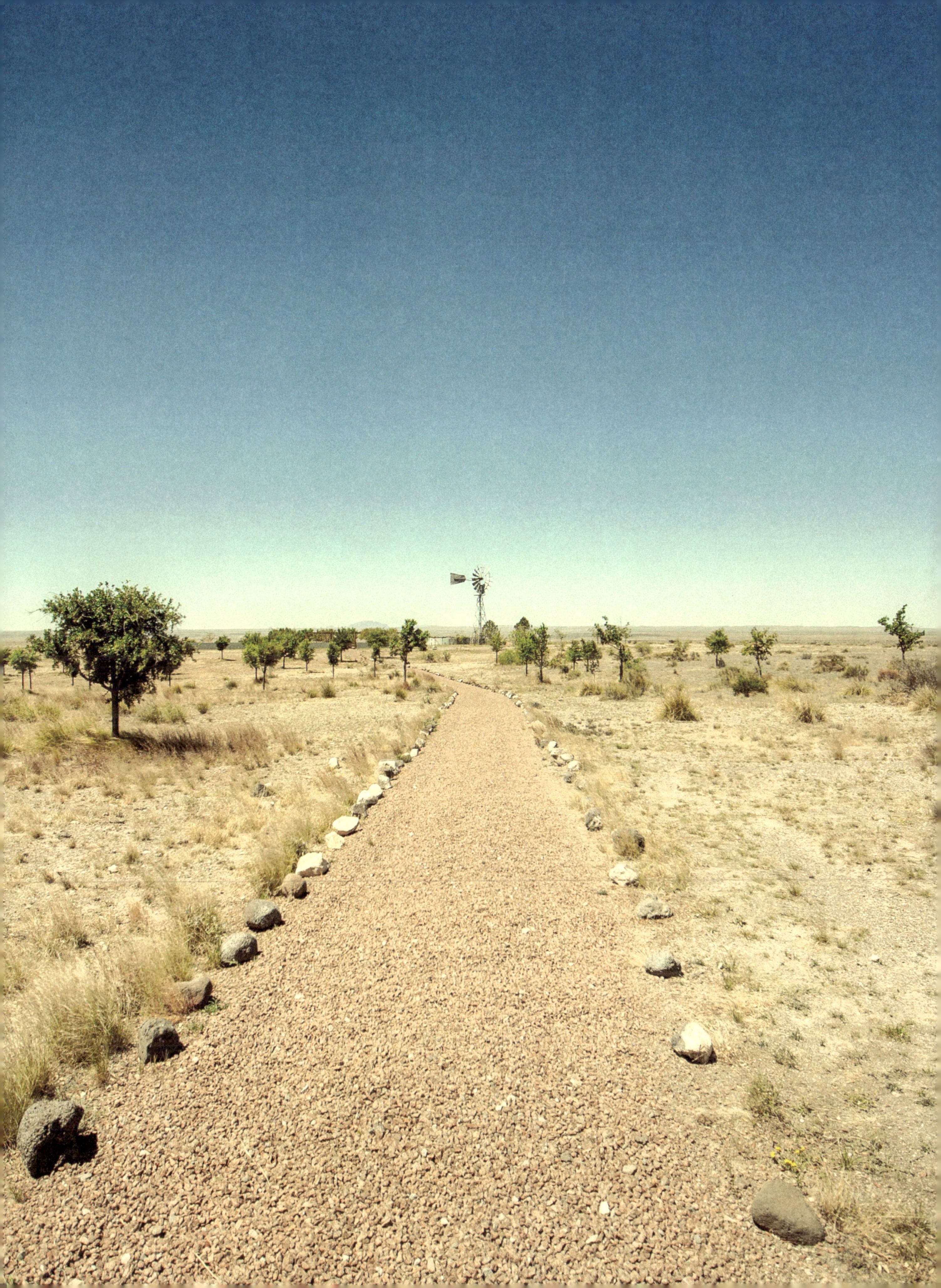

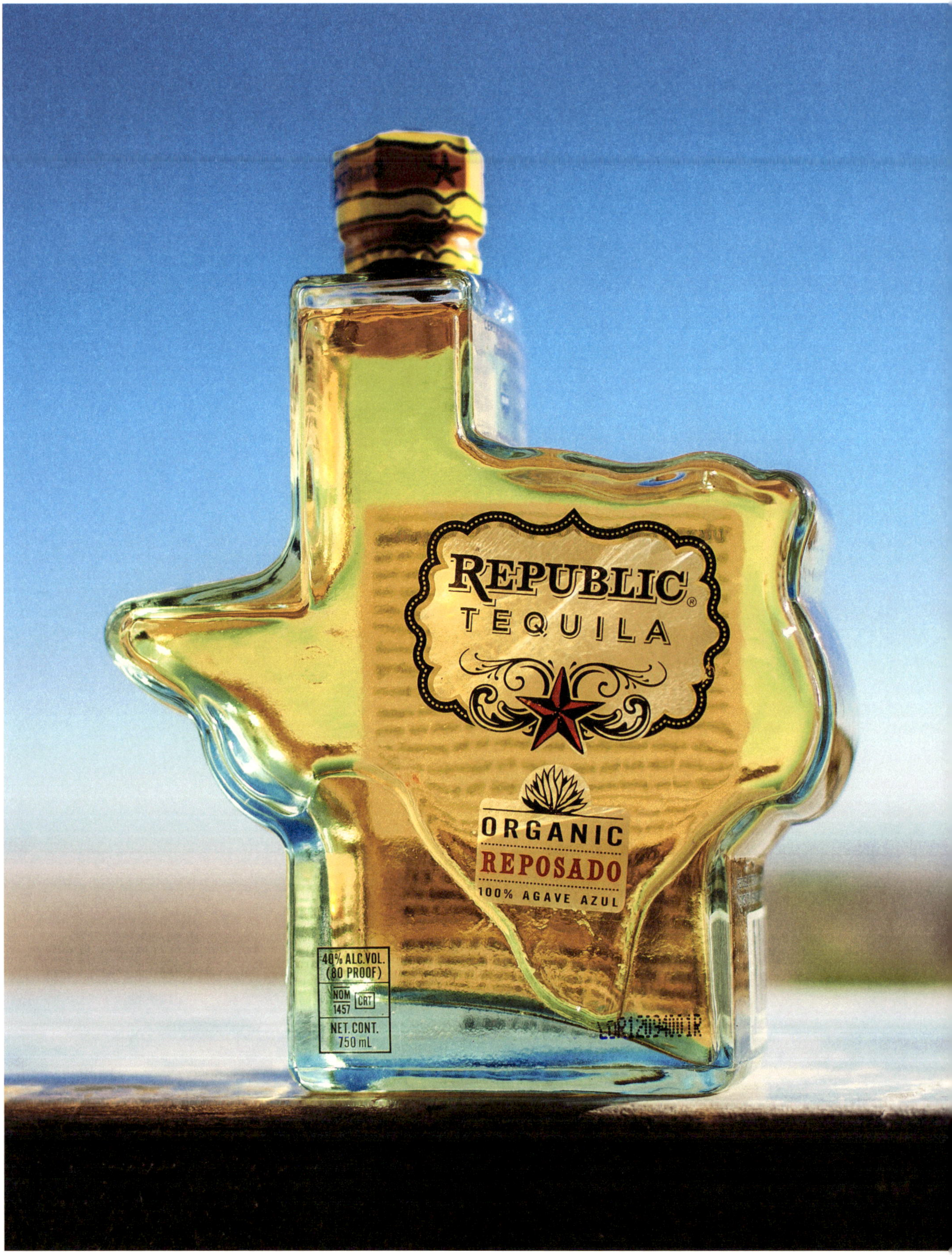
REPUBLIC®
TEQUILA
ORGANIC
REPOSADO
100% AGAVE AZUL
40% ALC.VOL.
(80 PROOF)
NOM
1457
CRT
NET.CONT.
750 mL

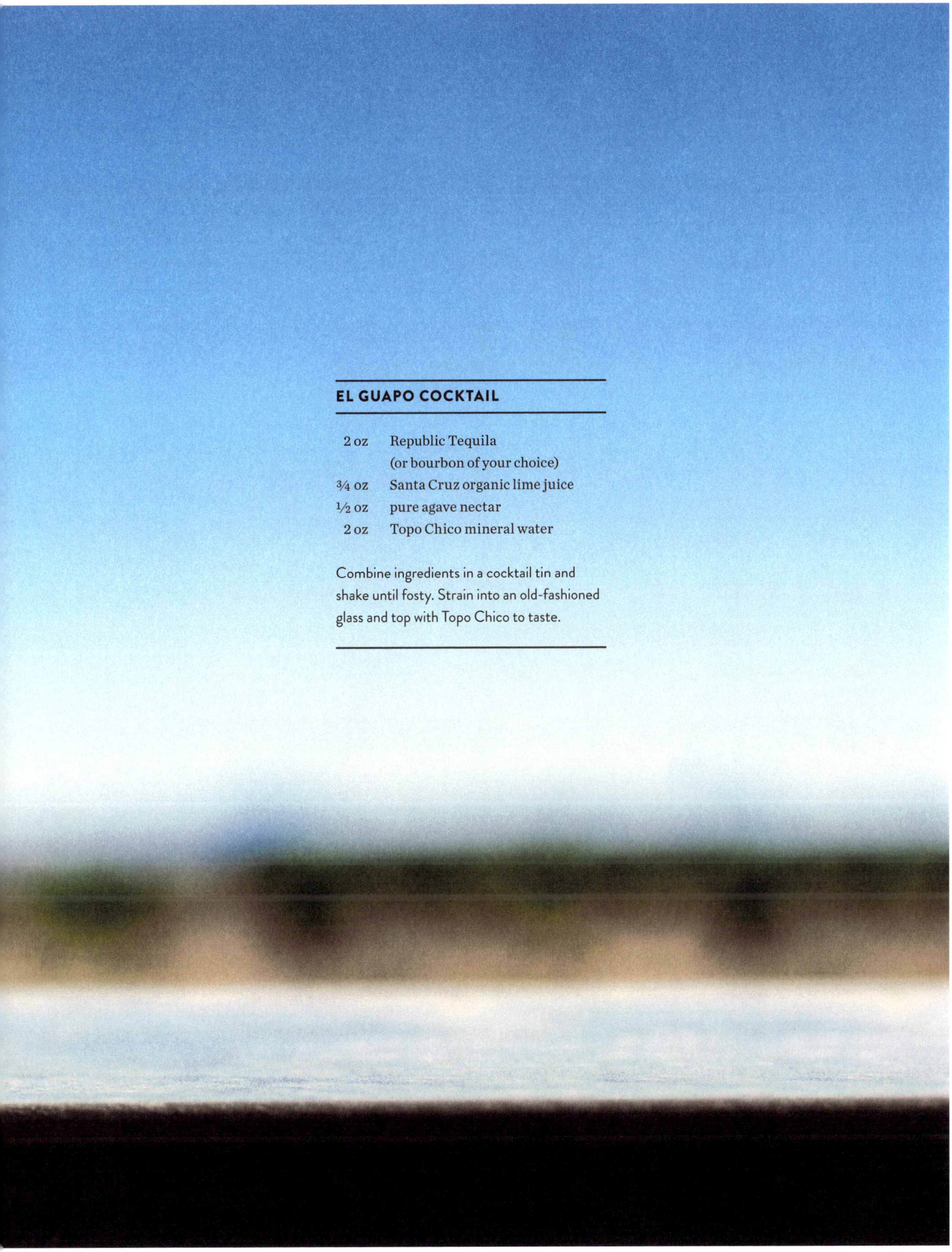

EL GUAPO COCKTAIL

2 oz	Republic Tequila (or bourbon of your choice)
¾ oz	Santa Cruz organic lime juice
½ oz	pure agave nectar
2 oz	Topo Chico mineral water

Combine ingredients in a cocktail tin and shake until fosty. Strain into an old-fashioned glass and top with Topo Chico to taste.

FED UP WITH SHOEBOX-SIZE GALLERIES & YEARNING FOR A WAY TO LINK LANDSCAPE & AESTHETIC, CONTEMPORARY ARTIST DONALD JUDD BACKED AWAY FROM THE BUSTLING NEW YORK ART SCENE TO PLANT A CREATIVE SEED IN MARFA'S KHAKI DESERT DIRT. THIS WAS THE EARLY 1970S, DECADES BEFORE THE ISOLATED RAILWAY STOPOVER WAS REBORN AS A CREATIVE MECCA. BEGINNING WITH SPORADIC INSTALLATIONS, JUDD'S INITIATIVE BLOSSOMED TO ENCOMPASS 340 ACRES OF SPACE THAT ONCE HOUSED US MILITARY OUTPOST FORT D.A. RUSSELL. THIS MINIMALIST SANCTUARY OPENED TO THE PUBLIC AS THE CHINATI FOUNDATION IN 1986.

MANY OF JUDD'S MOST RESPECTED CONTEMPORARIES, INCLUDING LIGHT ARTIST DAN FLAVIN & CAR-PART SCULPTOR JOHN CHAMBERLAIN, HAVE EXHIBITIONS SHOWCASED ACROSS CHINATI'S BARREN GROUNDS (EACH ARTIST RECIEVES A DEDICATED SPACE IN ONE OF 15 BUILDINGS). AN INSTALLATION THAT SITS ATOP THE SAND, HOWEVER, OFTEN SERVES AS THE CENTERPIECE OF CHINATI'S POSTCARDS AND PHOTOGRAPHS.

JUDD'S 15 UNTITLED WORKS IN CONCRETE— SMOOTH GREY BOXES OF THE SAME SIZE THAT DOT THE HORIZON— ARE ACCESSIBLE FOR FREE VIA A ONE & A HALF-MILE ROUND-TRIP GRAVEL PATH. THOSE LOOKING FOR A DEEPER IMMERSION INTO JUDD & COMPANY'S WORK SHOULD BOOK A GUIDED TOUR IN ADVANCE ($10-25; TOURS@CHINATI.ORG). THE ART'S CONTEMPORARY MESSAGE MAY BE UP FOR INTERPRETATION, BUT THE EERIE SILENCE & DESERT EMPTINESS AFFIXED TO THE WORK IS AN EXPERIENCE THAT IS TRULY MARFA. -A.R.

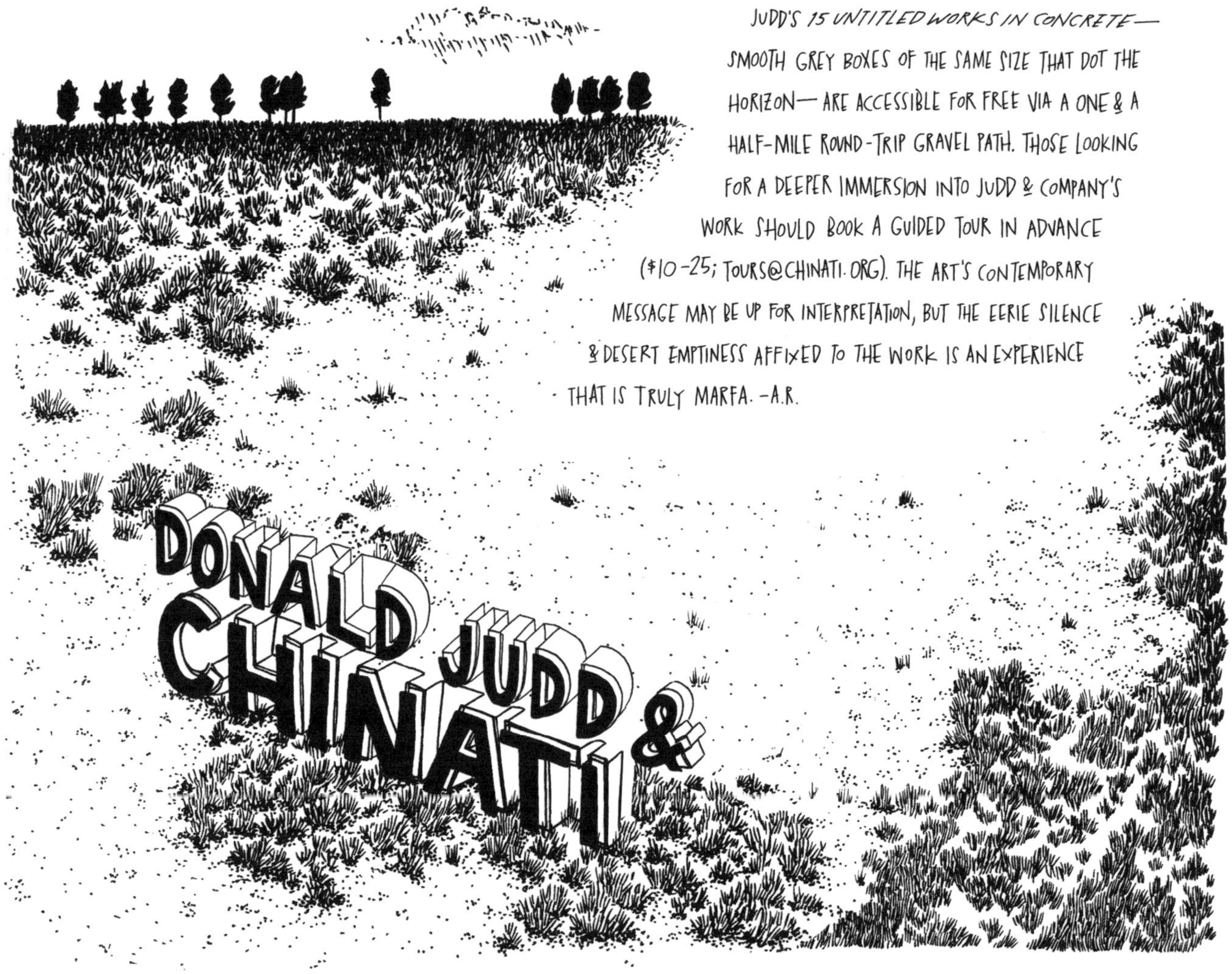

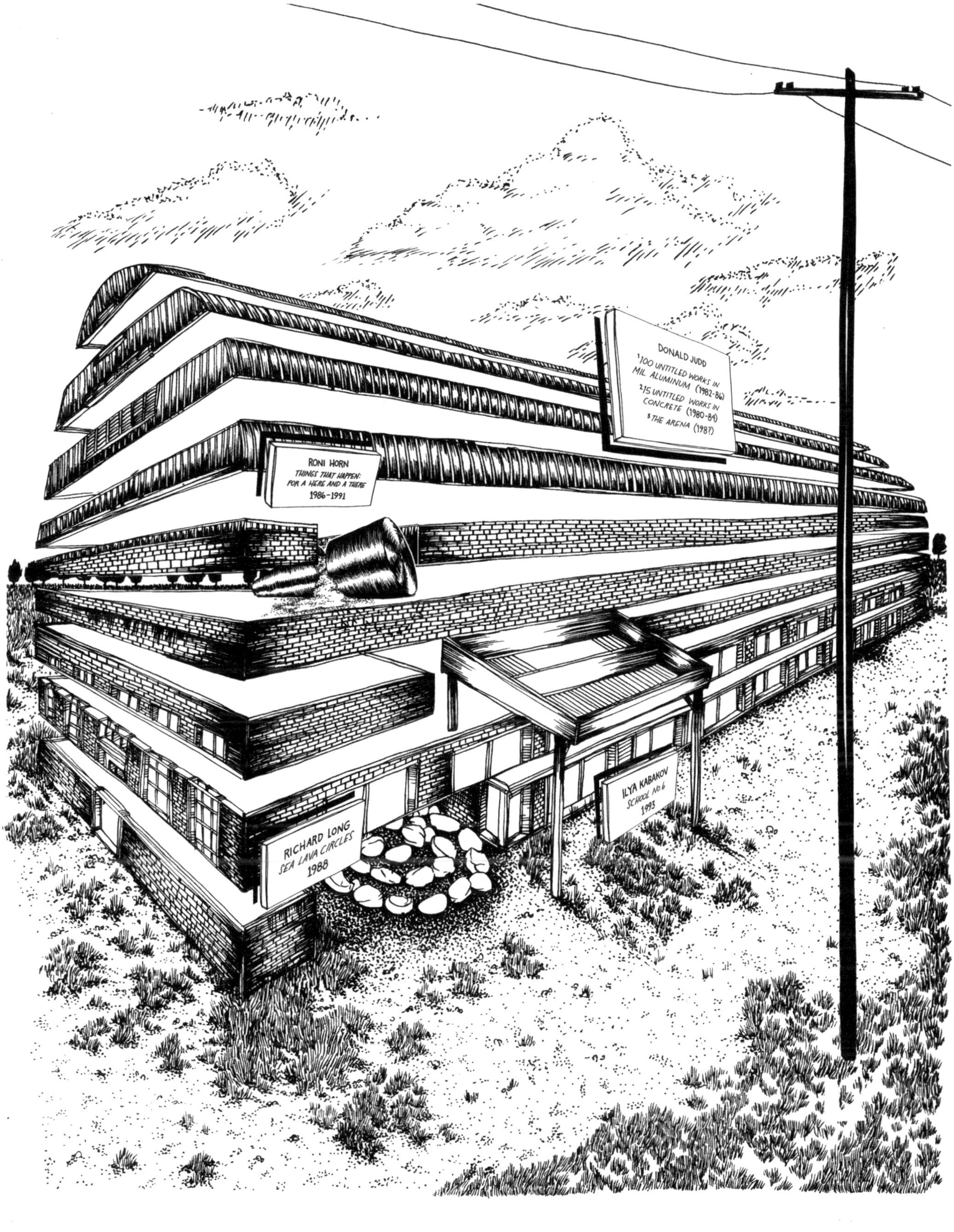

DONALD JUDD
1 100 UNTITLED WORKS IN MIL ALUMINUM (1982-86)
2 15 UNTITLED WORKS IN CONCRETE (1980-84)
3 THE ARENA (198?)
RONI HORN
THINGS THAT HAPPEN: FOR A HERE AND A THERE
1986-1991
RICHARD LONG
SEA LAVA CIRCLES
1988
ILYA KABAKOV
SCHOOL No.6
1993

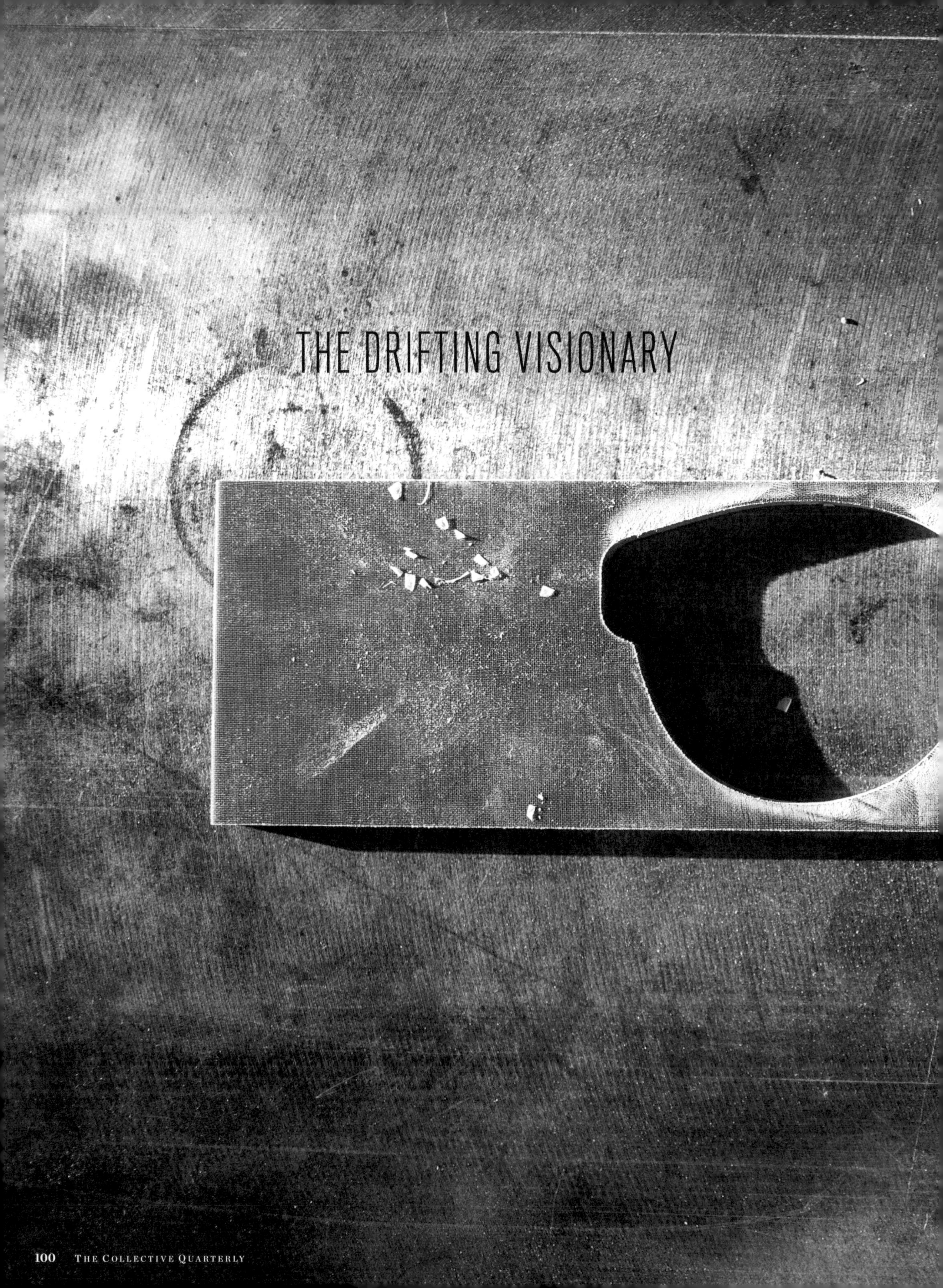

THE DRIFTING VISIONARY

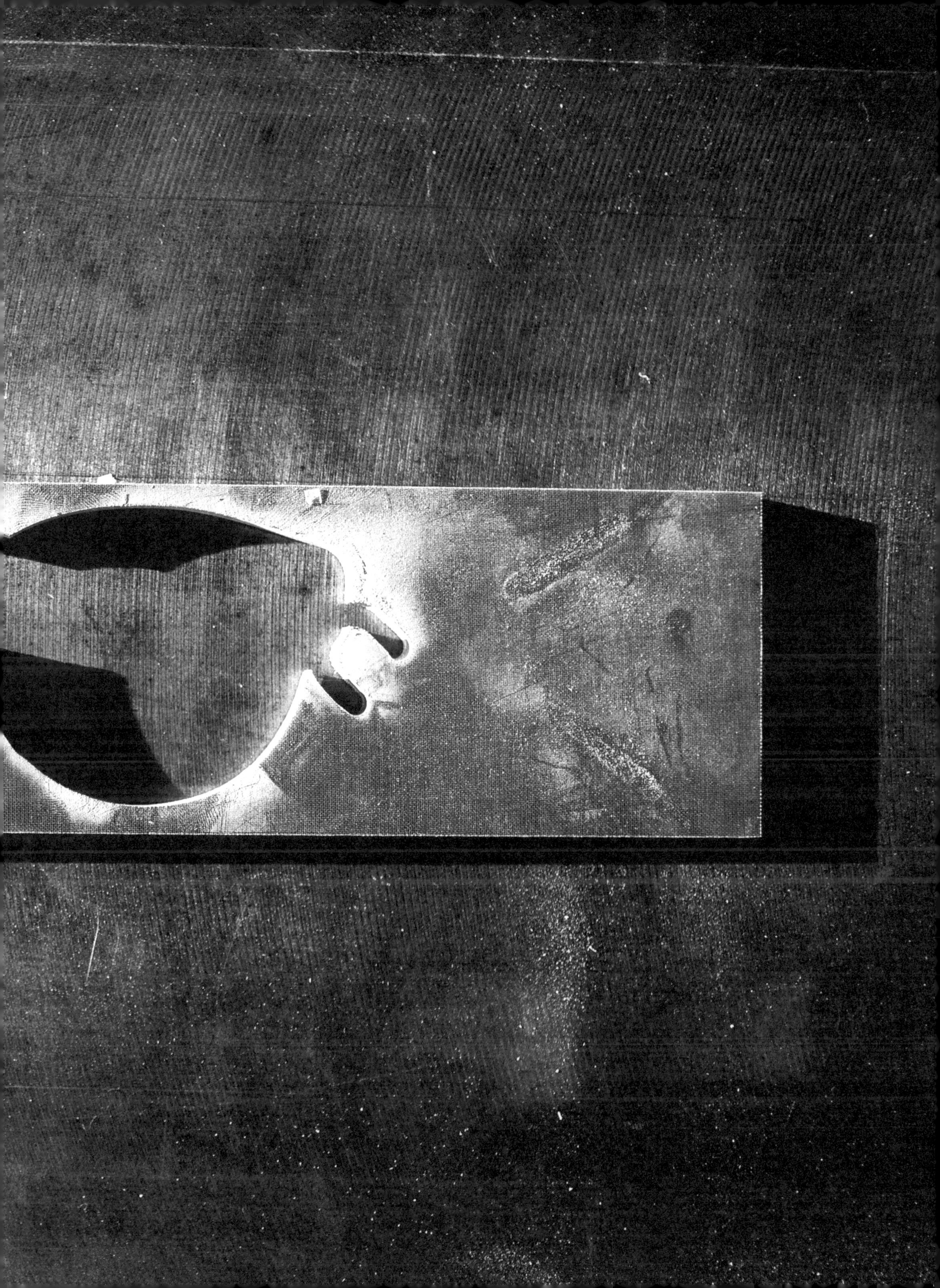

CHRIS MANTZ

IT BEGAN WITH A BEAT-UP SKATEBOARD: A SCARRED, chipped old deck in Chris Mantz's garage. His mom was going to throw it away.

"It was worthless," Chris says, trailing off. He may not have known why, but he saved it. And a use gradually came to him.

Chris is, at heart, an artist. He's the kind of guy who has so many thoughts careening around his skull that he will break himself off mid-thought, just as he was saying something you really wanted to hear, to begin a different one. He's the type of thinker who began a reaction paper in college about how the MP3 player was ruining music only to embark on a philosophical journey that led him to the conclusion that he should embrace technology for what it's worth.

But up to the moment in his garage, his creative process had been channeled into deeply practical work as a product designer for a company that manufactured valves and fittings for flammable carcinogens. He needed more. So he returned to that old skateboard deck and decided to make a pair of sunglasses out of it.

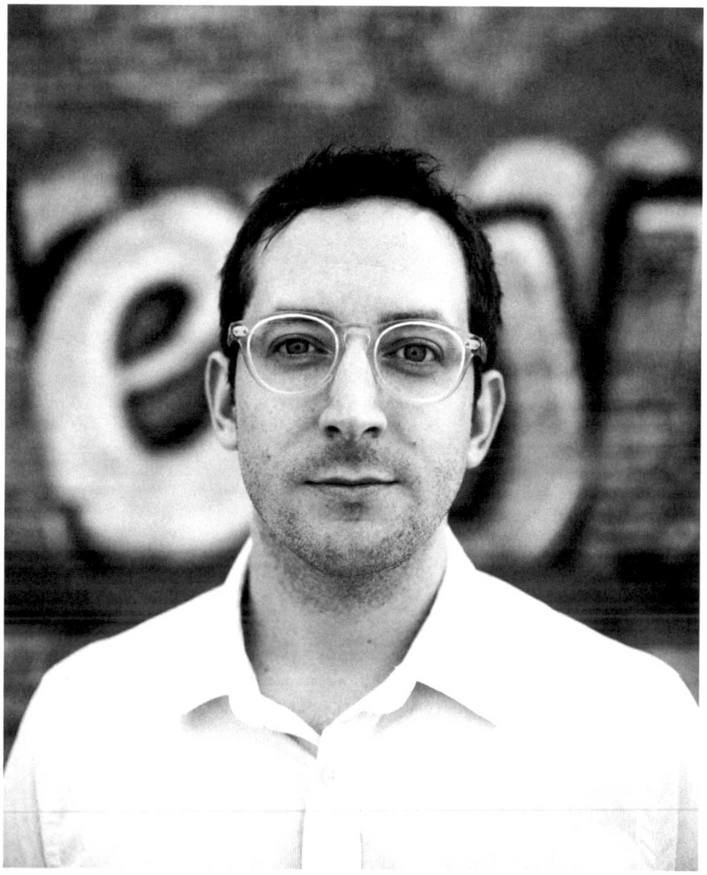

The next year, at a time when no one else was making sunglasses out of wood, Drift Eyewear was born. "What inspired me to do this was seeing other friends doing creative things and me not being able to play," he says. "This is how I play."

Chris was riffing on something that had irked him for a long time: There was a lack of substance in the accessories market. Sunglasses had become bedazzled, poor-quality rip-offs hiding behind designer names. Instead, he aimed to create his own eyewear line.

Each pair has an origin story. Limited edition releases go even deeper, like the "12Meter," Chris' interpretation of the legendary America's Cup sailing competition.

"The optical market was so shallow, and you were overpaying for very little," he says. "And what you were paying for, I felt, was the wrong thing. Even into the super high-end products that are $15,000, all they're selling are diamonds and gold, which have an inherent commodity value. But beyond that, there's nothing that special about the design. You can bejewel anything."

Instead, Chris wanted to use lines, metals, and woods to convey a strong message. The thought behind it sounds abstract, and it is. But it's packaged in a straightforward medium: Sunglasses made from high-quality, biodegradable, acetate frames with reclaimed wood temples.

Most forms of glasses are usually made the same way: The maker cuts out sheets of plastic, shoots steel inside the plastic, then polishes it down and bends it into shape.

Chris does none of that. Instead, he crafts temples from a wood lamination, taking layers and adhering them together with steel inside the laminate to make them more balance for the face and strong enough for daily use. Drift is one of only a handful of companies that still make their glasses in the United States, so Chris and his team (which he is quick to credit for the company's success) had to track down men in their 80s who could teach them how to perform very precise techniques. They even had to build their own machinery.

Unlike other popular eyewear makers, Chris doesn't sell his glasses online; he believes in the importance of buying directly from the experts and likes his customers to test the frames in person before buying them.

"The challenge was how to create that substance," Chris explains. "How do you give the customer that value that they didn't realize they wanted? It's not just that [the glasses] look cool. It's that they're really well-made, and they'll last a long time."

Chris even invented a new hinge. "There's a really cool bridge over Ashland Avenue [in Chicago], and there are these deco pillars that stick up," he says. "Every day I saw it, and finally I'm like, 'That's the hinge.' Nobody in the world is making any type of artistically inspired hinges."

When Chris revealed the "12Meter" collection to his retailers, he credited the frame's inspiration: the America's Cup sailing competition. "We sent out messages in bottles to all our stores inviting them to come and meet us at the trade show," he says. "I worked with a glass blower to put our frames in a bottle. So they received the message in the bottle to invite them, and then they saw the frame in the bottle, and those frames were teak, which was salvaged decking from the USS California, which relates to the America's Cup."

The frames' colors? Mint and blue for the yachts Intrepid and Freedom, which won the competition in 1967 and 1980, respectively. (If that wasn't enough, Drift released the glasses to coincide with the 34th America's Cup, in which Oracle Team USA won eight races in a row to beat the Royal New Zealand Yacht Squadron 9–8.) The coloration, the material, the way of creating an experience around the piece—it all matters.

Chris accompanied the Collective Quarterly to Marfa partly because he needed to recharge and partly because he's the kind of guy who soaks up inspiration from physical places. His appearance, up early in the sun-drenched morning, sketching at Ranch 2810's breakfast table or lounging by the pool, could have been mistaken as leisurely. But appearances are deceptive: He was drinking in the scenery, letting it ferment in his brain so he could distill it into inspiration. Because, for Chris, every detail matters.

"Frank Lloyd Wright didn't just design the building, he also designed the furniture you sat in, which complemented the cabinets, the floors, the utensils," he says. "Everything was made for a full user experience. And that's what I want for Drift." *—S.P.*

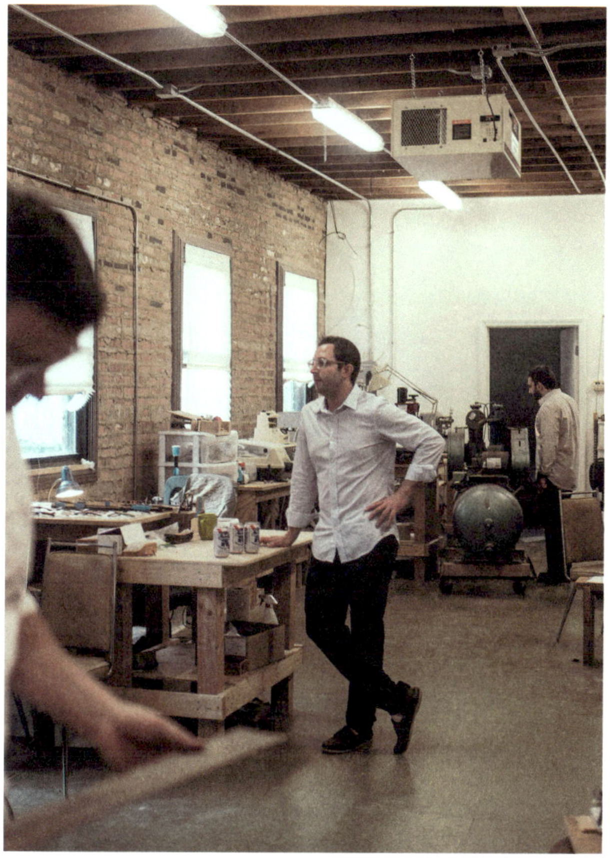

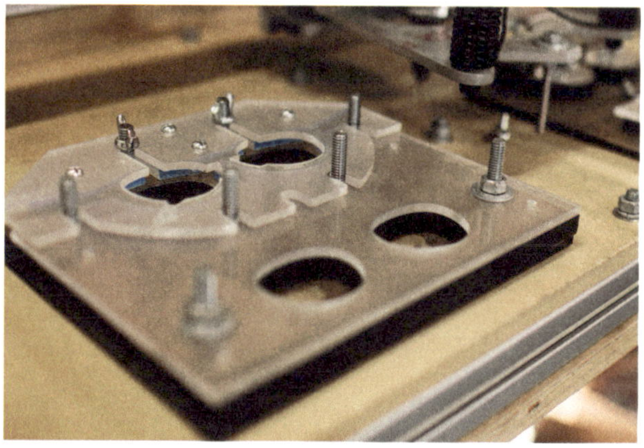

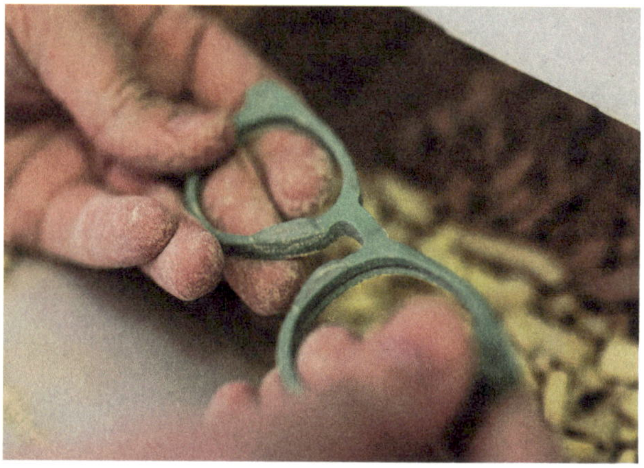

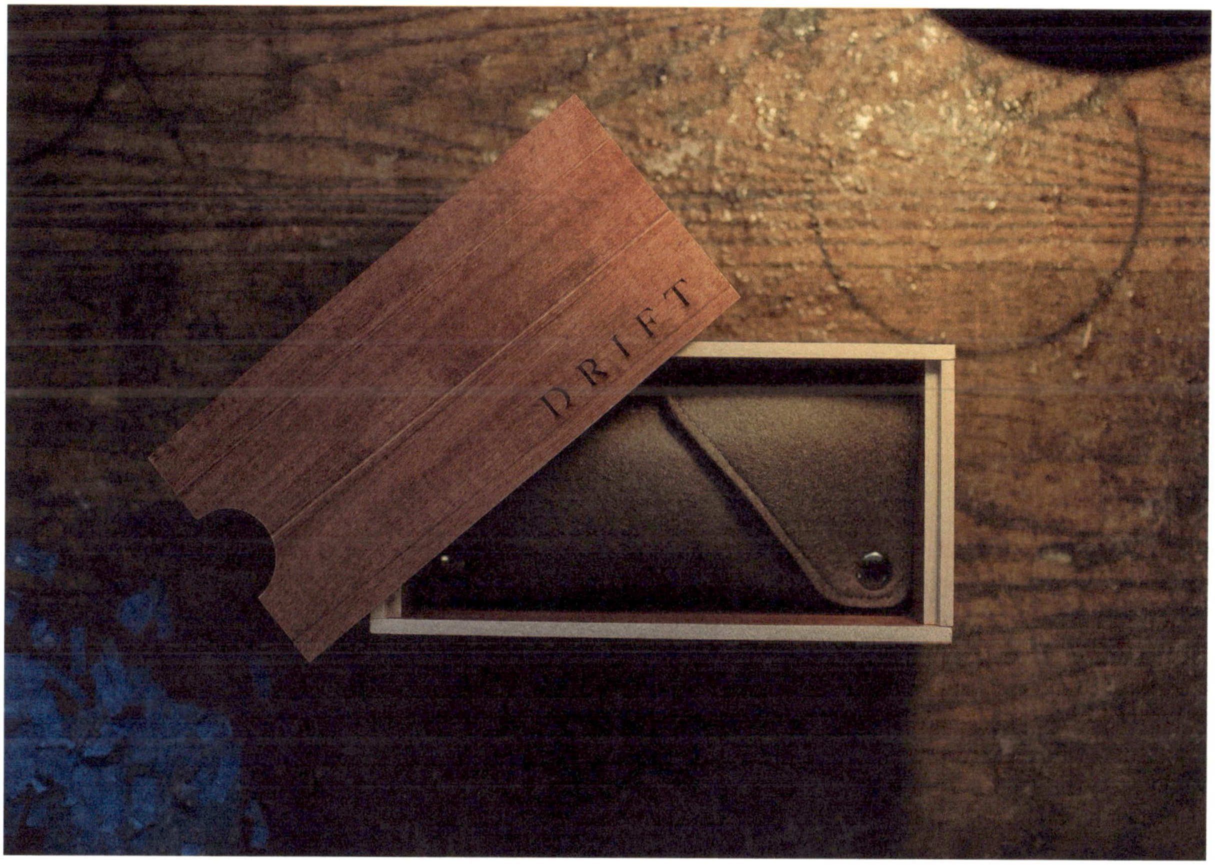
DRIFT

Drawing upon a rich knowledge of art in architecture, Chris scours the spaces around him for inspiration few others notice:

"IT DIDN'T MAKE SENSE WHY THEY DESIGNED THE LATTICES AT RANCH 2810 UNTIL I SAW THEM IN A CERTAIN LIGHT. ONCE THE SHADOWS APPEARED, IT ALL CLICKED."

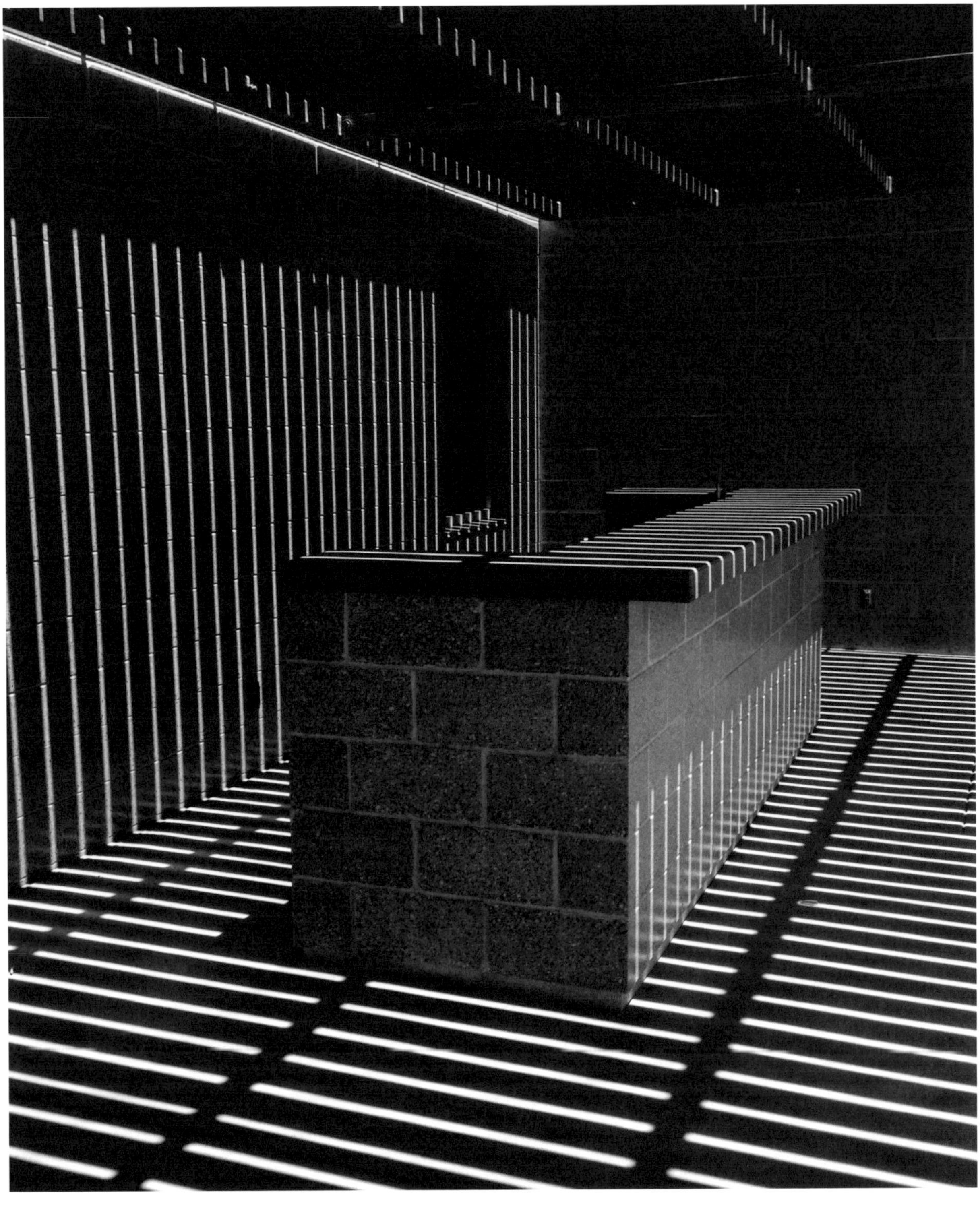

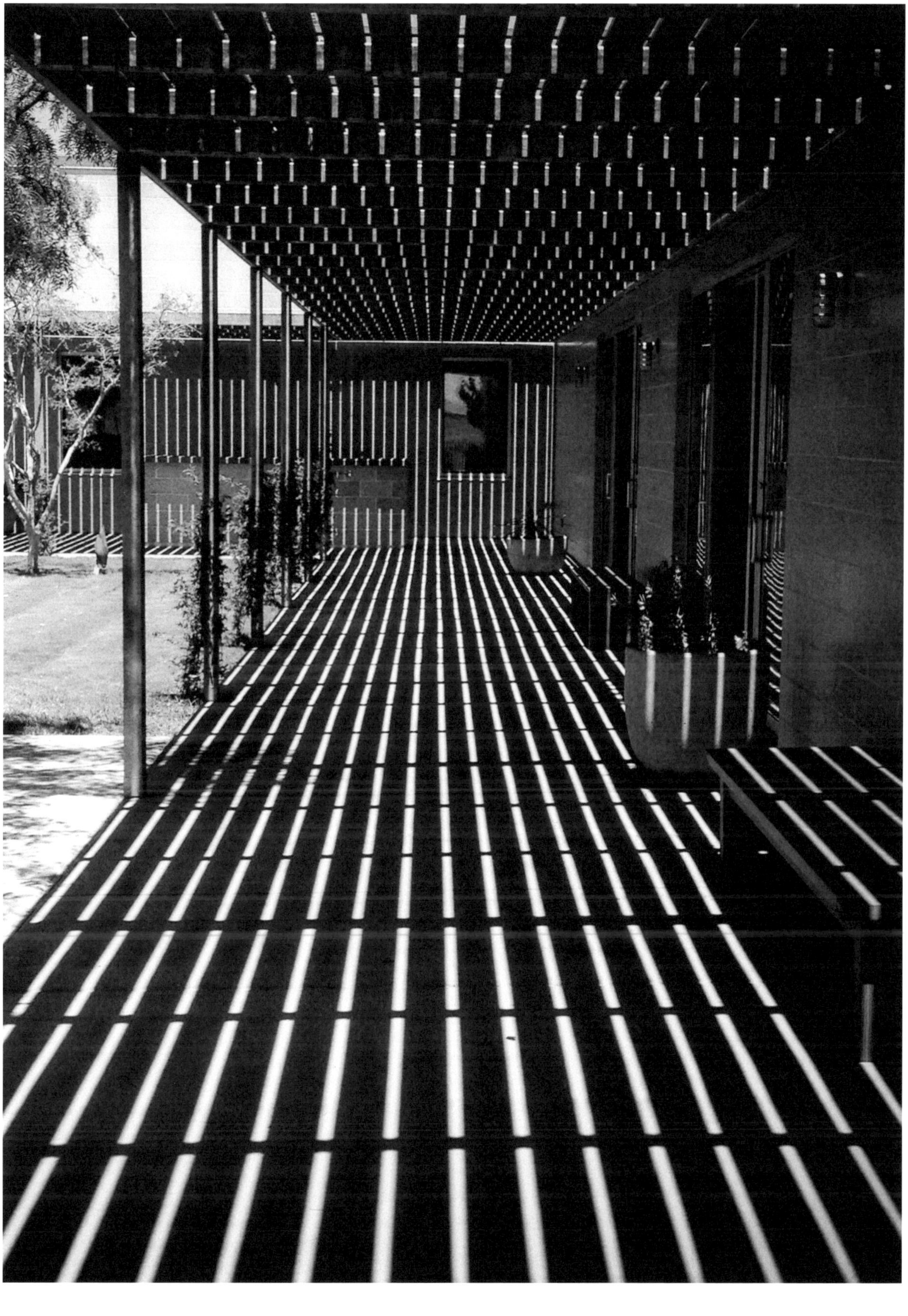

Reflecting on the Reflection: As told to Seth Putnam.

GOOD DESIGN HAS THAT POWER WHERE IT DOESN'T matter if someone realizes what's going on; it's still happening. Most people don't ever get the whole thing. They'll know in the back of their head that it reminds them of something but they can't quite put their finger on it. Nor do they need to.

It's all about interpretation, not mimicry. And that's been the biggest challenge for me: knowing when to not do something. It's not just about margins or numbers; it's about doing real good and making an impact in the world even through a luxury accessory.

If you put your stamp a product, it used to mean you were giving your word that you were making something worthwhile. I look at old machines, old coffee presses, even industrial machinery. People made them to be functional and beautiful and to last.

After the Marfa trip, I designed "The Kerouac." It was a struggle because when I started I felt like I was trying to design for Marfa. And I don't like designing for anyone else but myself.

Marfa is peculiar because it has big-city vibe, but it's a tiny town. For some reason, I really struggled to figure out what to make of it. It was actually through conversations with Jesse Lenz [creative director of the Collective Quarterly] that it began to make sense. He told me: "Don't think about designing for Marfa. Think about where you were standing when you were there and what it made you feel."

Do these frames fit outside of Marfa? I didn't want to copy Donald Judd or El Cosmico [the town's iconic airstream motel]. It had to make sense standing alone within the Drift brand. In the end, I don't feel like I did design a frame for Marfa. Looking back in 10 years, will I wish I had done something different? I don't think so.

I'm not automatically in love with the desert. What was interesting to me was the people, the mentality. There's a freedom there to do what they want as long as they respect each other and the environment. That's a Texas idea I'm attracted to: You can come and go as you please.

I respect Donald Judd and Dan Flavin [two of the contemporary artists who drew attention to Marfa], but before going there, I had always found their work difficult to relate to. I think it was important in its time and place, but I experienced so much later than the height of its relevance. And it's difficult to interpret if you don't see it in its original context.

At the Chinati museum, Judd built these glimmering aluminum boxes that don't seem like they should make sense with the landscape. But when you look at them from different angles they reflect different light: bluish, pinkish hues. They reflect the light of their surroundings, and it, and it almost makes them look like a mirage. And it was beautiful. I realized that whatever Judd was trying to do made sense there.

I feel the same way about the concrete blocks that are outside. Each one has different wall characteristics: Some of them you can see through; some of them have partitions. Each one has the same external dimensions, but they all have different orientations and partitions. They're not the same material as their natural surroundings, but they're really not that outlandish. With the bright sunlight and the grey tones, it's fascinating: I felt like they were almost camouflaging themselves.

That whole era can sometimes be difficult to relate to. There weren't a lot of rules. Though, it's interesting that Judd had such a specific set of rules for his exhibitions. Judd was so particular. Everything was made for him, so he would spec out what he wanted, and he was very specific about where the pieces should be placed in gallery shows. To think that he was able to get all that done without physically doing it himself was really fascinating.

I wanted to make a frame that would be seamless in that desert environment, but modern from any other vantage point. For inspiration, I pulled from the materials and the surroundings. The way color changes throughout the day in the desert. So I decided on a browed frame that mimics the skyline. I imagined it, perched on the horizon, almost invisible against it.

When you ask what color aluminum is, people say silver. It isn't. It's a reflection of the surroundings. Wherever you go, aluminum will reflect the color of your environment. If you're stopped at a traffic light and you look over at the car next to you, your frames will glow red. And that seemed to be a parallel with the human existence: we take on the characteristics of our environment. ★

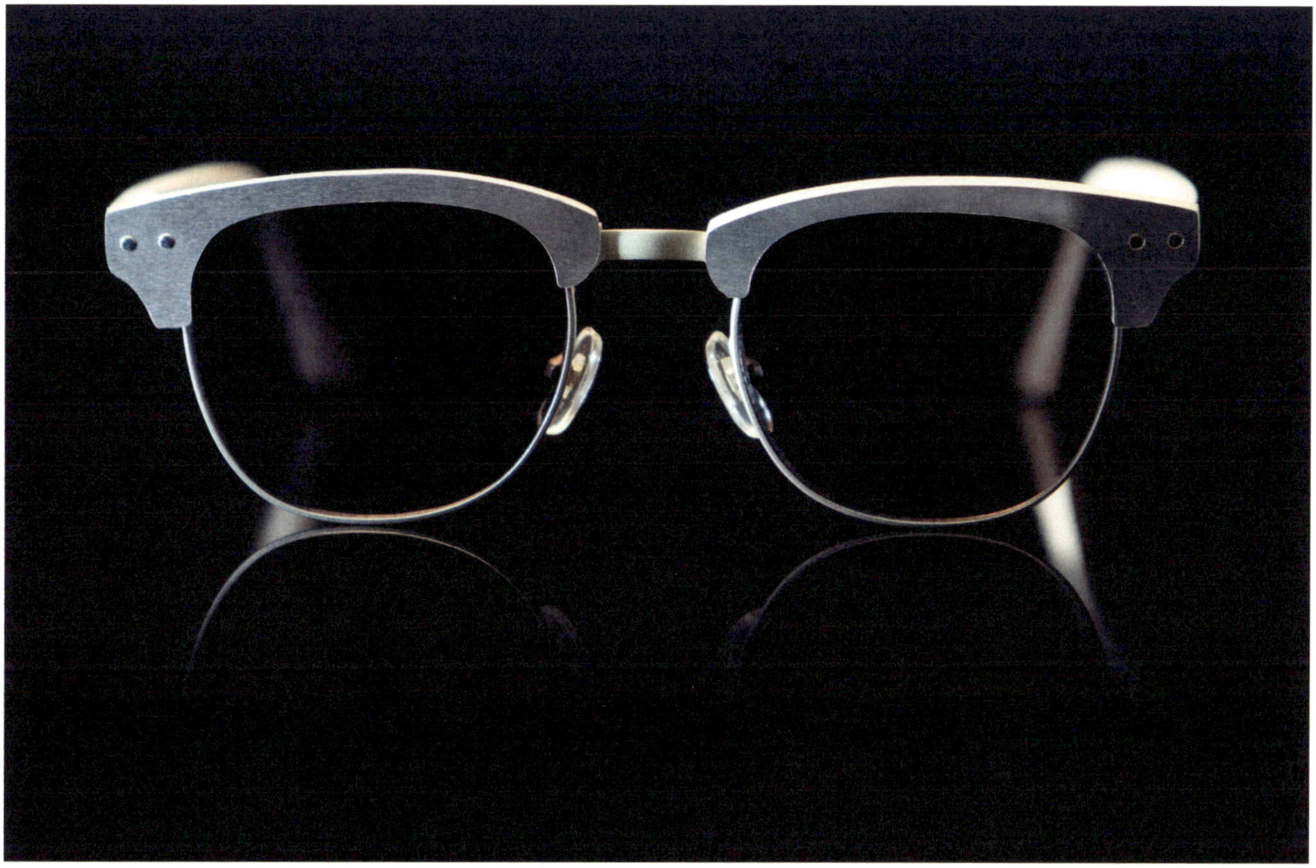

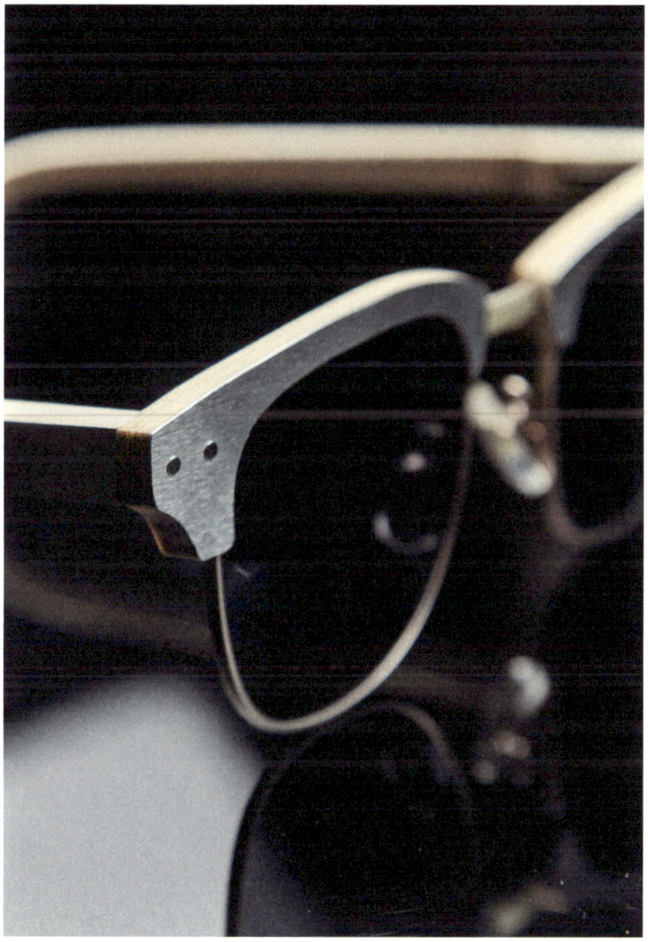

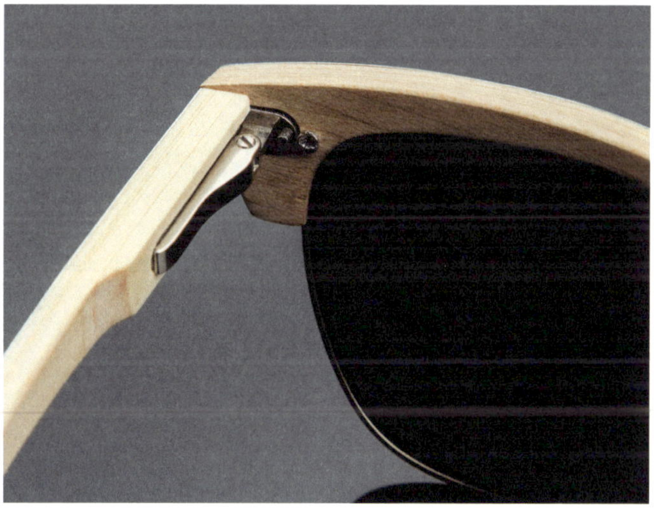

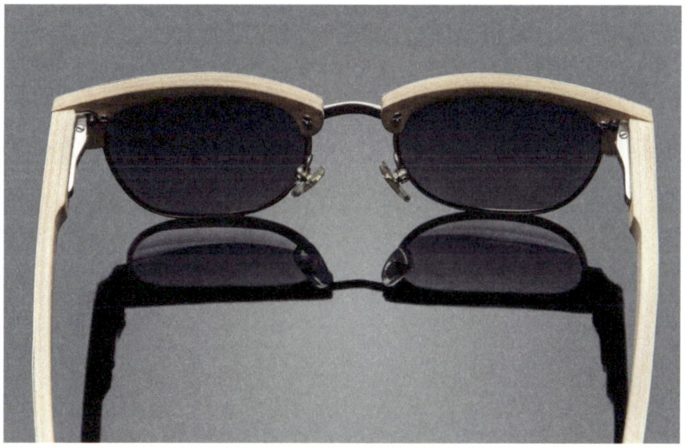

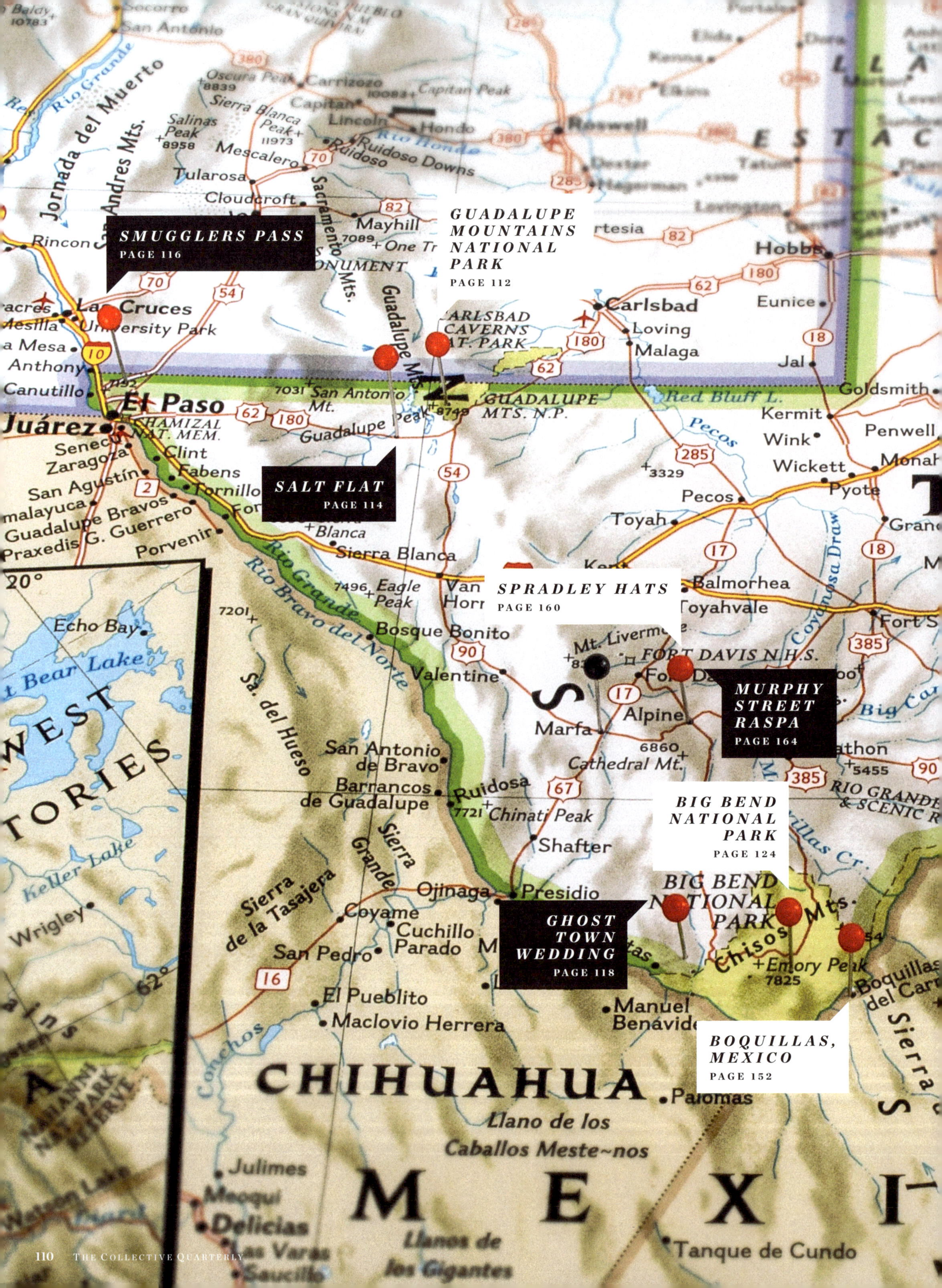
SMUGGLERS PASS
PAGE 116
GUADALUPE MOUNTAINS NATIONAL PARK
PAGE 112
SALT FLAT
PAGE 114
SPRADLEY HATS
PAGE 160
MURPHY STREET RASPA
PAGE 164
BIG BEND NATIONAL PARK
PAGE 124
GHOST TOWN WEDDING
PAGE 118
BOQUILLAS, MEXICO
PAGE 152
El Paso
Juárez
Las Cruces
Carlsbad
Marfa
Alpine
Presidio
Ojinaga
CHIHUAHUA
M E X I

ON THE ROAD

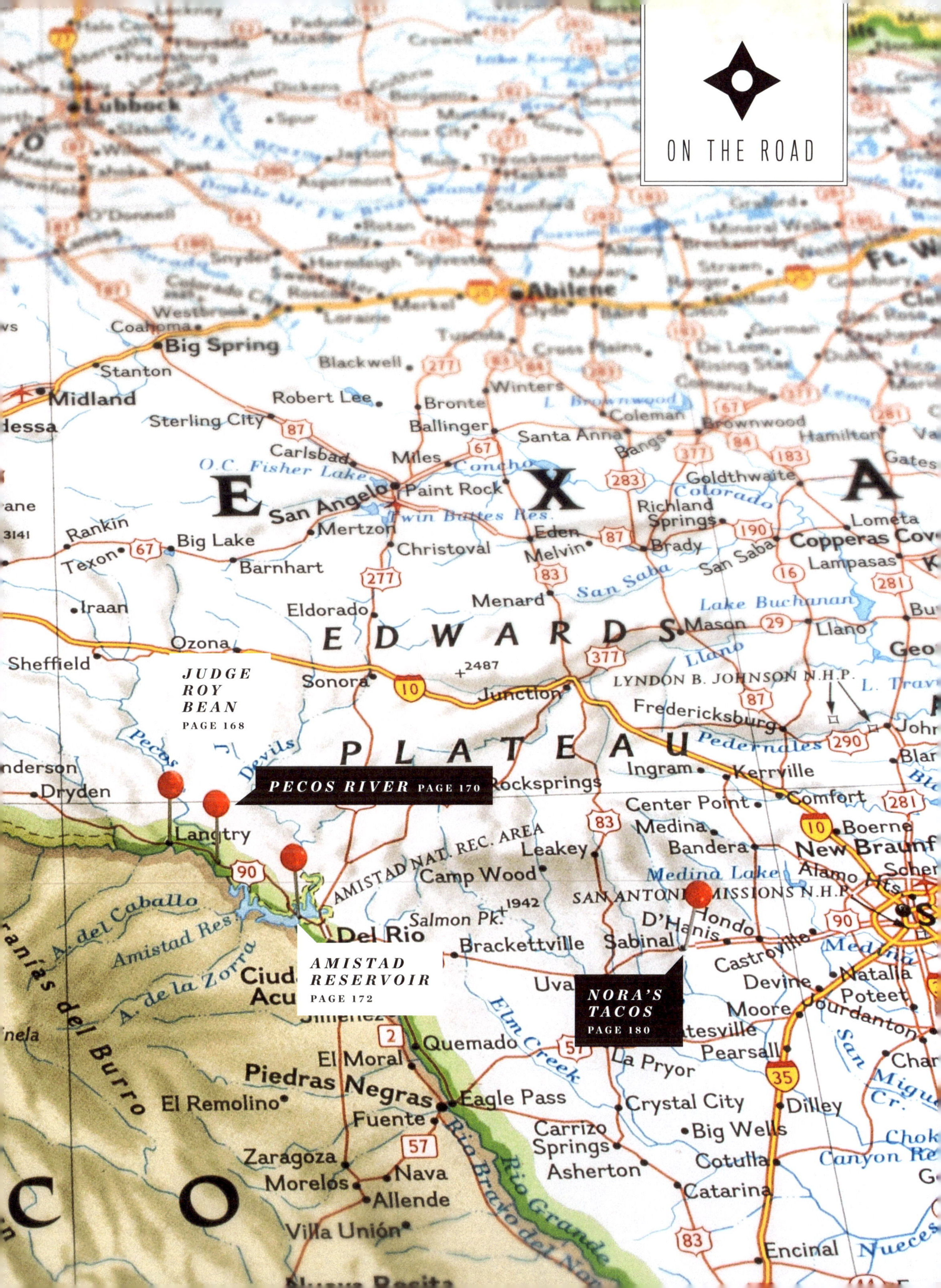
JUDGE ROY BEAN
PAGE 168
PECOS RIVER PAGE 170
AMISTAD RESERVOIR
PAGE 172
NORA'S TACOS
PAGE 180
EDWARDS PLATEAU
LYNDON B. JOHNSON N.H.P.
AMISTAD NAT. REC. AREA
SAN ANTONIO MISSIONS N.H.P.

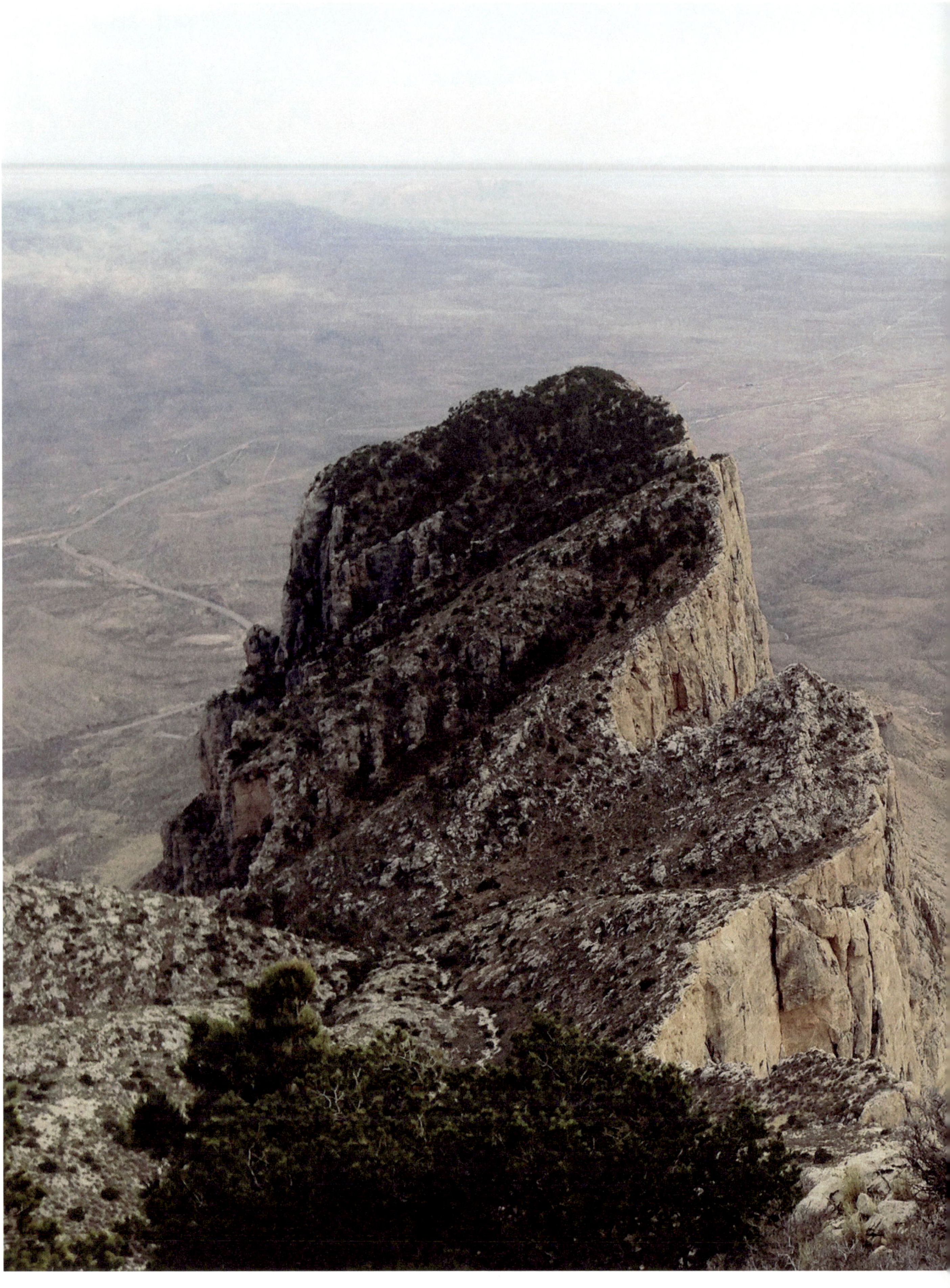

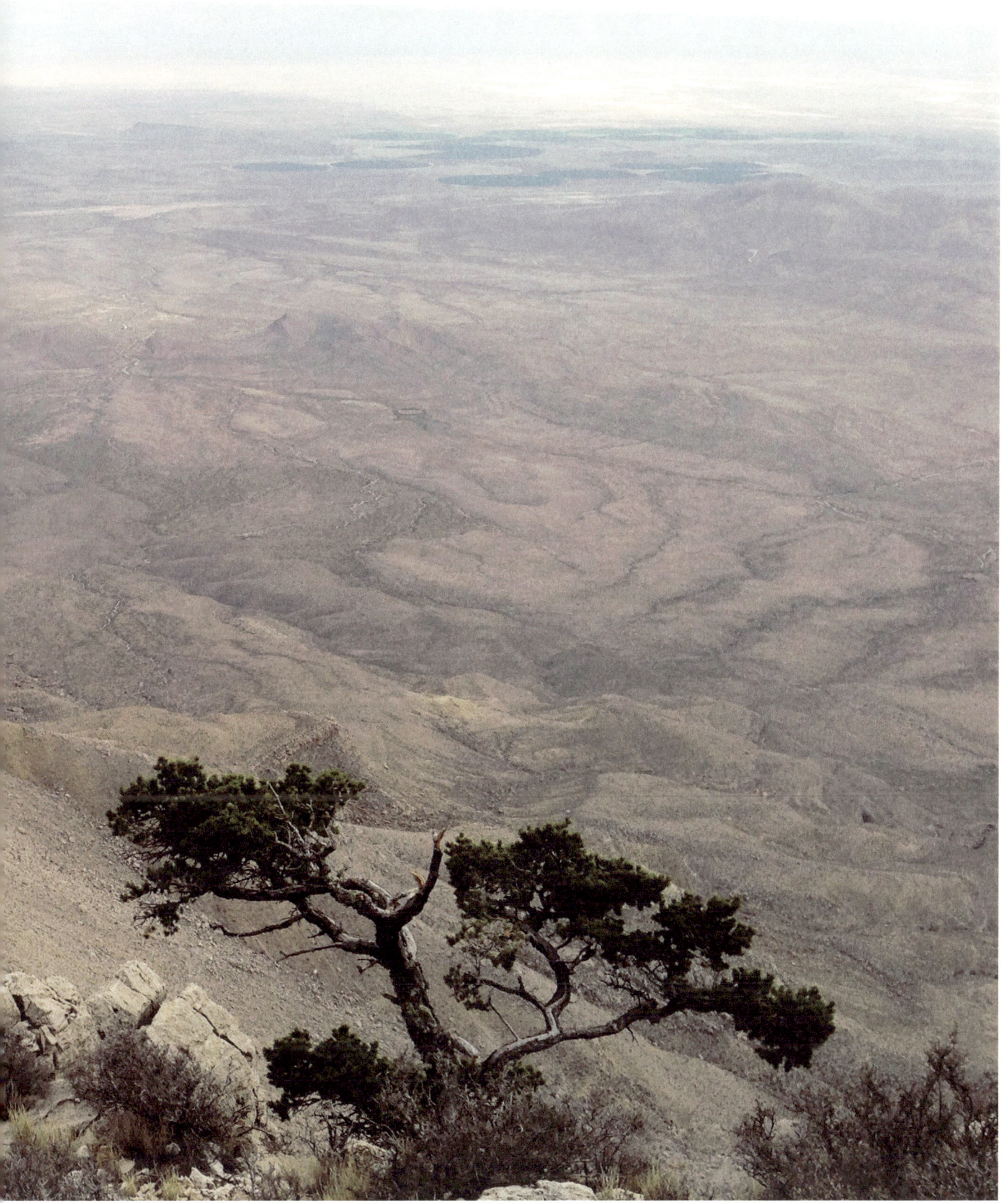

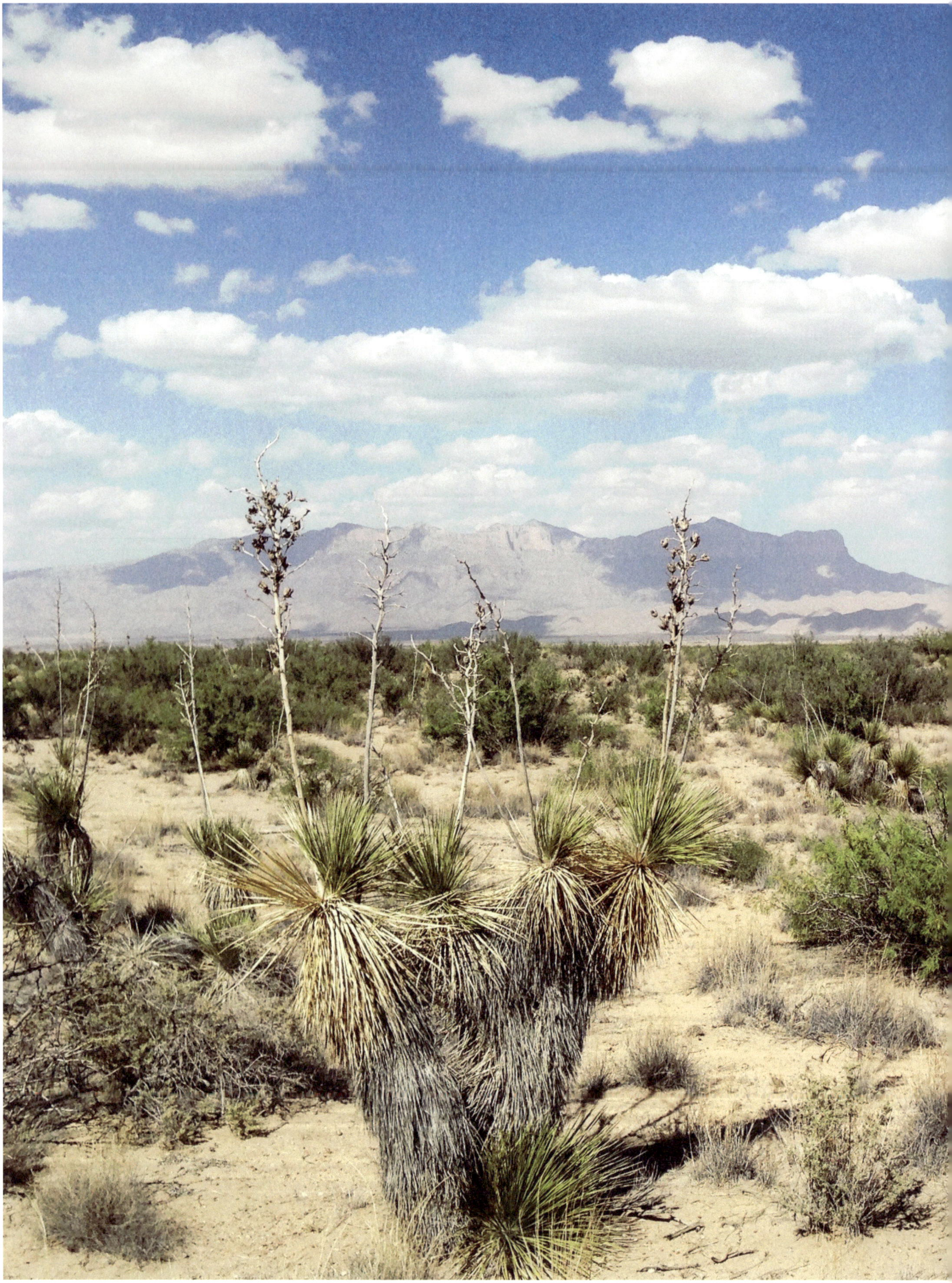

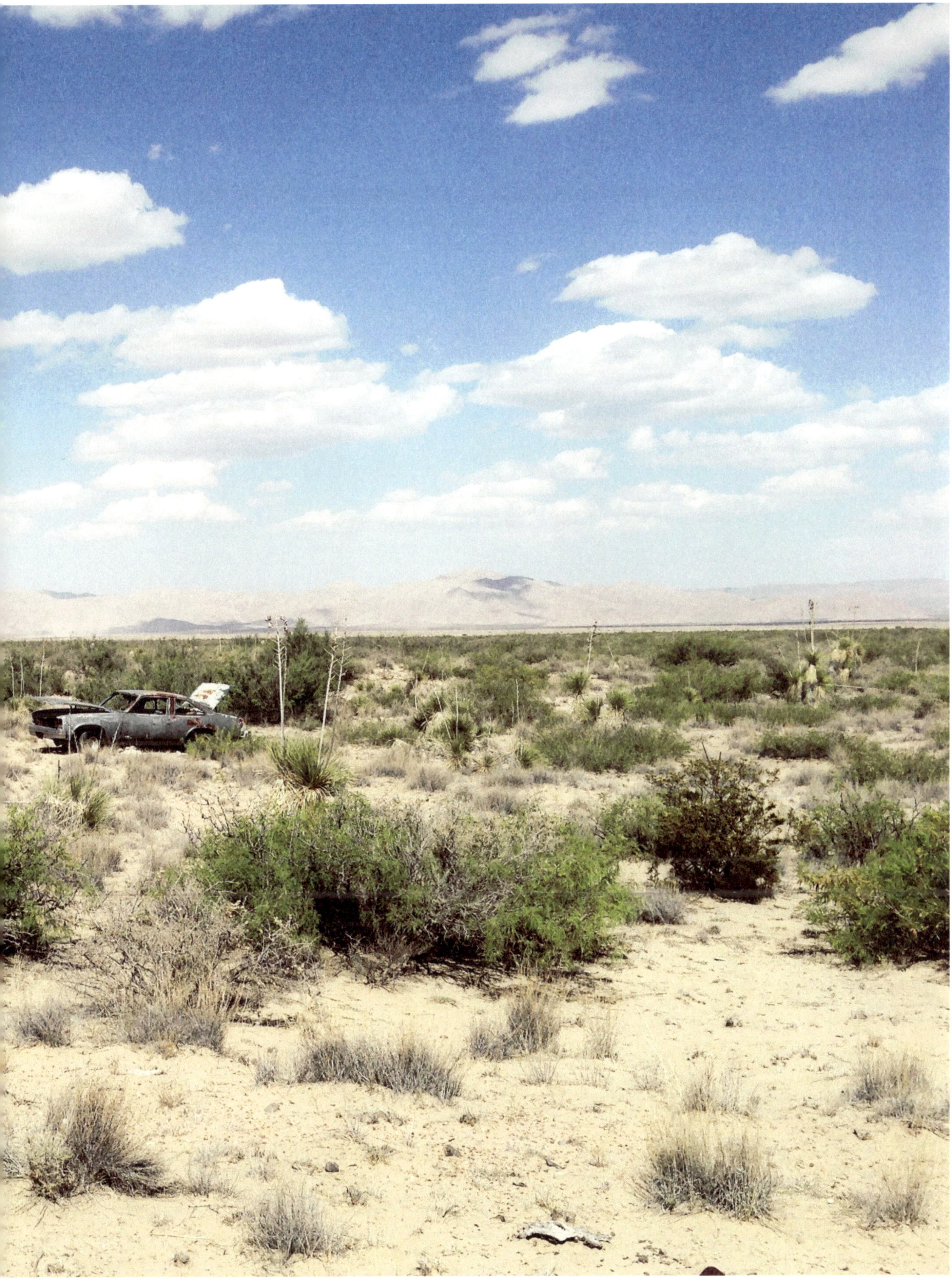

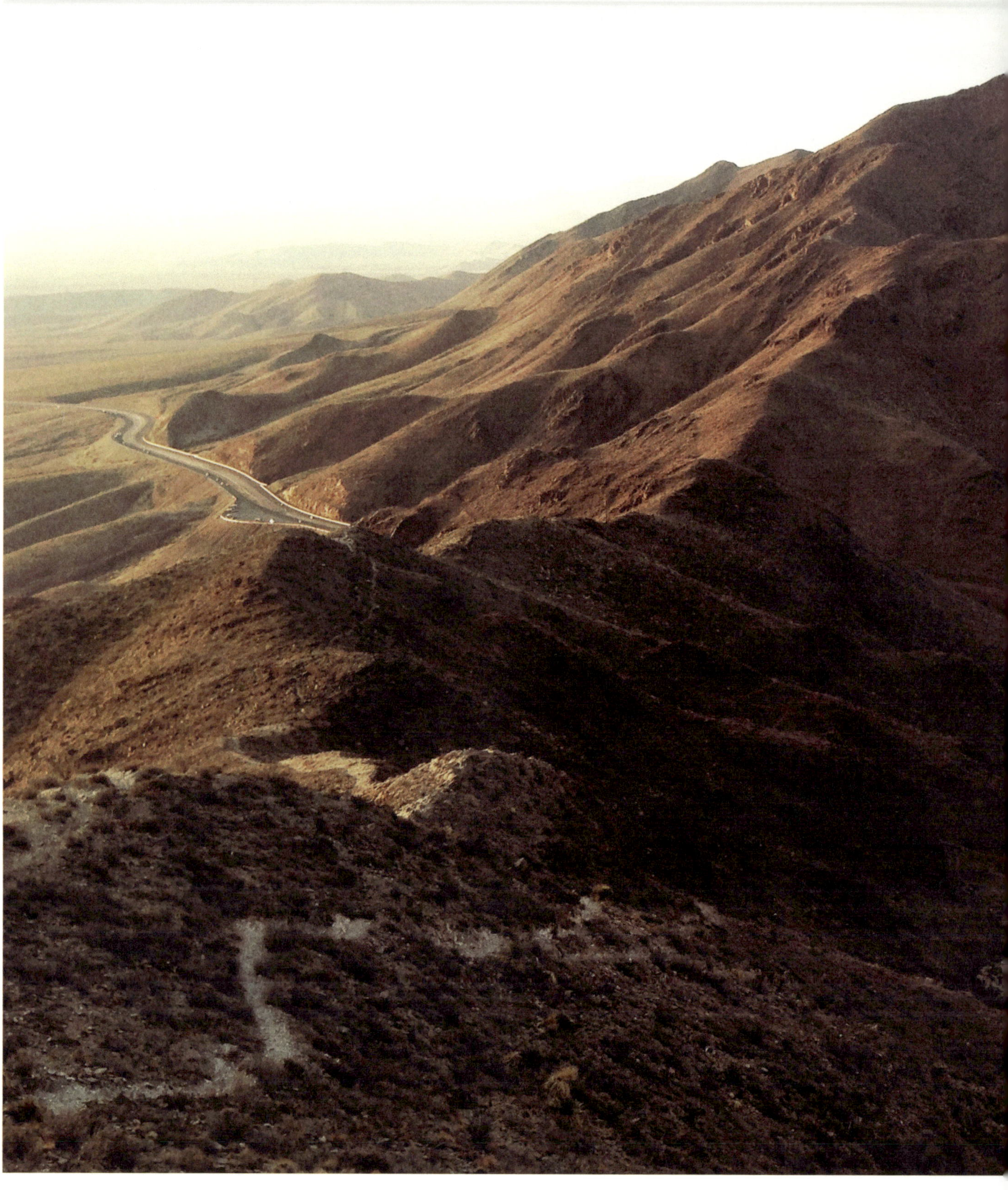

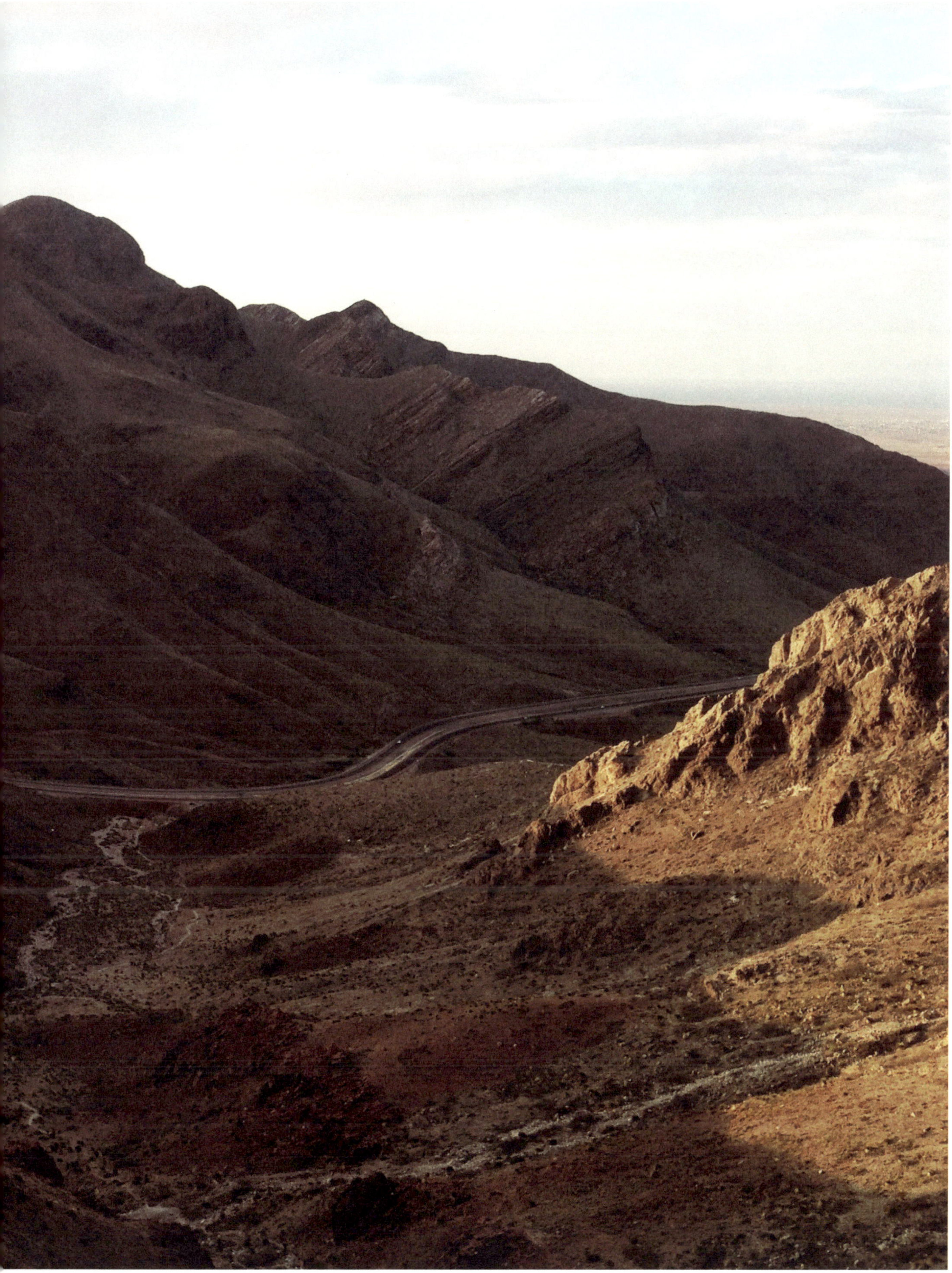

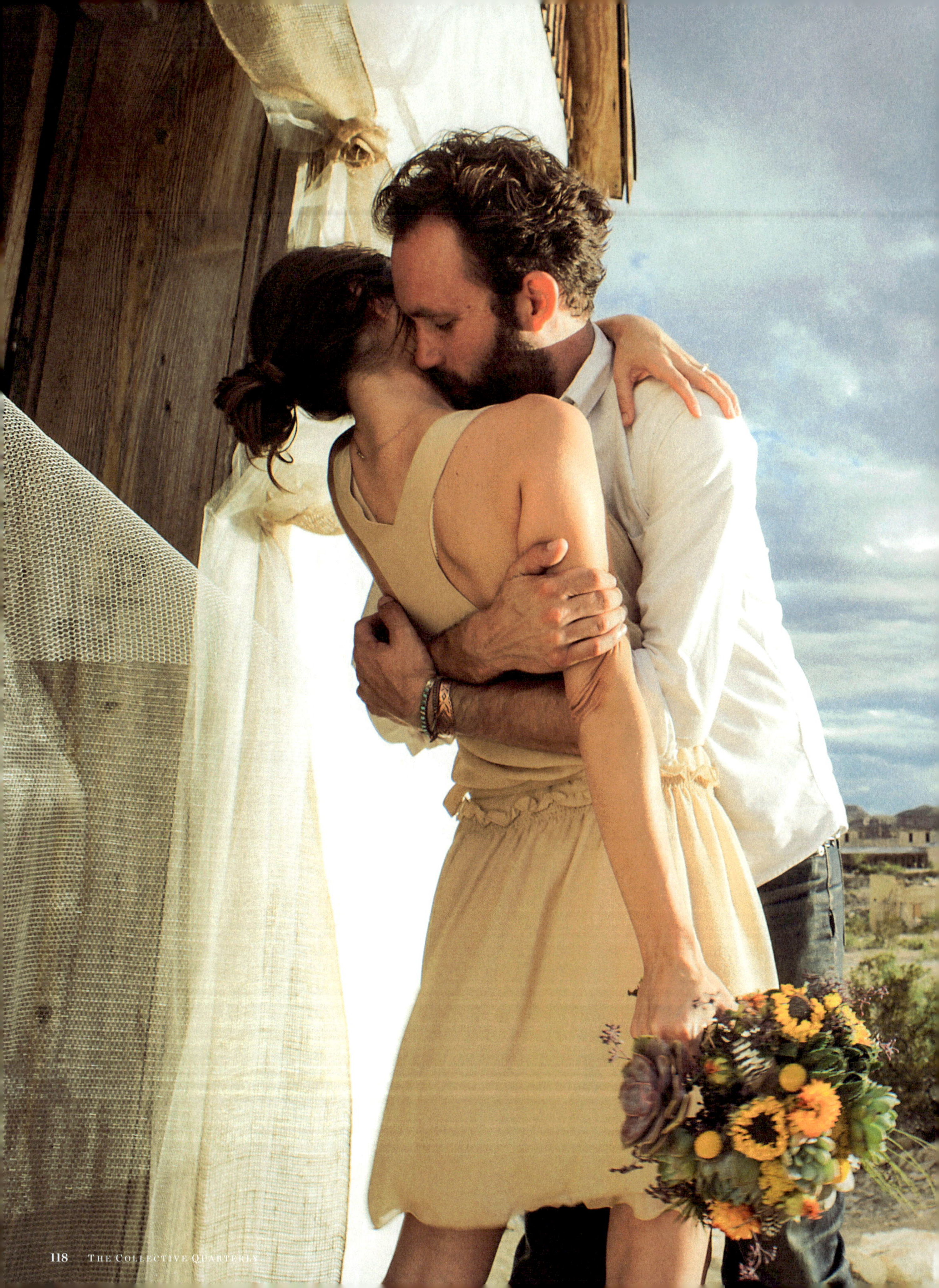

GHOST TOWN WEDDING

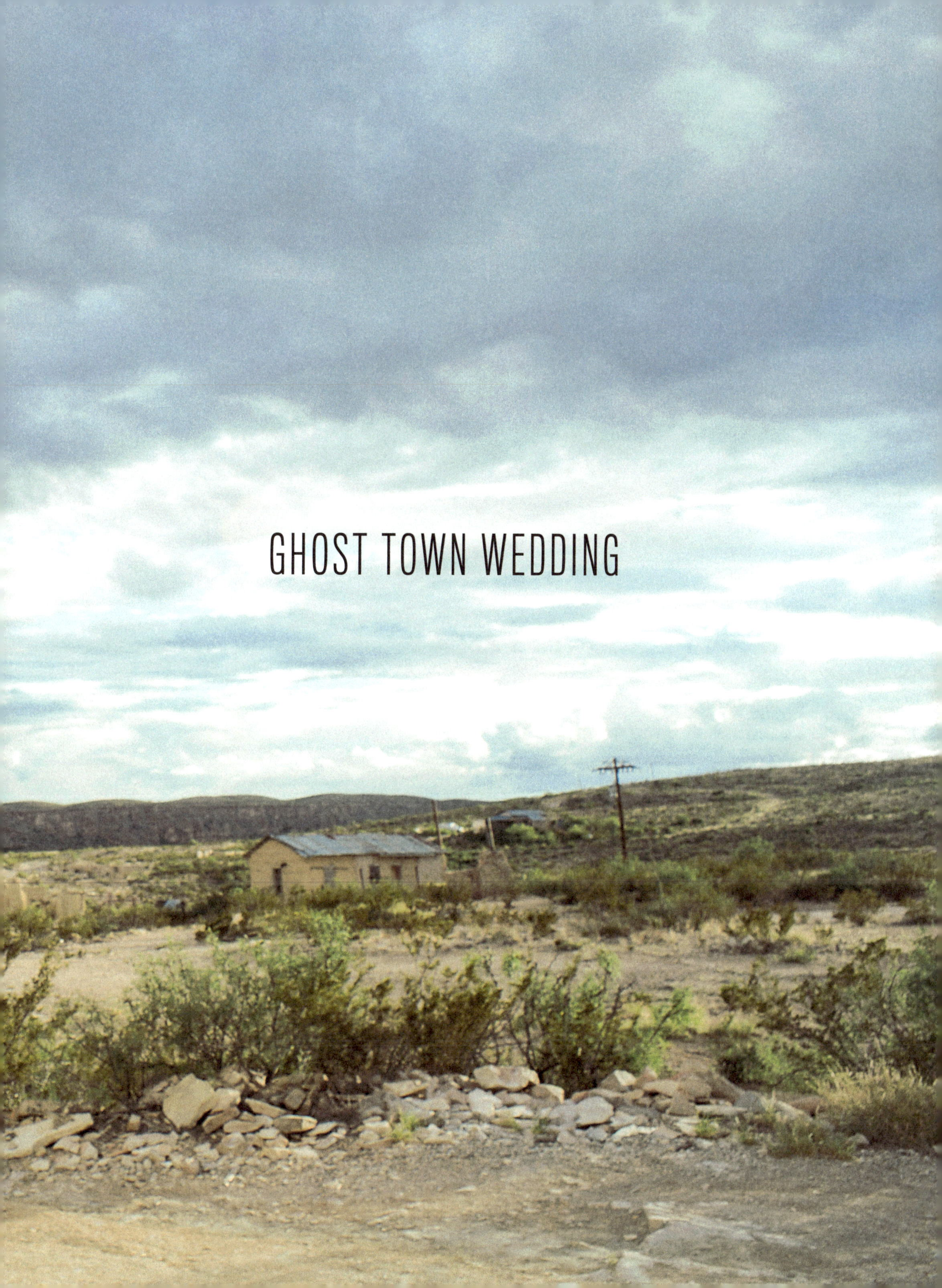

AIN'T TOO MANY PEOPLE WHO WOULD GET MARRIED in a ghost town. But then again, Lauren Wilkins and Josh Block aren't most people. She's of Detroit's wristwatch-bicycle-and-leather-goods maker Shinola, and he drums for Texas sensation White Denim.

Cut to Terlingua, a bizarro settlement about a hundred miles south of Marfa, established in the late 1800s as a quicksilver-mining outpost. The veins dried up, and today it's little more than a patch of earth where the tan, mud-brick ruins blend into the hillside. There's usually only a handful of people in town at any given time, hanging out on the porch of the Starlight Theatre, except for the several thousand fanatics that converge every November for a giant chili cook-off. It's a place where everyone's got a nickname: Suitcase Sally, Jackass Judy, Just Bob.

It's also the perfect place to elope. Lauren tells the story of their journey, and Josh replays tunes they listened to during their eight-hour drive through the desert.

(Scan the pages to listen.)

LAUREN WILKINS: We met at my boutique in Austin called Arrow and Arrow. We had mutual friends, and I knew Josh was in a band. He used to invite me to shows and put me on the list. Basically, he wanted to get me out of the store so he could ask me out, which was good, because it creeped me out to be hit on in the store. But something always seemed to come up. So for about a year and a half I never went. Somehow I ended up playing it really cool and hard to get, but it was completely on accident ,because I don't play anything cool.

Finally we had this fumbling email interaction: He happened to be close to my apartment (but didn't have my phone number), and he asked if I wanted to hang out. I was free. We've been inseparable from that point on. We found out later that we actually went to preschool together; there's a Polaroid of me on my fifth birthday with a paper crown, and there's Josh sitting next to me.

After two months of dating, he abandoned ship in the little town of Driftwood where he was living in this 1960s Spartan trailer attached to a cabin. We moved in together in the "big city."

Josh and I travel a lot. He's constantly jetting to Europe and South America and all over the world because he's a musician. So we're always trying to find a place for just the two of us. We had been going to Marfa for several years. And we kept hearing about Terlingua.

Our friends would tell us these crazy stories, like the one about a local woman who was the lover of Pablo Acosta, a Mexican drug lord who was on the run from the US government. They say she was one of the last people to see him alive in 1987 before he died in a helicopter raid, brandishing an assault rifle in one hand and clutching a pistol in the other.

Eventually, we drove out there, rented a house, and fell in love with it. That was our spot. When we decided to get married—there was no formal engagement—we knew we wanted do it by ourselves. It wasn't a secret, but we wanted to have a wedding for just us.

Two weeks out, we rented the church online for like $50. Then I thought: "Shit! Flowers. Do I even need them?" Josh said: "Yeah, you need flowers. We are getting married." You can't really get flowers in Terlingua, but we found a florist who does dry wildflower arrangements.

All the locals hang out at the Starlight, and we figured: Someone's gotta be a minister. Or at the very least they can get set up online in like 15 minutes. We're having a beer at the bar, and it turns out the bartender was ordained. He said, "Know what? I'm working the day of the wedding, but the church is right behind the bar. I'll get someone to cover my shift for 20 minutes."

There was a woman sitting nearby, and she looked exactly like this friend of mine whose mother had moved to Terlingua in the '90s. I said, "This could be a weird question, but are you Stephanie's mom?" It was her, and she agreed to be our witness. So in 30 minutes over Shiners, we had found our minister and our witness.

All of this was on a Wednesday. Friday rolls around, we were hanging out, and we were like: Okay, time to get married! We hiked up the hill to the chapel. Jeff, the bartender, had brought out his special sport coat and had decorated the entryway of the church. We said our vows, and afterward we had tequila shots at the Starlight with the locals, because they had all heard there was a wedding going on.

West Texas is my absolute favorite place on the planet. I just think it's so magical there. I love Marfa, but in Terlingua you can literally get away. You can hang out with people at the bar or be completely on your own. And every time, it feels like it's just for us.

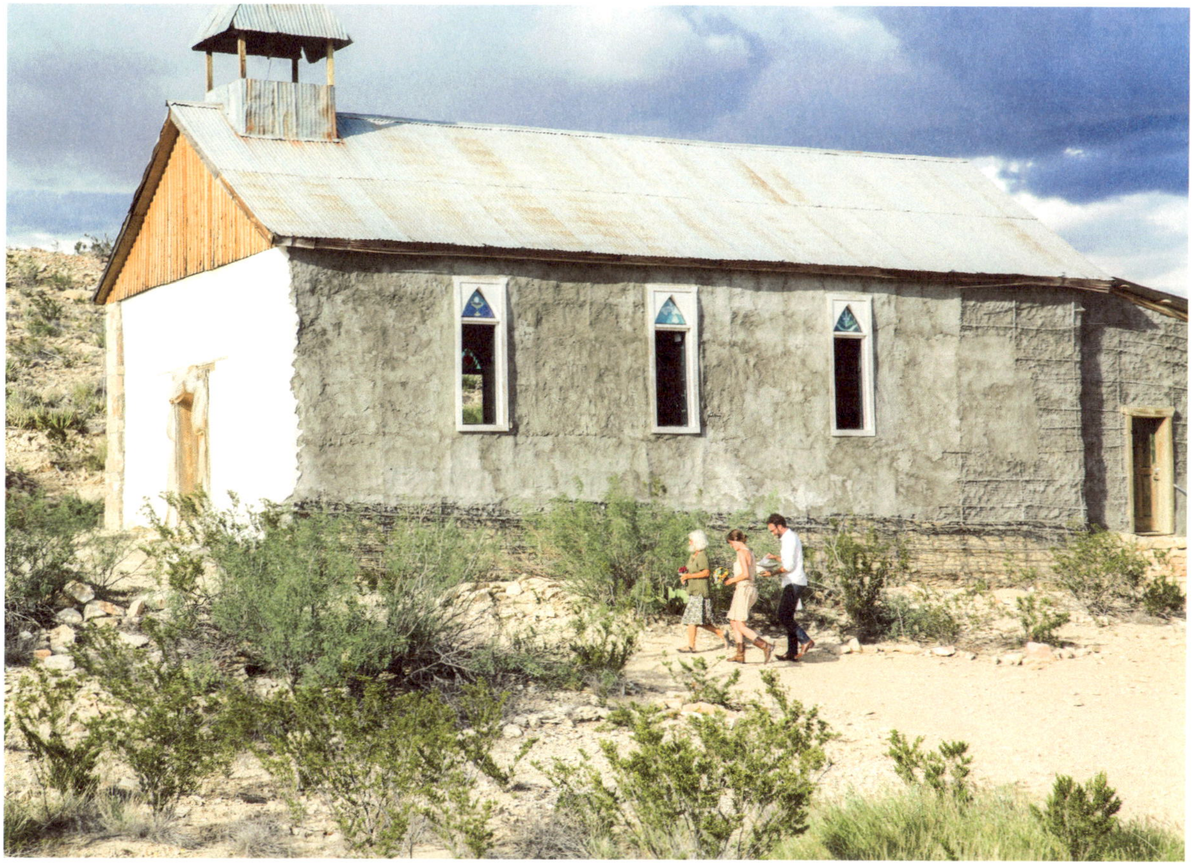

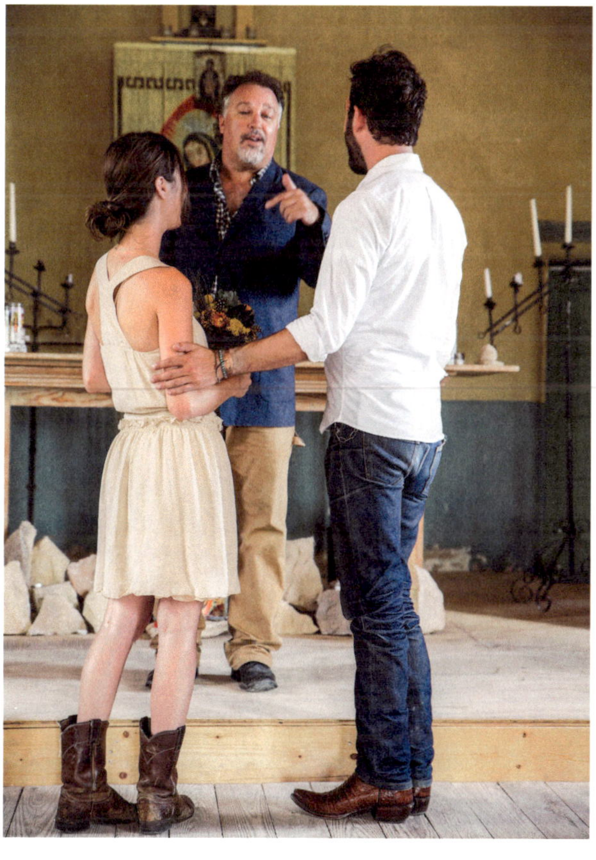

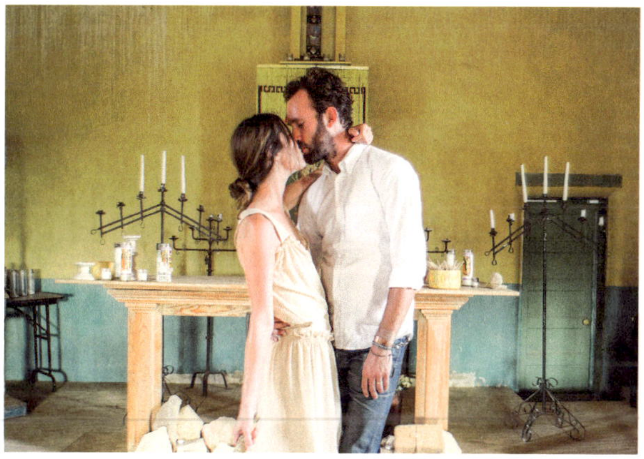

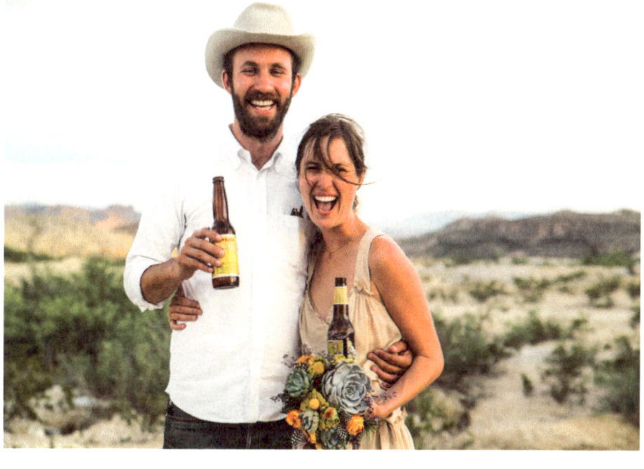

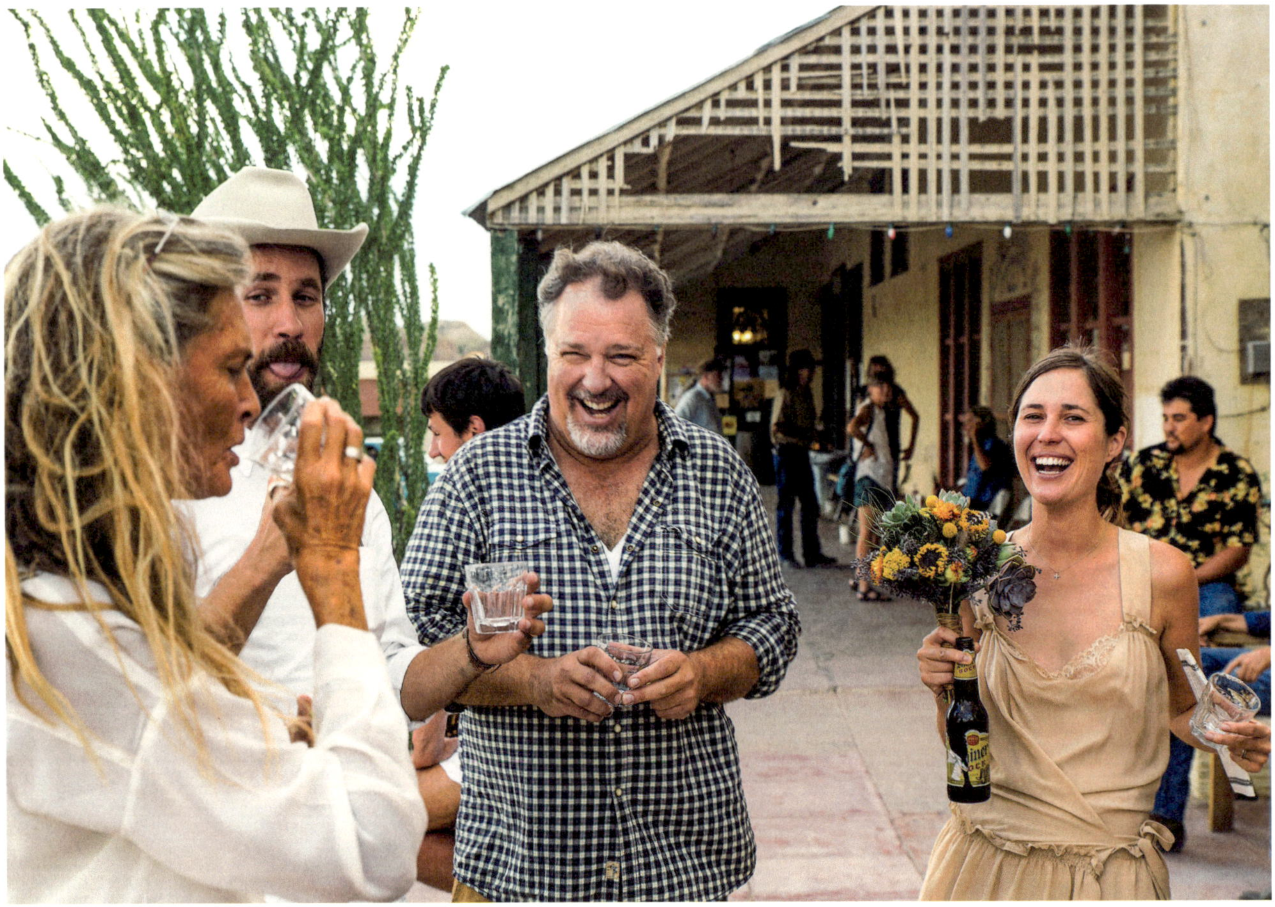

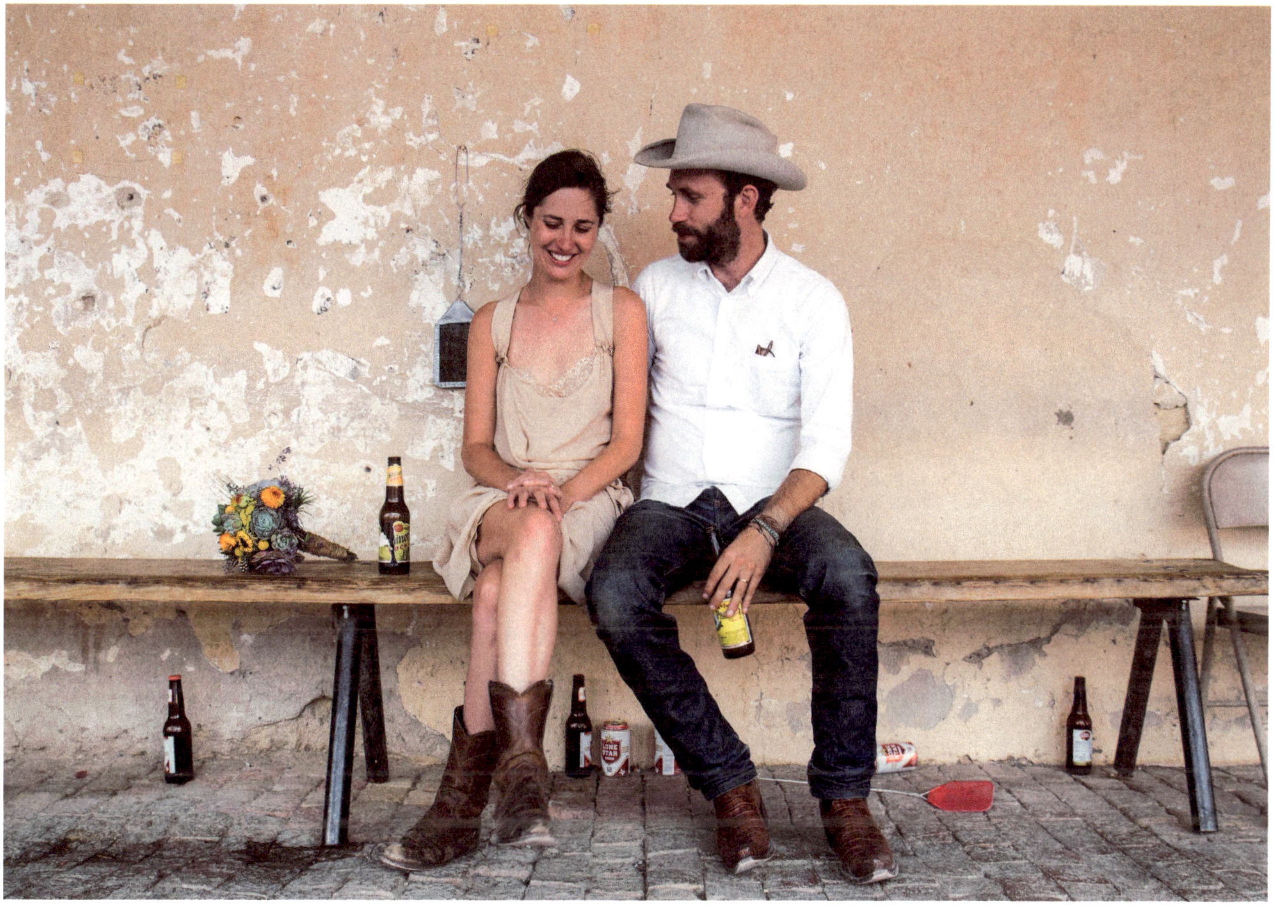

BIG BEND NATIONAL PARK

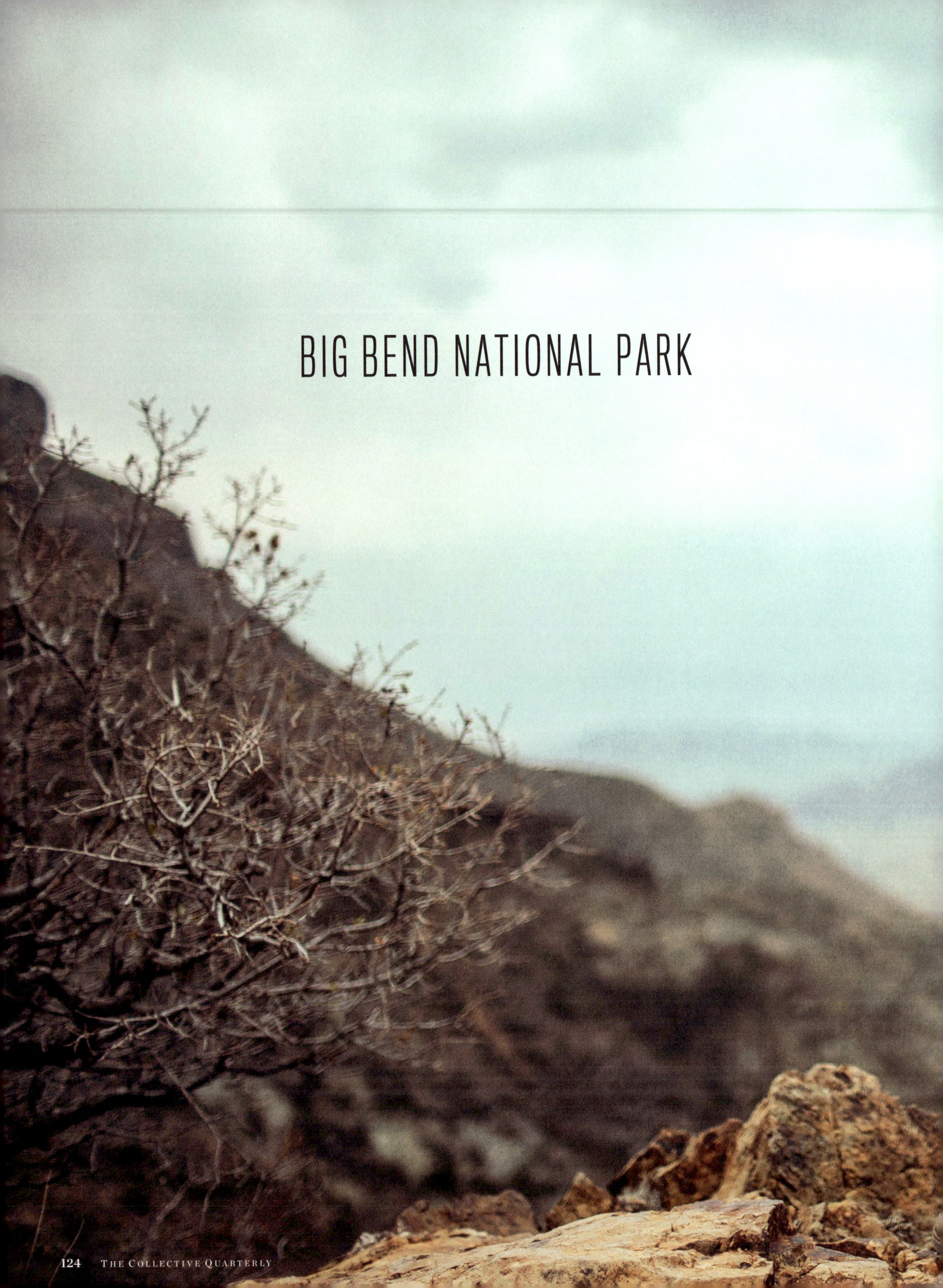

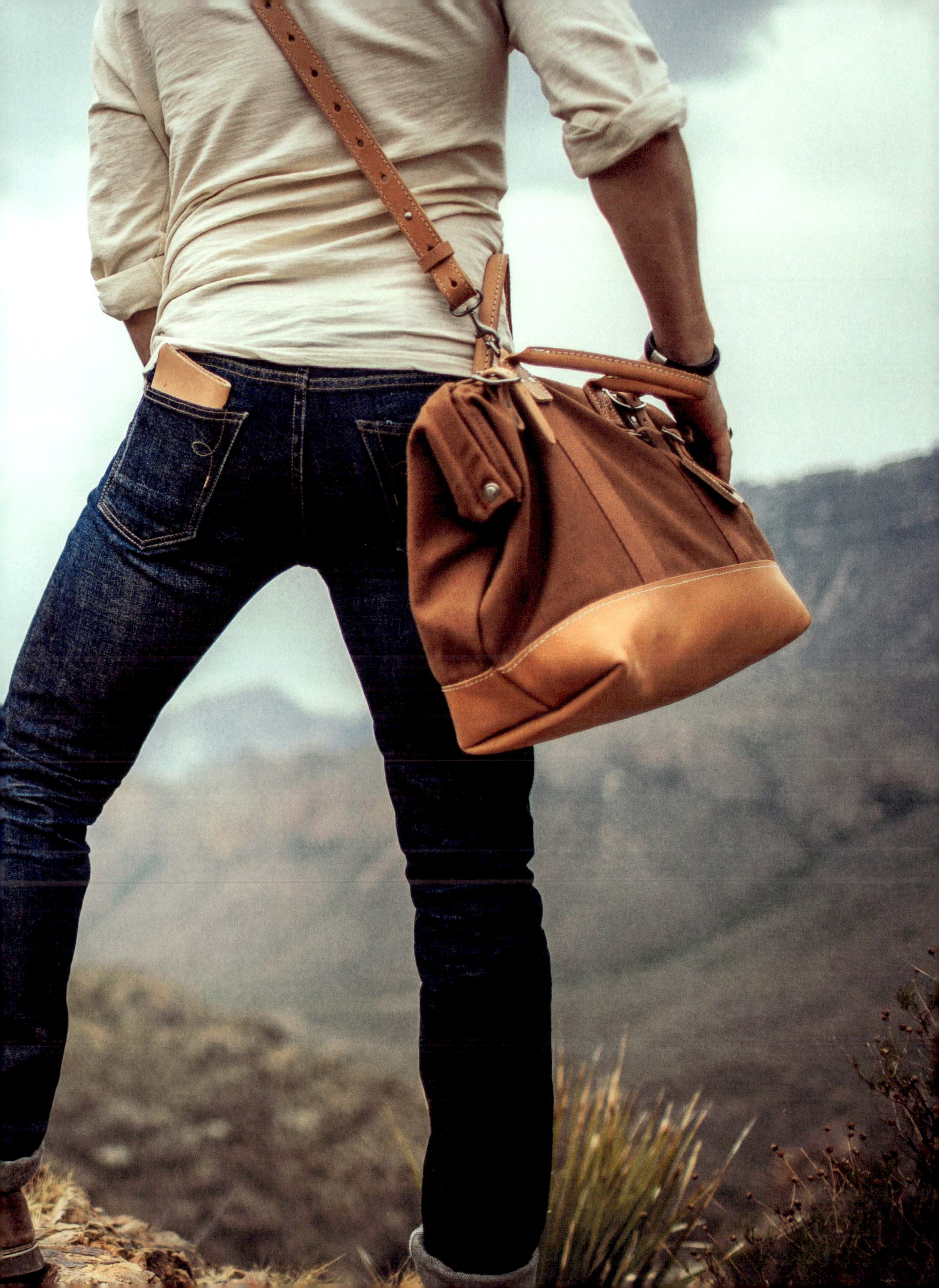

SANTA ELENA CANYON

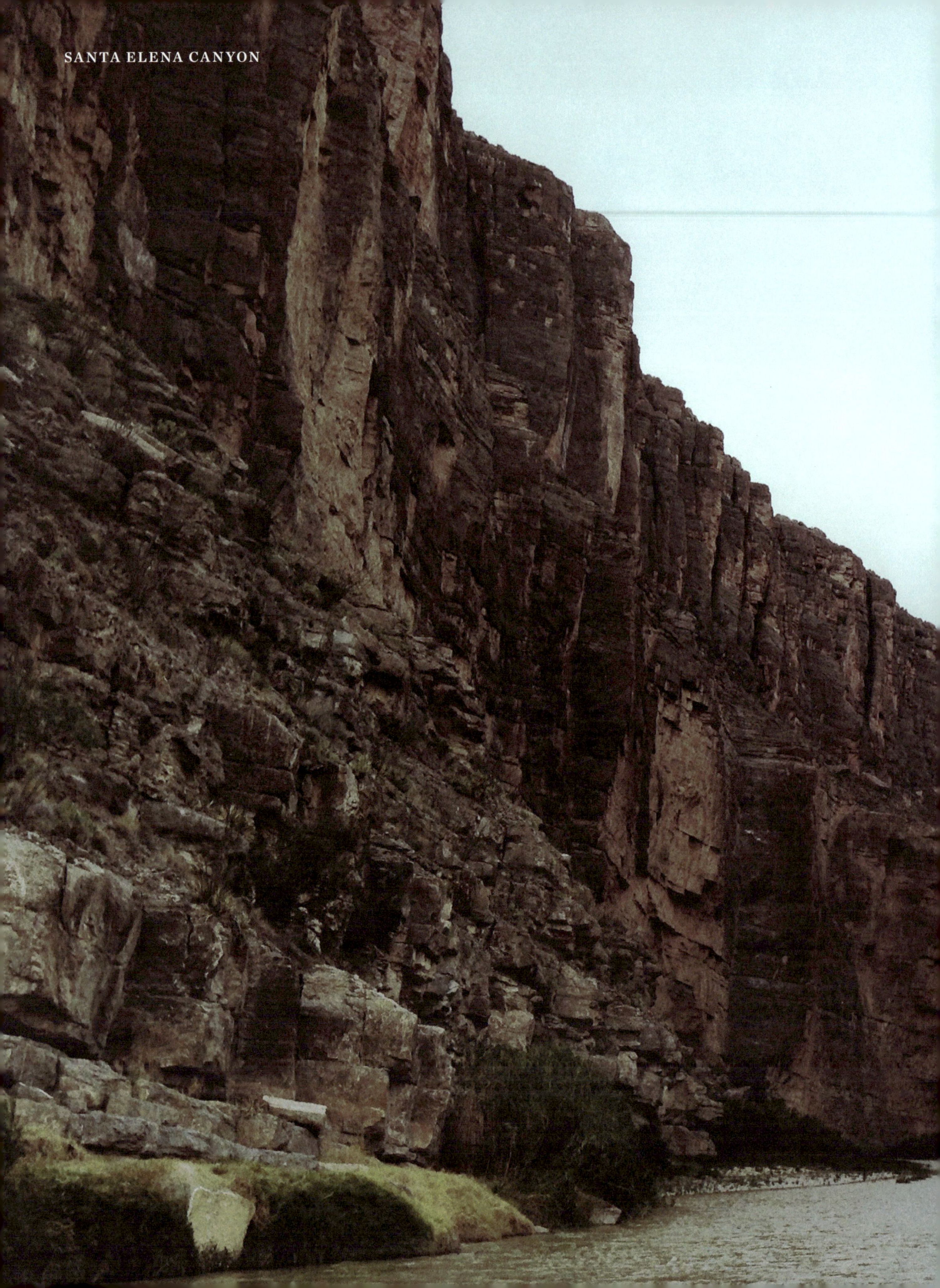

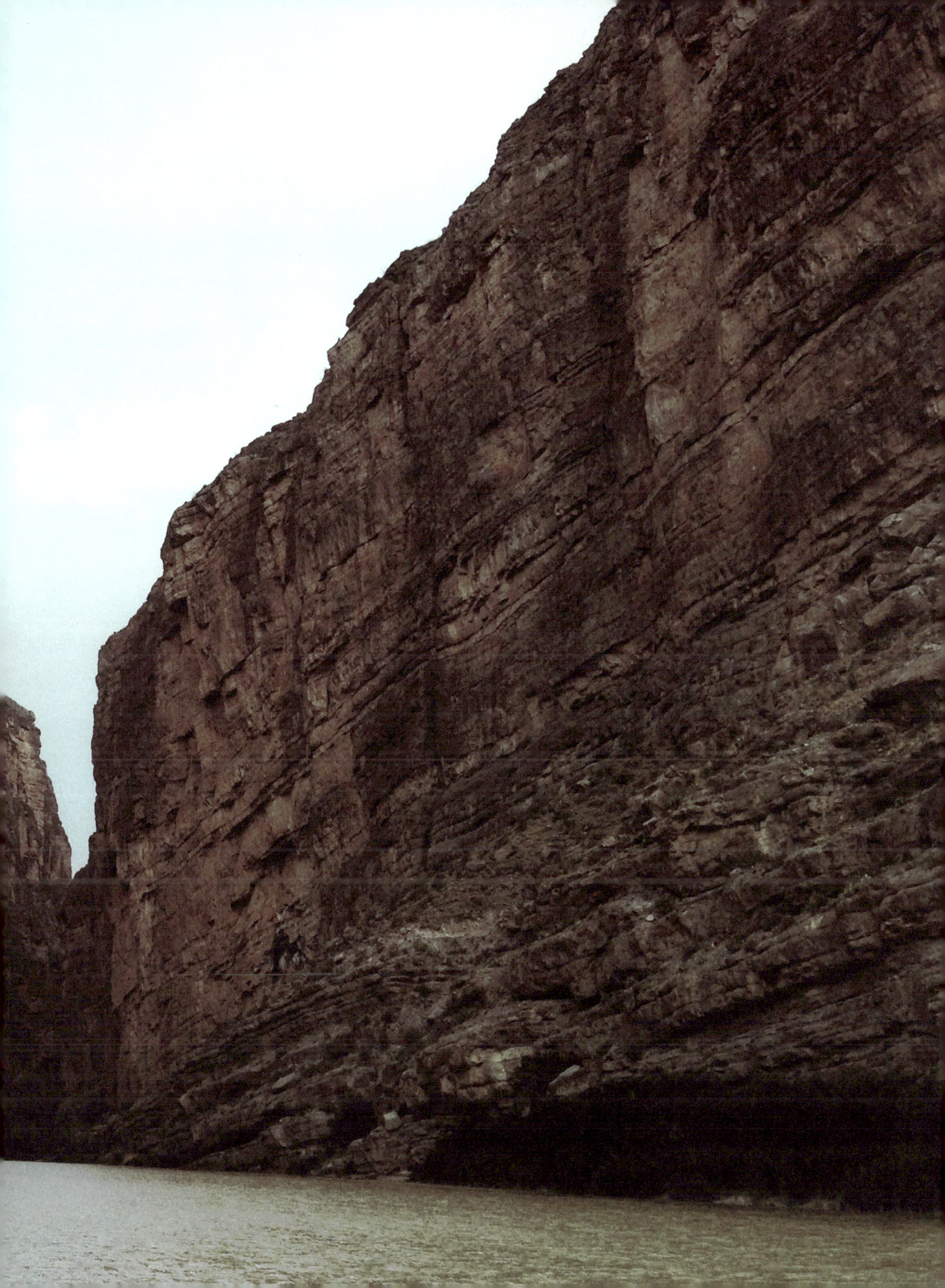

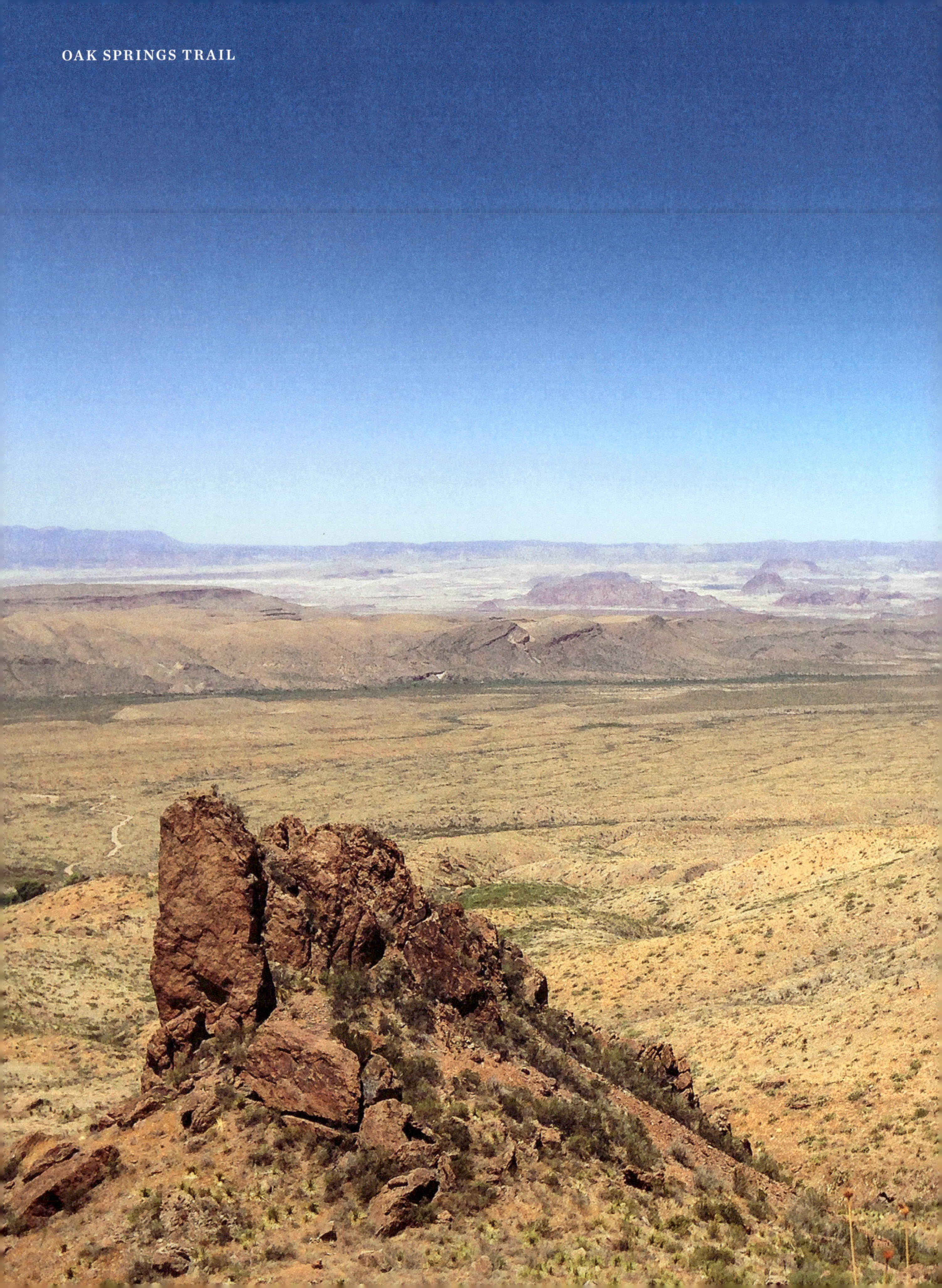

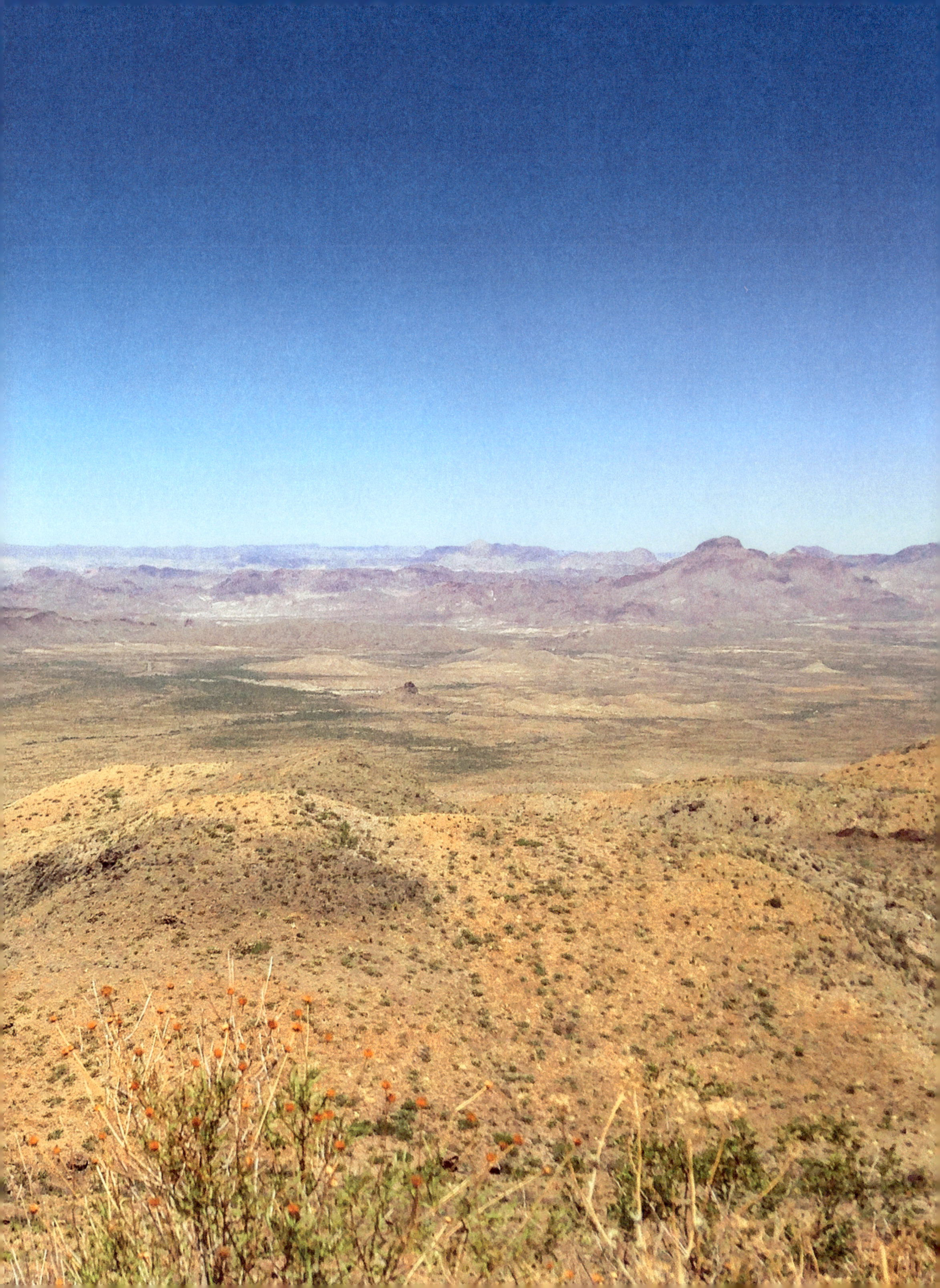

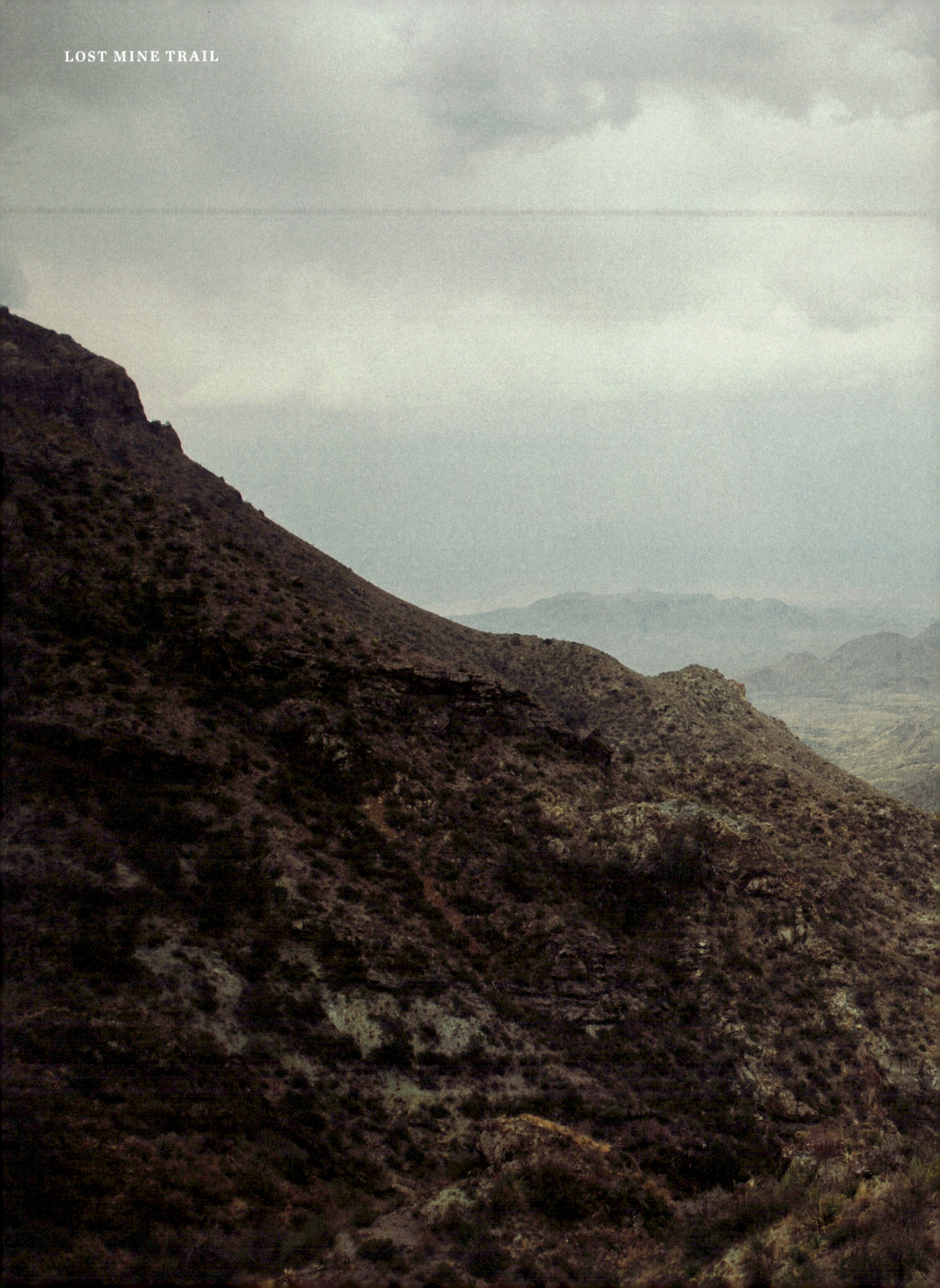

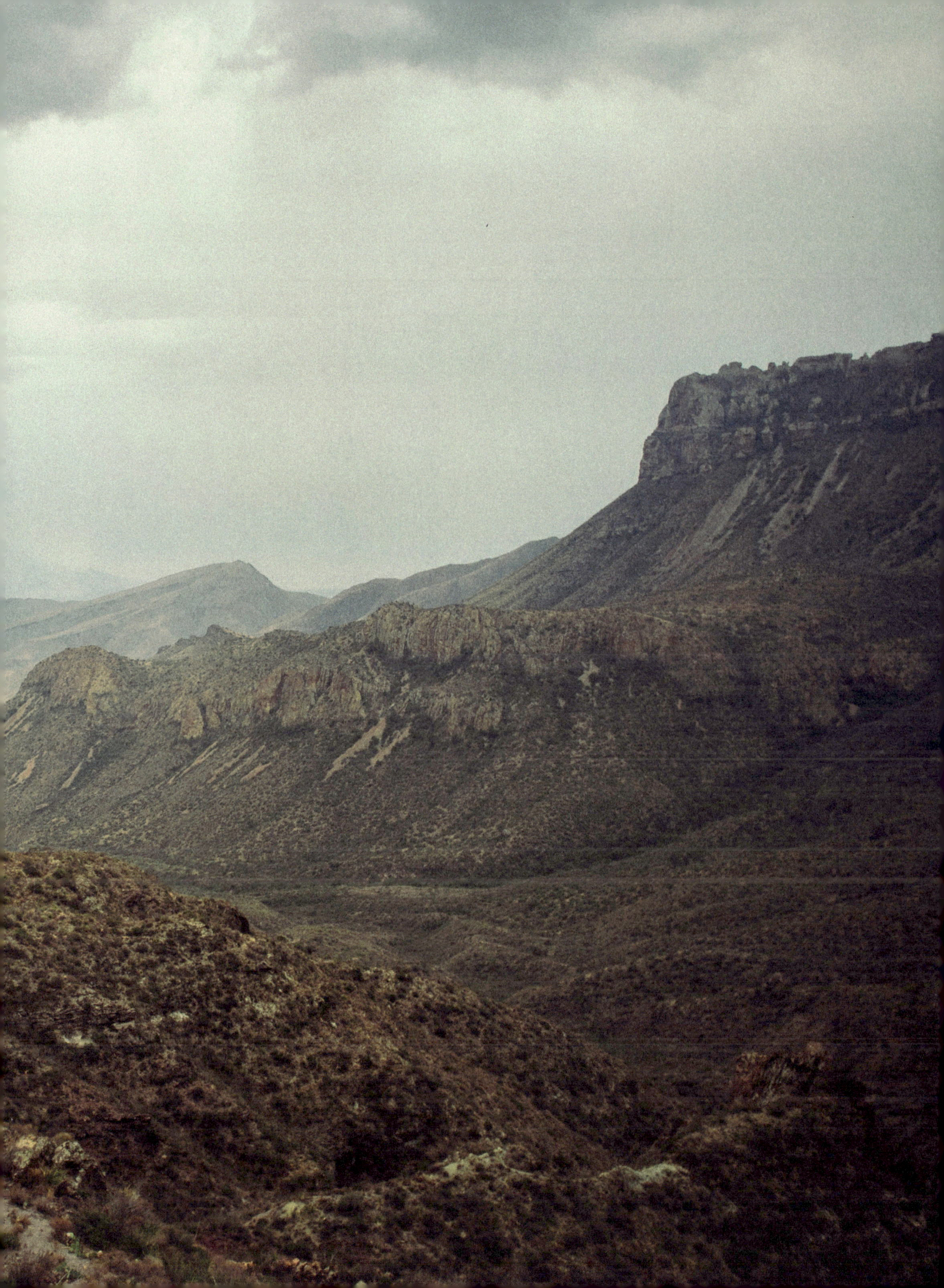

THE EXPERIENCE COLLECTOR

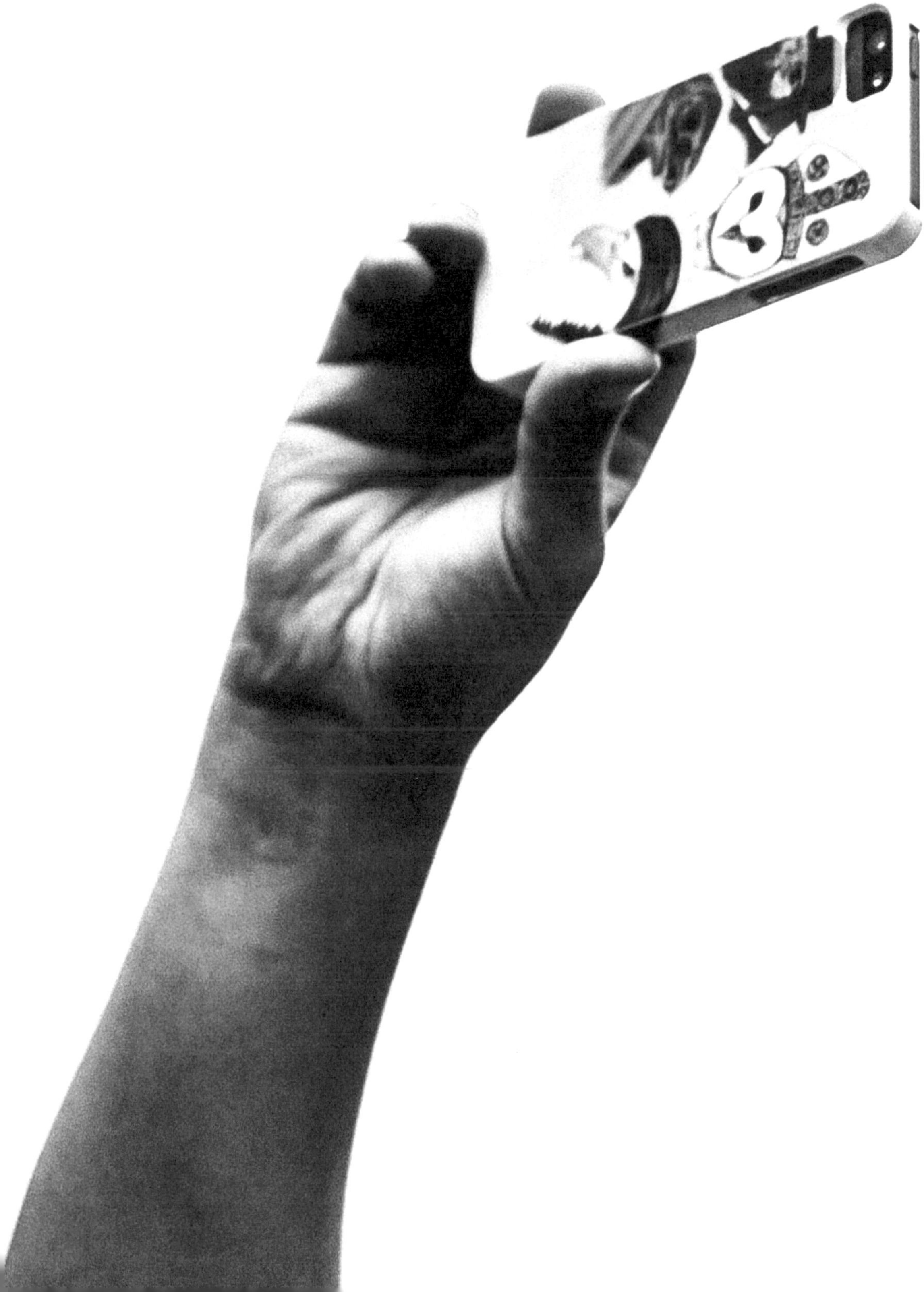

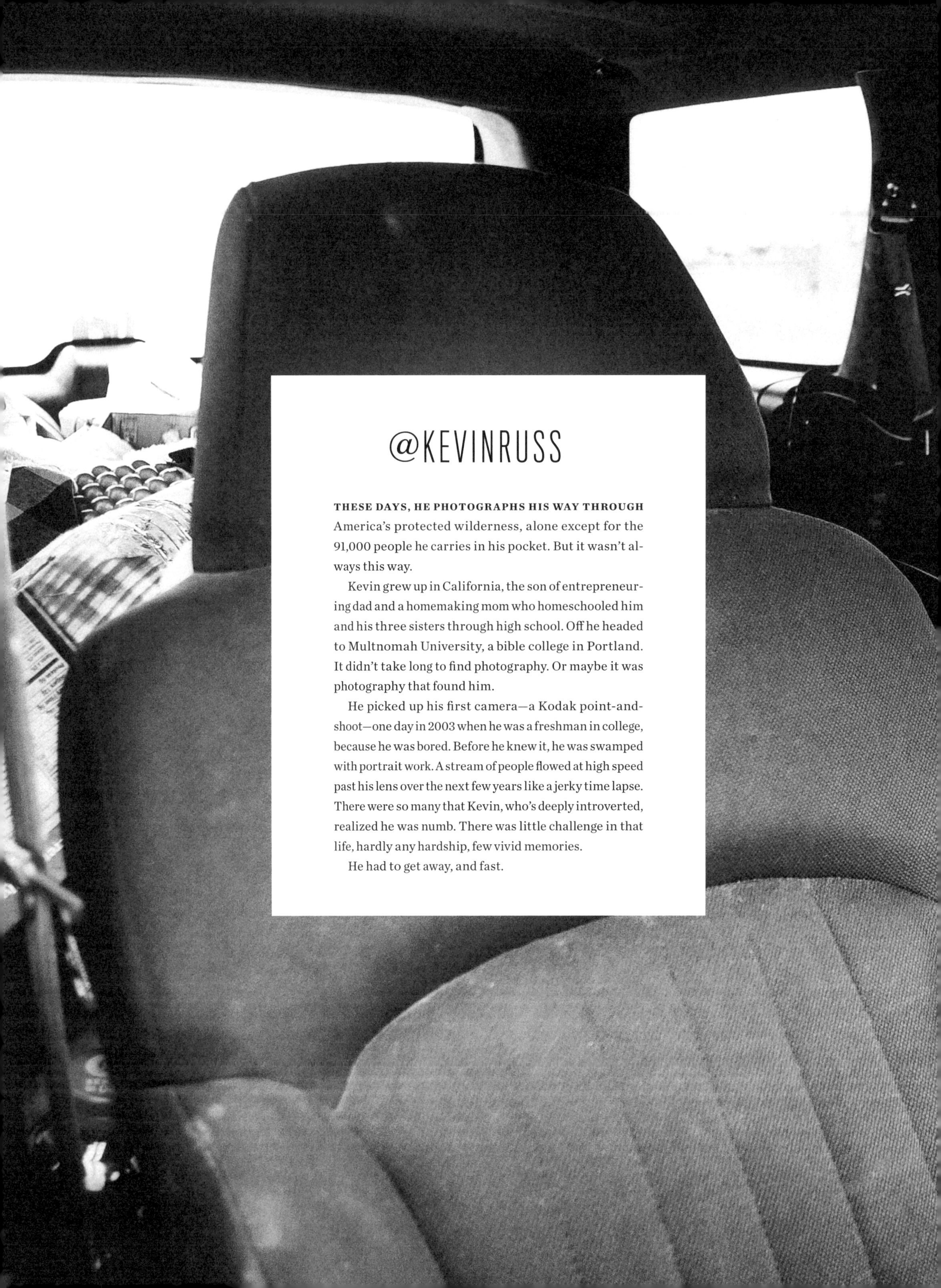

@KEVINRUSS

THESE DAYS, HE PHOTOGRAPHS HIS WAY THROUGH America's protected wilderness, alone except for the 91,000 people he carries in his pocket. But it wasn't always this way.

Kevin grew up in California, the son of entrepreneuring dad and a homemaking mom who homeschooled him and his three sisters through high school. Off he headed to Multnomah University, a bible college in Portland. It didn't take long to find photography. Or maybe it was photography that found him.

He picked up his first camera—a Kodak point-and-shoot—one day in 2003 when he was a freshman in college, because he was bored. Before he knew it, he was swamped with portrait work. A stream of people flowed at high speed past his lens over the next few years like a jerky time lapse. There were so many that Kevin, who's deeply introverted, realized he was numb. There was little challenge in that life, hardly any hardship, few vivid memories.

He had to get away, and fast.

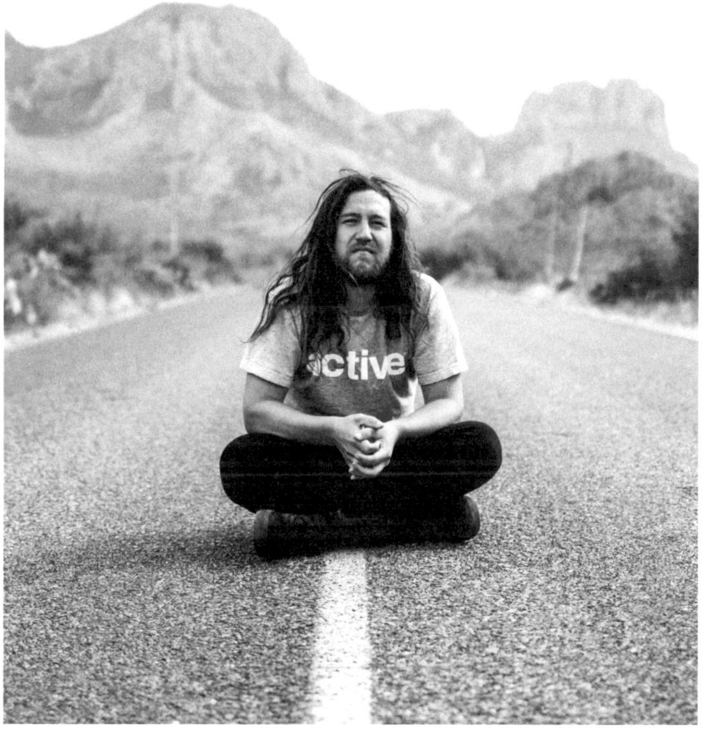
active

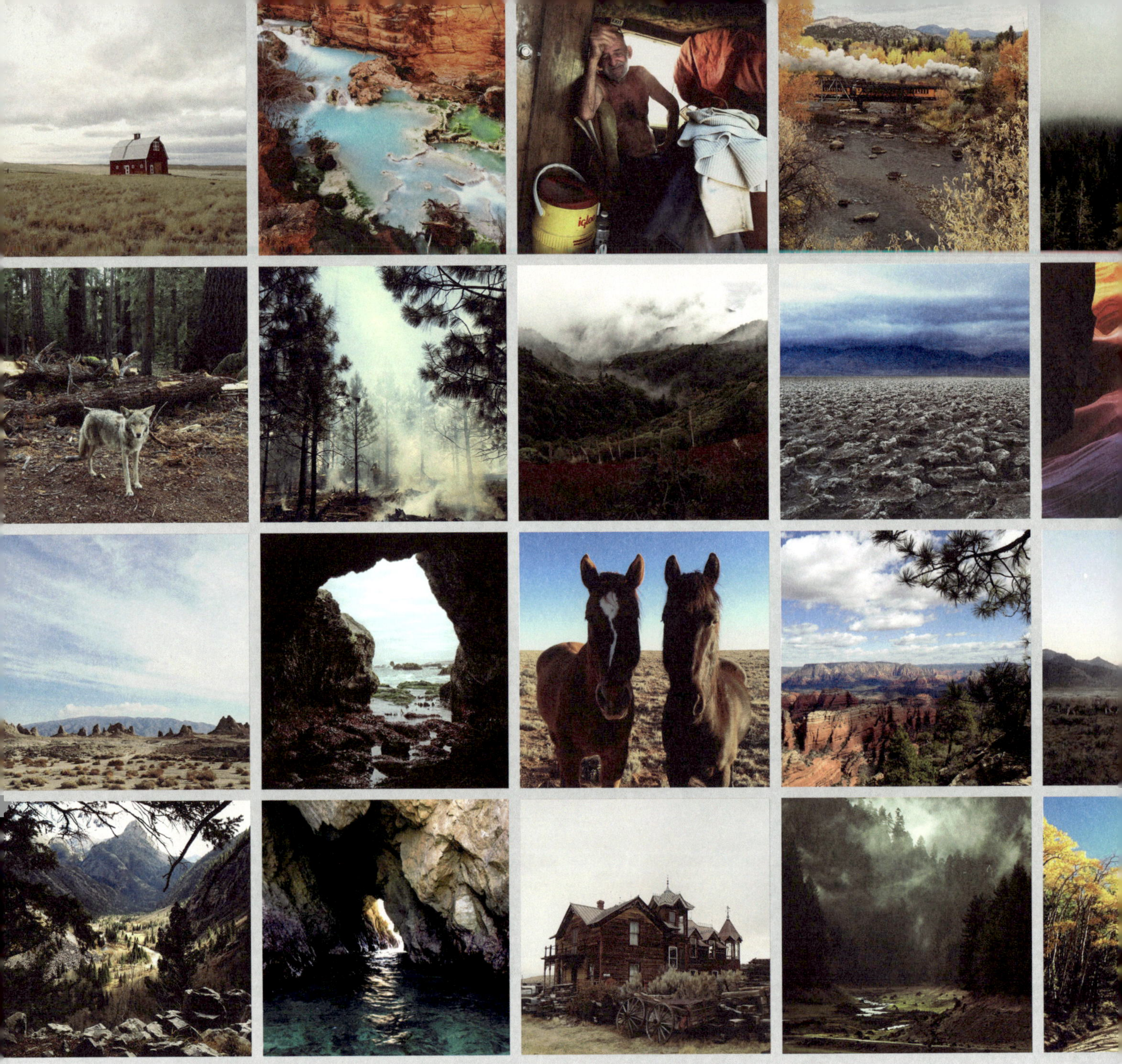

HE'S A TRAVELING MAN.

For the better part of the past couple of years, Kevin has been on an odyssey. He remembers the colorlessness of his old life, and he's not keen to return. His story now is one of getting lost, getting hurt, getting stranded. Once, he sheltered with homeless mechanics who got his car up and running during a strange week without transportation. "In Portland, where my friends and house are, I don't even have a room anymore," he says. "It's packed into a garage." He's been driving around America, through Havasu Canyon and Oneonta Gorge and Monument Valley and others, taking pictures of the *land*. There's a wildness out here, and most of us don't get to witness it often.

HE'S A QUIET MAN.

Silent, sleeveless, and bearded, with tangled hair that by now hits pretty close to his biceps, Kevin is the least pretentious character you're likely to meet. He has an agreeable, easy-going laugh. When he does talk, it's matter-of-factly, and though he's fully invested in the conversation, you can see his eyes are always scanning the landscape for the beauty in nature that others may not be as quick to see. He prefers to listen and discover. "My first night in Slab City [an RV oasis in Niland, California] I met a couple of guys who had some regrets with their children and hadn't seen them for a long time," he says. "I don't meet people every day but when I do it's usually people like that."

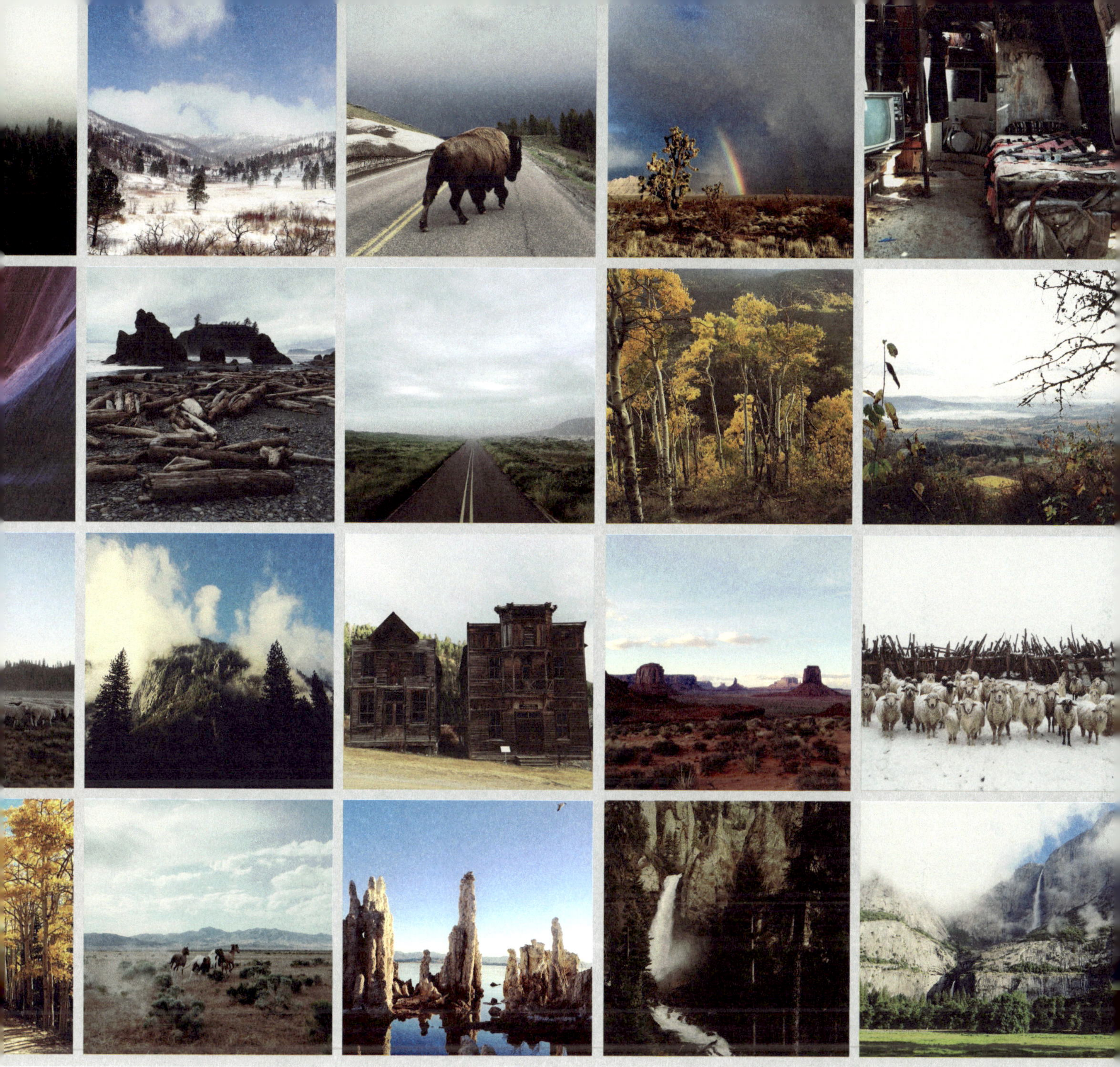

HE'S A FRUGAL MAN.

Four dollars a day doesn't buy much food, but it keeps Kevin alive. His menu is simple: oatmeal for breakfast, a tuna sandwich for lunch, and ramen noodles for dinner. Water is free at gas stations, or the odd pump at a pet cemetery. That leaves the rest of his money for his biggest expense: the unleaded fuel he pumps into his dusty, white 1998 Toyota 4Runner, with its 18-gallon gas tank. It's an ascetic existence, but Kevin has learned from his travels that hardship is what allows him to grow, which is why he dilberately seeks out experiences that will stretch his idea of comfort and safety. "You learn things when you have difficult experiences," he says.

HE'S AN ARTIST, MAN.

He sees in rectangles. And though some might view the 4-inch screen of Kevin's iPhone 5 as a constraint, he has turned it into a world whose pixel limitations pale next to the multitude of doors they fling open. An iPhone is relatable because everyone has one, and it releases a mover like him from the moorings of a computer's bulky editing software. He'll go to great lengths to get the shot: "I will often run and literally chase light," he says. "I have to capture it. I'll also do hikes to tops of mountains, and the sun will be setting and I'll want to shoot it. I know it's going to be dark coming back, but it's hard to leave the mountaintop. I know the pictures can be better if I just wait another half an hour, so I'll often be hiking in the dark."

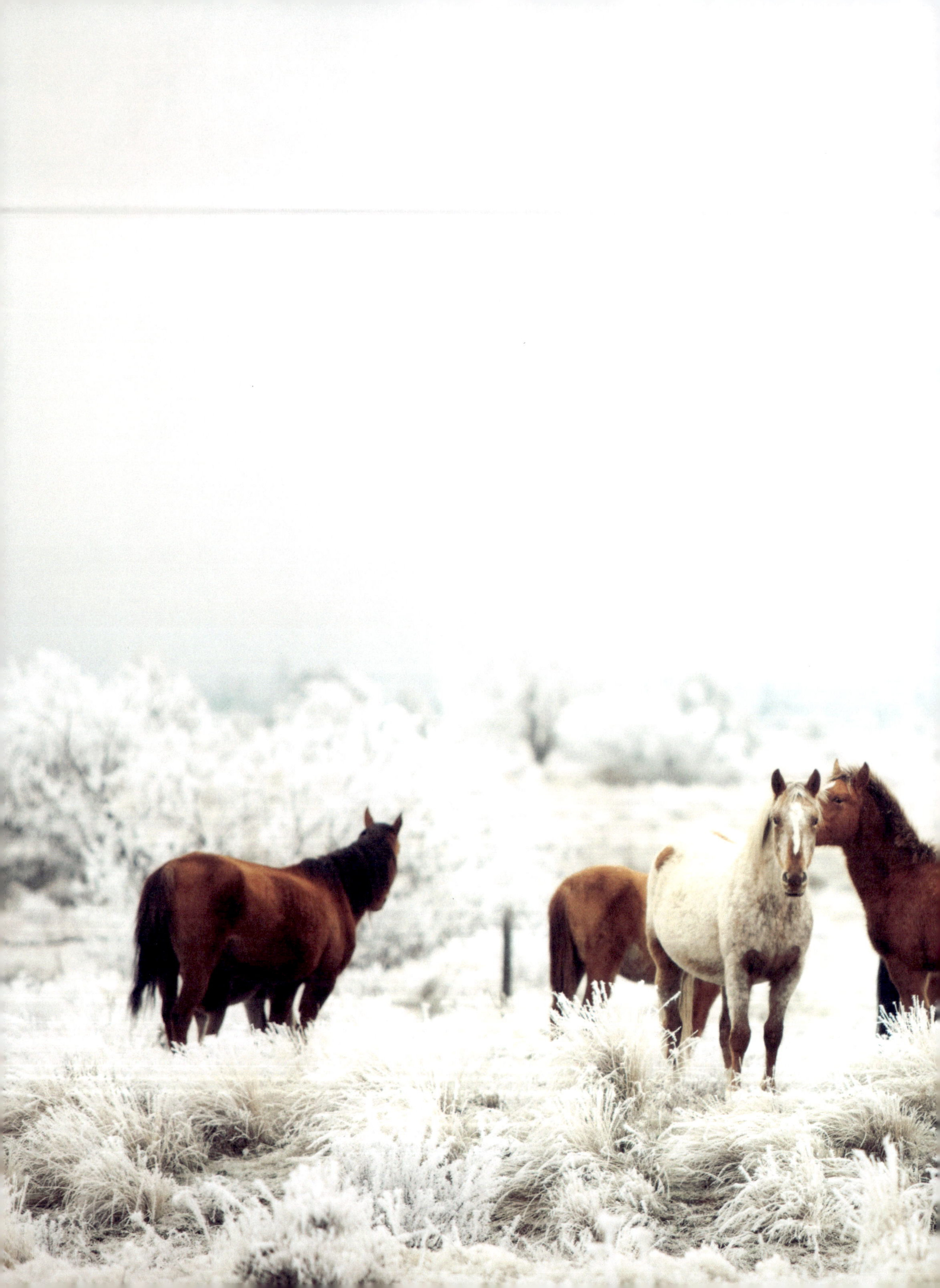

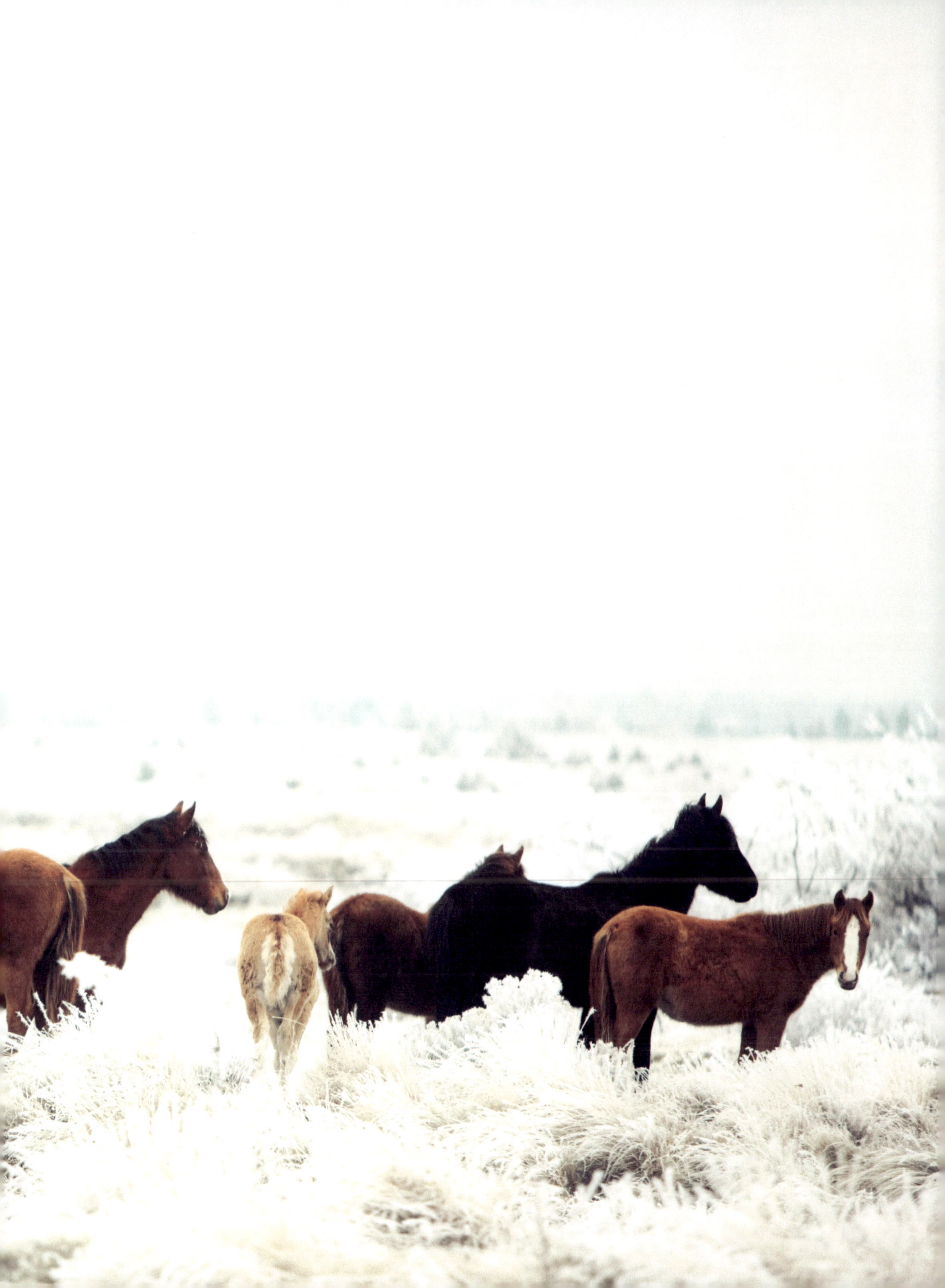

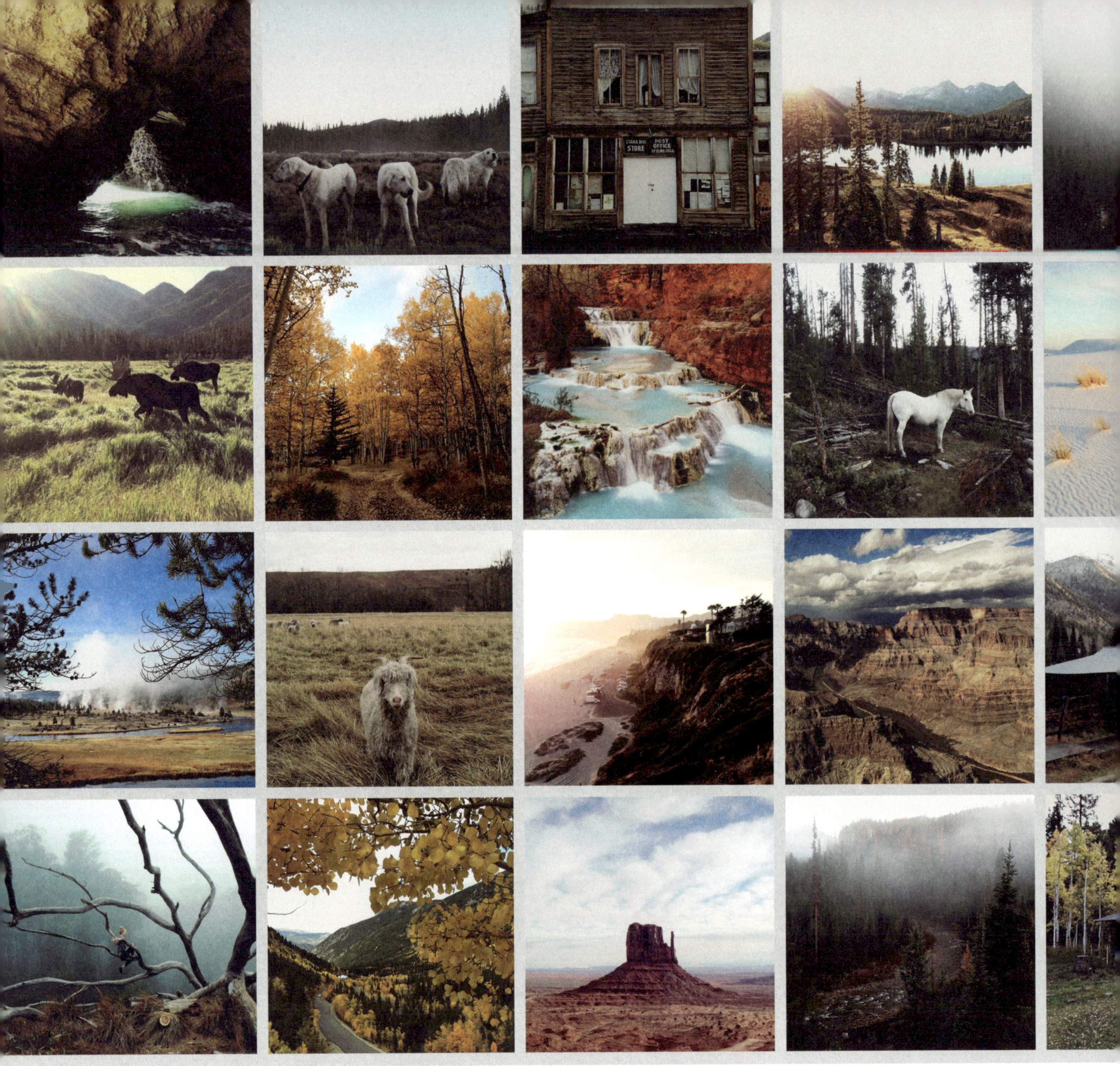

HE'S AN UNPREDICTABLE MAN.

He has the tendency to disappear, following his eyes on a treasure hunt of photographic gold. There was the time in Big Bend National Park, when the Collective Quarterly crew hiked up Lost Mine Trail to take in the view on top of the ridge. Kevin wasn't quite satisfied, though, and before they knew it he was gone, having vanished into a thicket where the trail ended. It began to rain, hard. Thunderous whip cracks were getting closer and closer, and lightning seemed to strike in front of their faces. They didn't know whether to spread out and look for him or trust that he could take care of himself in the downpour. As they began to make their way toward the trailhead, he suddenly appeared, dashing down the path, hair trailing behind him.

HE'S A CURIOUS MAN.

There was another time in the little pueblo in Mexico, when his feet took him on a walkabout toward the Rio Grande, where he had seen man bathing his horse behind a row ramshackle houses. In broken language, he made friends with a family who invited him inside and proudly showed him their living room. It was 5.50 p.m., 10 minutes before the border crossing closed, and he would have been stuck for the night. The Mexican agent on duty had stamped Kevin's passport when he crossed a couple of hours earlier, and now he looked worried. The United States of America doesn't wait around for tourists who dilly-dally. But then came Kevin, unhurried, and he made it back to the boat across the Rio Grande and into his country with a few minutes to spare.

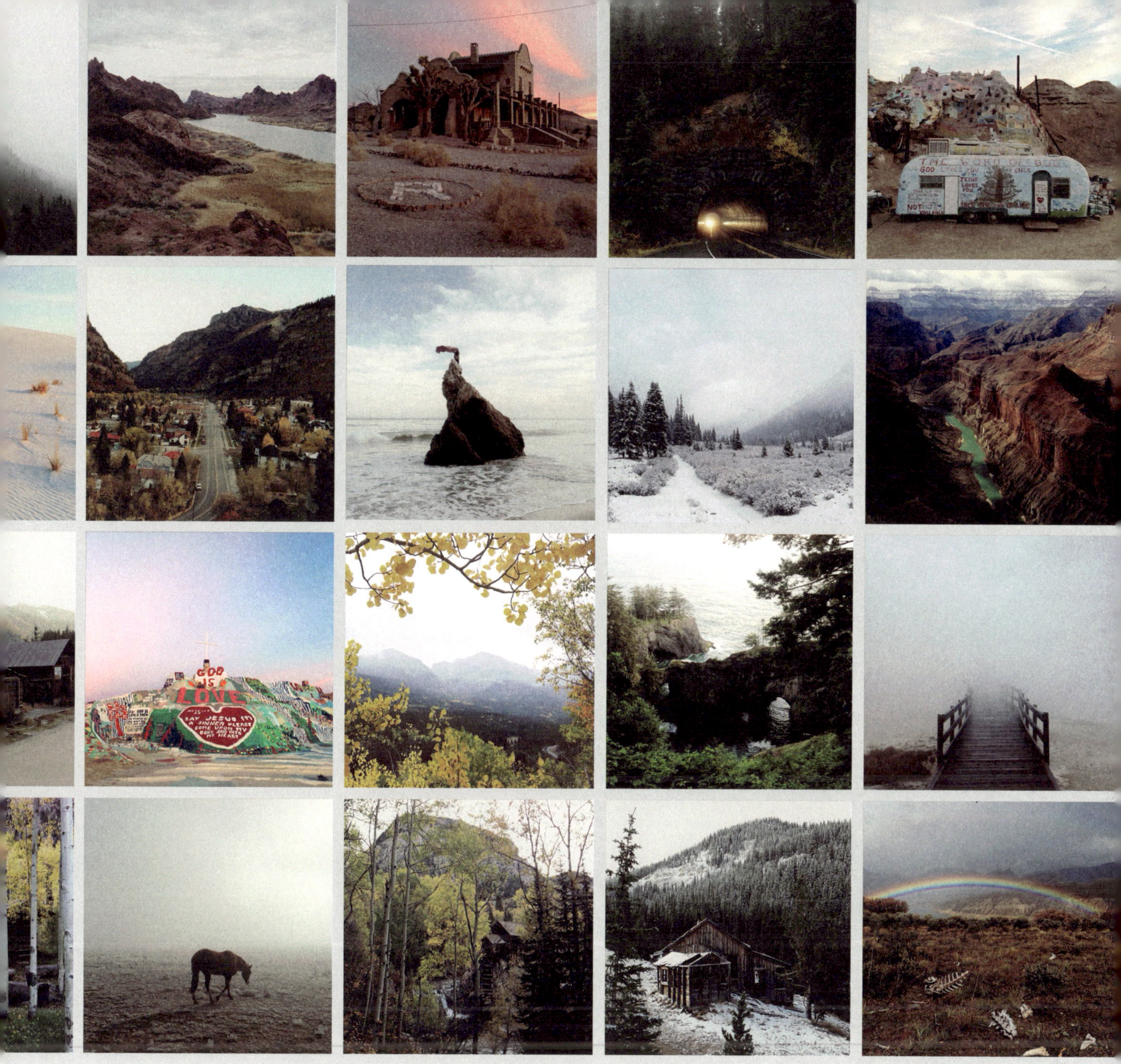

HE'S A POWERFUL MAN.

He'd never see it quite that way, but it's true. You see, the smartphone has become an object of intimacy—as much as your bedroom, bathroom, or Internet search history. For many, it's the first thing you look at when you wake up, and the last thing you take in before you drift off. When people choose to follow you, they're choosing to put you in front of their eyes during some of the most intimate moments of their lives: the times when they're alone. And nearly 100,000 Instagrammers have chosen to do that with Kevin's vivid, tiny photographs of the natural world. His work has connected his audience with vistas they don't often get to see, and his journey has opened their eyes to the idea that seeing the world can be a way of life. *–S.P.*

Sustainable Stock Stocksy United Co-op Photography

Kevin makes his living in part thanks to Stocksy United, an ethically conscious stock photography website, founded by Bruce Livingstone. The British Columbia-based photo licensing co-op's first commitment is to its artists. Livingstone and his team handpick Stocksy's contributors and compensate them fairly, thus developing a vibrant community of talented photographers who offer a vibrant body of high-quality images. *Scan to learn more about Stocksy and how to license Kevin's work.*

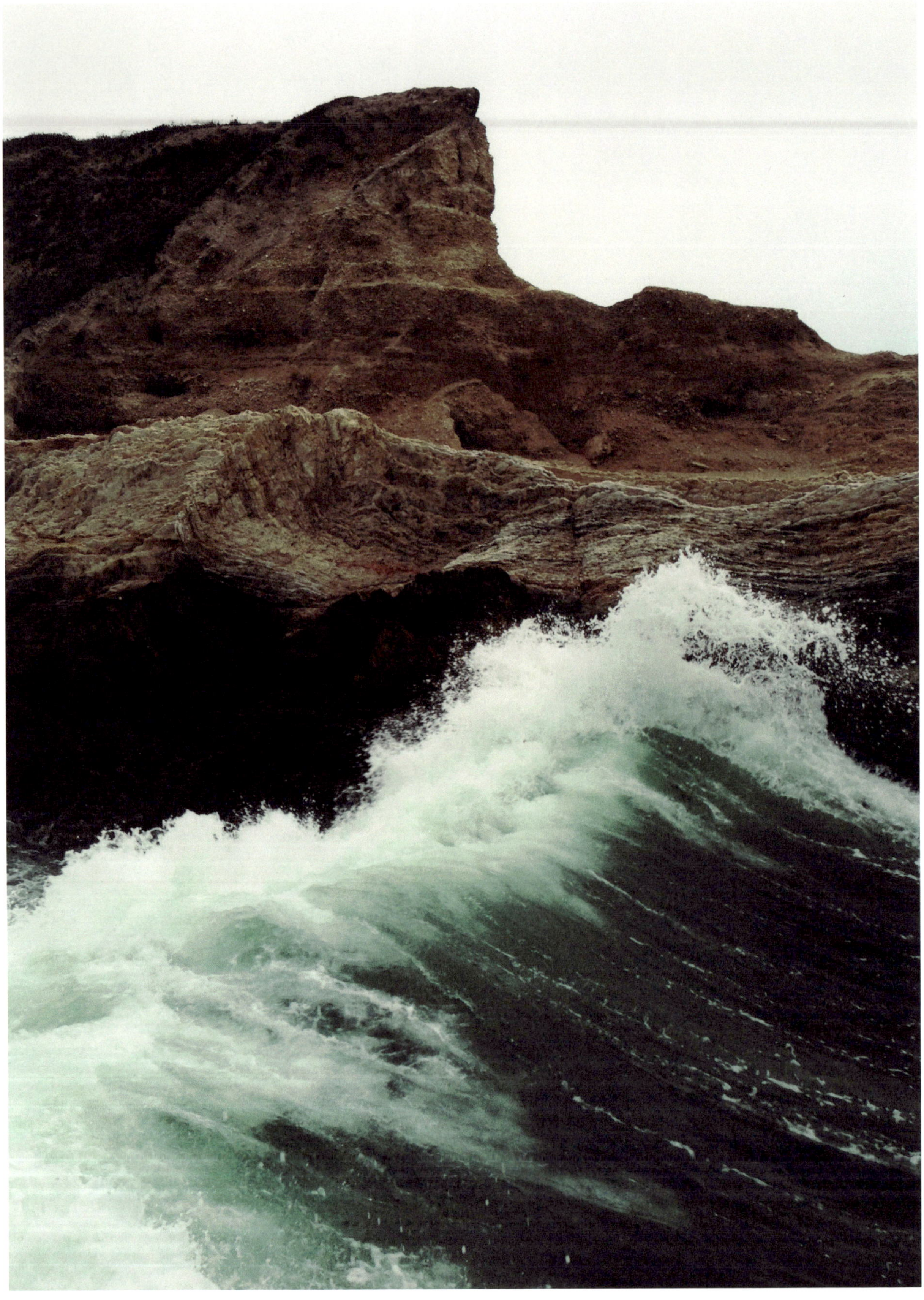

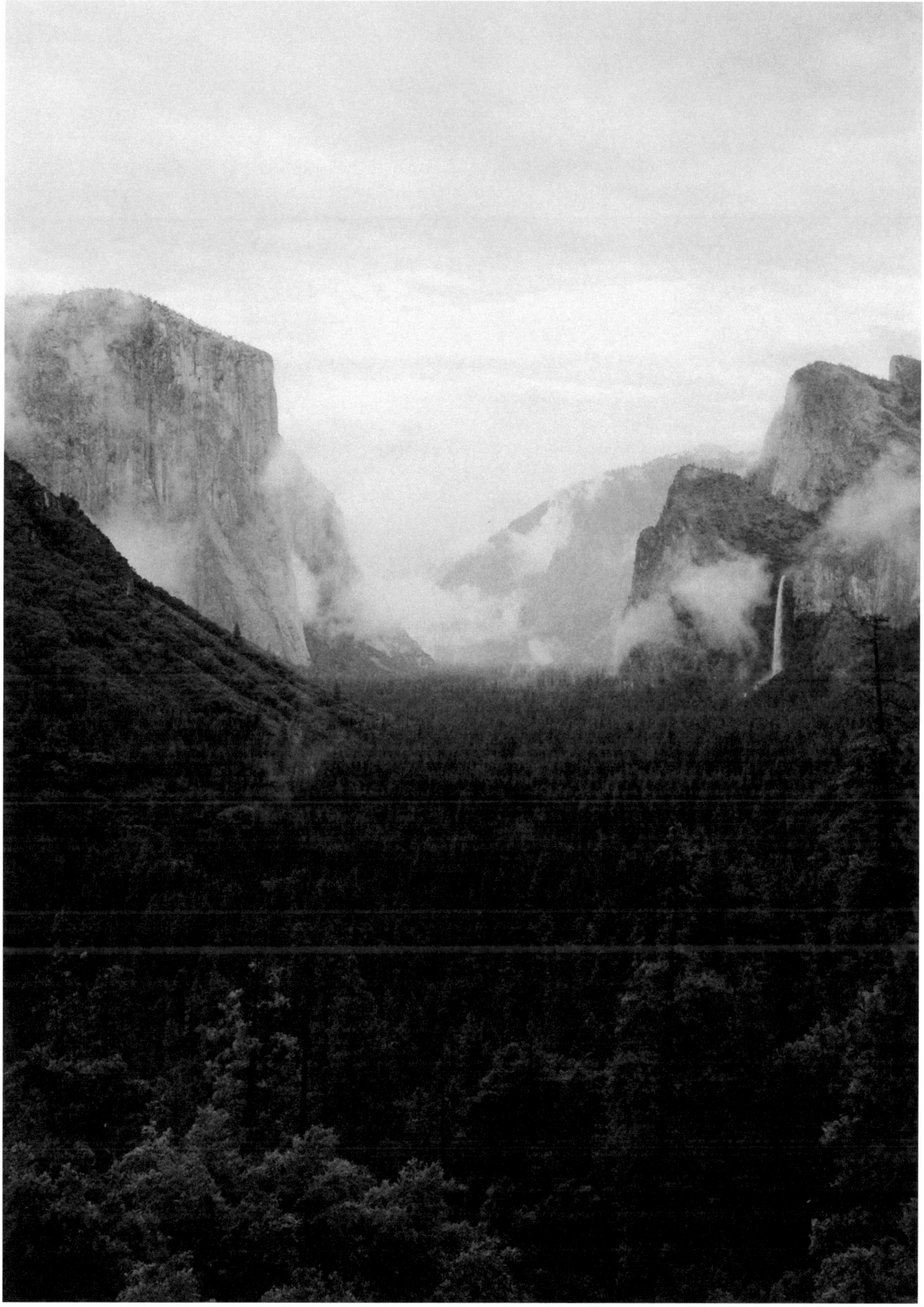

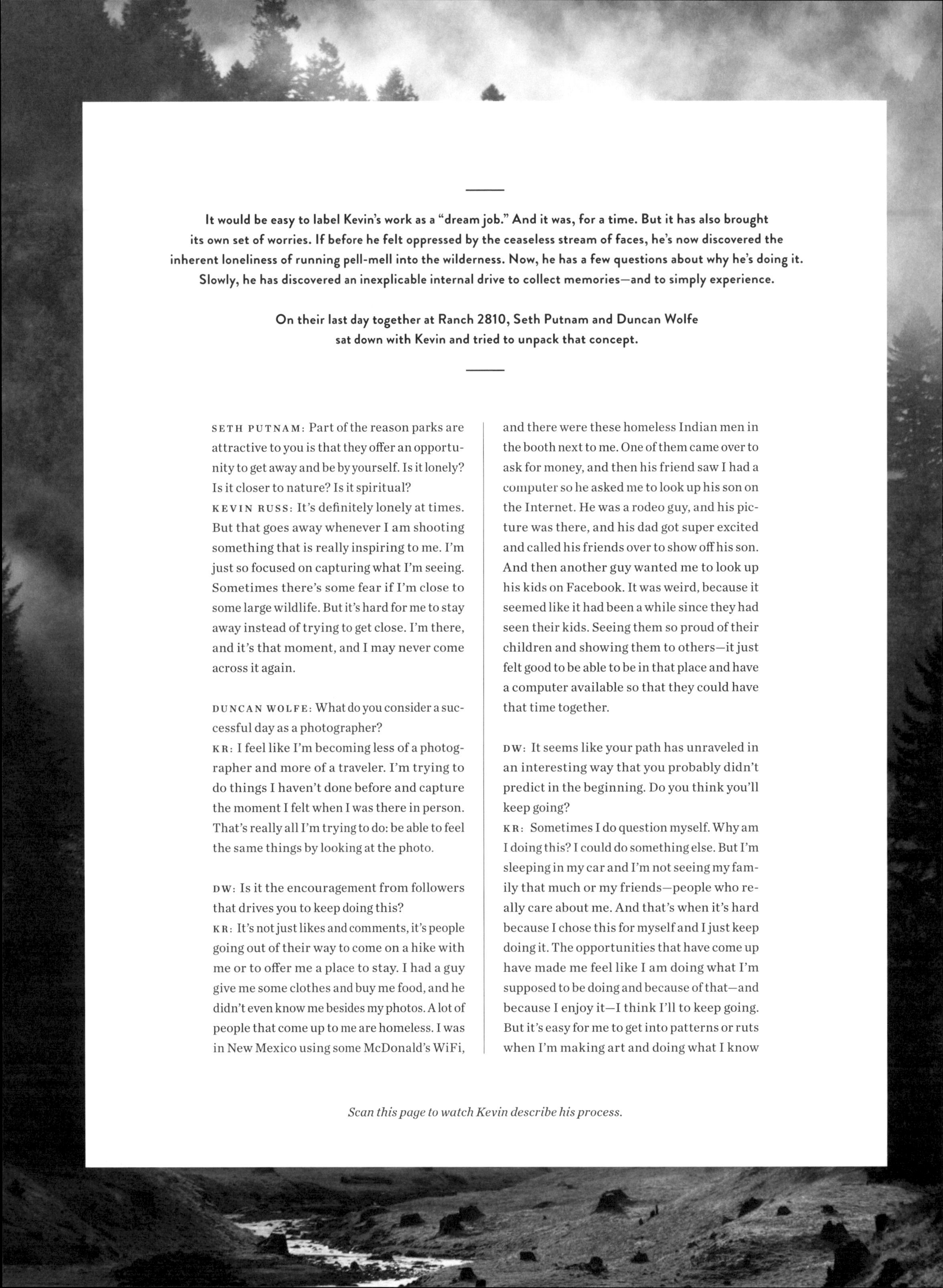

It would be easy to label Kevin's work as a "dream job." And it was, for a time. But it has also brought its own set of worries. If before he felt oppressed by the ceaseless stream of faces, he's now discovered the inherent loneliness of running pell-mell into the wilderness. Now, he has a few questions about why he's doing it. Slowly, he has discovered an inexplicable internal drive to collect memories—and to simply experience.

On their last day together at Ranch 2810, Seth Putnam and Duncan Wolfe sat down with Kevin and tried to unpack that concept.

SETH PUTNAM: Part of the reason parks are attractive to you is that they offer an opportunity to get away and be by yourself. Is it lonely? Is it closer to nature? Is it spiritual?
KEVIN RUSS: It's definitely lonely at times. But that goes away whenever I am shooting something that is really inspiring to me. I'm just so focused on capturing what I'm seeing. Sometimes there's some fear if I'm close to some large wildlife. But it's hard for me to stay away instead of trying to get close. I'm there, and it's that moment, and I may never come across it again.

DUNCAN WOLFE: What do you consider a successful day as a photographer?
KR: I feel like I'm becoming less of a photographer and more of a traveler. I'm trying to do things I haven't done before and capture the moment I felt when I was there in person. That's really all I'm trying to do: be able to feel the same things by looking at the photo.

DW: Is it the encouragement from followers that drives you to keep doing this?
KR: It's not just likes and comments, it's people going out of their way to come on a hike with me or to offer me a place to stay. I had a guy give me some clothes and buy me food, and he didn't even know me besides my photos. A lot of people that come up to me are homeless. I was in New Mexico using some McDonald's WiFi, and there were these homeless Indian men in the booth next to me. One of them came over to ask for money, and then his friend saw I had a computer so he asked me to look up his son on the Internet. He was a rodeo guy, and his picture was there, and his dad got super excited and called his friends over to show off his son. And then another guy wanted me to look up his kids on Facebook. It was weird, because it seemed like it had been a while since they had seen their kids. Seeing them so proud of their children and showing them to others—it just felt good to be able to be in that place and have a computer available so that they could have that time together.

DW: It seems like your path has unraveled in an interesting way that you probably didn't predict in the beginning. Do you think you'll keep going?
KR: Sometimes I do question myself. Why am I doing this? I could do something else. But I'm sleeping in my car and I'm not seeing my family that much or my friends—people who really care about me. And that's when it's hard because I chose this for myself and I just keep doing it. The opportunities that have come up have made me feel like I am doing what I'm supposed to be doing and because of that—and because I enjoy it—I think I'll to keep going. But it's easy for me to get into patterns or ruts when I'm making art and doing what I know

Scan this page to watch Kevin describe his process.

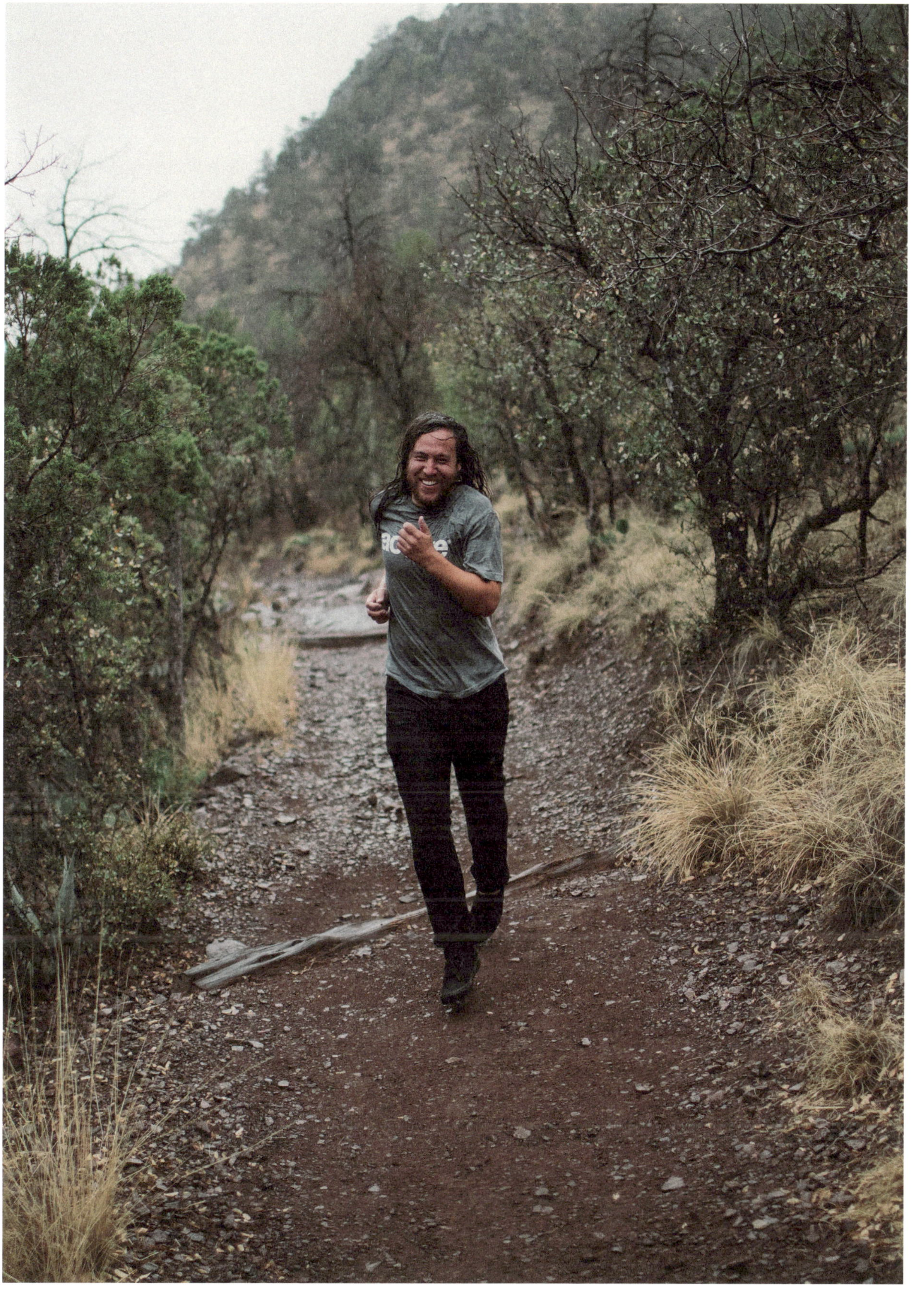

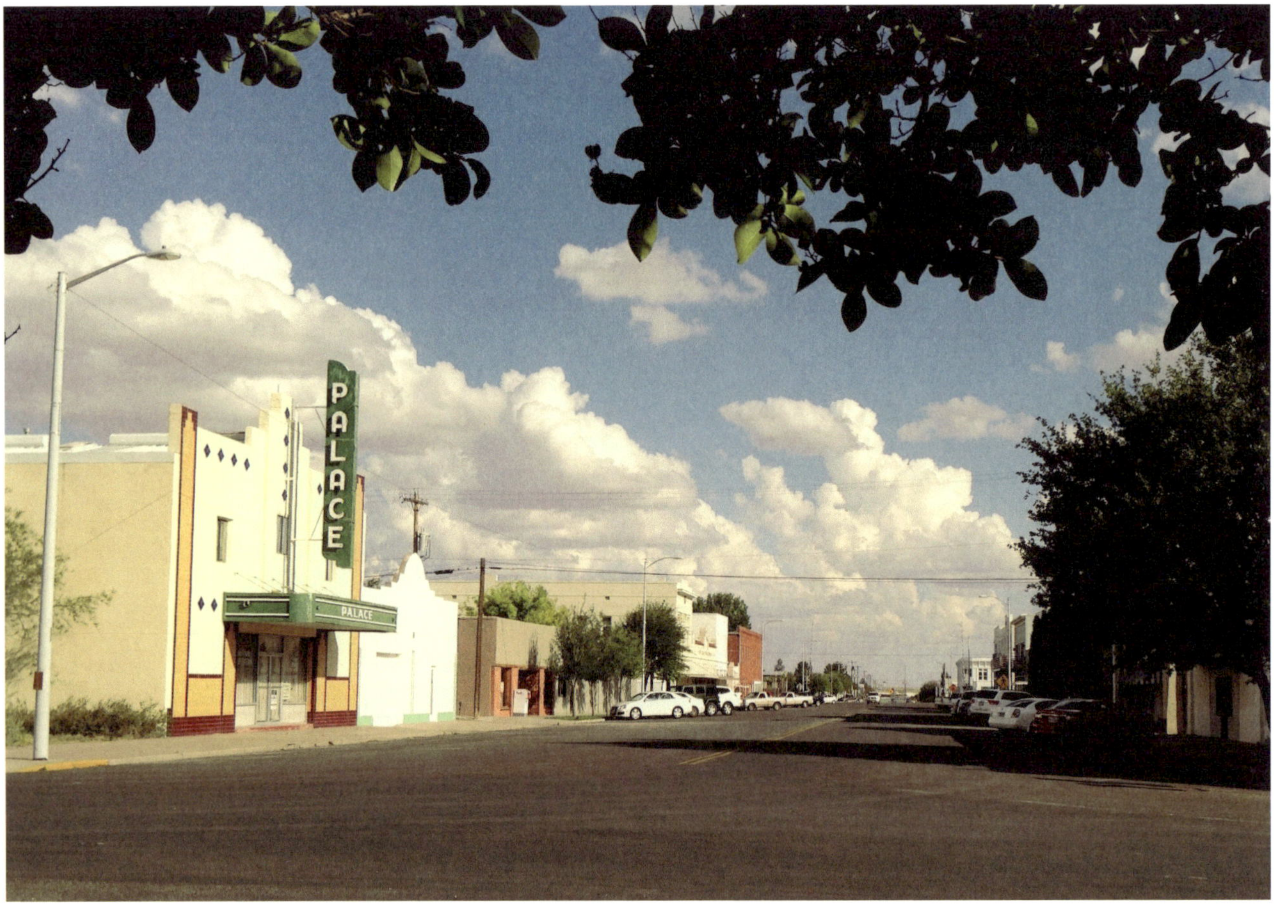
PALACE
PALACE

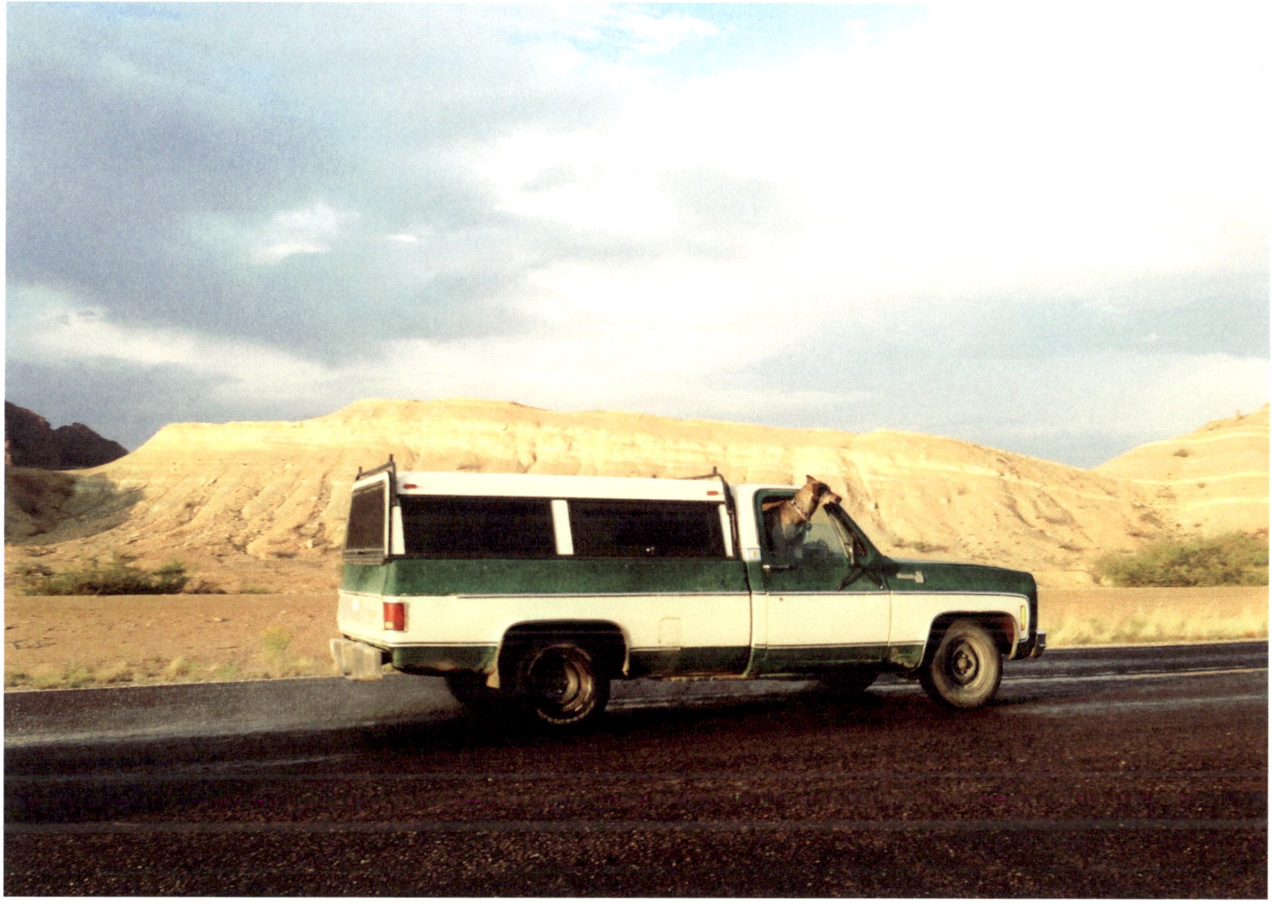

"IF YOU KNOW WHAT YOU'RE DOING, YOU'RE NOT REALLY MAKING ART; YOU'RE JUST GOING THROUGH THE MOTIONS."

works and is comfortable. That can get old to me. That's part of the reason why I stopped shooting portraits of people. I couldn't pull myself out of that and shoot different, so I just changed everything.

SP: It seems like you're chasing happiness by choosing to be vulnerable up to hardship.
KR: You learn things when you have difficult experiences. And maybe that's why I went to Mexico, where I can't speak the language. The way I was raised, we never had any money issues or anything tragic happen around the house. Not that I'm seeking out tragedy, but if you don't have difficult experiences, how do you grow as a person? If you know what you're doing, you're not really making art; you're just going through the motions. I'm just realizing this now: When I am in situations that I'm comfortable with, I'm not inspired.

SP: What was it about Marfa that was inspiring to you?
KR: Marfa seemed to be an offbeat artists' community in the middle of nowhere. It's cool because I don't really know any other place like it. I remember one photo I took, the one with the truck and the dog: It was such a one-off, quick moment. I turned around, and he was driving by, and I only got one shot. But it was during that time we pulled off the road and had a beer and were hanging out, watching the sun go down. It meant something to me, and I wanted to remember what it was that I felt there.

Marfa came along right after my longest solo trip, which was four months. Spending a week with you guys and being in a community every day—I was kind of craving that, and I was only just realizing that I was. Talking with John Mooty on his last night, we were saying goodbye, and I got emotional because I think for both of us this trip was a moving experience.

DW: Do you think there's a compulsion to explore every last bit of America?
KR: It's kind of just an obsession to see everywhere. That feeling that you have when you're climbing a mountain or going around a bend in a canyon: You just have to see what's on the other side. Even if it's not good, you don't know that, but you're compelled to see what's around there...what's next.

DW: So what happens when you go all over the world, and you're 85. Is there a 'done'? Is there a finish line, or is it not about that?
KR: No, there isn't a finish line because the landscape is always changing. The light is always going to be different, and encounters with wild life are always going to be different. There's always going to be something to see. There is no end. There's an end to a checklist of countries or cities, but there's no end to taking photos or exploring or chasing light. It's going to be there to chase all the time.photos or exploring. Or chasing light. It's going to be there to chase all the time.

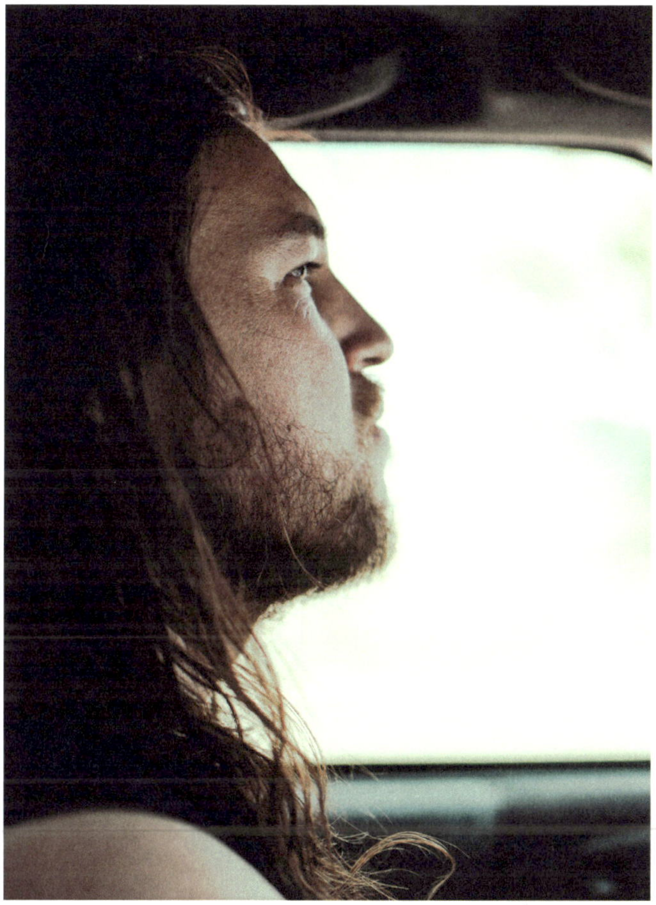

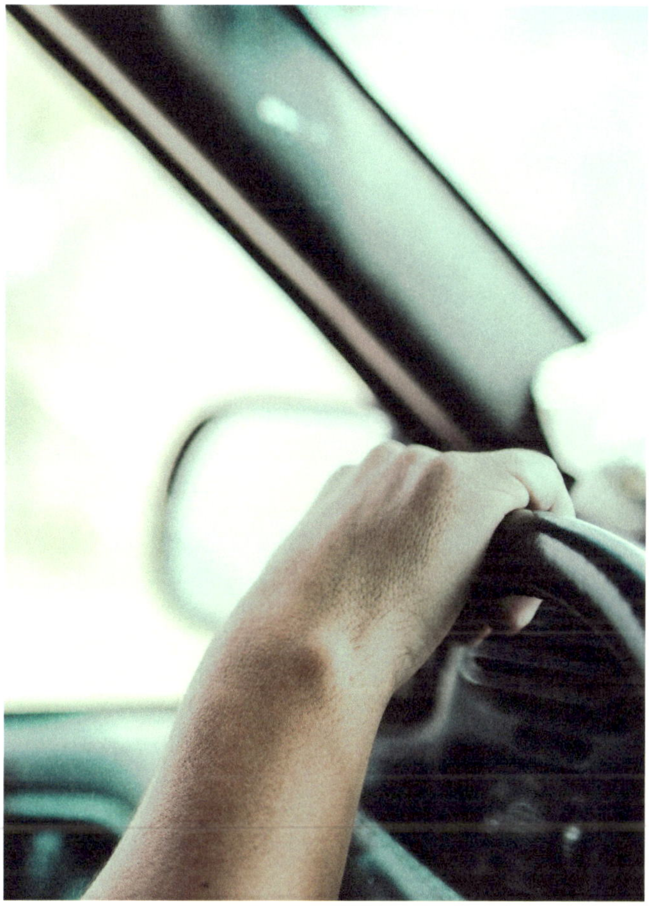

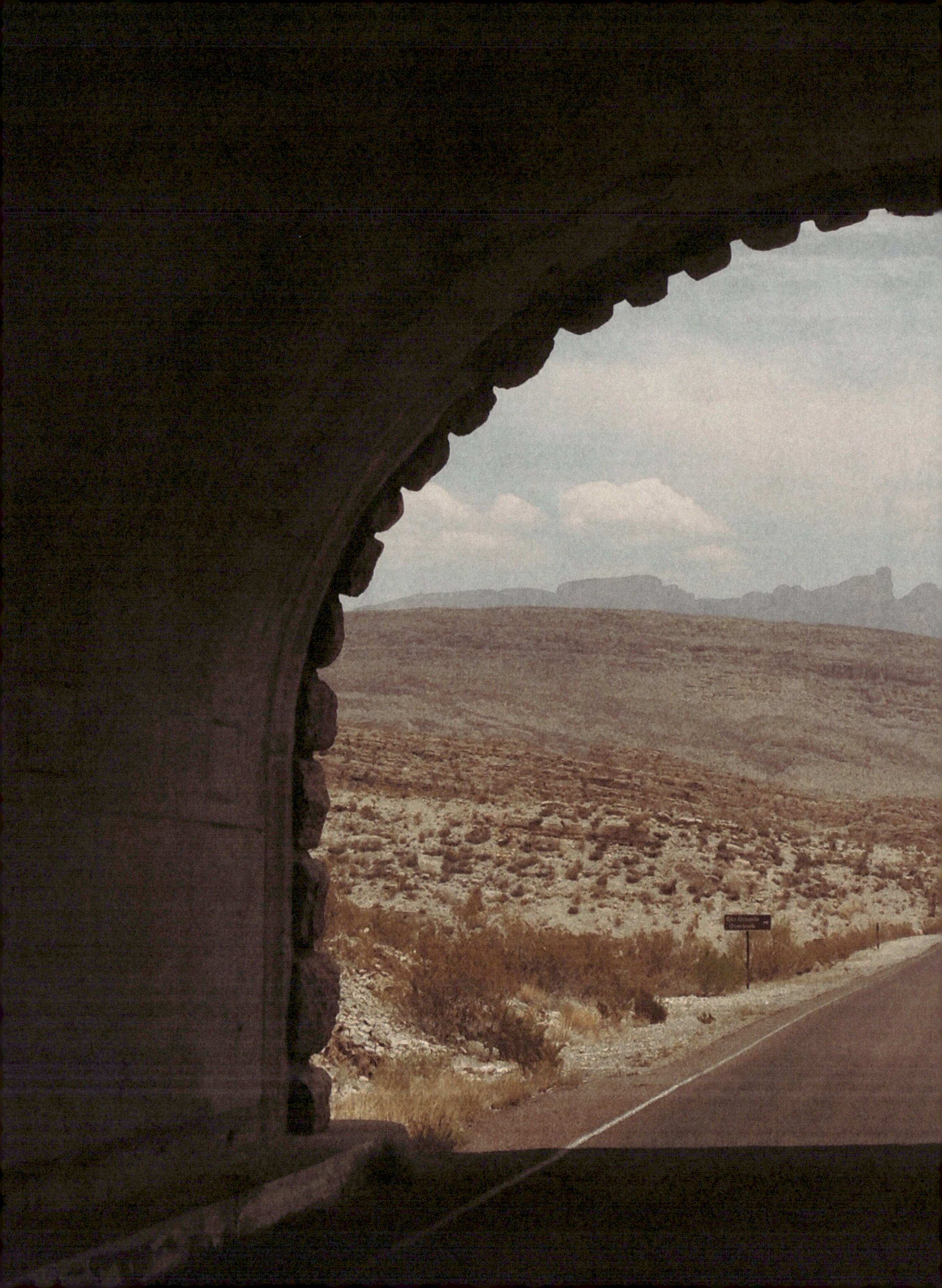

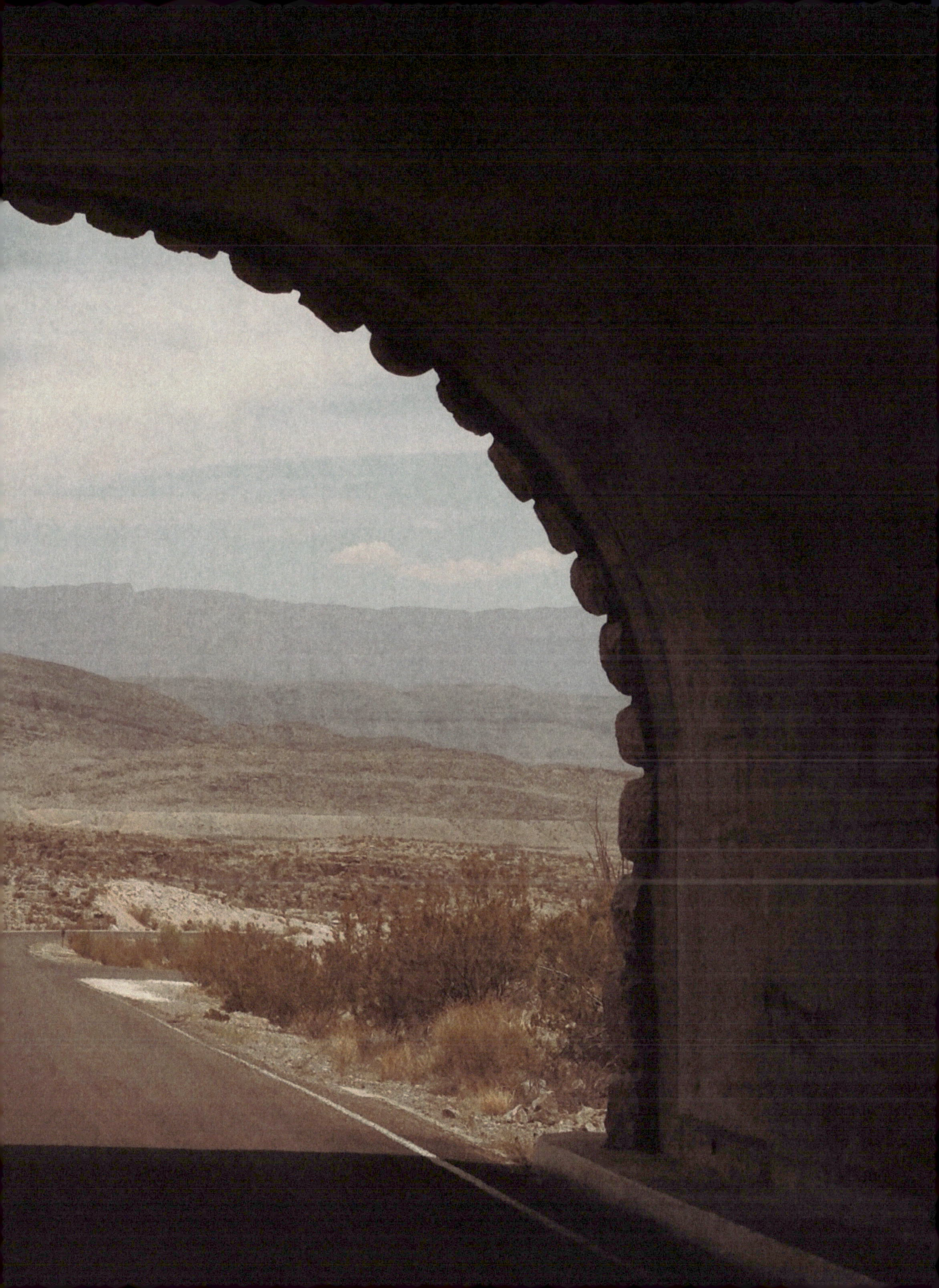

THE LOST PUEBLO

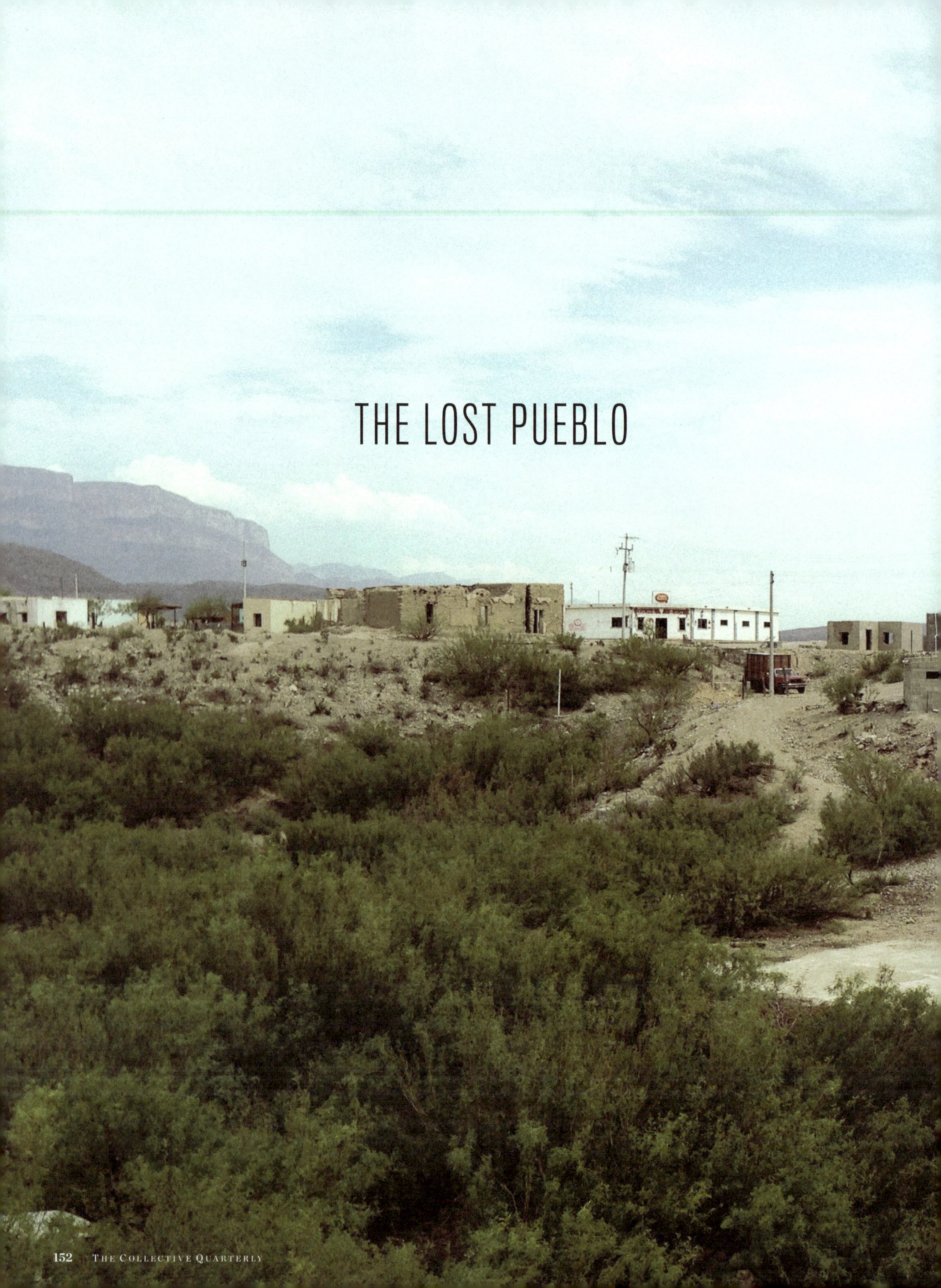

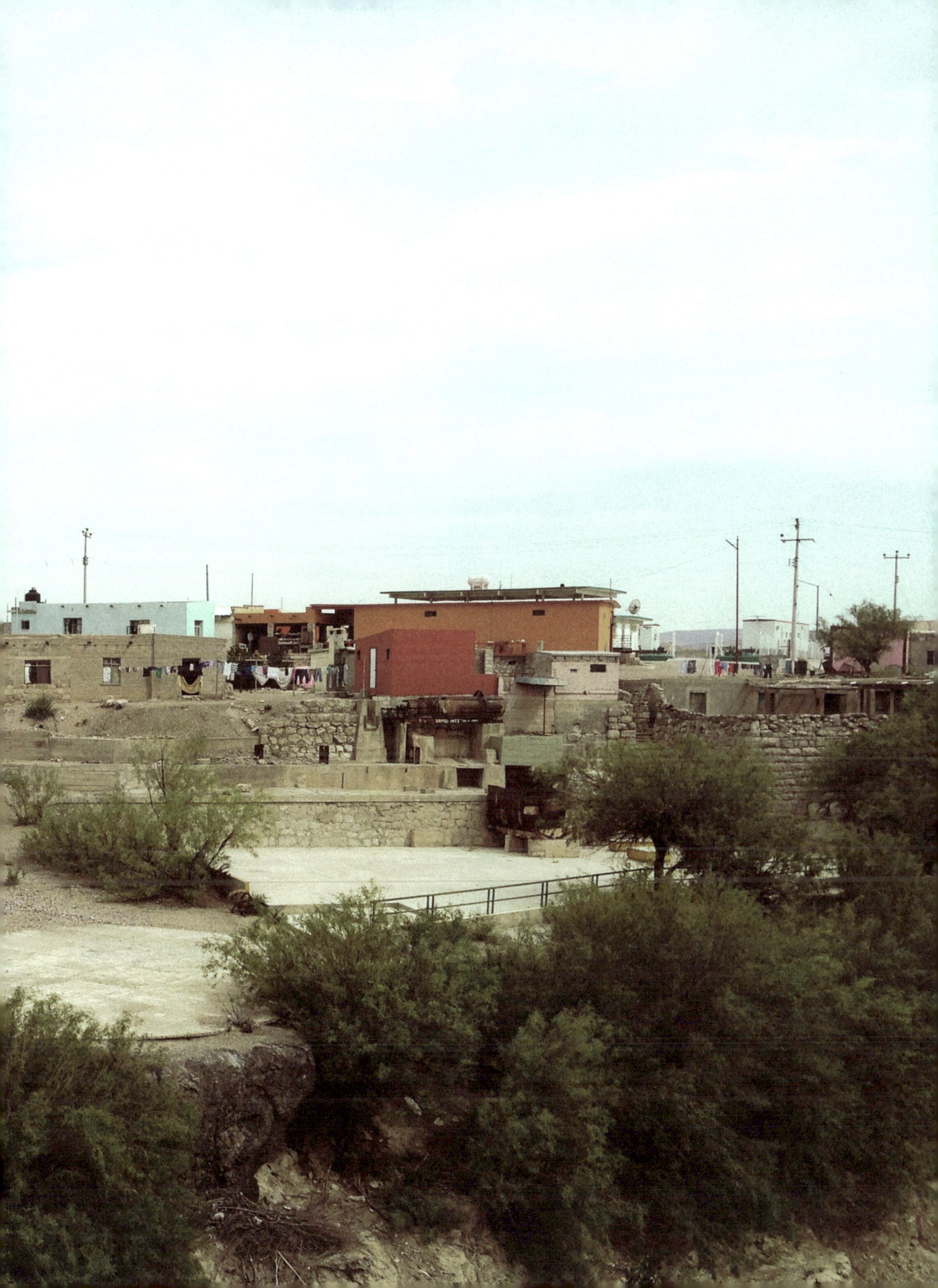

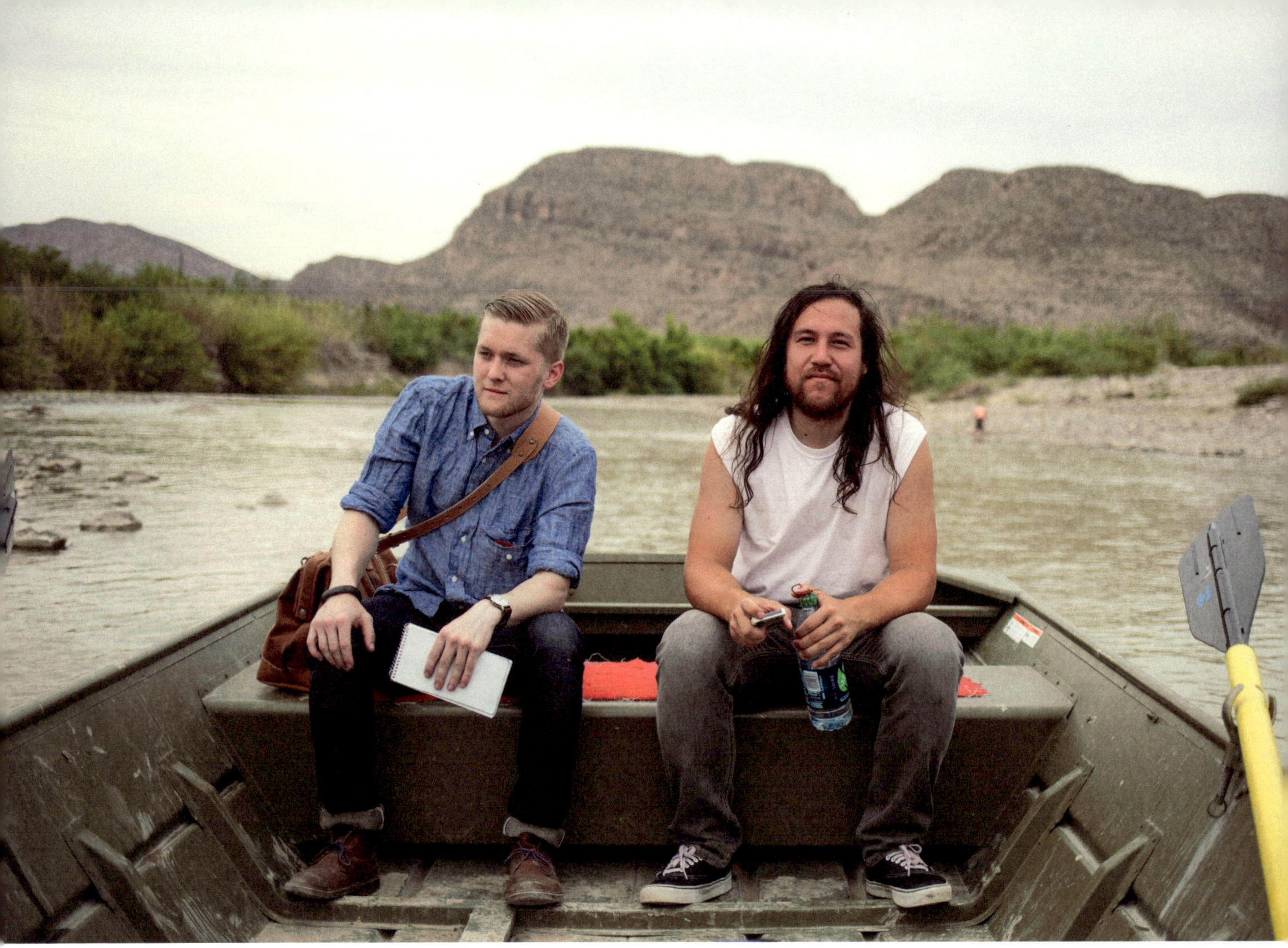

FOR $5, A MAN WILL ROW YOU ACROSS THE RIO GRANDE to a tiny Mexican town called Boquillas del Carmen.

In truth, the Big River isn't so big. You could wade across if you wanted to. But it's running today, so Kevin Russ, Duncan Wolfe, and I pile into a flat-bottomed boat. We shove off, and Victor Valdez's lilting voice sings us across the river, warbling a song about seagulls looking for love nests that they will never find. The dark-skinned, barrel-bellied 62-year-old croons ballads across the river, making his living off of tips from visitors to the little pueblo.

As we step out of the barquito onto Mexican soil, it's hard to imagine that only a few weeks ago, what we were doing would have been illegal. Just before we arrived in Texas, the US government re-opened this defunct crossing about 145 miles south of Marfa in the bottom crook of Big Bend National Park. The port of entry had been closed for 11 years—since shortly after the Sept. 11 attacks, a faraway event that bizarrely wrecked life in Boquillas by slamming the door to tourists.

"The people over in the village have a chance to make money now," Valdez says, explaining that the town's artisans will finally have customers for their blankets, artwork, and copper scorpions. He walks with us up the river bank, where we have the option of truck, horse, or burro to get into town. "Just be back by 5:30. That's when the last boat leaves."

He means: The border closes at 6 p.m., and if we don't make it back in time, we'll be stuck in Mexico for the night. We choose wheels, and man named Esteban loads us ihnto a rusted Ford pickup, which lurches along a dried up creek into the hills.

The tiny town used to cater to Americans who were visiting Big Bend and wanted to pop across, have some tacos and a cerveza, and say they'd been to Mexico. It's easy to feel cut off simply on account of being outside the country, but we quickly realize that Boquillas is isolated even within its own homeland. As we hand over our passports in the mobile trailer serving as the Customs Office, the lone border patrol agent tells us that he's an out-of-towner from several hours away, who rotates with other officers to spend a week at a time at this remote outpost.

We head across the street to José Falcon's Restaurant, one of two food joints in town. Lilia Falcon and her husband, Bernardo Rogel, greet us and quickly produce sweating Carta Blanca beers and fresh bean tacos smothered in

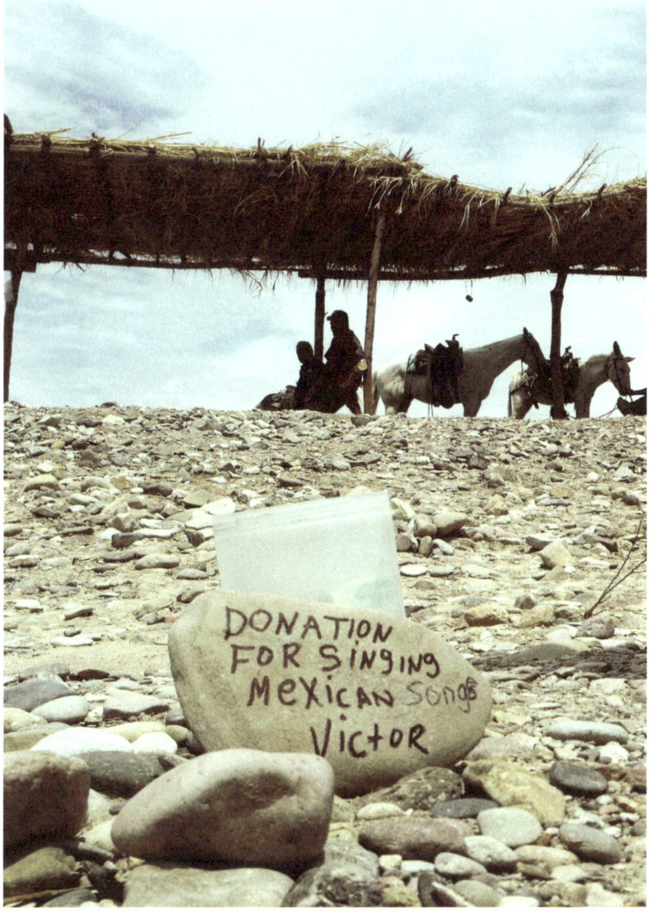
DONATION
FOR SINGING
MEXICAN Songs
Victor

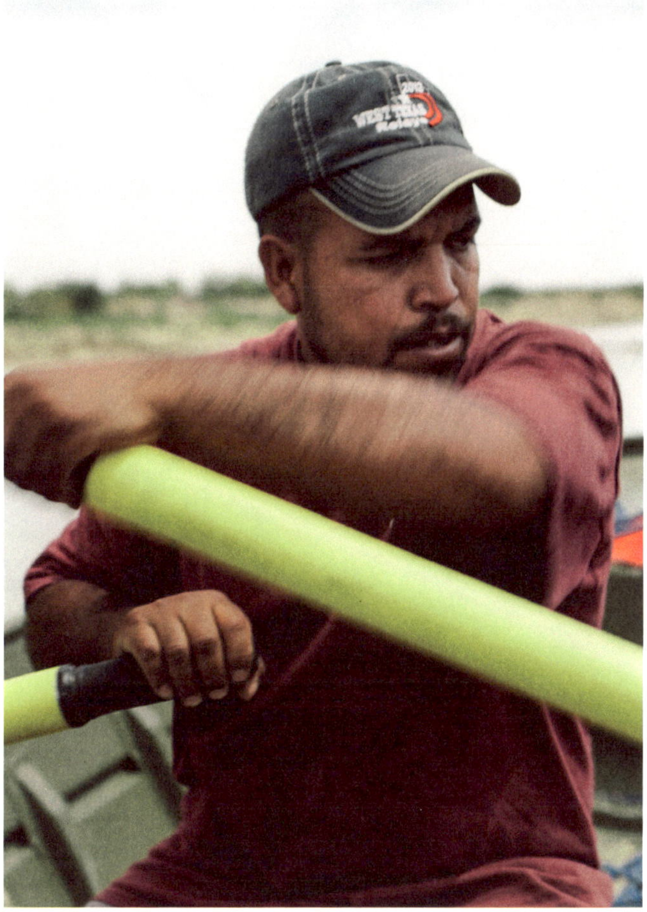

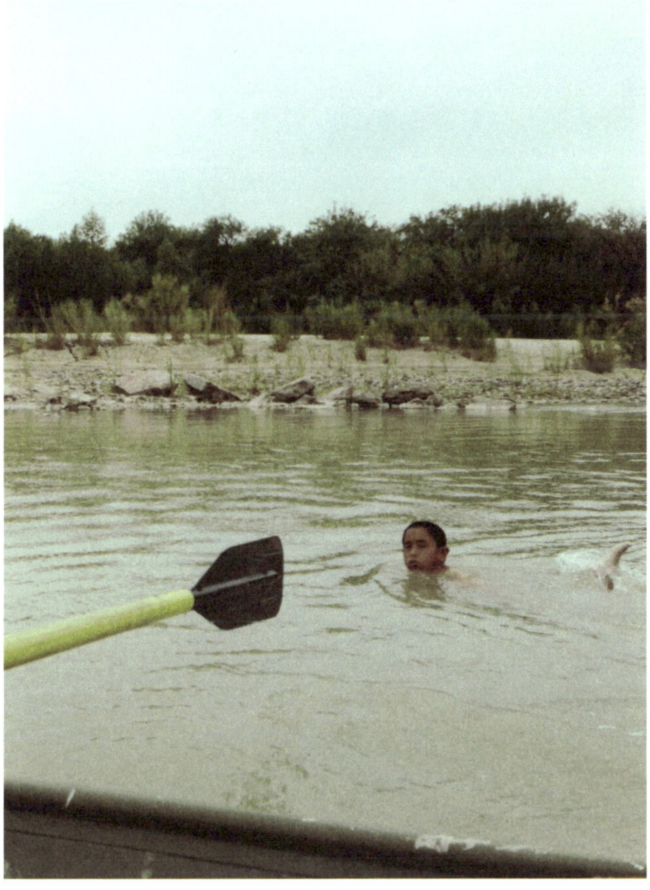

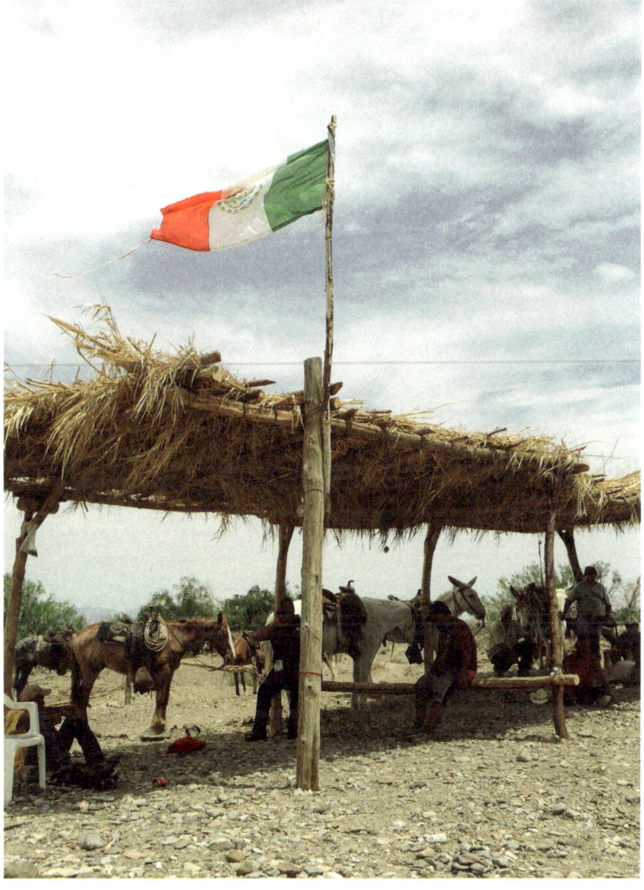

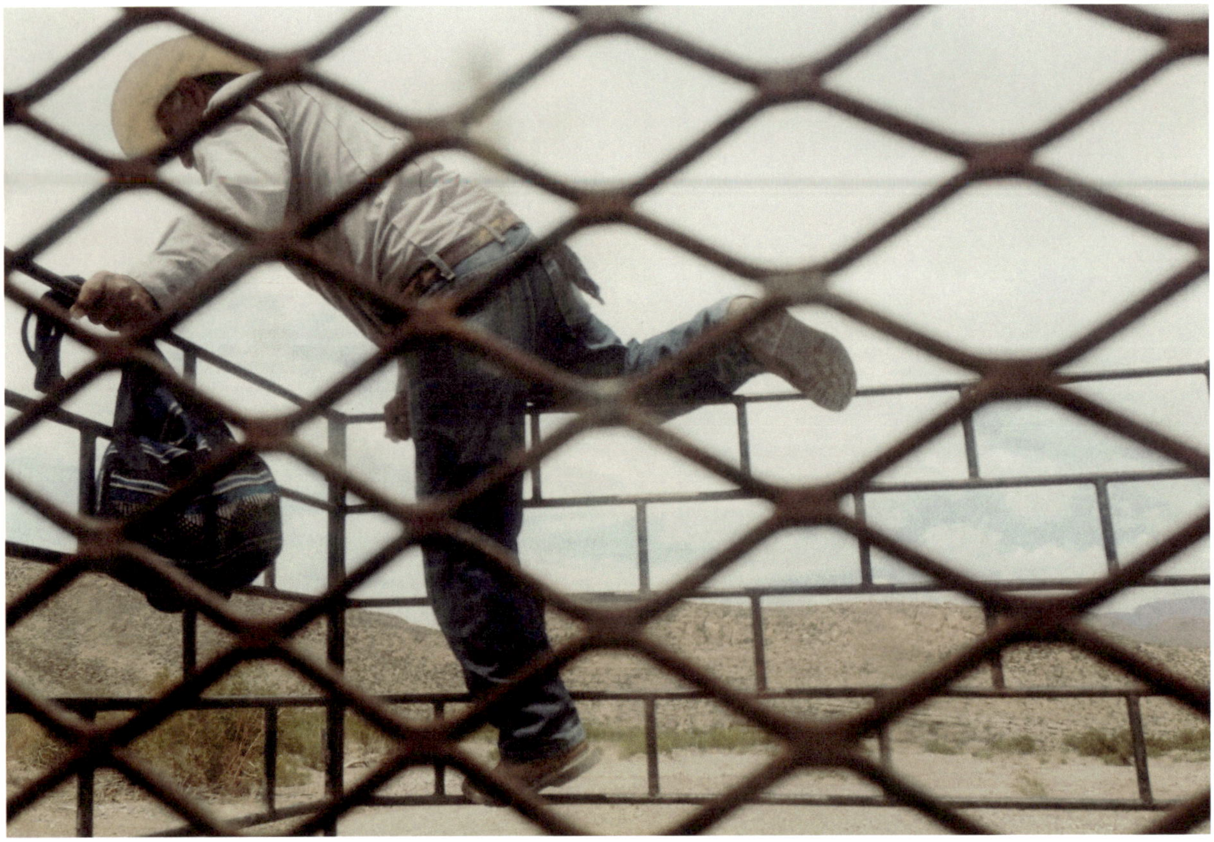

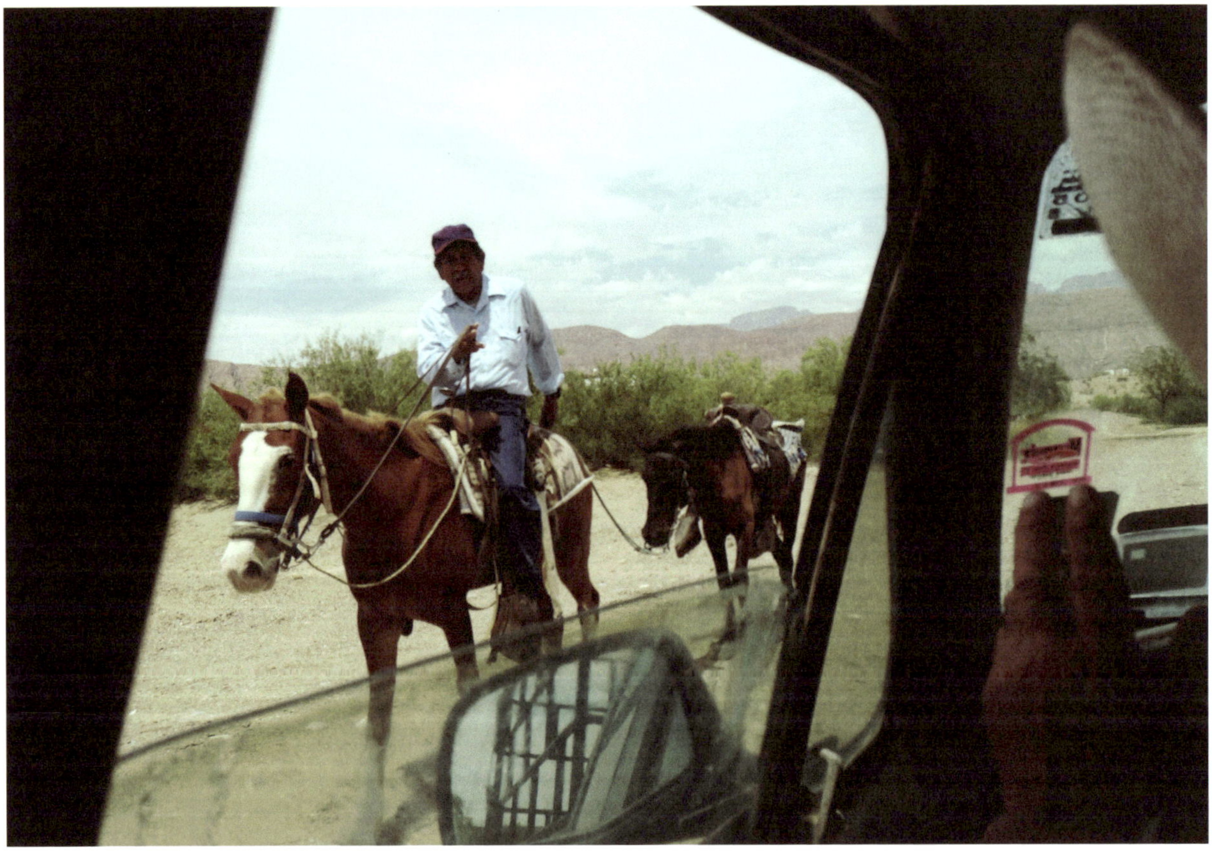

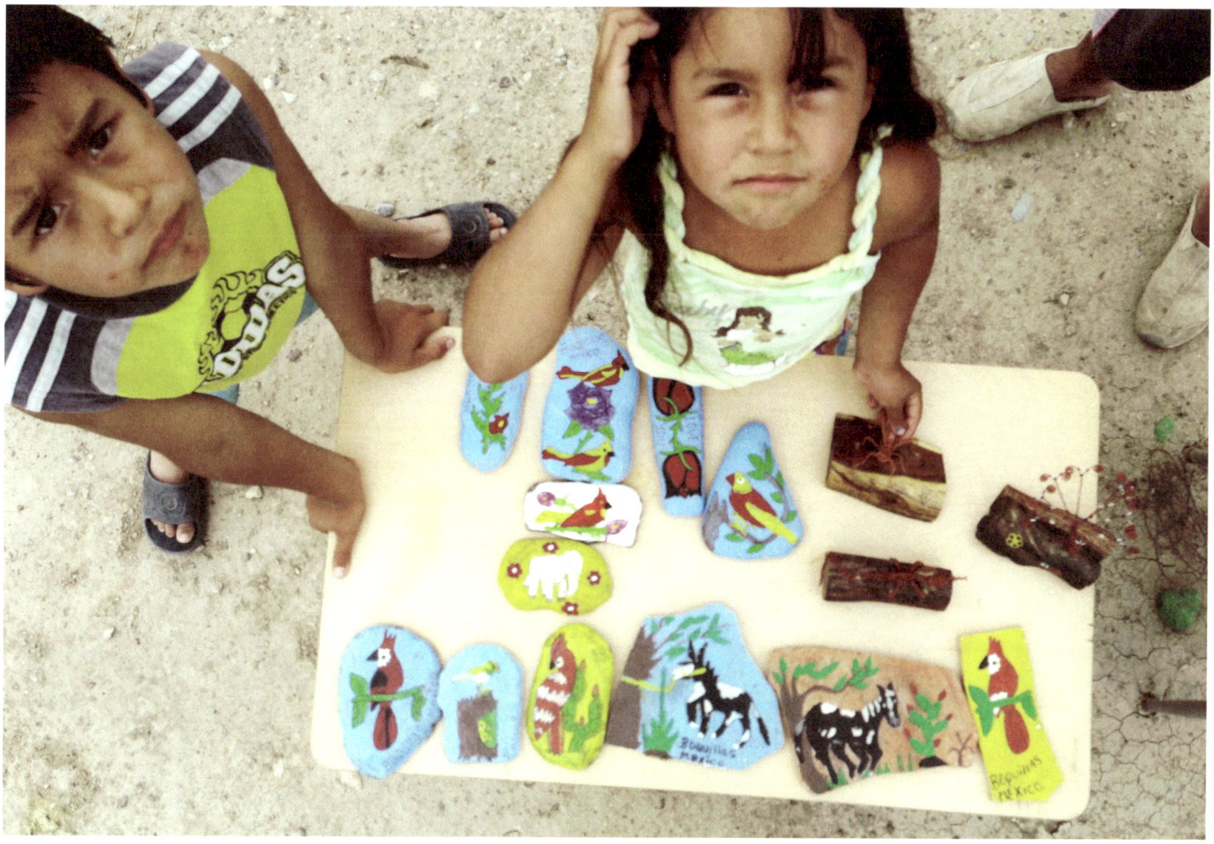

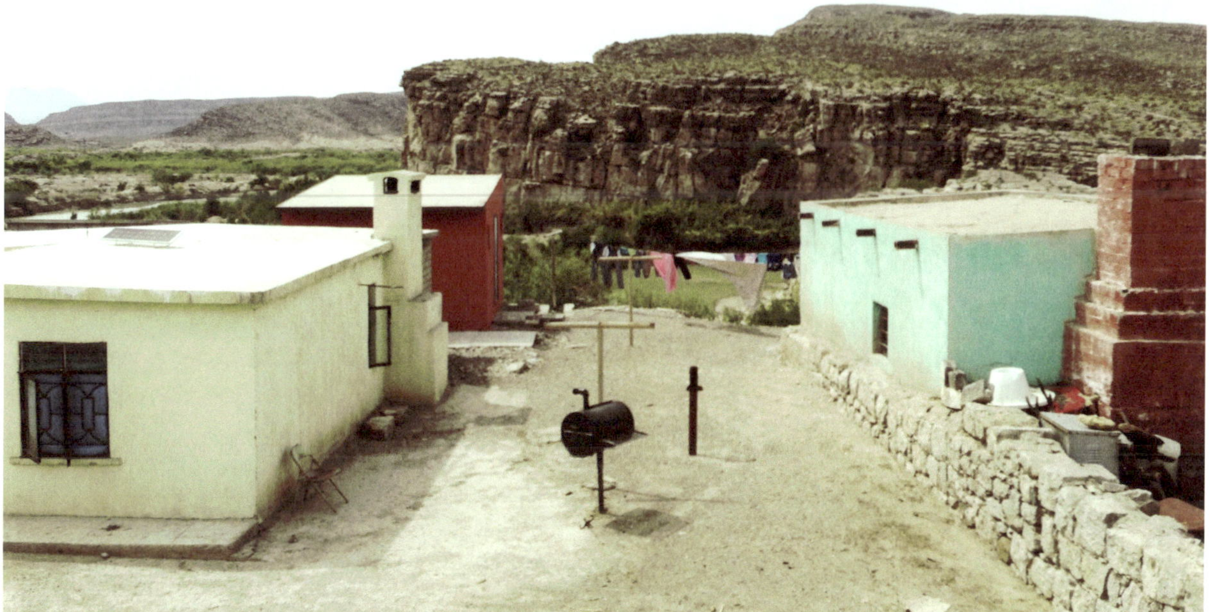

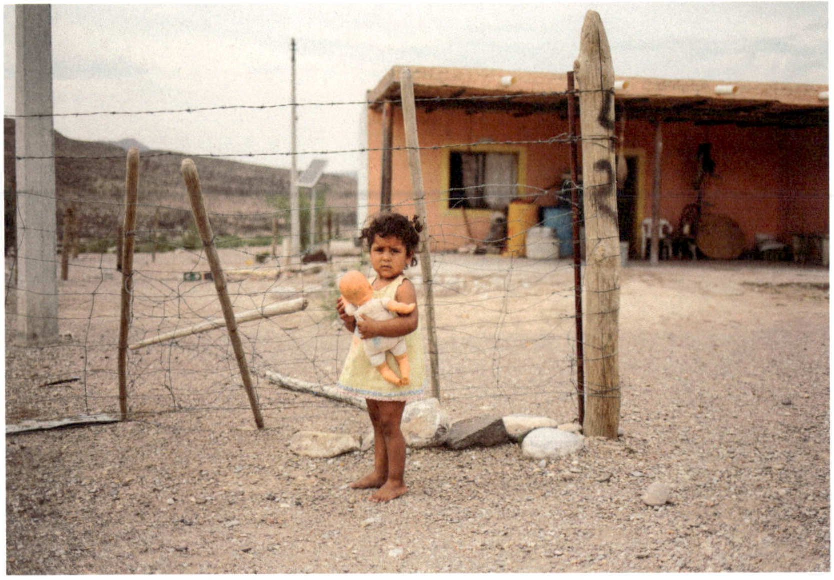

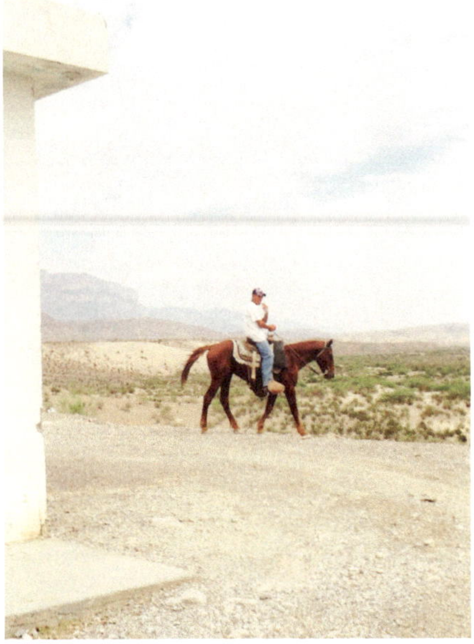

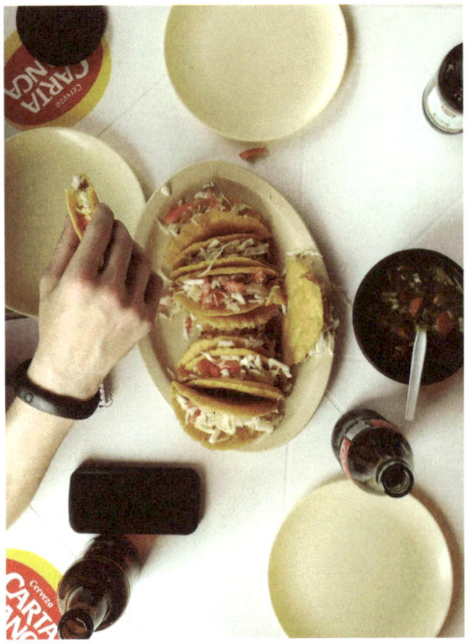

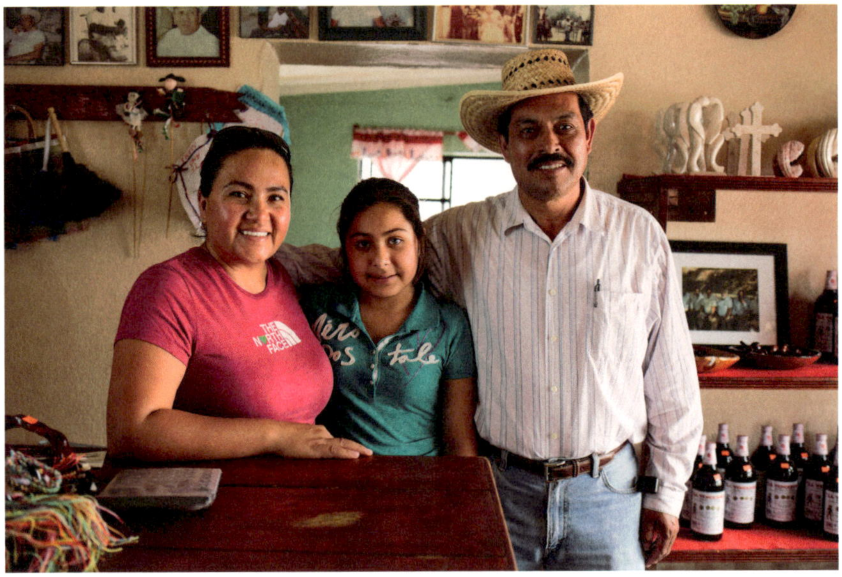

cheese and giardiniera. Falcon explains that she keeps the restaurant open as a tribute to her father, who established and operated it even while he was confined to a wheelchair until he died in 2000. She introduces us to her daughter Josie, who was born exactly a week after the planes crashed into the World Trade Center. The border closed the following May. For the entirety of her life, she's been unable to see the reason for her hometown's existence.

A bearded river guide named José Ernesto Hernadez Morales joins us for lunch. His neck is red from the sun, and a green fish-skeleton pendant is visible in the opening of his red polo. (His sign is Pisces, and he doesn't eat fish.) He's employed by both the Mexican and US governments through a consulting firm called Solimar International, and he's on assignment in Boquillas to help the village develop the tourism options into sandboarding, river kayaking, or hiking to Maderas de Carmen, an imposing, jagged rock face that offers unexplored territory.

The pueblo is a case study in the life and death of a frontier town. Accurate records are difficult to find, but Morales says that at Boquillas' height as a mining outpost at the turn of the 20th century, there were upwards of 2,000 people living there. At its lowest, perhaps three or four people remained. As the slim strains of gold and mercury dried up, the town's economy transitioned to cattle. But that export would never become particularly profitable, since the nearest market, a town called Múzquiz, is a 150-mile trek, a large part of which traverses washed-out river beds that pass for roads. Just before the US door clanged shut, Morales tells me, 300 people called Boquillas home. Now, there are about 135.

Everything here costs $5. The ride into town in the rusted out Ford? Cinco. The colorful, thread-wrapped ballpoint pens

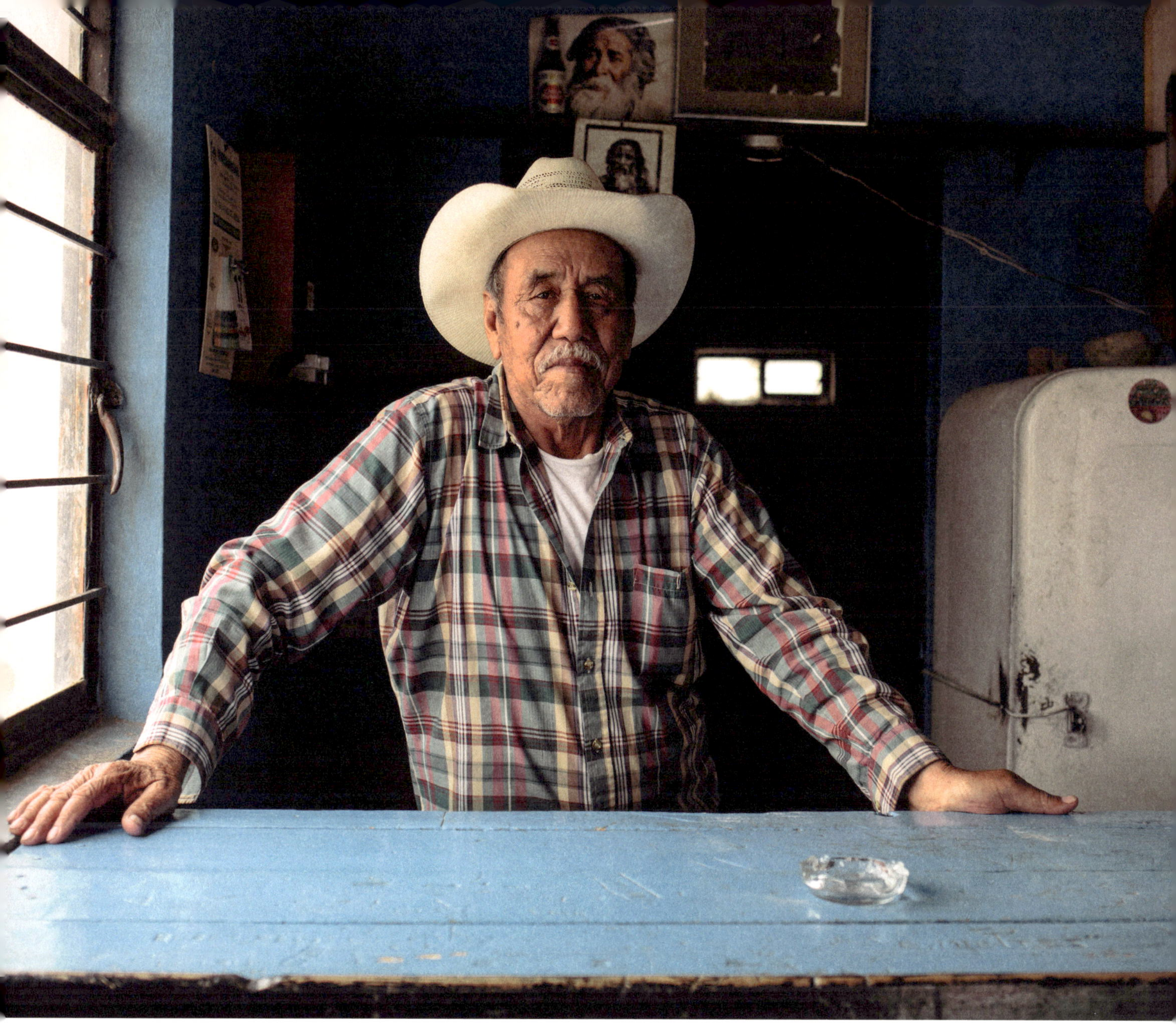

hawked by a gaggle of tanned children? Cinco. A wire scorpion sold by Singing Victor? Cinco. You could haggle. But you're there to spend money, not get a deal. Say the average visitor spends $20. That goes a long way in a town whose name is Spanish for "little mouths."

The talk turns to immigration. Sitting in the shade within eyeshot of the deadly blazing wilderness, I ask Morales what leads so many people to risk their lives crossing the border. "It's desperation," he says. "Going to Muzquiz is not an option because you have no skills and no education. If you cross the border, there is always the chance to make a dollar. You can do things that maybe Americans don't want to do anymore.".

After we finish our tacos, Duncan and I wander into the Park Bar, Boquillas' lone watering hole. Seventy-year-old Candelario Valdez, Victor's older brother, pours us shots of mescal as we eye the two pool tables. Based on their dusty, ripped felt, it looks like it's been a while since they last saw a break shot.

We glance at our watches: 5:50 p.m. Late for Victor's boat. Shooting the mescal, we careen out the door and sprint for the truck. Everyone we've met so far has been beyond hospitable, and if it came to it, we probably could find someone willing to put us up for the night. But by the look of the buildings we pass, abandoned and unfurnished, three beds might be hard to come by. Kevin appears from his walkabout, and the three of us barely make it back to the river in time to hop in the boat.

At the border station on the American side, an electronic kiosk awaits, with a telephone and a camera trained on our faces. We speak to a faceless border agent in El Paso, who asks us a few questions about what we did while we were abroad and whether we've brought anything back into the country. We answer that we haven't.

"Free to go," he says. Then he hangs up. – *S.P.*

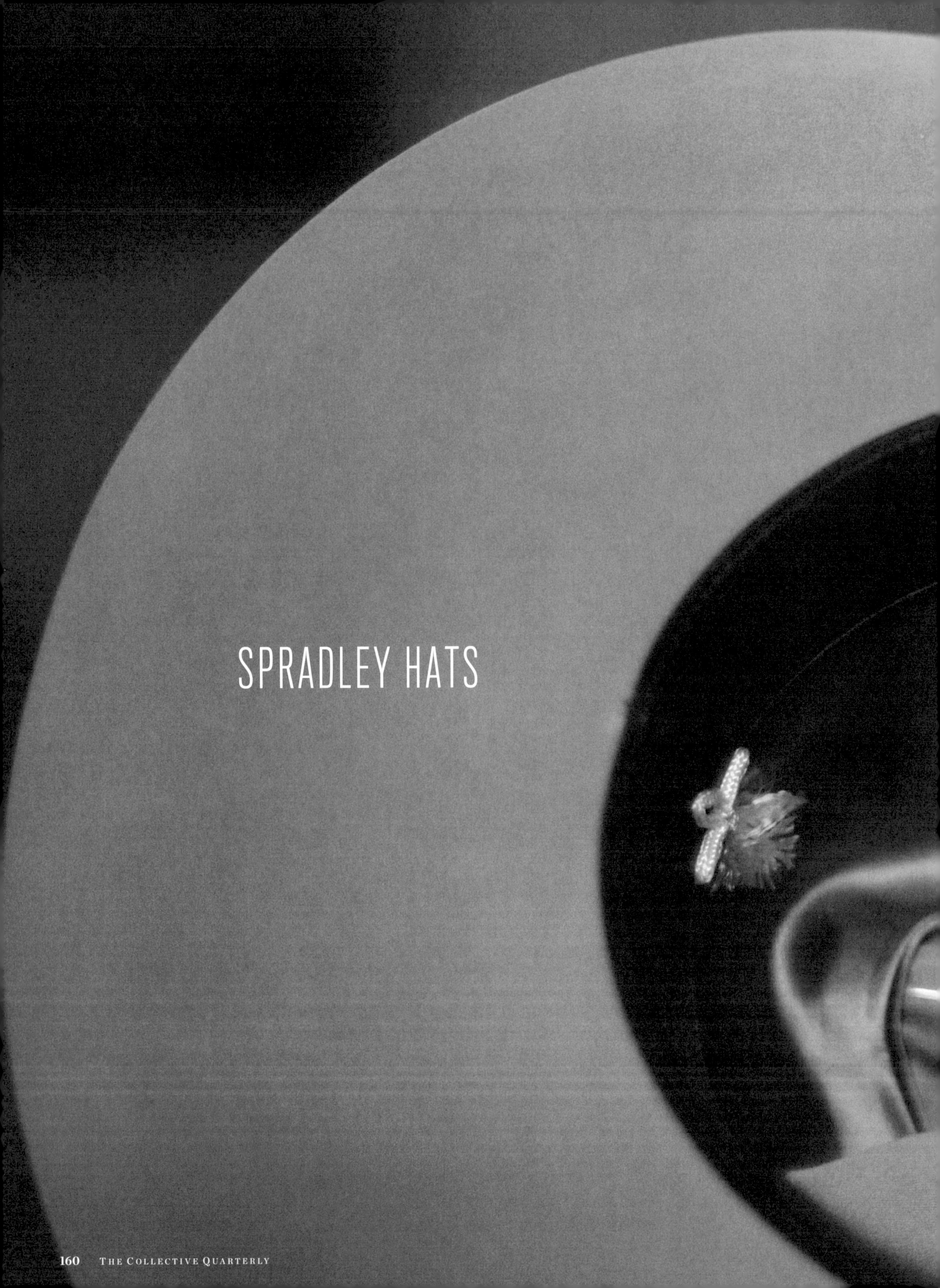

SPRADLEY HATS

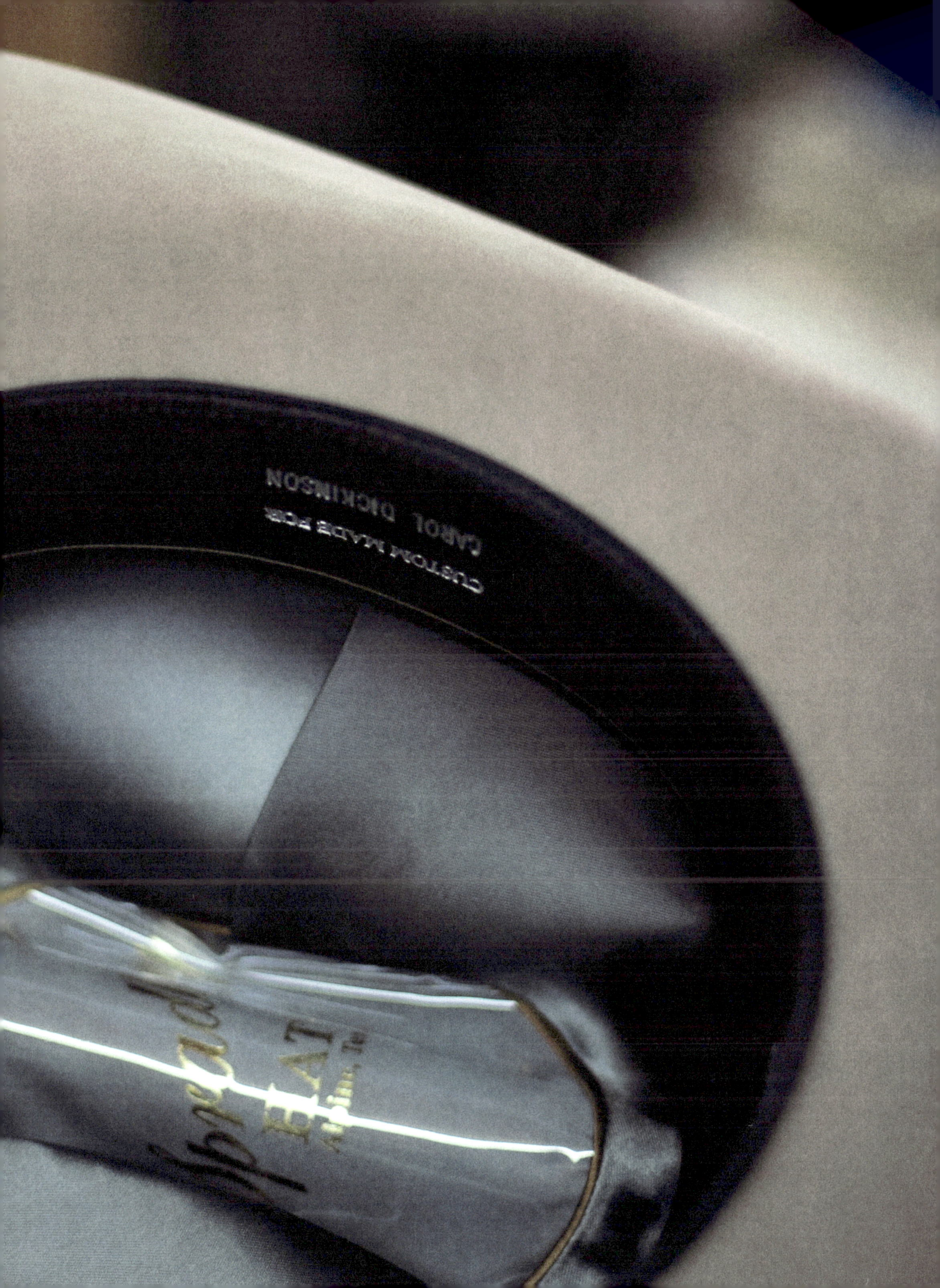
CUSTOM MADE FOR
CAROL DICKINSON

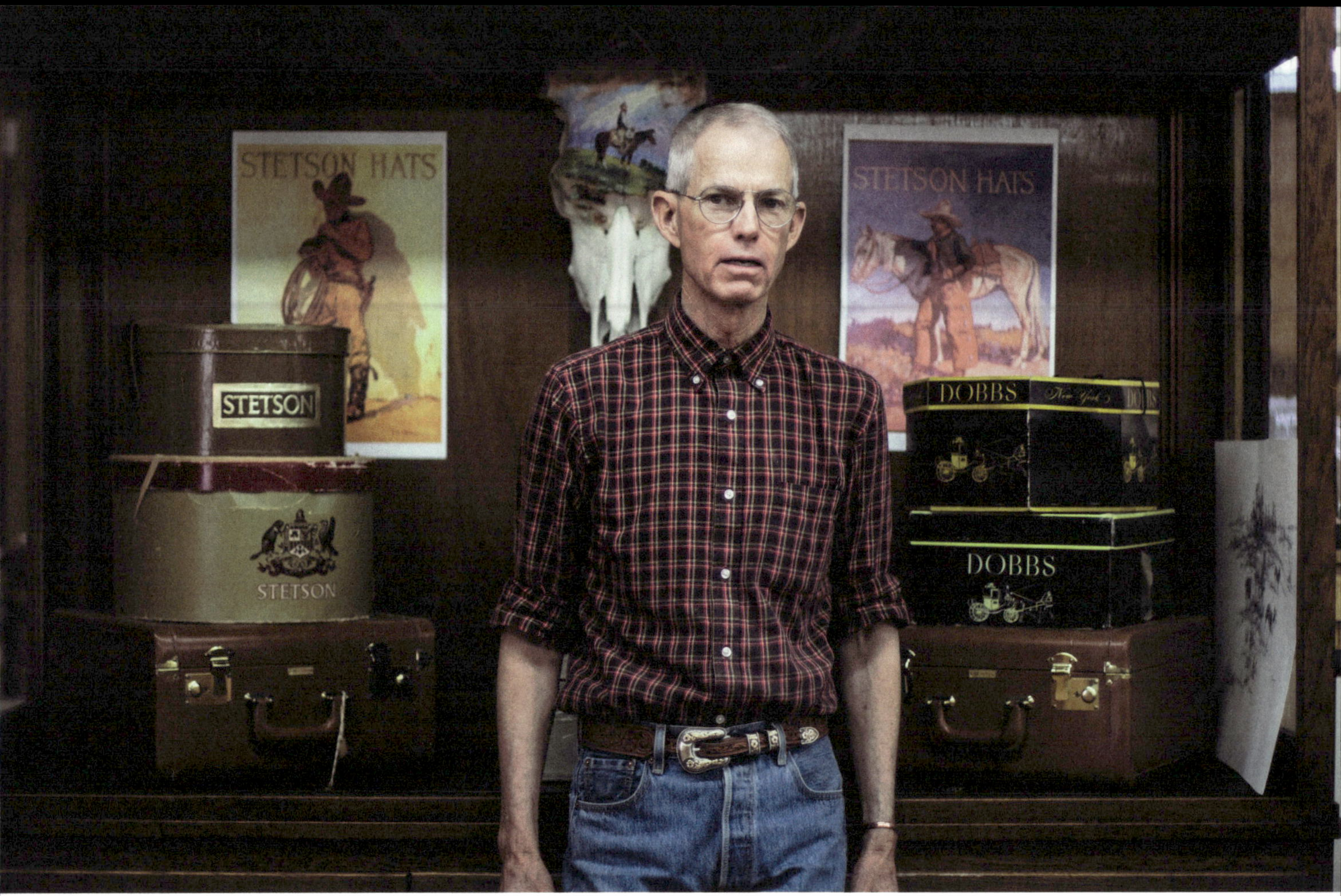

JIM SPRADLEY CAN BE DESCRIBED AS GOD-FEARING, humble, ornery, and a bit cool.

And why wouldn't he be? He's a man who respects his art form, a man who takes great care in the arduous process of turning a beaver pelt and into a hat suitable for cattlemen and cityfolk alike. He has a polite and pious nature, but he is careful to keep his distance. As the flow of tourism increases, with more and more city slickers rolling into to his small town of Alpine (population: 5,972), he's allowed to be skeptical. When asked to show how he makes a hat, he becomes wary.

"I'm not gonna show you that," Spradley says. "That's special. That's my process. We can talk hats all you want, but unless you're gonna buy something, I can't really talk about it."

Just then, a customer crouches to fit through the front door: a humongous, dust-covered cowboy in from a ranch nestled deep within the surrounding desert. His face is beet red and raccoon-tanned, burned by the sun's blaze. Pulling off a beat-up straw hat, he nods hello.

"Hey Jim, she ready?" he asks.

Without saying a word, Spradley scurries to a rack in the back of his shop, pulling off a drop cloth. "Wall-ah," he says, with a warbly drawl, more Paris, Texas, than Paris, France.

The cowboy flashes a lily white smile and affixes the stiff grey chapeau to his balding head. "Perfect," he says.

Spradley turns and declares, as though preaching: "You can't rush this. He was tryin' to get me to build this in a week. Thing took a month. When I build a hat, I really take my time."

After a bit of small talk—wives, grandkids, and the like—the giant rancher is back in the saddle, and Spradely has warmed up a bit.

"It's funny that I'm building hats, when 40 years ago I was selling 'em in a Western store to go to college, never, never thinkin' I'd ever do this," he once told a videographer who was making a short film about him. "I like working with my hands. I like picking up something and making it better than what it was when I got a hold of it."

Spradely has a deep reverence for the Lord, and believes he's called to be an imitator of Him. Building hats just happens to be the way he does that.

As for his comprehension of French? It goes deeper than you'd think. Spradley uses equipment made in Paris in the 1850s to size the customer's head.

The oval metal contraption, called "The Conformateur," with wires like the feet of a millipede, looks like something found in a Brooklyn steampunk shop.

When asked who his best clients are, he's been known to answer, simply: "All of 'em. Now, look: I've been asked if we've done anything for 'important people,' and I say the same thing: Every single one of 'em's 'important people.'"

Then, Spradley boils it down exactly the way you'd expect a Texan to do: "You come here because you just want a good hat. There's some good hatters out there. And hopefully, I'm one of 'em."

But he never reveals how he's one of 'em. The hats do that for him. – *M.W.*

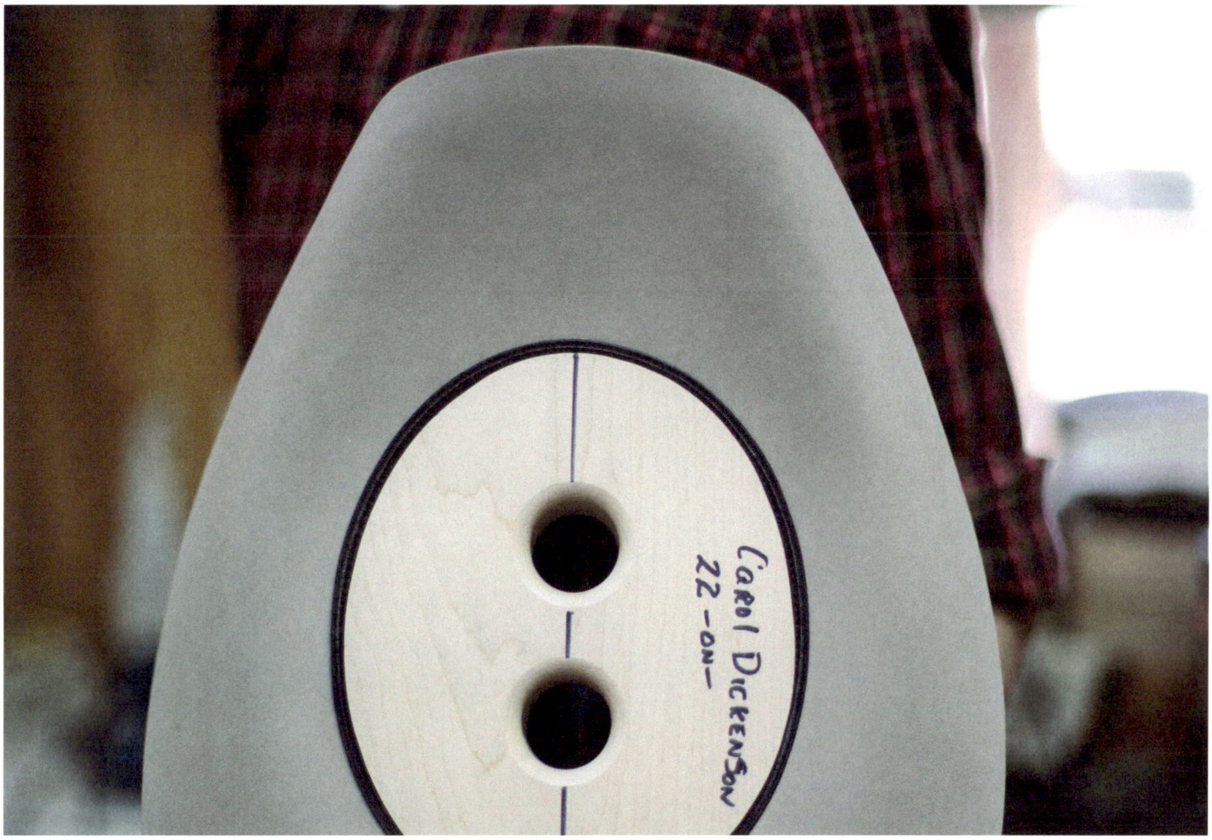
Carol Dickenson
22 -on-

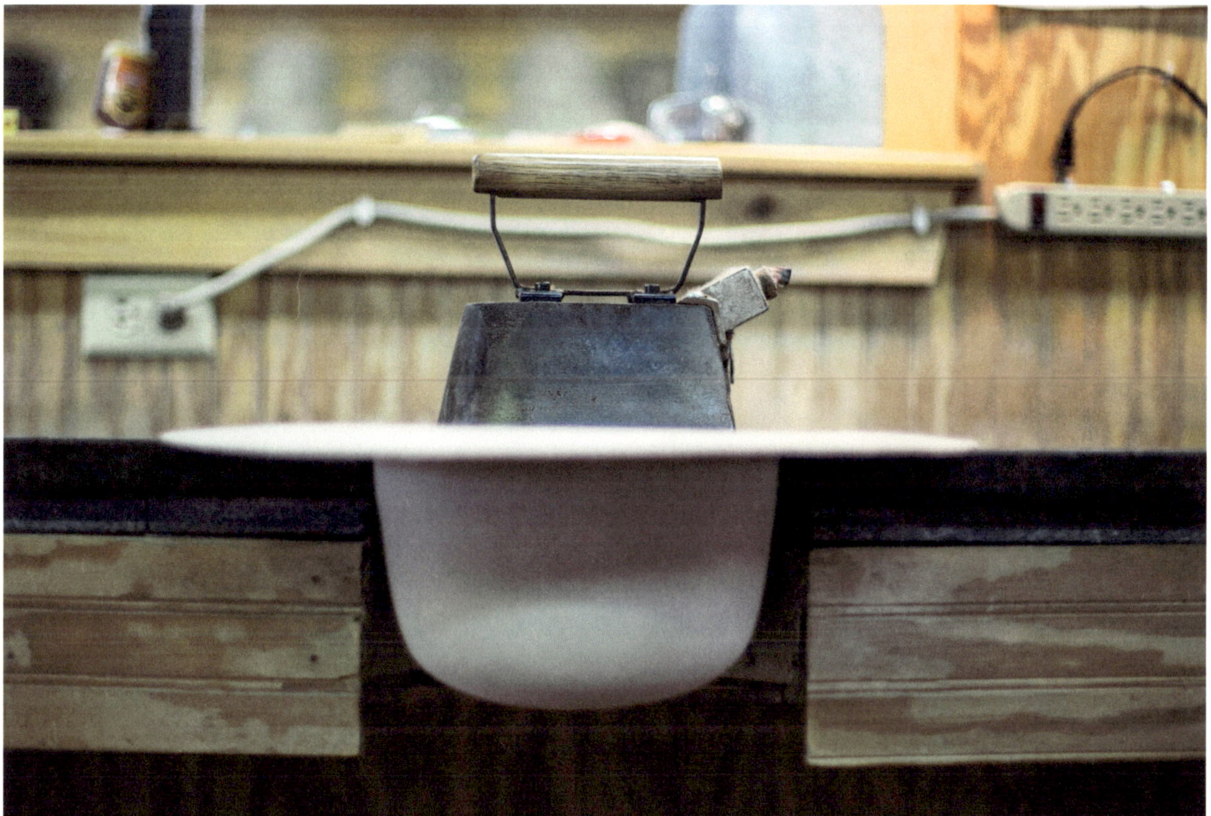

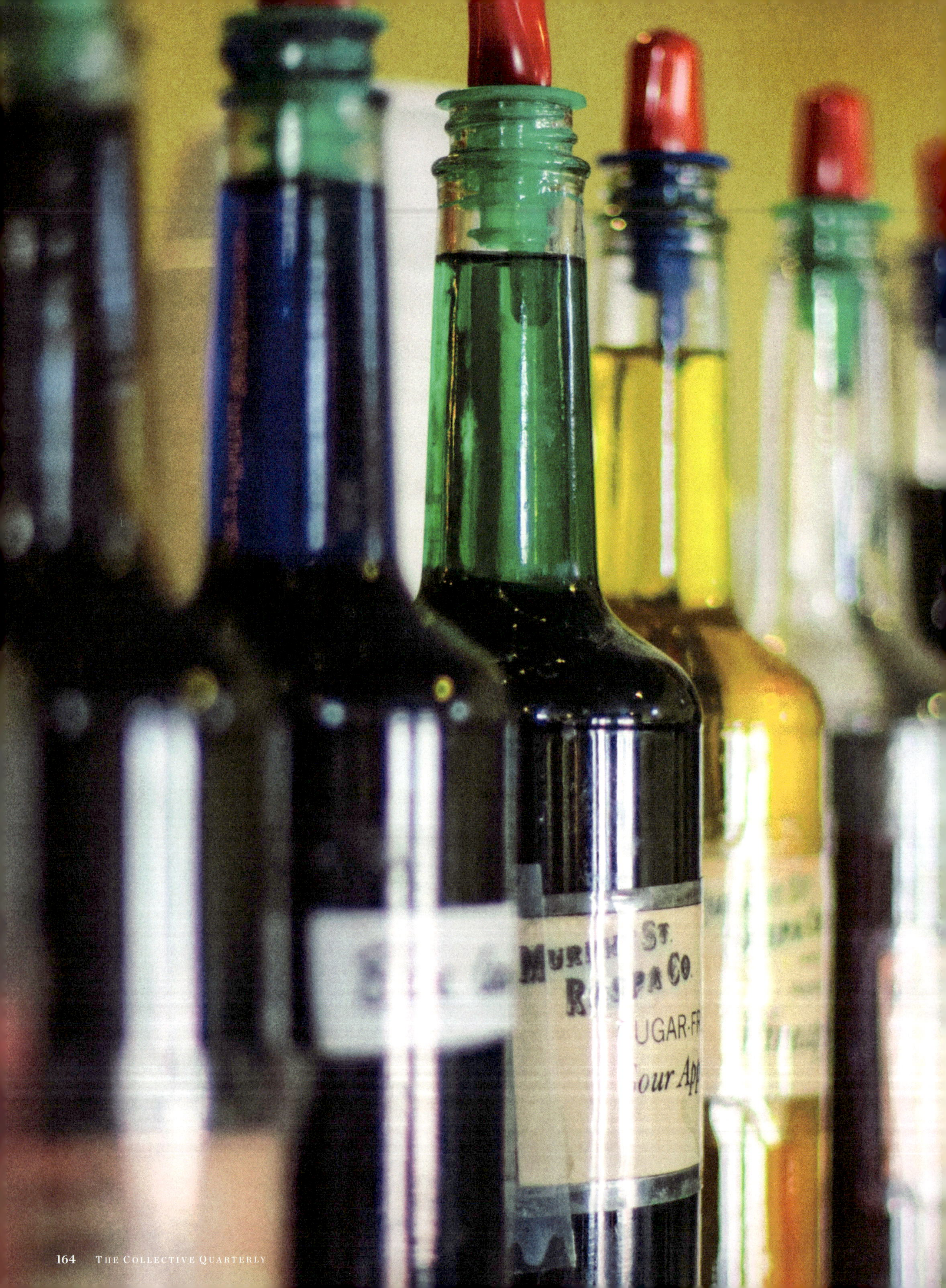

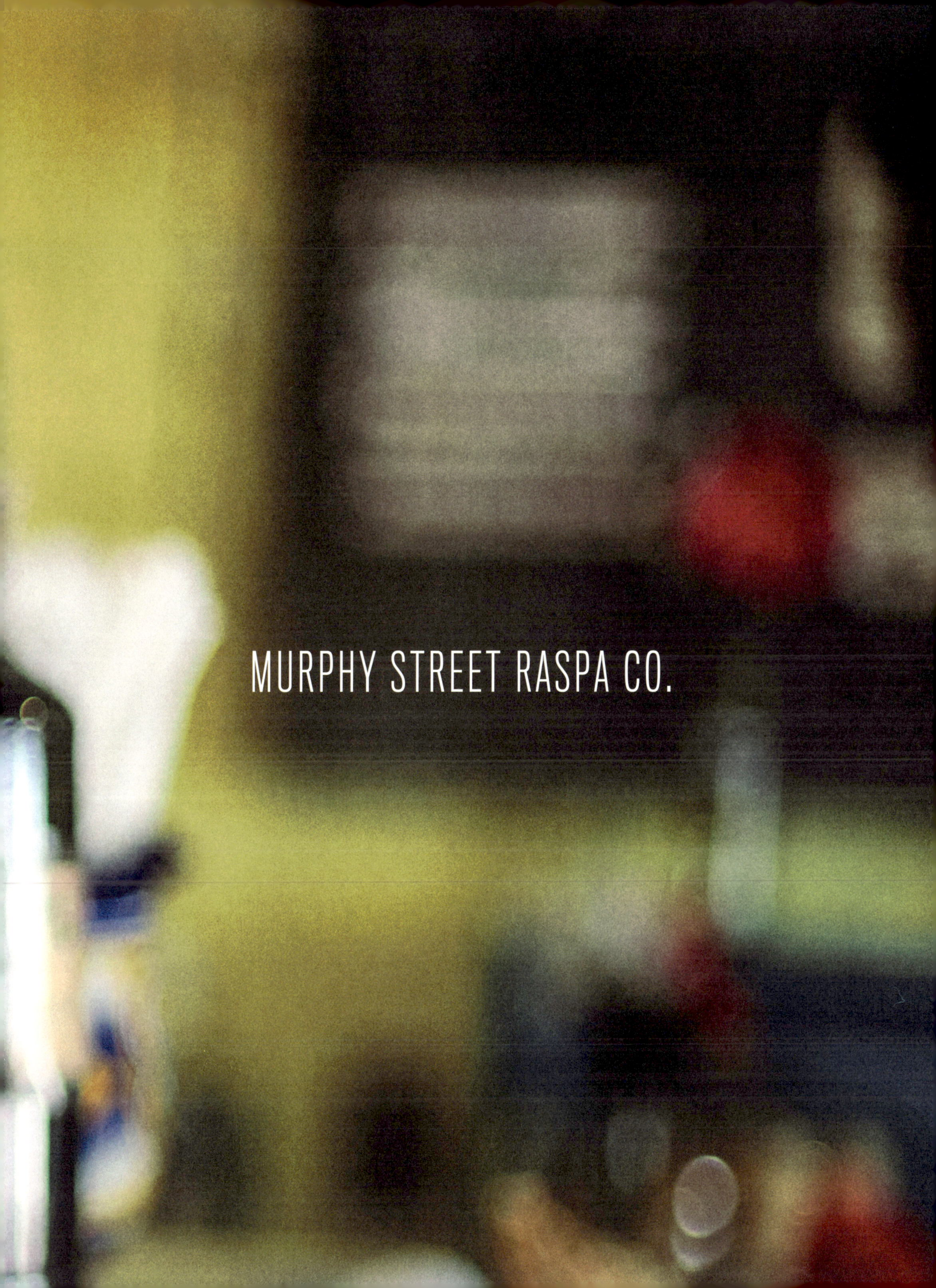

MURPHY STREET RASPA CO.

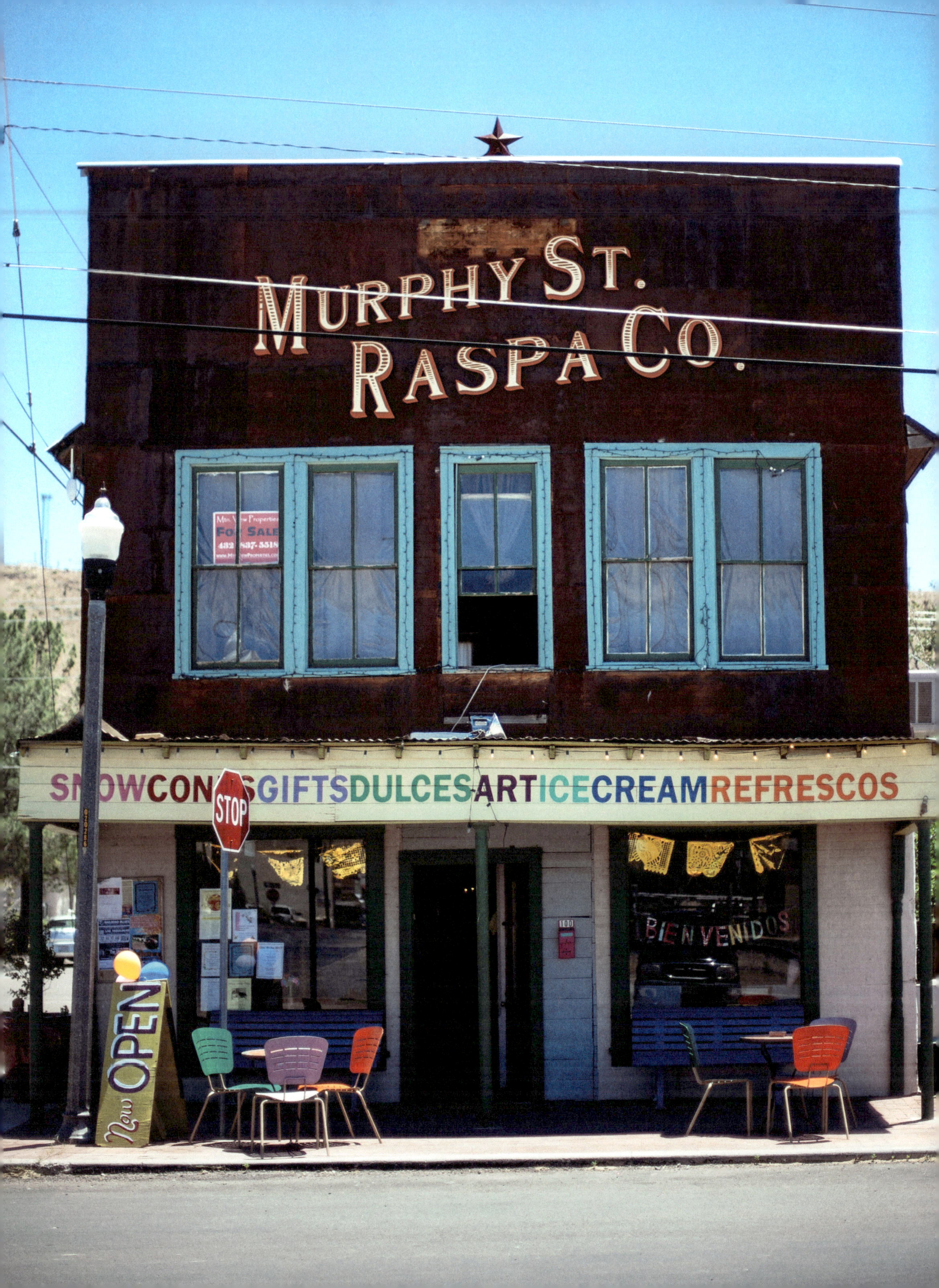
MURPHY ST.
RASPA CO.
FOR SALE
STOP
GIFTS DULCES ART ICE CREAM REFRESCOS
BIENVENIDOS
New OPEN

RASPA. IT'S SORT OF AN ODD MONIKER FOR A SNOW CONE, NO?

In Spanish, "raspar" means "to scrape," and as Murphy Street Raspa Co.'s owner Jessie Temple likes to tell it, "'Raspa' is so much more fun to say than 'shaved ice' or 'snow cone.'"

As fun as it is to say, her cold, cold raspas are just as fun to scarf. Starting with a block of solid ice, Jessie hand-cranks her SnoWizard machine, and fluffy white shaved ice shoots from the machine and into a cup.

A hot day in Alpine, Texas, has locals lining the block for Jessie's creations. I brought her a bottle of Basil Hayden's bourbon, and when she closed for the day, we whipped together her take on a Manhattan: cherry syrup, bourbon, chamoy—a spicy, Mexican pickled plum sauce—and, of course, plenty of scraped ice.

It was the chamoy that made it. As sweet as it was spicy, I craved the tart concoction all summer, and set to making my own version of the sweet, picante sauce. *–M.W.*

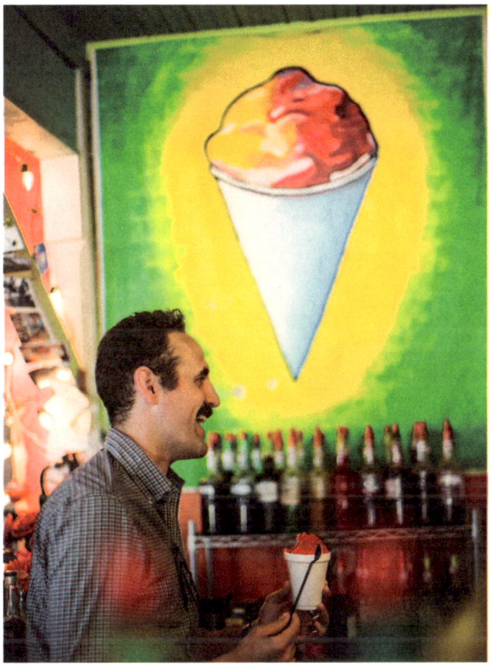

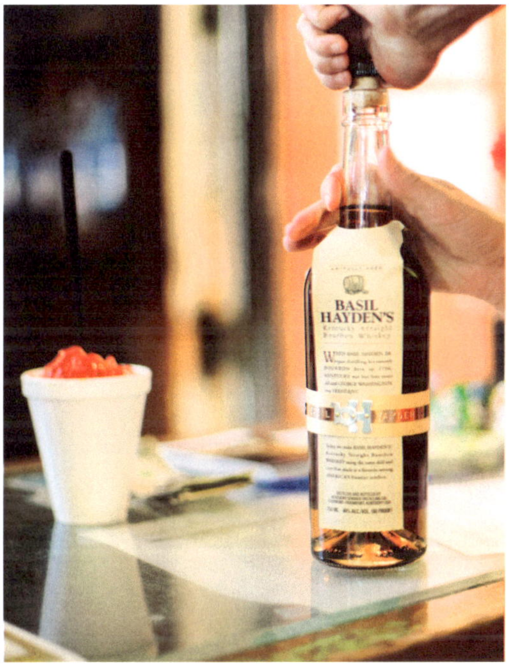

"ALPINE" CHAMOY

2 to 3	dried ancho chili peppers
1 cup	apricot jam
½ cup	lime juice
½ tsp	salt
⅓ cup	sugar

Let the ancho chilies sit in warm water for half an hour to soften. Once saturated, remove seeds and stems. Combine the rest of the ingredients in a blender until smooth.

MAX WASTLER'S MANHATTA-RASPA

1½ parts	Basil Hayden's bourbon
½ part	sweet vermouth
½ part	dry vermouth
½ part	maple syrup
2 dashes	Angostura bitters
2 tsp	"Alpine" chamoy

Combine ingredients and shake in a cocktail tin with ice. Pour over crushed or shaved ice and garnish with a cherry. Spicy.

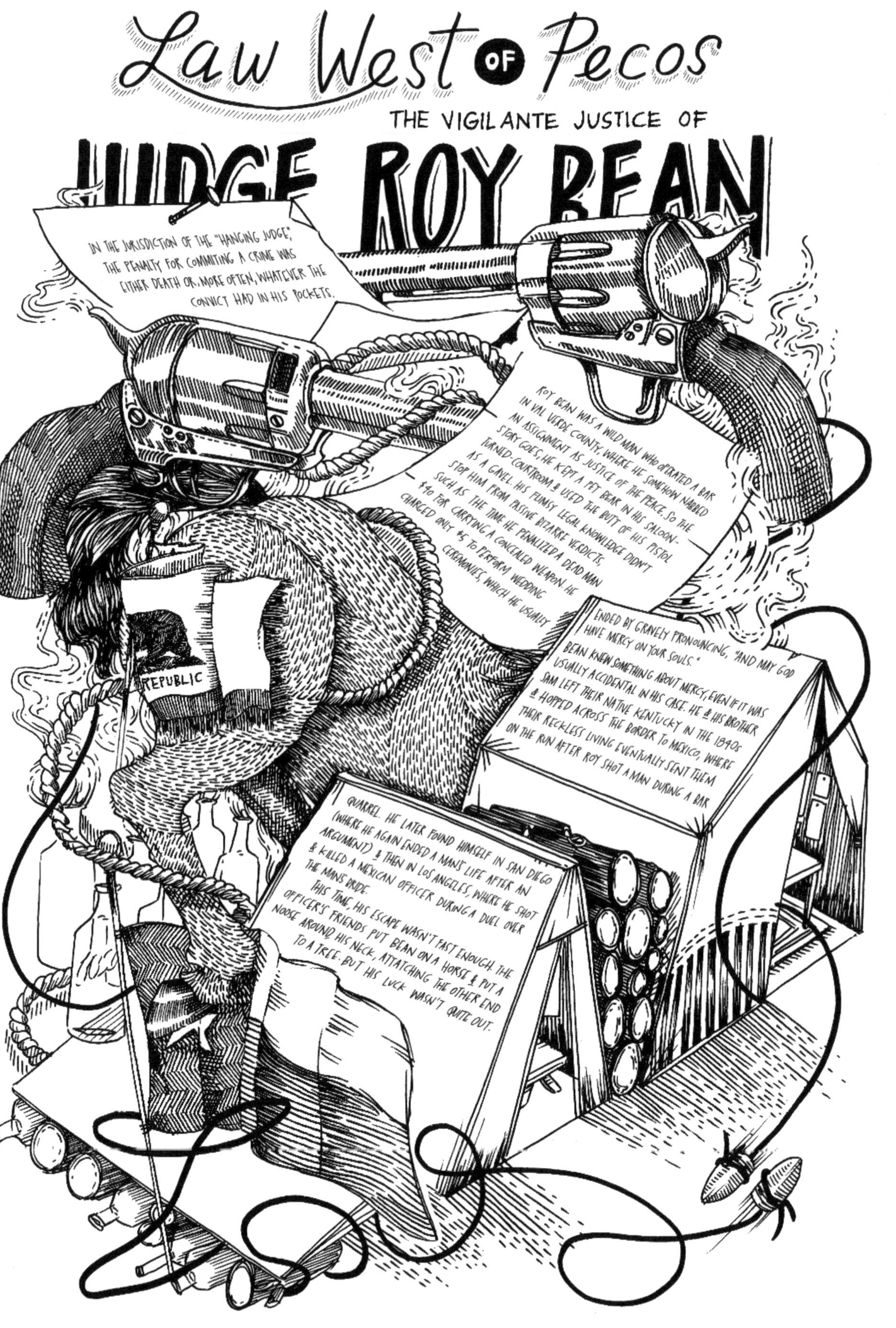

Law West of Pecos
THE VIGILANTE JUSTICE OF
JUDGE ROY BEAN
IN THE JURISDICTION OF THE "HANGING JUDGE," THE PENALTY FOR COMMITING A CRIME WAS EITHER DEATH OR, MORE OFTEN, WHATEVER THE CONVICT HAD IN HIS POCKETS.
ROY BEAN WAS A WILD MAN WHO OPERATED A BAR IN VAL VERDE COUNTY, WHERE HE SOMEHOW NABBED AN ASSIGNMENT AS JUSTICE OF THE PEACE. SO THE STORY GOES, HE KEPT A PET BEAR IN HIS SALOON-TURNED-COURTROOM & USED THE BUTT OF HIS PISTOL AS A GAVEL. HIS FLIMSY LEGAL KNOWLEDGE DIDN'T STOP HIM FROM PASSING BIZARRE VERDICTS, SUCH AS THE TIME HE PENALIZED A DEAD MAN $40 FOR CARRYING A CONCEALED WEAPON. HE CHARGED ONLY $5 TO PERFORM WEDDING CEREMONIES, WHICH HE USUALLY
ENDED BY GRAVELY PRONOUNCING, "AND MAY GOD HAVE MERCY ON YOUR SOULS."
BEAN KNEW SOMETHING ABOUT MERCY, EVEN IF IT WAS USUALLY ACCIDENTAL IN HIS CASE. HE & HIS BROTHER SAM LEFT THEIR NATIVE KENTUCKY IN THE 1840s & HOPPED ACROSS THE BORDER TO MEXICO, WHERE THEIR RECKLESS LIVING EVENTUALLY SENT THEM ON THE RUN AFTER ROY SHOT A MAN DURING A BAR
QUARREL. HE LATER FOUND HIMSELF IN SAN DIEGO (WHERE HE AGAIN ENDED A MAN'S LIFE AFTER AN ARGUMENT) & THEN IN LOS ANGELES, WHERE HE SHOT & KILLED A MEXICAN OFFICER DURING A DUEL OVER THE MAN'S BRIDE.
THIS TIME, HIS ESCAPE WASN'T FAST ENOUGH. THE OFFICER'S FRIENDS PUT BEAN ON A HORSE & PUT A NOOSE AROUND HIS NECK, ATTACHING THE OTHER END TO A TREE. BUT HIS LUCK WASN'T QUITE OUT.
REPUBLIC

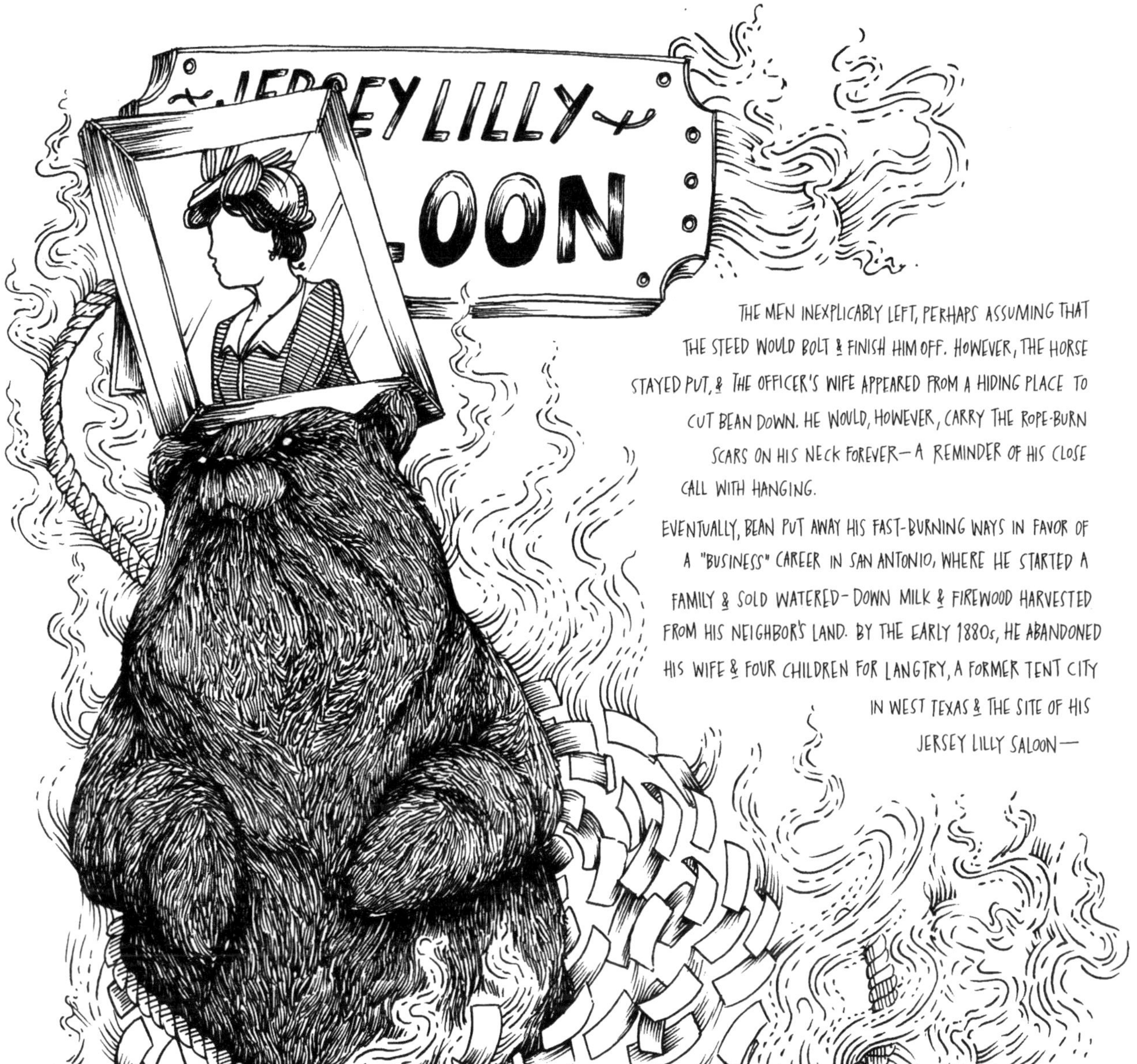

THE MEN INEXPLICABLY LEFT, PERHAPS ASSUMING THAT THE STEED WOULD BOLT & FINISH HIM OFF. HOWEVER, THE HORSE STAYED PUT, & THE OFFICER'S WIFE APPEARED FROM A HIDING PLACE TO CUT BEAN DOWN. HE WOULD, HOWEVER, CARRY THE ROPE-BURN SCARS ON HIS NECK FOREVER—A REMINDER OF HIS CLOSE CALL WITH HANGING.

EVENTUALLY, BEAN PUT AWAY HIS FAST-BURNING WAYS IN FAVOR OF A "BUSINESS" CAREER IN SAN ANTONIO, WHERE HE STARTED A FAMILY & SOLD WATERED-DOWN MILK & FIREWOOD HARVESTED FROM HIS NEIGHBOR'S LAND. BY THE EARLY 1880s, HE ABANDONED HIS WIFE & FOUR CHILDREN FOR LANGTRY, A FORMER TENT CITY IN WEST TEXAS & THE SITE OF HIS JERSEY LILLY SALOON—

BOTH OF WHICH HE CLAIMED HE NAMED AFTER FALLING IN LOVE WITH A PICTURE OF A BRITISH ACTRESS NAMED LILLIE LANGTRY.

IN THE END, THE "HANGING JUDGE" ONLY SENT TWO MEN TO THE GALLOWS, & ONE OF THEM ESCAPED. BEAN DIED IN 1903, SOME SAY AFTER BEING GUNNED DOWN ON THE STEPS OF HIS SALOON BY A MEXICAN OUTLAW. OTHERS SAY THAT HE SIMPLY WENT ON A DRINKING SPREE IN DEL RIO & DIED IN HIS SLEEP. IN A TWIST OF FATE, LILLIE LANGTRY FINALLY VISITED HER NAMESAKE TOWN, BUT 10 MONTHS TOO LATE FOR BEAN TO MEET HER.

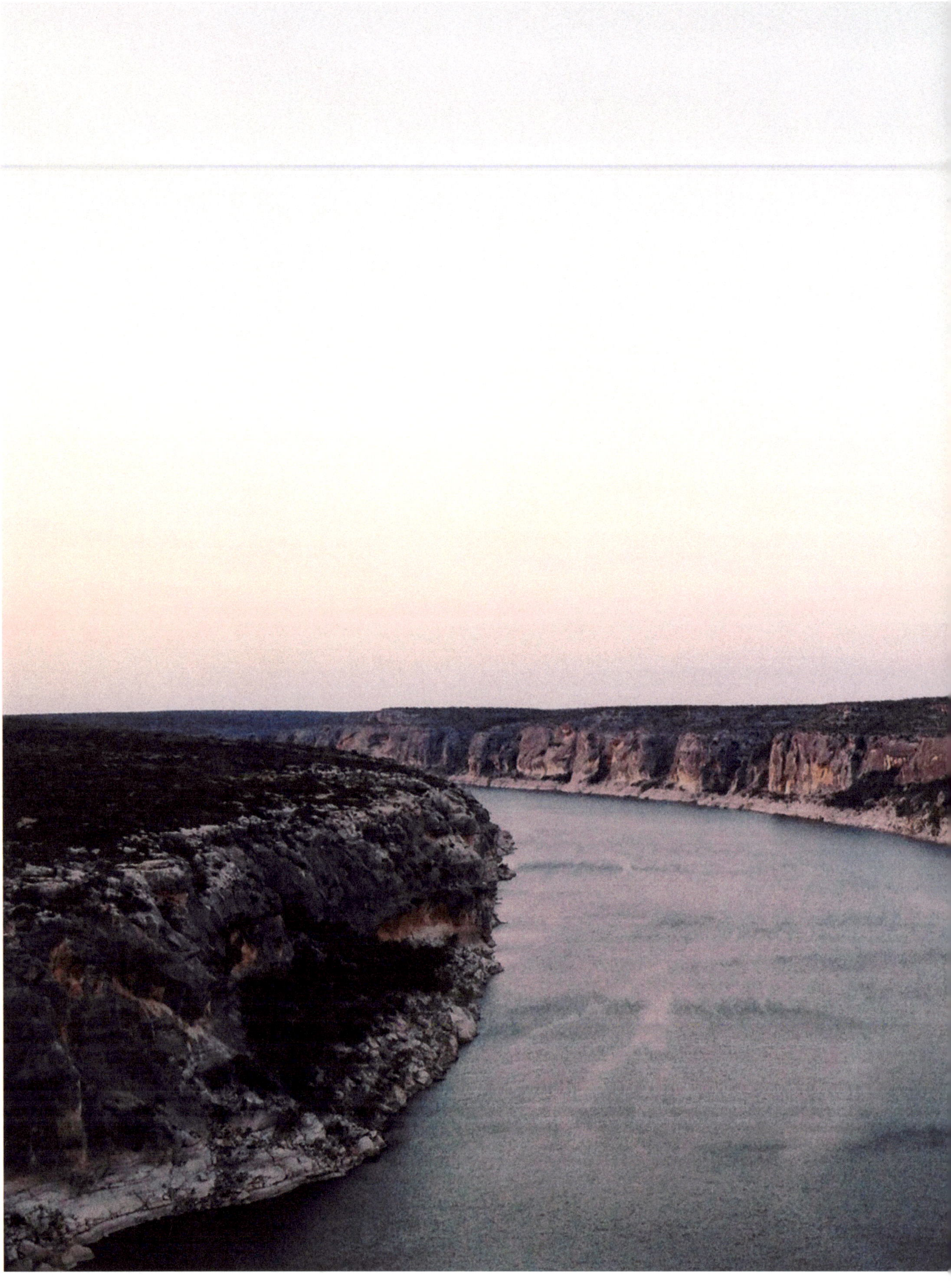

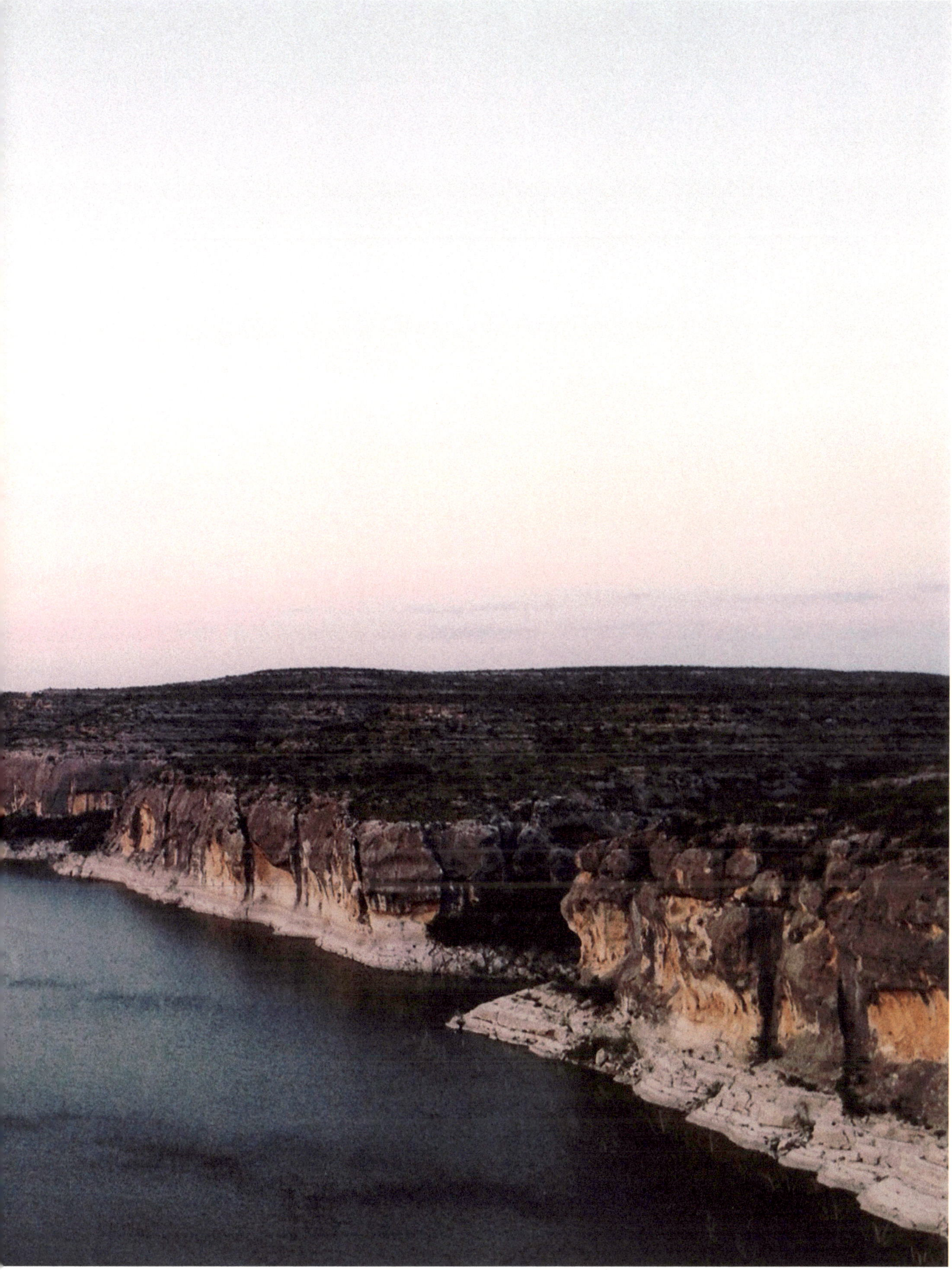

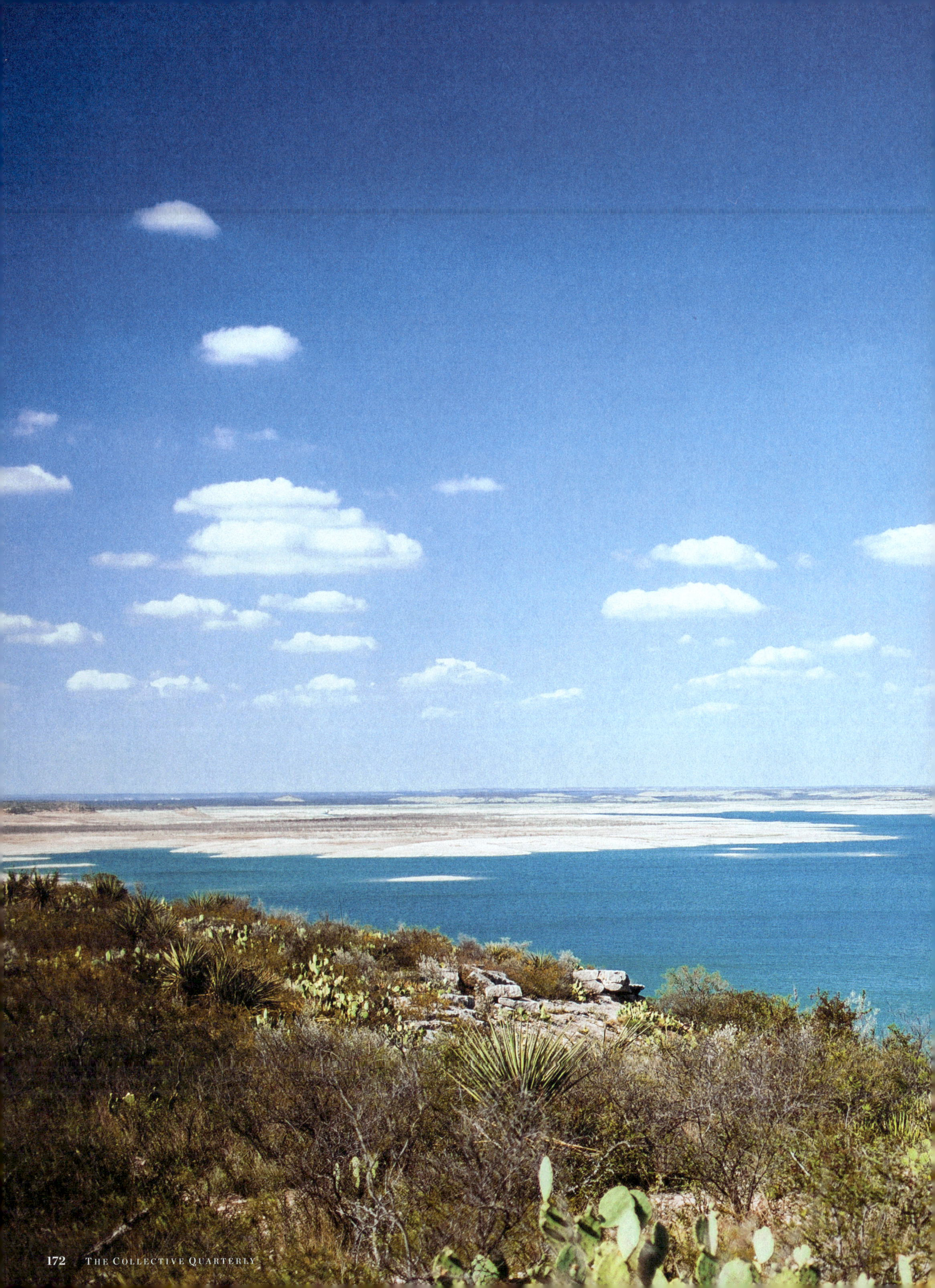

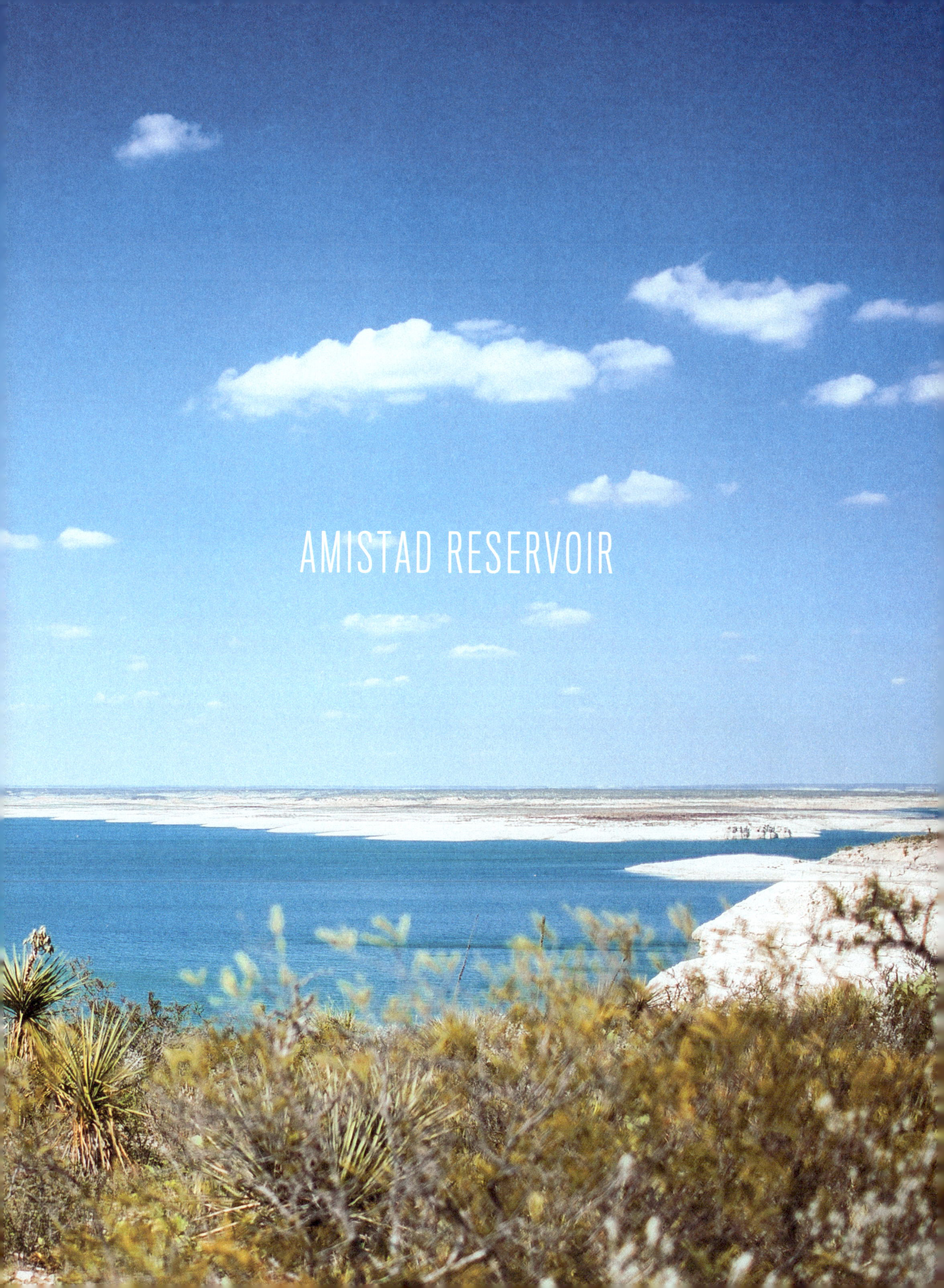
AMISTAD RESERVOIR

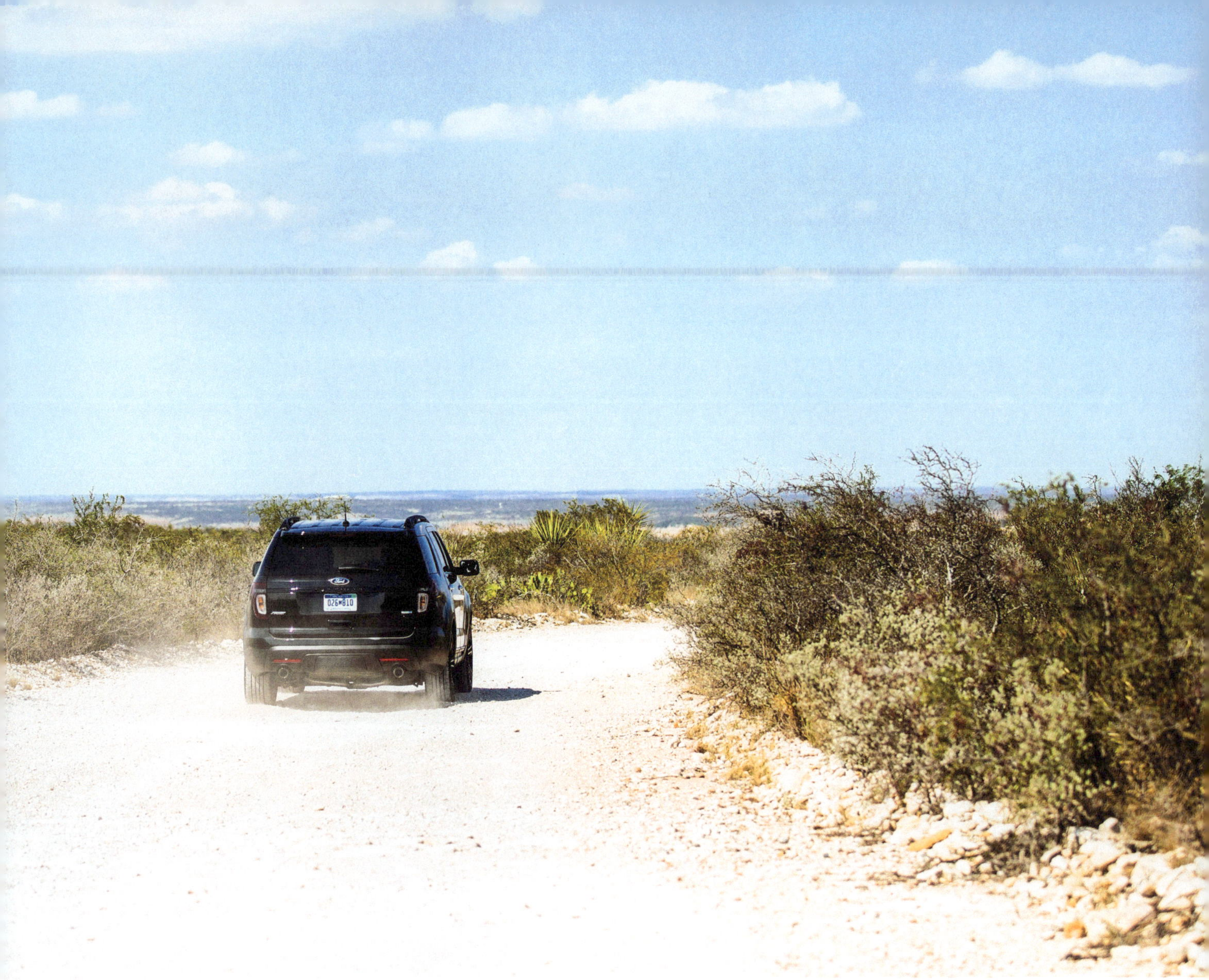

HIGHWAY 90 STRETCHED AHEAD OF US, COVERED IN dust and heat.

It was a few hours after the incident at Nora's Tacos, and we were motoring to the sounds of the Eagles, Willie Nelson, and Dwight Yoakam. We had grown quiet, hypnotized by the road and the way it snaked along the desolate Mexican border.

Suddenly out the window, our eyes caught a tinge of blue rising out of the scorched earth. The shock of color we had just seen disappeared quickly beneath a ridge, as if it were a mirage. But convinced that what we had seen was real, we pulled over and consulted the map.

It showed a giant lake just ahead, straddling the border. With Texas on one side and Coahuila on the other, the US and Mexican governments jointly own the giant basin. They built a dam where the Devil's River meets the Rio Grand and flooded the reservoir in order to provide power and recreation for the surrounding areas. Fittingly, they named it Amistad, the Spanish word for "friendship."

We drove farther, searching for a way to get close to the water. Slowly, the color reappeared: a 65,000-acre oasis sprawling out in front of us. The azure blue water beckoned through the heat. The contrast was stark against the blinding white cliffs.

Hopping out of the car, we hiked past signs warning visitors to dive off the cliffs at their own risk. After exploring the area thoroughly, we kicked off our shoes and tossed our shirts in a pile. We tiptoed toward the precipice and peered over the edge at the water 40 feet below.

There was nothing left to do but jump. *–S.P.*

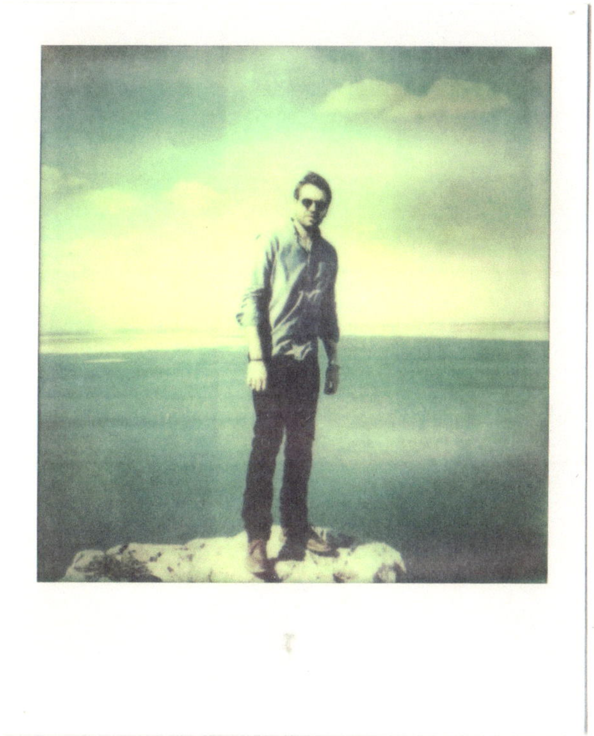

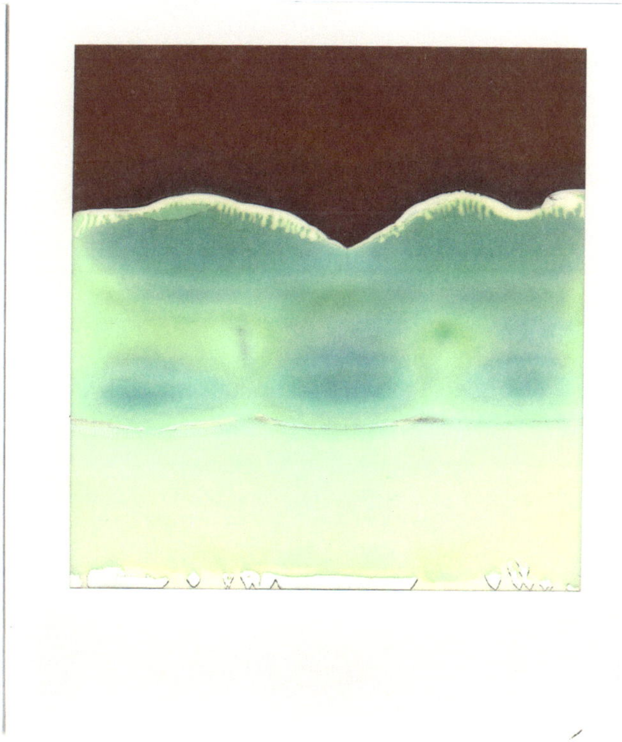

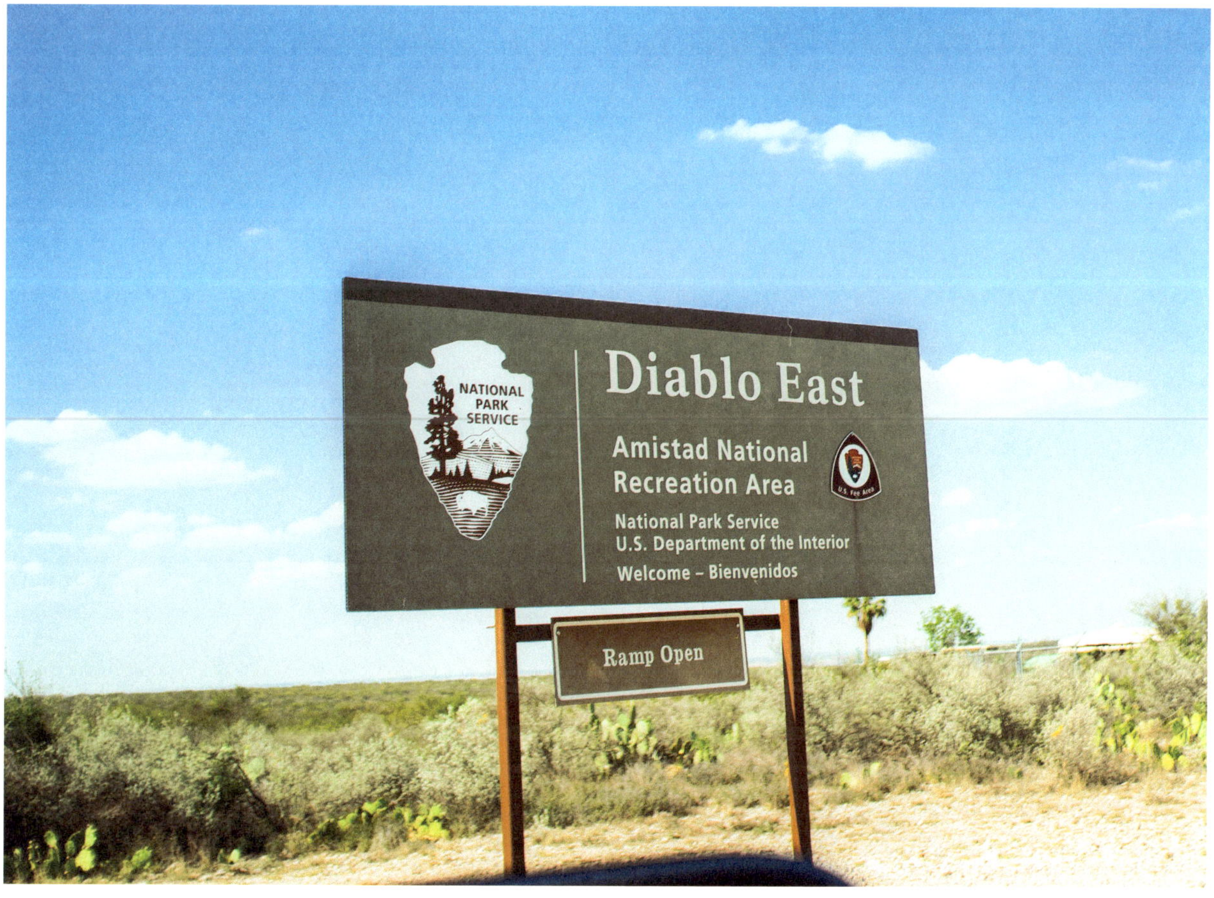
NATIONAL PARK SERVICE
Diablo East
Amistad National Recreation Area
National Park Service
U.S. Department of the Interior
Welcome – Bienvenidos
Ramp Open

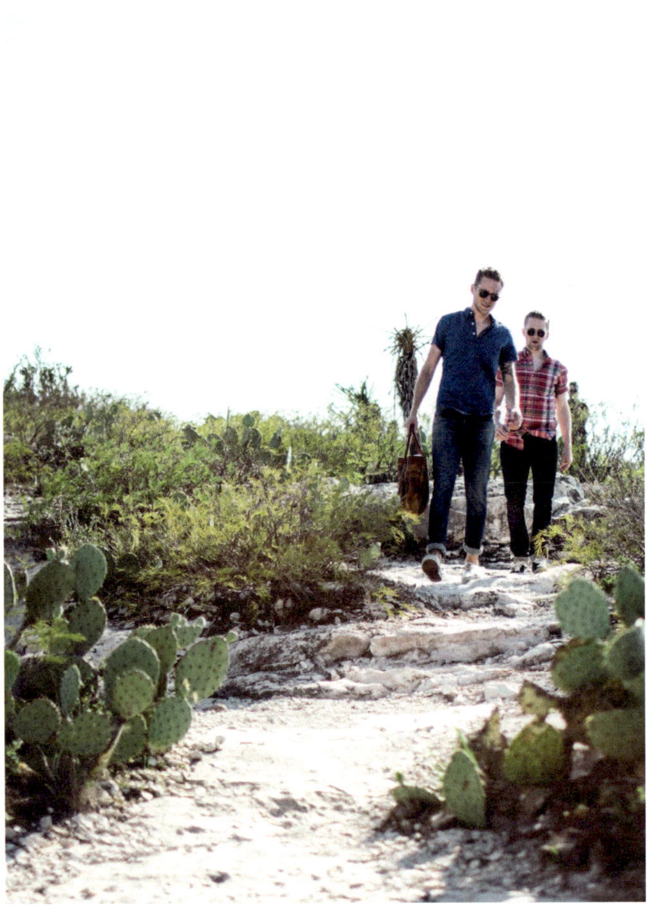

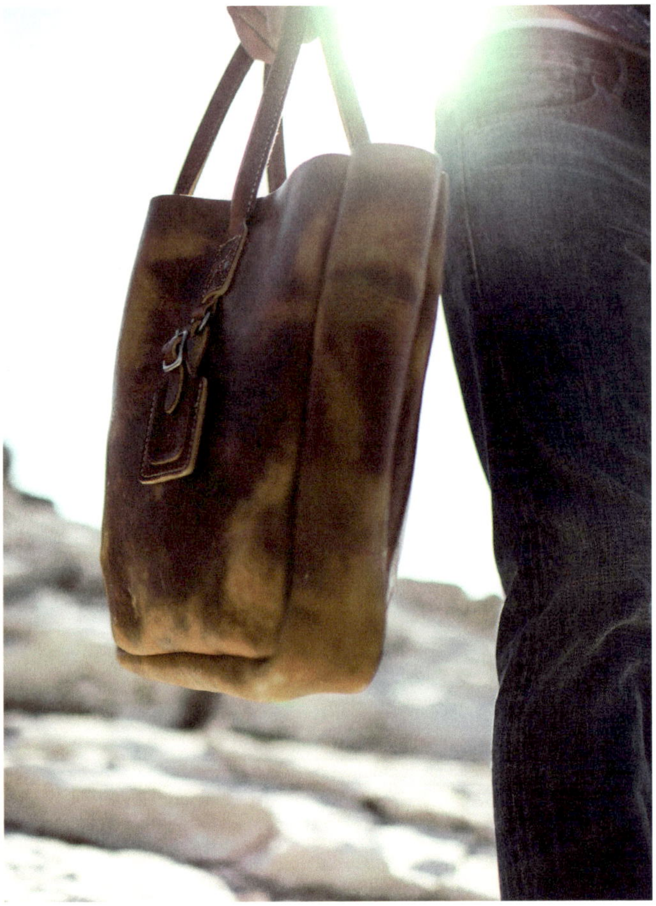

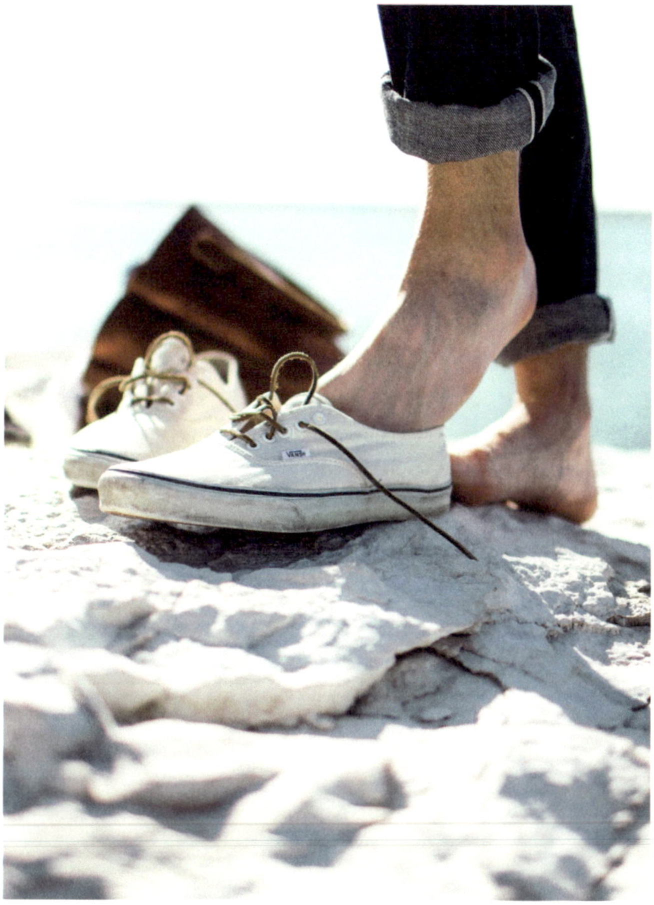

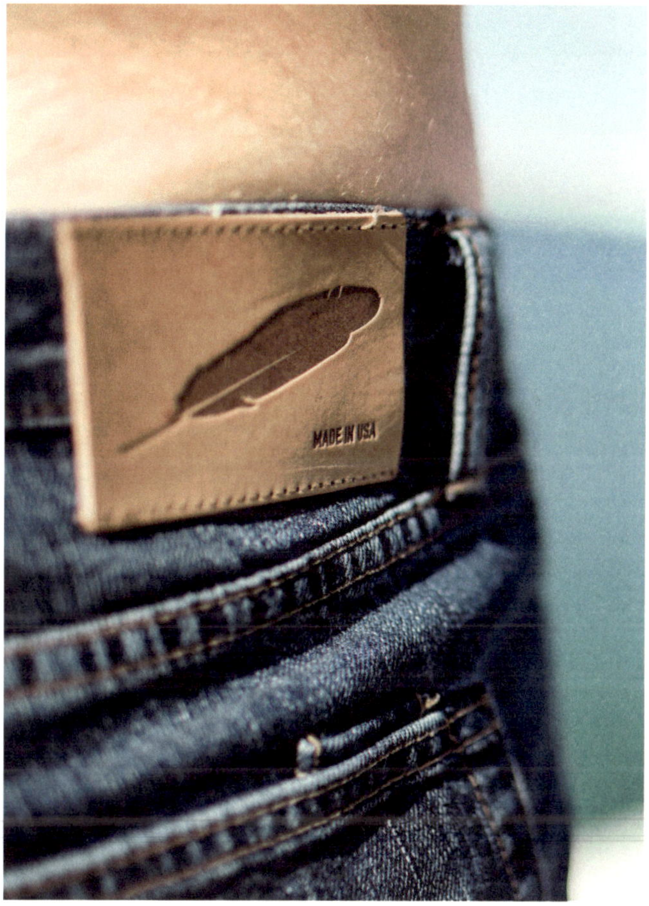
MADE IN USA

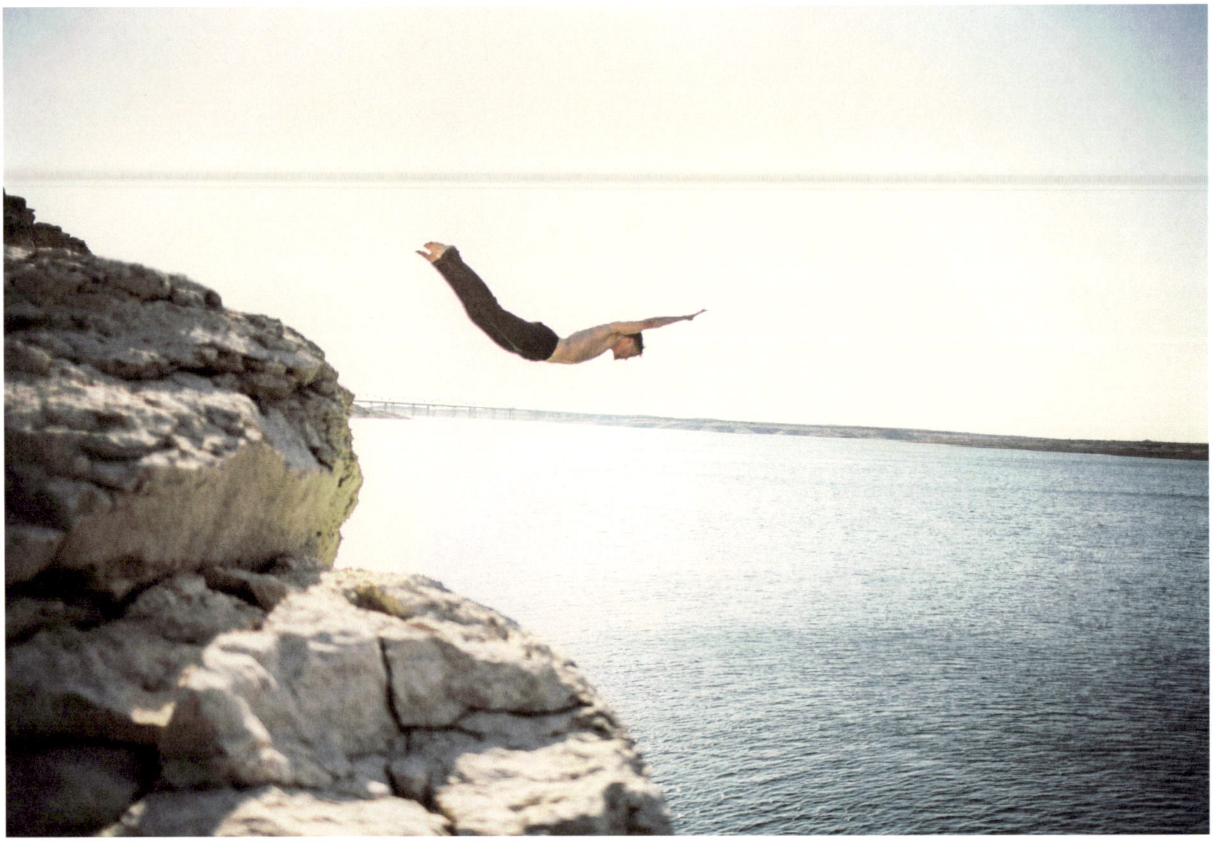

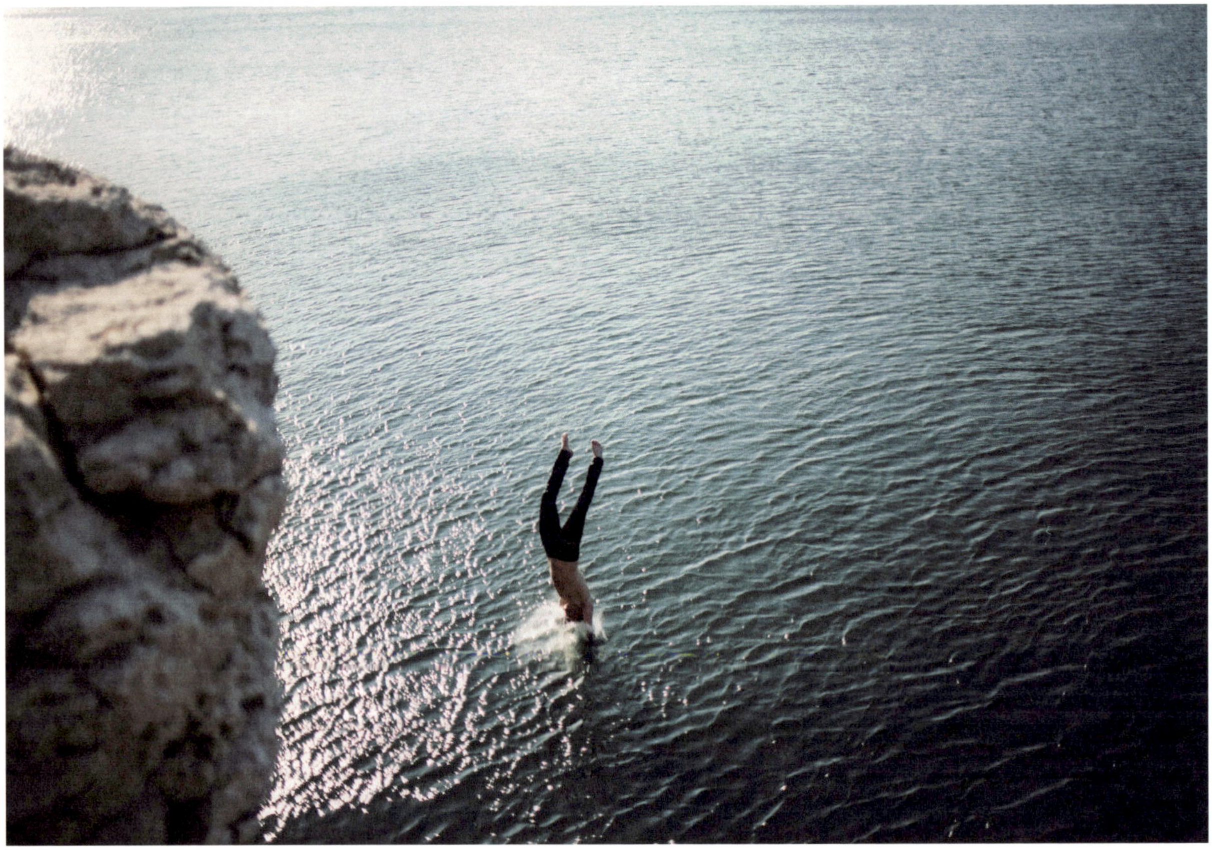

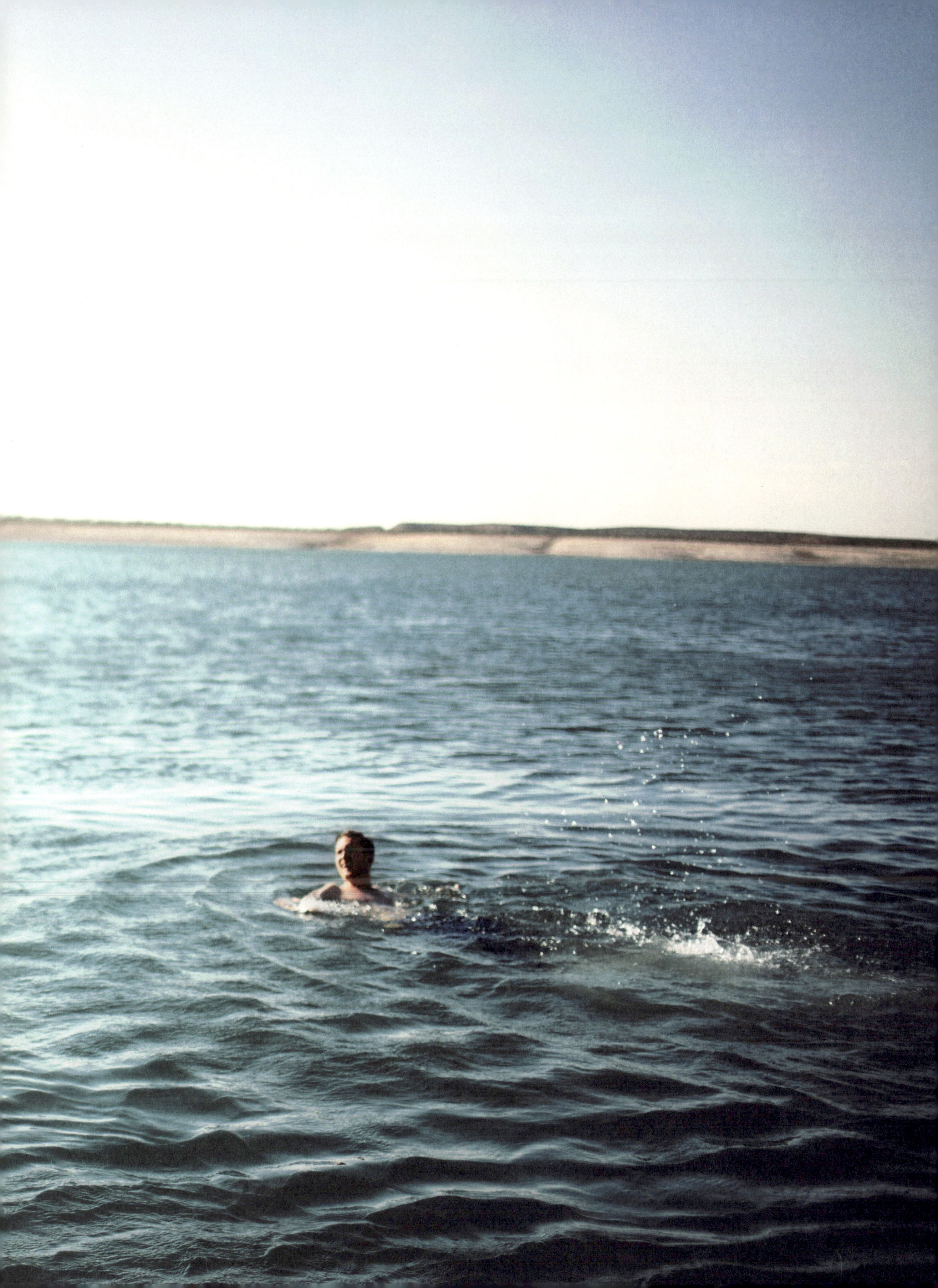

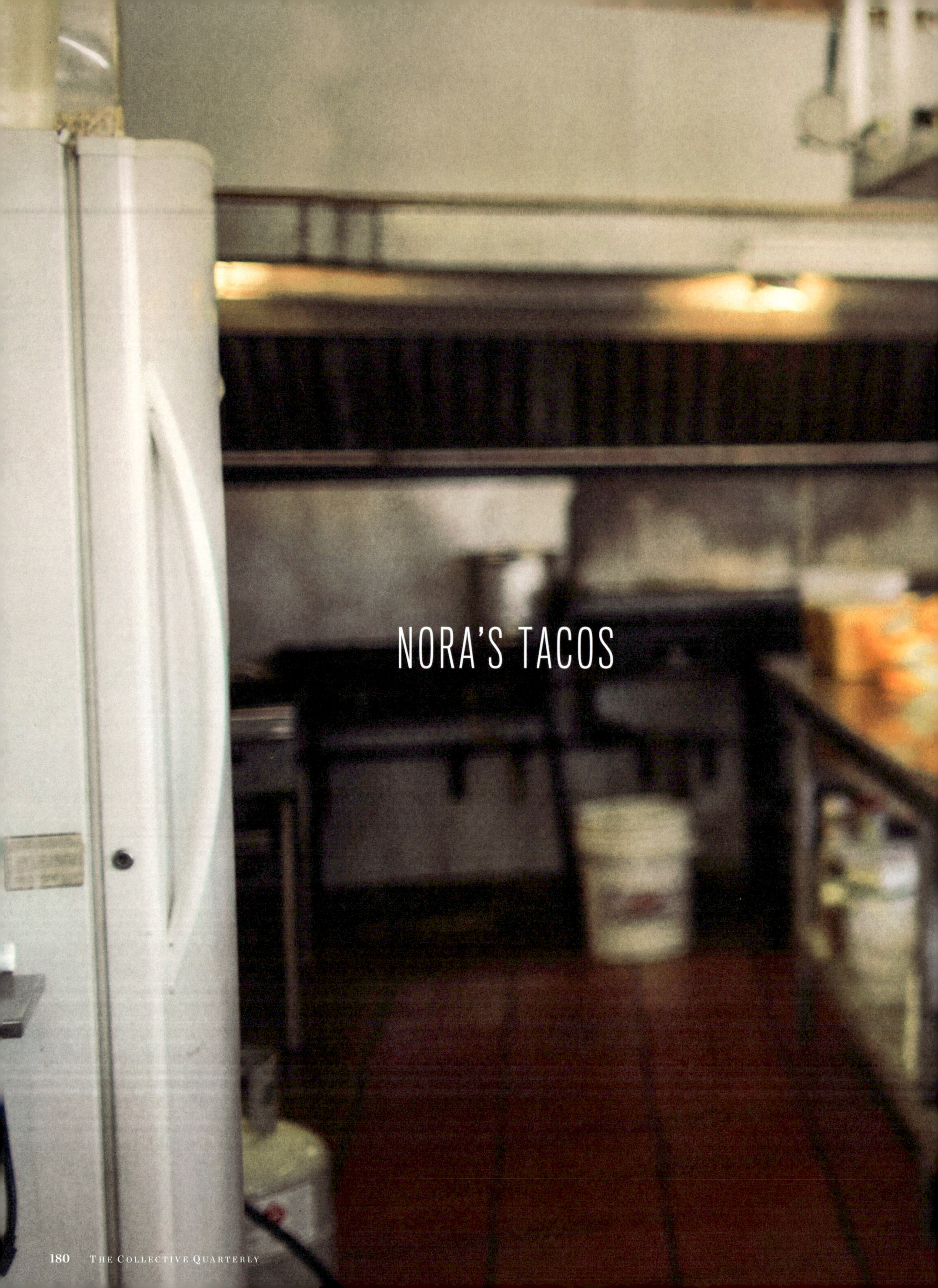

NORA'S TACOS

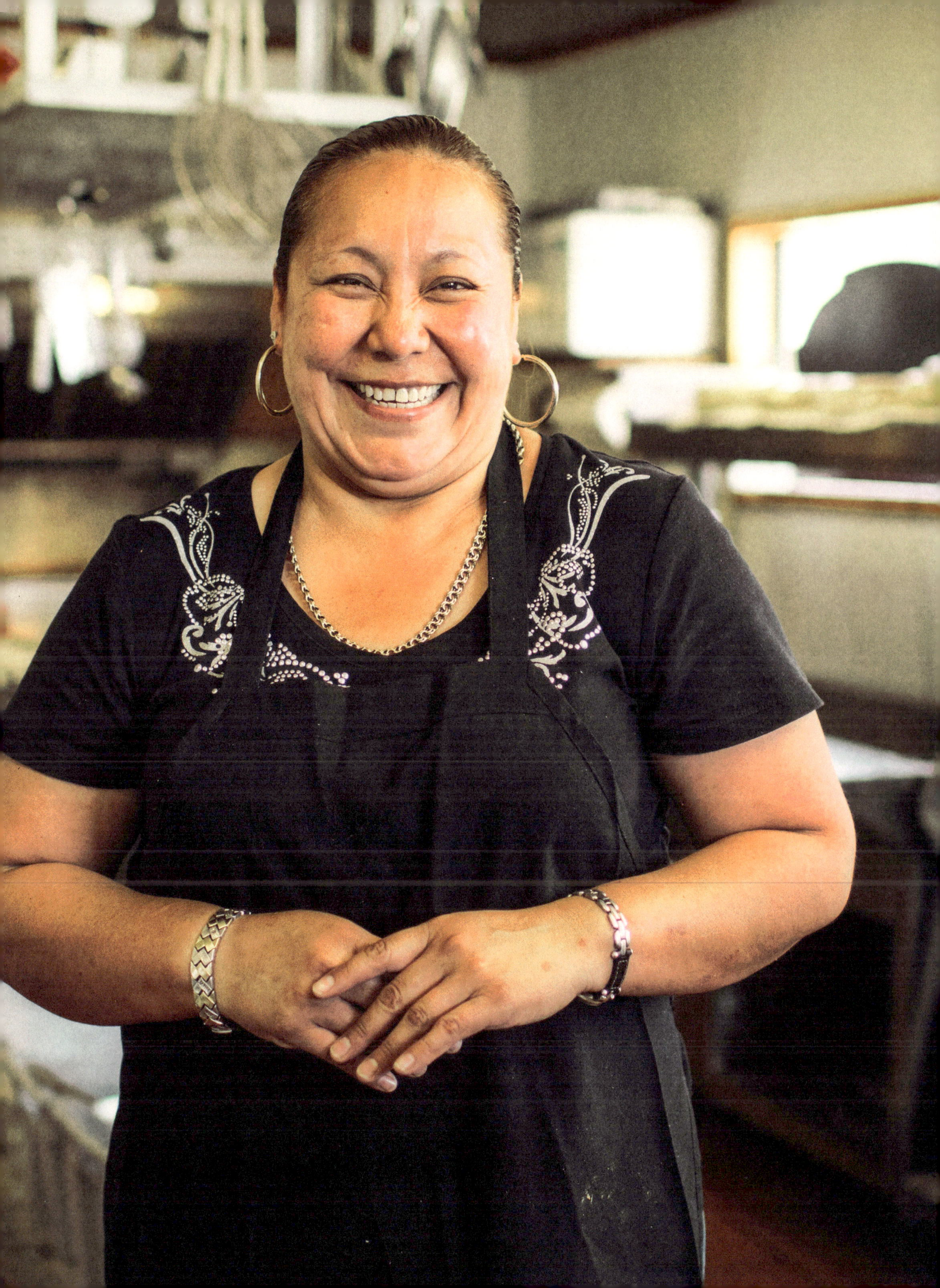

HALFWAY BETWEEN SAN ANTONIO AND THE MEXICAN border, there's a patch of ground about a mile square called Sabinal. That's where you'll find Nora Herrera and her tacos.

There's a word in Spanish, *el campo,* that describes anything outside the big city. Literally, it means "field." In English, "countryside" comes close to a synonym, but it still lacks a feeling of remoteness. For example in Argentina, anything outside the federal capital of Buenos Aires (where a full third of the country's population lives) is considered *el campo*: the hinterland.

Based on the landscape here—the two-lane highway, the dust swirling underneath hot tires—there's a temptation to paint with clichés of isolation: It's miles from anywhere. Just a peck of dirt. A one-stoplight town. Sabinal is indeed a small burg, but truth be told, it's about an hour outside of San Antonio, and in the grand scheme of our week-long odyssey to Marfa, we'd hardly gotten started.

It may have been that we were a handful of dudes overeager to experience *el campo* of Texas, or it may have been the minor disaster that had already struck so early in our trip, but Nora's Tacos were what the road required.

By the time we rolled up a little after 1 p.m., things had already gone a little haywire. One member of the group left his wallet in Walgreens after we stopped to pick up water and sunscreen. By the time we caught the mistake and circled back to recover the billfold, it was gone—and with it, credit cards, cash, identification, and all. Anxiety ensued.

While the victim paced around on the phone canceling his cards, the rest of us ambled up to the window of the trailer that is Nora's Tacos and placed our orders. A lot of fellas in cowboy hats were doing the same, and when our cameras came out, they eyed us warily from beneath their brims. Most of Herrera's customers are dove hunters, *rancheros,* and construction workers—some of whom travel 70 or 80 miles for work. Out here, in *el campo,* "far" is relative.

Every morning at 4:30, Herrera arrives at her trailer to hand-press 400 fresh flour tortillas. She's proud of the fact that her tacos are *personalizados,* and that each of her regulars adds his or her own spin to her base model. (Like "El Frank," not advertised on the menu but named for a customer who likes bacon, eggs, and cheese.)

"Aqui, no son mis tacos; son tus tacos," Herrera says. (Here, they're not my tacos; they're your tacos.)

"La unica cosa de mi es el sabor, porque soy Mexicana," she says with a smile. (The only thing of mine is the flavor, because I'm Mexican.) Herrera came here eight years ago from her home just across the border in Piedras Negras, in the Mexican state of Coahuila. About 150,000 people live there, compared to the 1,700 in Sabinal. Now, she runs the taco stand with her husband, mother, and children, and she says there's steady traffic. "Best tacos in town," the sign reads.

Herrera cracks open the lids of five Mexican Coca-Colas—the legit kind made with cane sugar—and sends us on our way. And for our part, we're happy to have met someone who puts so much flavor into her work. —S. P.

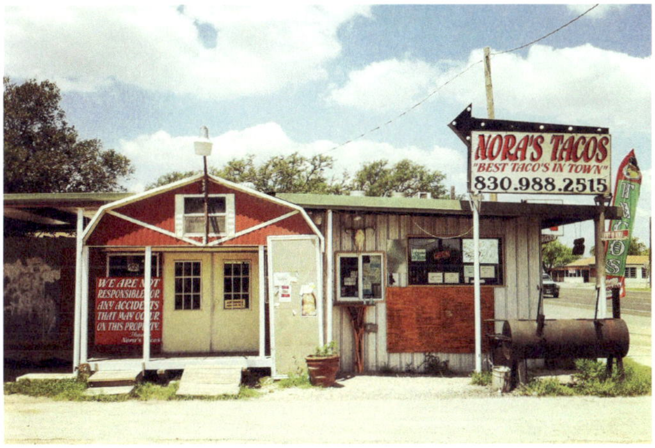
NORA'S TACOS
"BEST TACO'S IN TOWN"
830.988.2515

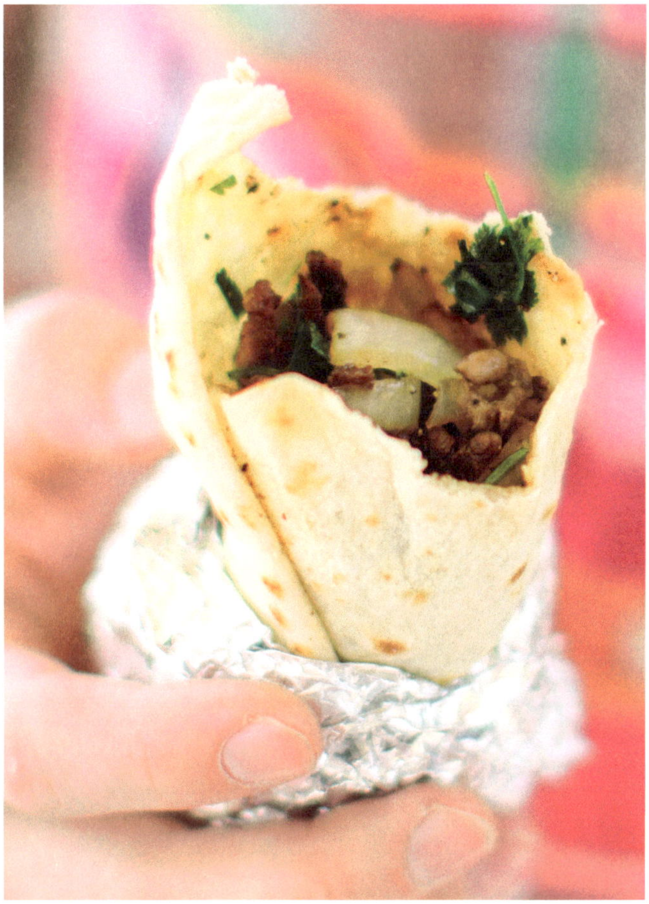

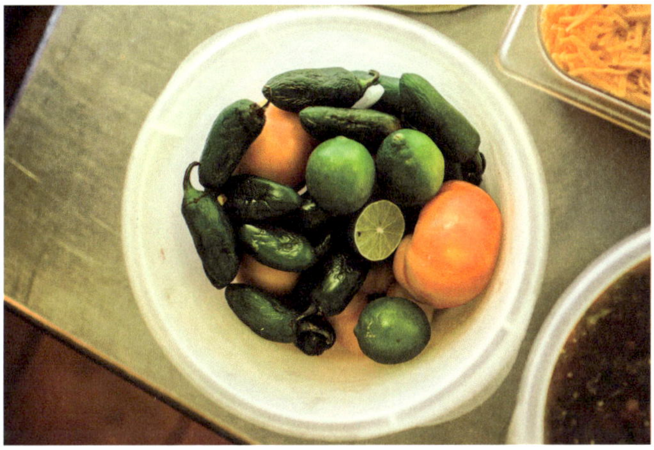

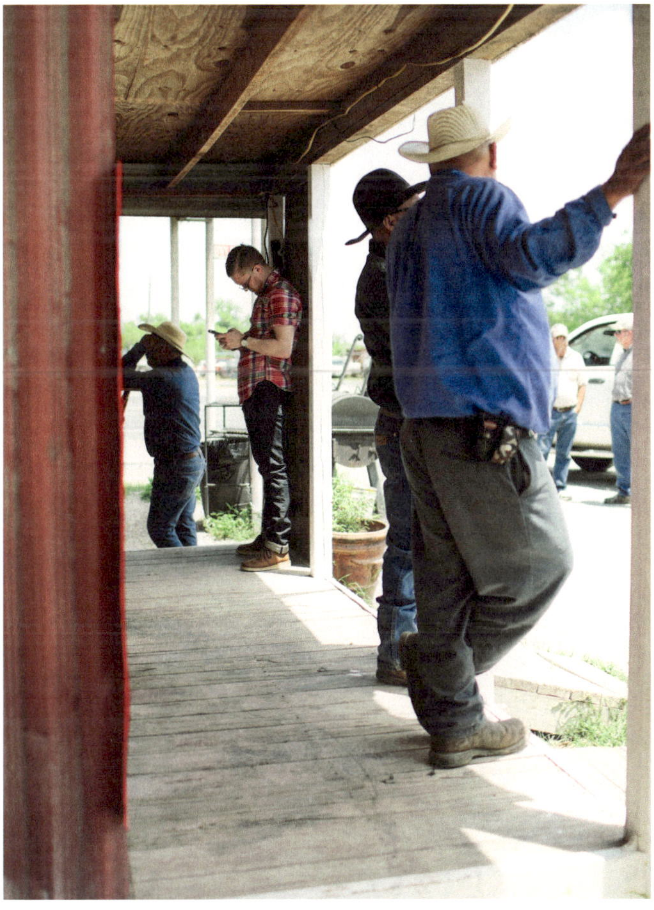

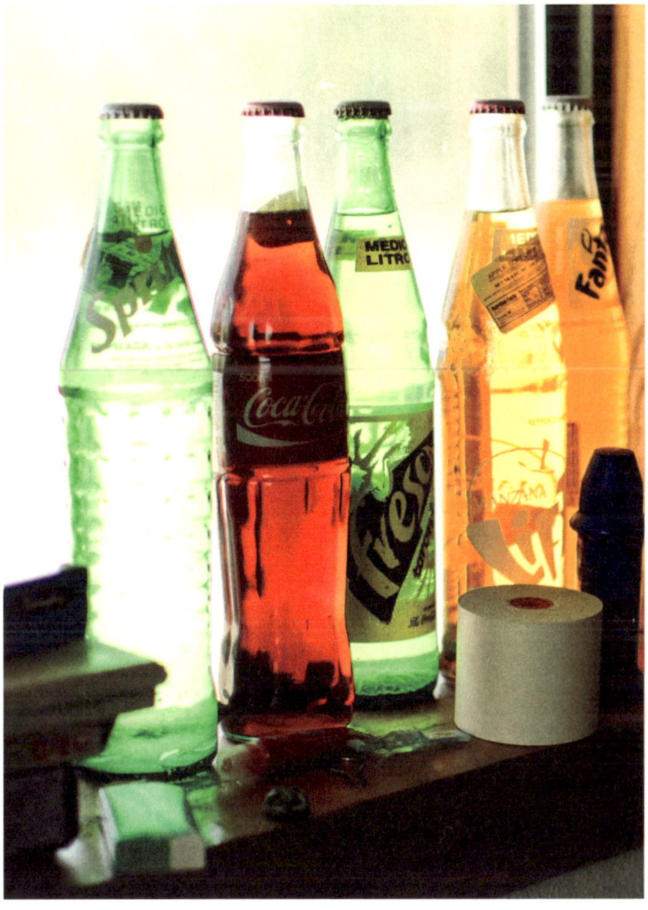
MEDIO LITRO
Coca-Cola

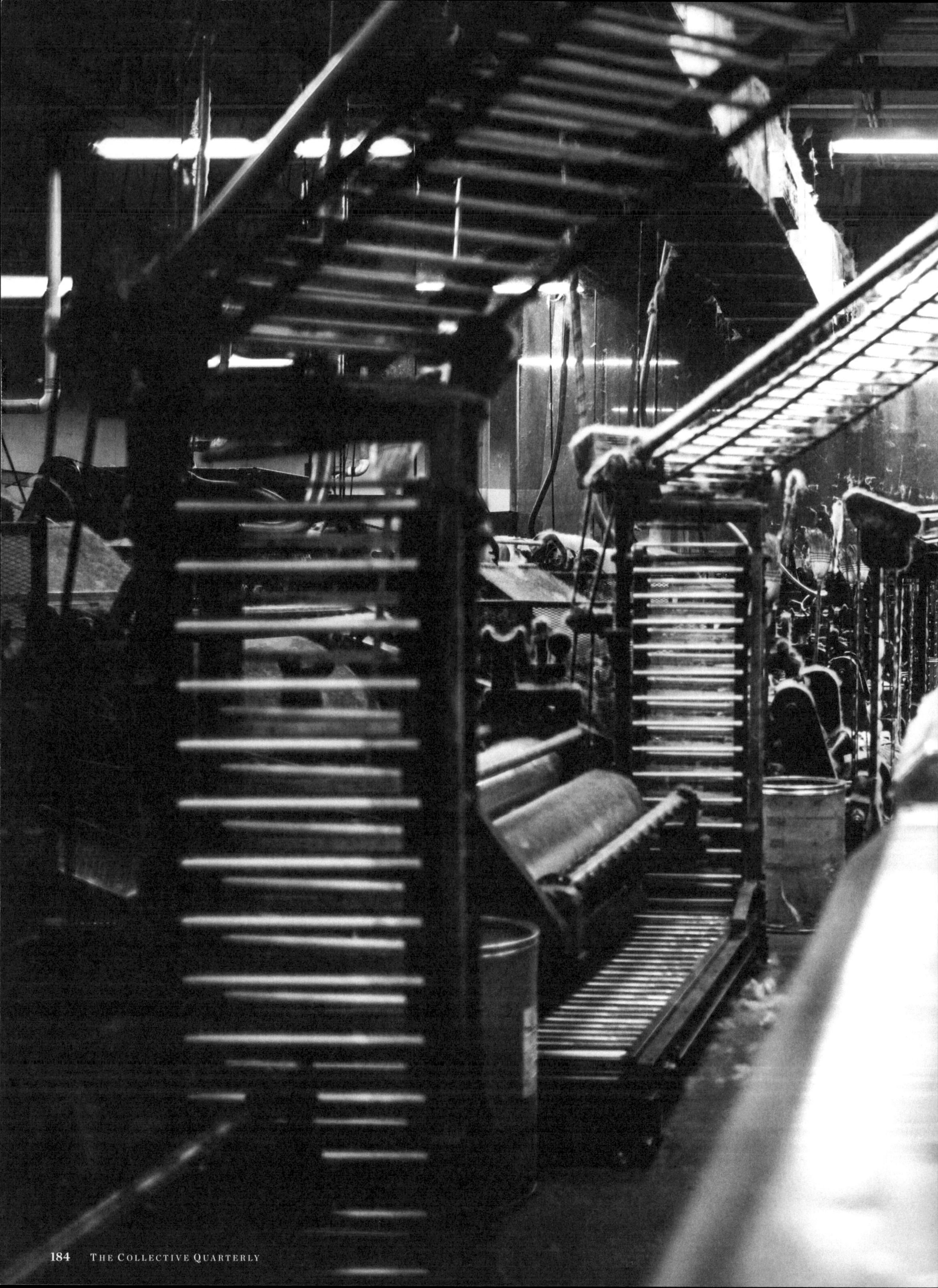

THE WARP AND THE WEFT

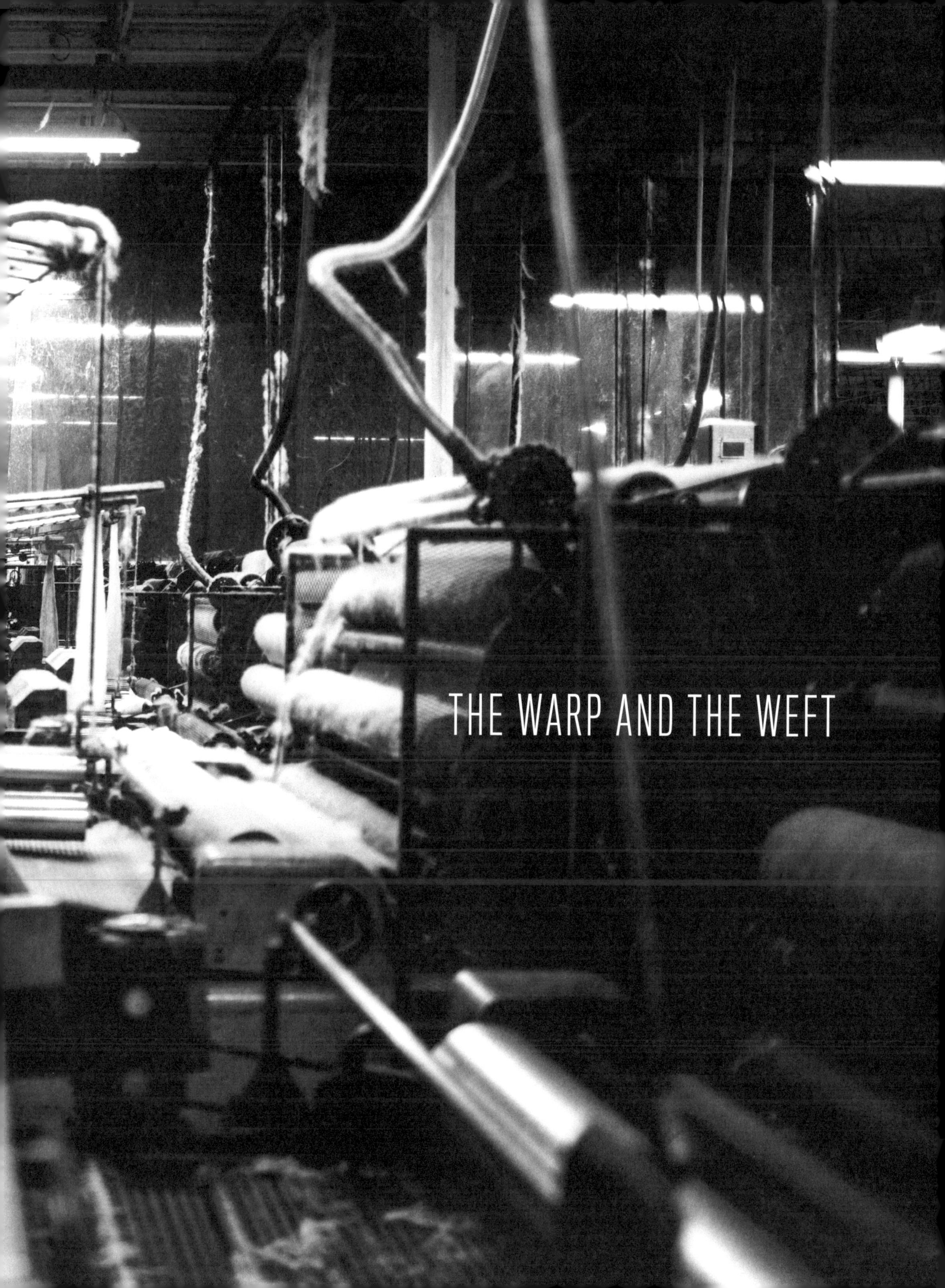

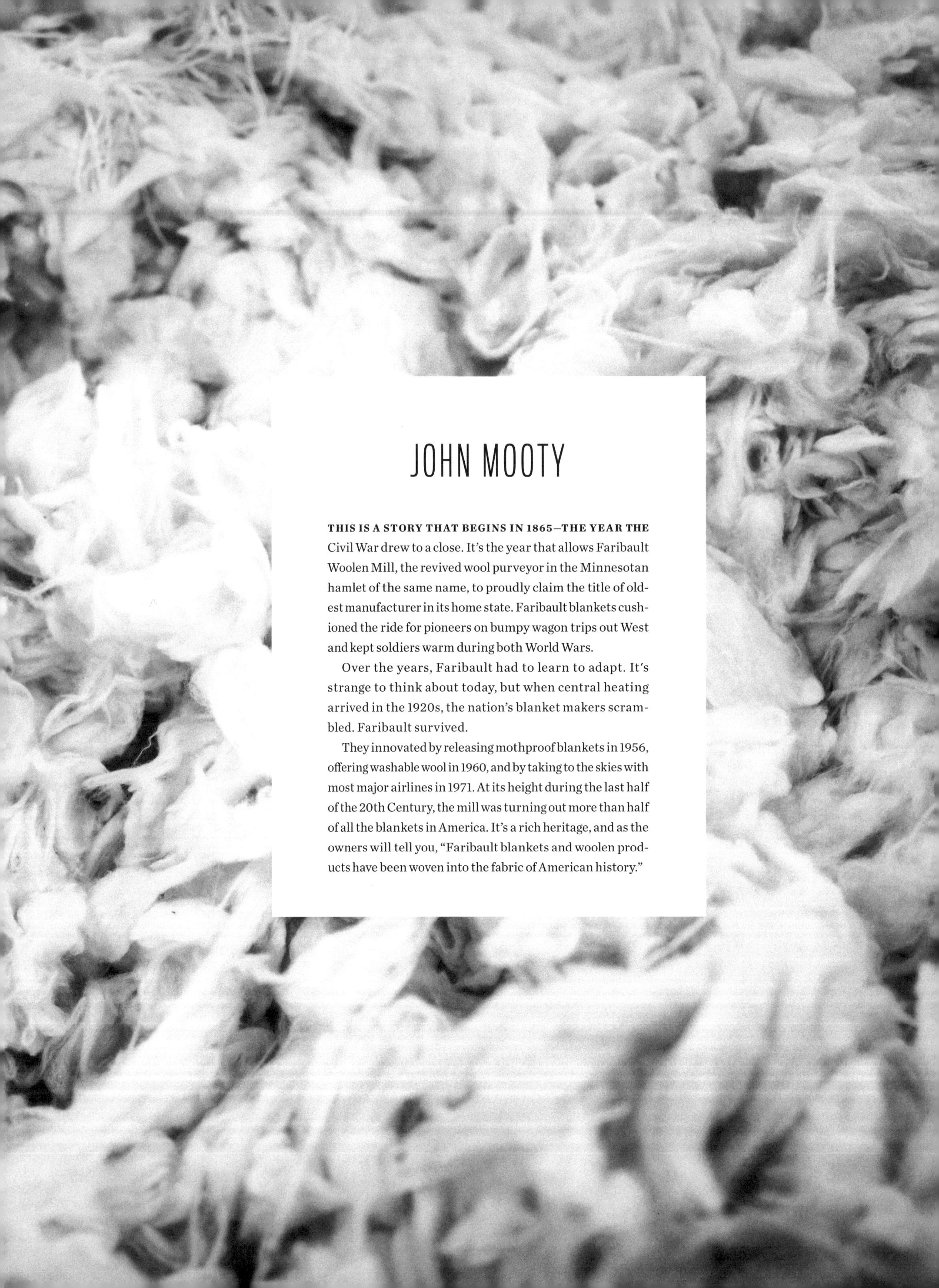

JOHN MOOTY

THIS IS A STORY THAT BEGINS IN 1865—THE YEAR THE Civil War drew to a close. It's the year that allows Faribault Woolen Mill, the revived wool purveyor in the Minnesotan hamlet of the same name, to proudly claim the title of oldest manufacturer in its home state. Faribault blankets cushioned the ride for pioneers on bumpy wagon trips out West and kept soldiers warm during both World Wars.

Over the years, Faribault had to learn to adapt. It's strange to think about today, but when central heating arrived in the 1920s, the nation's blanket makers scrambled. Faribault survived.

They innovated by releasing mothproof blankets in 1956, offering washable wool in 1960, and by taking to the skies with most major airlines in 1971. At its height during the last half of the 20th Century, the mill was turning out more than half of all the blankets in America. It's a rich heritage, and as the owners will tell you, "Faribault blankets and woolen products have been woven into the fabric of American history."

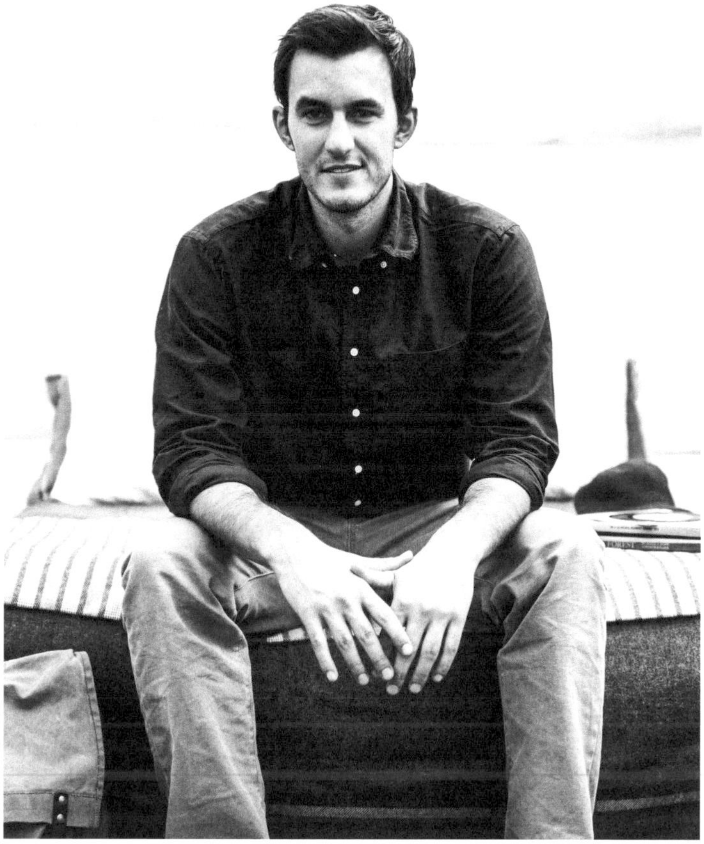

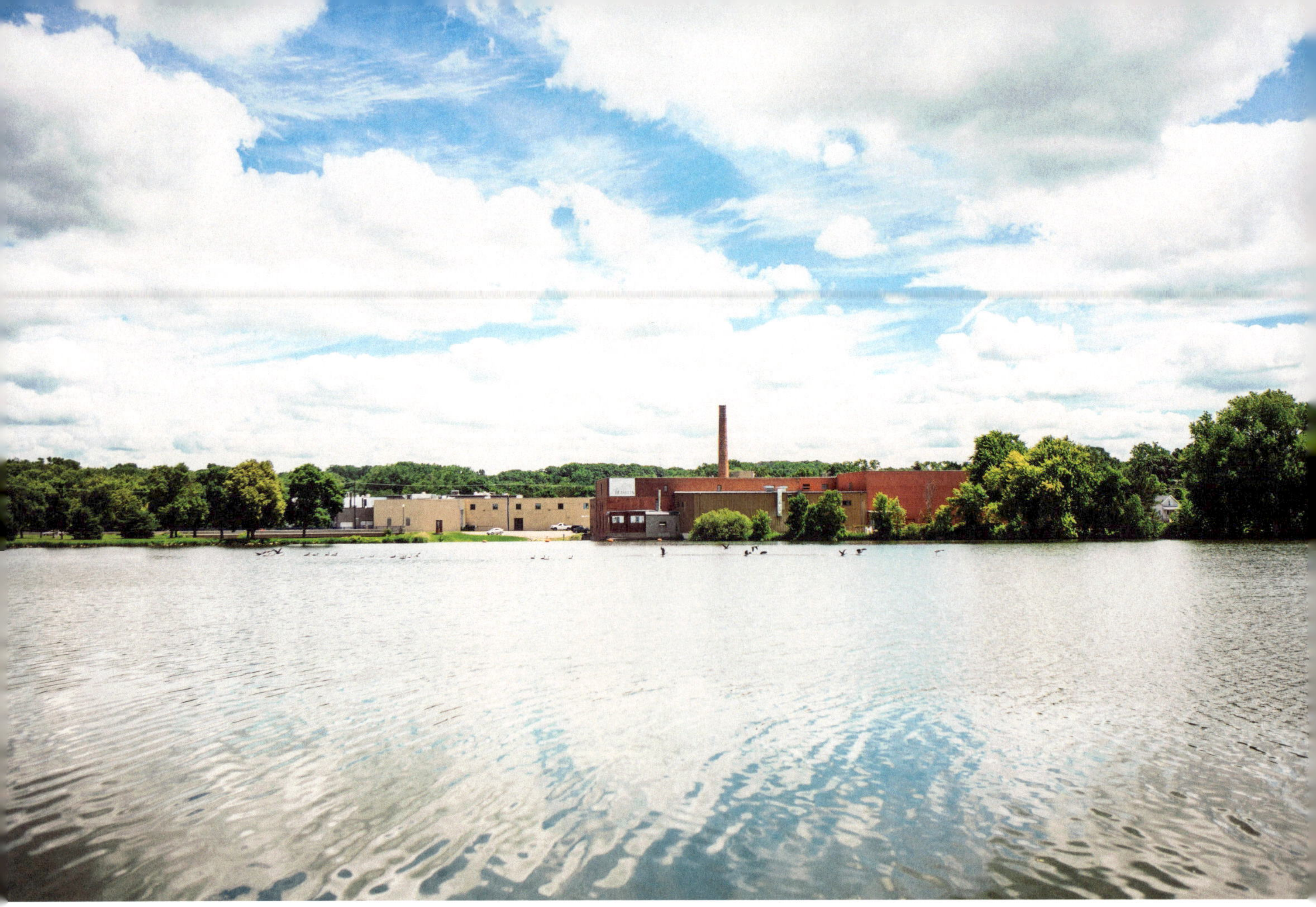

It's stories like this that help create the lore surrounding Minnesotan craft—a lore not even the drought of the Recession has quite been able to dry up, even though it certainly has come close.

Faribault shuttered in 2009. Happily for one of the most iconic names in American wool production, that turned out to be merely a hiatus. Two years later the Mooty family bought the mill. They were in a mood to bet large on the American excellence of their hometown. Since its rebirth, they've claimed Engineered Garments, Ebbets Field Flannels, and West Elm among their clients.

CUT TO: THE RAUCOUS ESQUIRE TAVERN IN SAN ANTONIO. The mood was beyond merry by the time John Mooty, the 26-year-old creative director behind Faribault, strolled past the longest bar top in Texas and took his place among the crew of writers and photographers who had assembled for the Collective Quarterly's inaugural journey. It was the night before they set out on their road trip through West Texas, and some of them were just meeting for the first time. More than making a magazine merely about travel, the group also aimed to pull back the veil on the creative process. To properly show such an abstract concept, they brought artisans like John with them so they could document the people they met and the materials that inspired them. Over drinks, it became obvious that a week in Marfa with John was going to be an adventure.

John exudes humility. Character qualities aren't often the stuff of first impressions, especially when there are other things to focus on like stature (the man is built like a redwood). But one of the immediate things that sticks out about the northerner is the way he makes no pretenses. He's quick with a firm handshake and huge smile; then he lets his work at Faribault speak for itself.

The classics are still very much alive at the mill—with pure and simple solids alongside military patterns for foot soldiers and medics—but John and his team have done a first-rate job of freshening the line in the form of updated offerings, like iPad cases and intriguing backpack collaborations with Duluth Pack.

As the team drove through the wilderness, slept in teepees and hiked the desert with John, it was easy to see that Faribault's history is just as important to him and his family as it must have been to the original owners. There's a rule in business when heritage comes into play: In order to safely steer the ship into new waters, innovation must come within the company's core principles, not at the expense of them.

With the past two years as proof, John and his family have passed that test. They remain "purveyors of comfort and quality"; it's all right there on the Faribault label. —*S.P.*

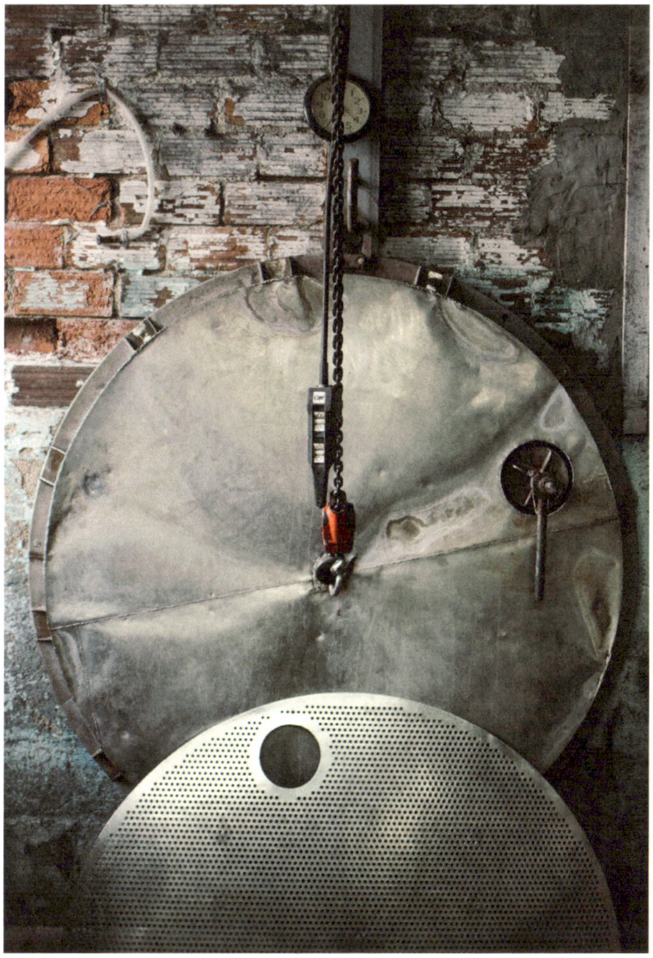

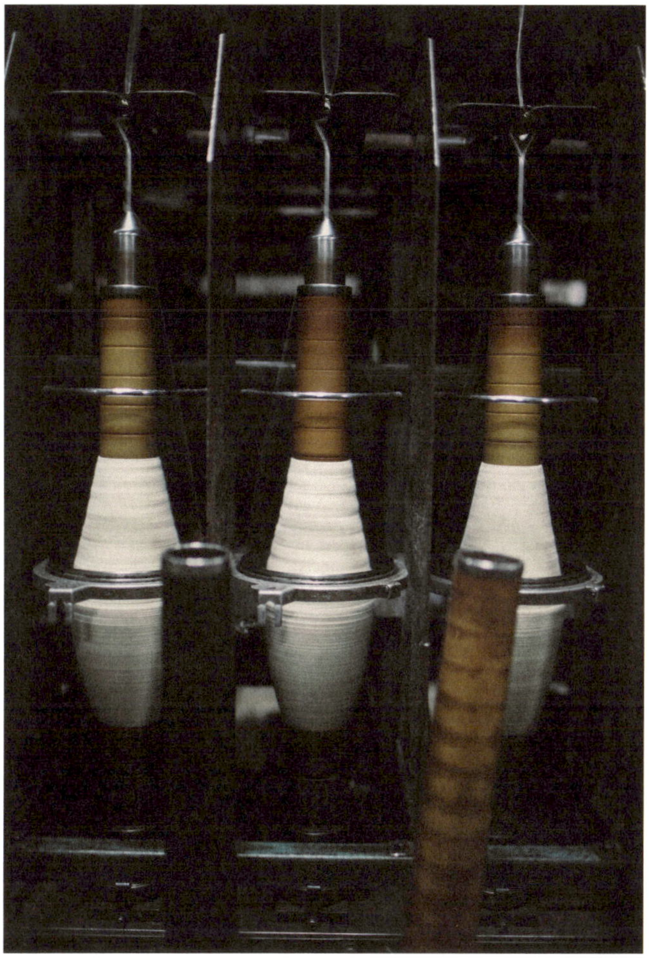

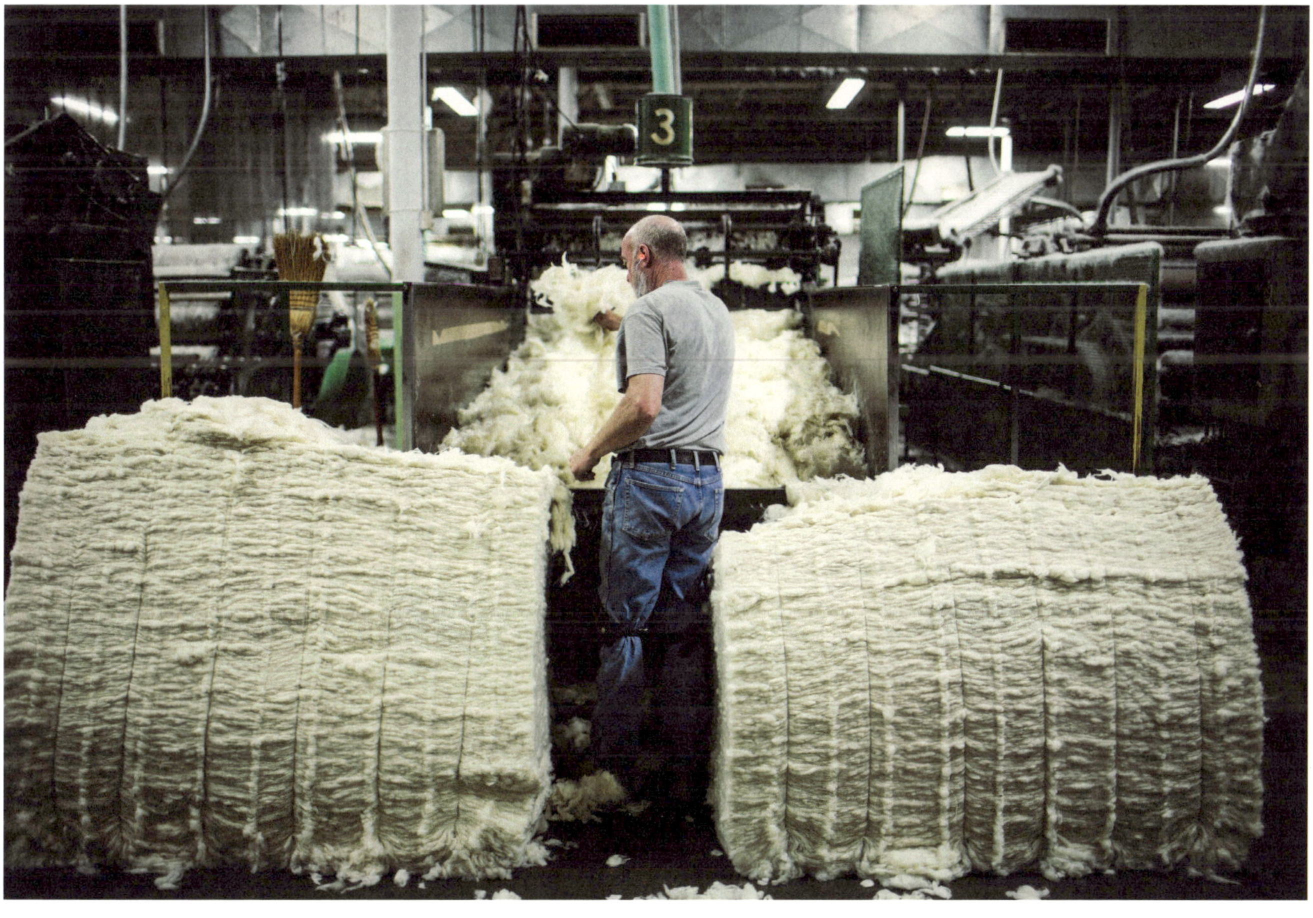
3

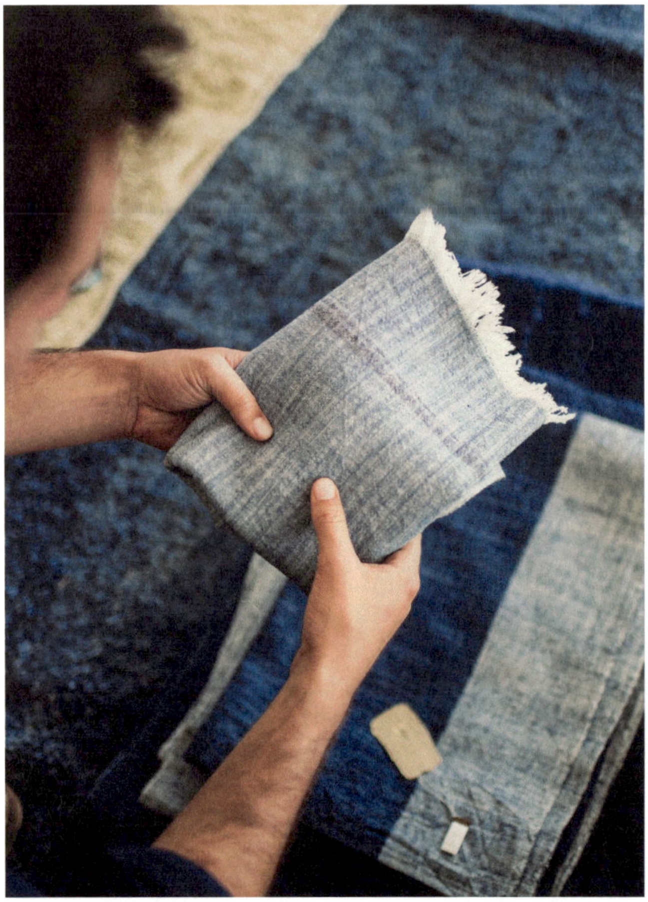

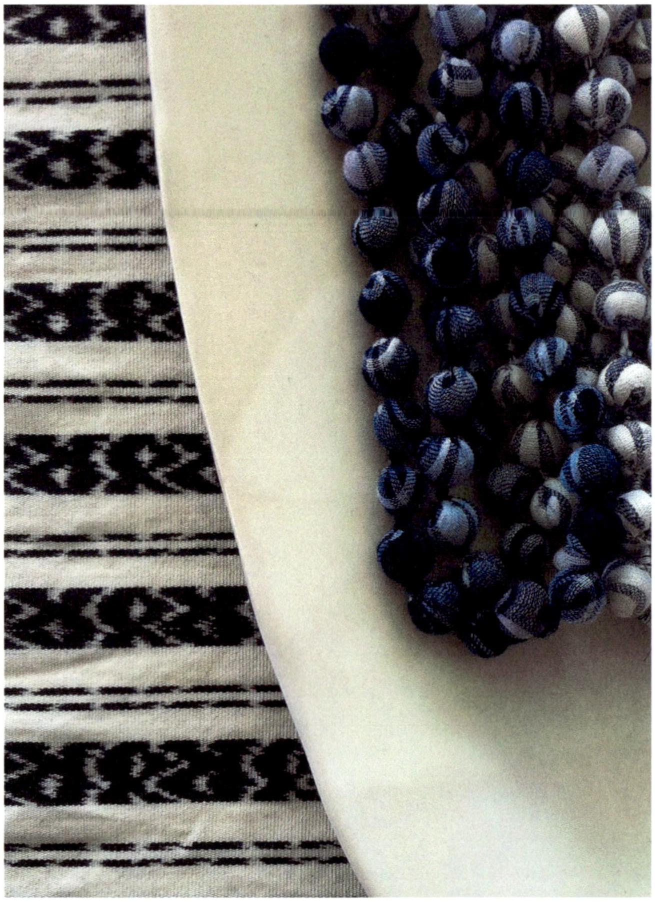

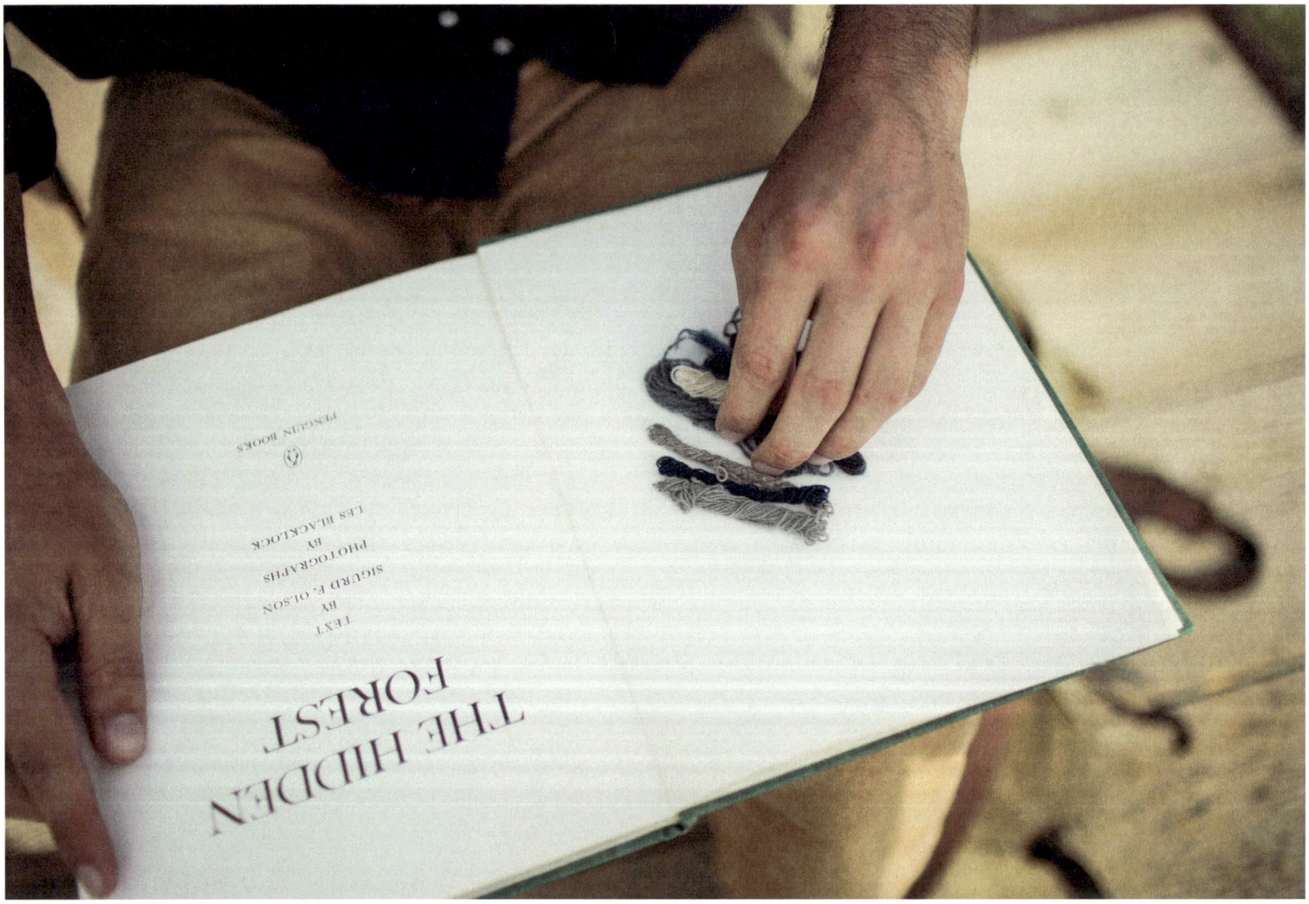
THE HIDDEN FOREST
TEXT BY SIGURD F. OLSON
PHOTOGRAPHS BY LES BLACKLOCK
PENGUIN BOOKS

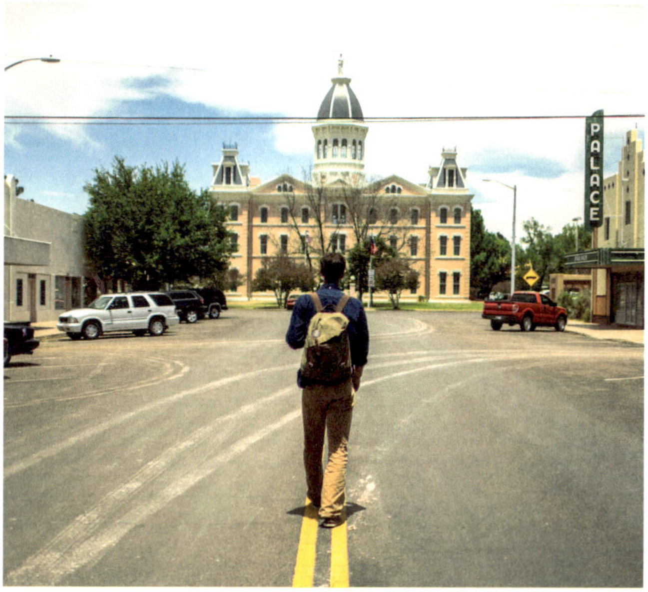

The Story Behind the Stripes: As told to Seth Putnam.

When I came back from Marfa, my thought was, "How does the trip I've just taken translate to a cohesive product line?"

For inspiration, I looked most to the colors of the landscape, the colors of the daytime and the sunset, and the difference between them. Then there were the textures we came across, from the clean lines of the minimalist architecture to the jagged lines of the desert. There was this combination of streamlined, contemporary art, but it had meshed with this really rugged landscape and way of life. How do those two live together? How do they combine into something that's ultimately beautiful?

In the Stripe Series, the pattern gets really contemporary. However, the way it's woven draws from the rugged textures we saw. The goal was to blend those two: the clean, modern lines compared to the rough textures of the landscape. And ultimately the colors chosen were reflections of that as well.

To bring out the texture we wanted, we used a plain white warp (which are the yarns held in tension to form the base of the weave). When we crossed blues and reds over that natural warp, it created this broken, heathered texture. This kind of weave is called a "broken twill." It takes the original base and breaks it up a little bit.

The moment this all really clicked was when we were walking around right before grabbing lunch at Food Shark. We went into Tienda M at the corner of Highland Avenue and El Paso Street, and they had these beautiful southwestern and Mexican textiles laid out on the floor. There was a series of different stripes and solids that had this indigo hue to them. The way they balanced against each other became a huge influence on the Stripe Series.

My process is less about reproduction and much more about interpretation. When something catches my eye, I only give it a glance and then move on so I can let it resonate in my brain. Rather than taking a photo or measuring out the stripes, I'll just take a quick look and then spend the rest of my time dwelling on the feeling it sparks.

When you look at something that inspires you, you get a certain sensation. If you're trying to create a product that spurs that feeling in others, rather than replicating it perfectly, you have to figure out how to make your own design, which you can put out with the confidence that you're not ripping off someone else's work. But you appreciate so much the feeling it gave you that you want to produce your own interpretation of it.

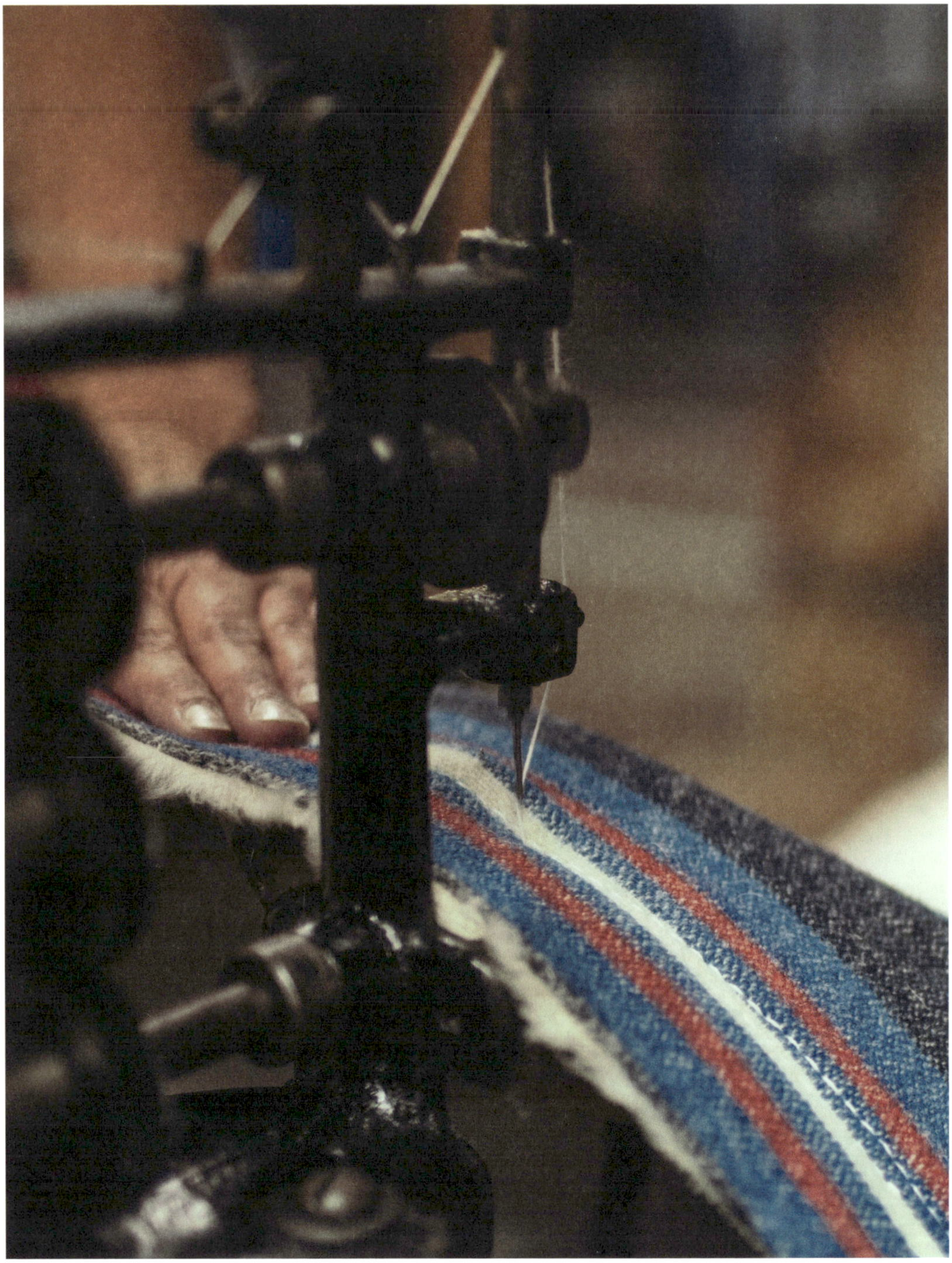

For this pattern, we're starting with what we're best at: blankets. When you're creating a line based around particular pattern, the natural extension is to take that blanket material and put it in other applications. So, the Stripe Series will include a throw pillow, a vest with Fischer Clothing, and a tote and Scoutmaster bag with Duluth Pack.

It boils down to this: You get the flavor of the thing that inspires you, and then you put it away. That way, your own original ideas can simmer and permeate the process.

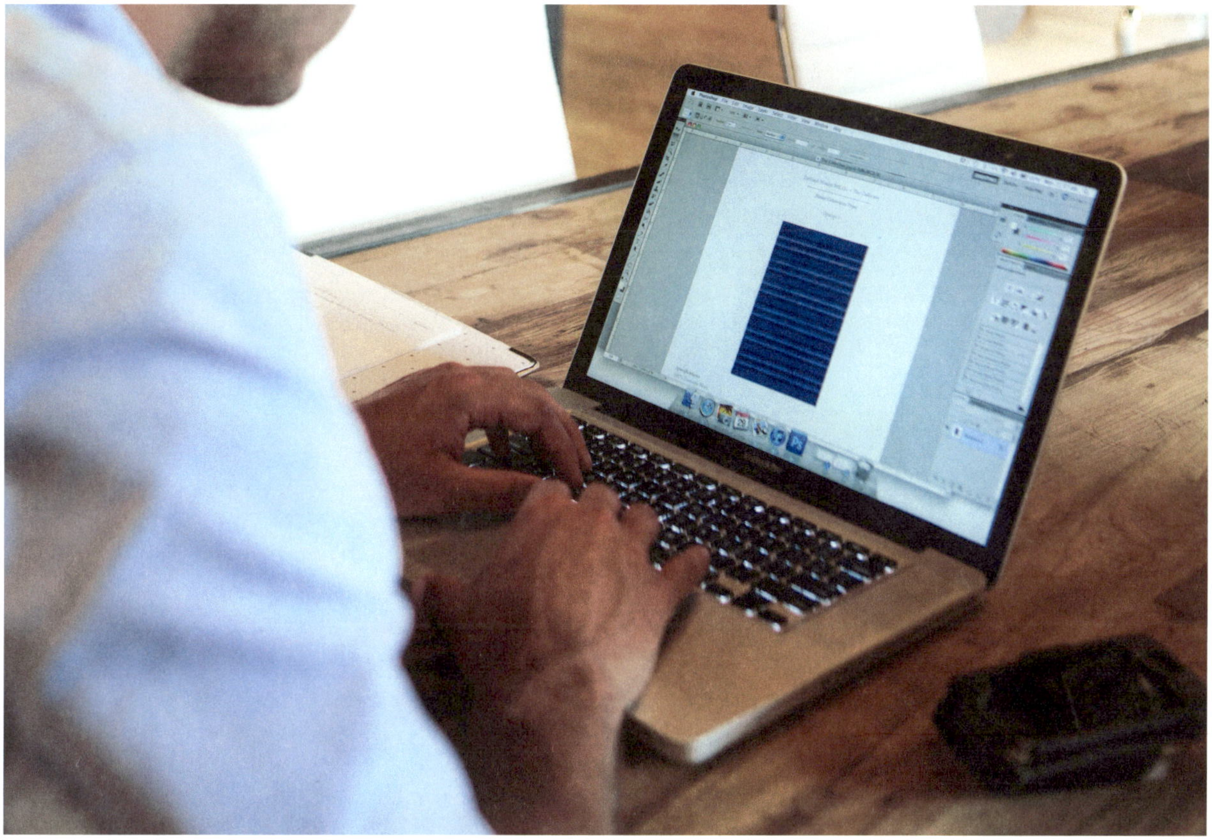

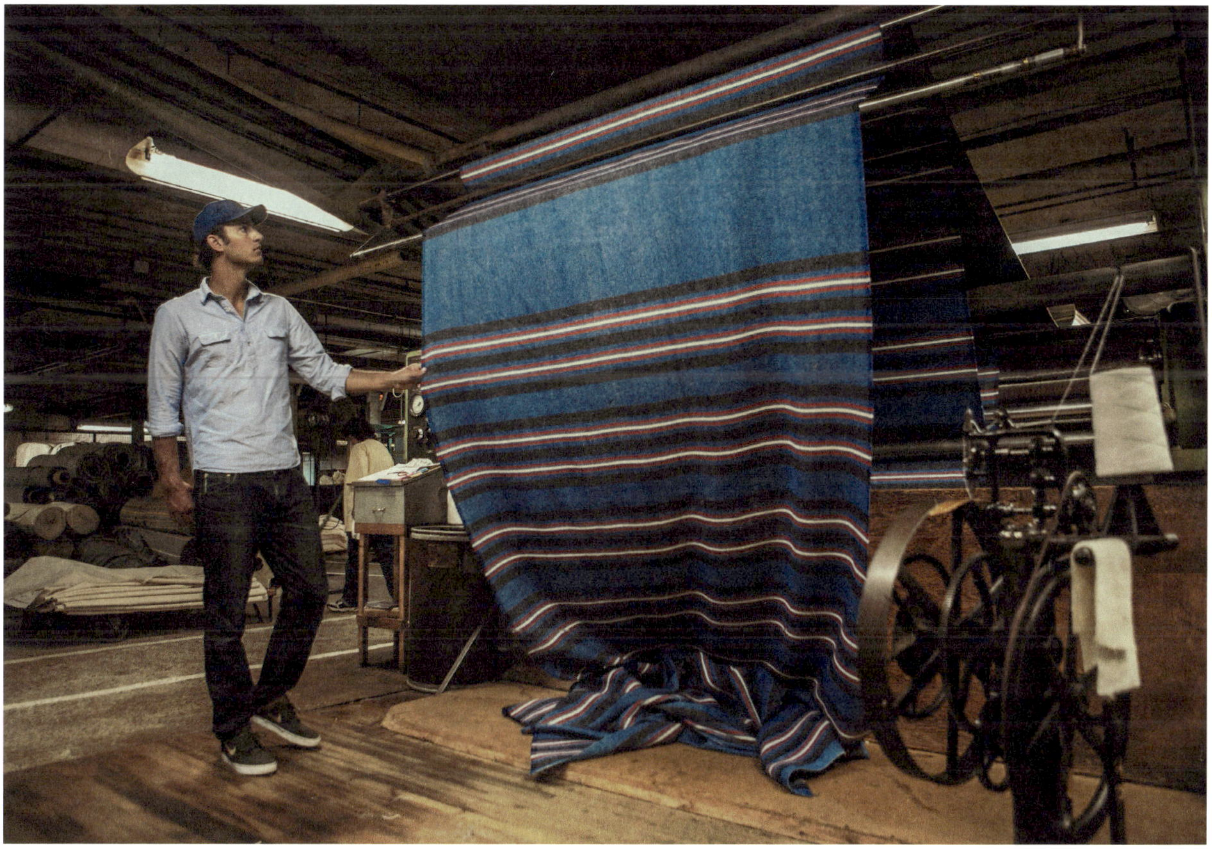

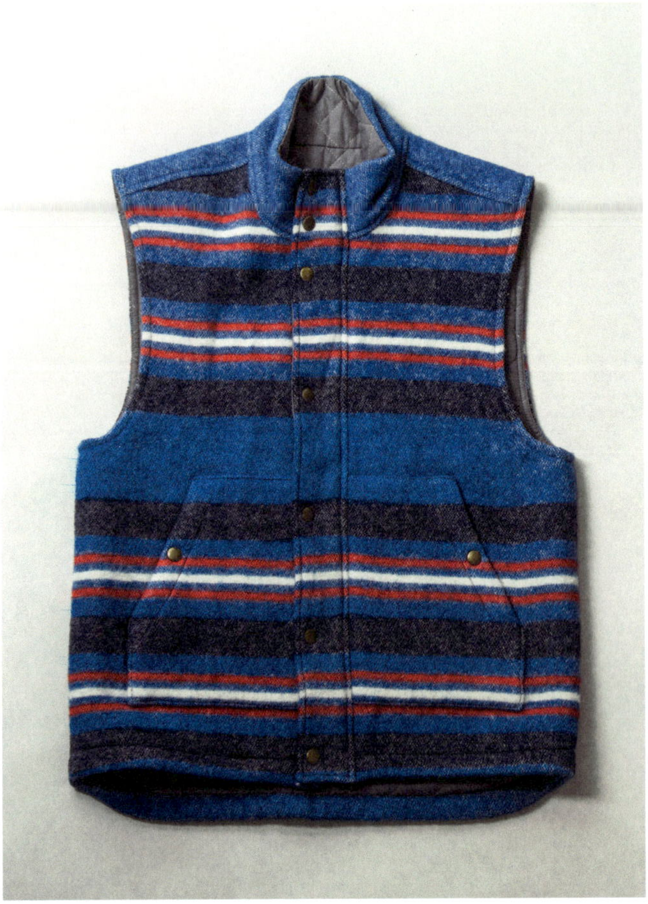
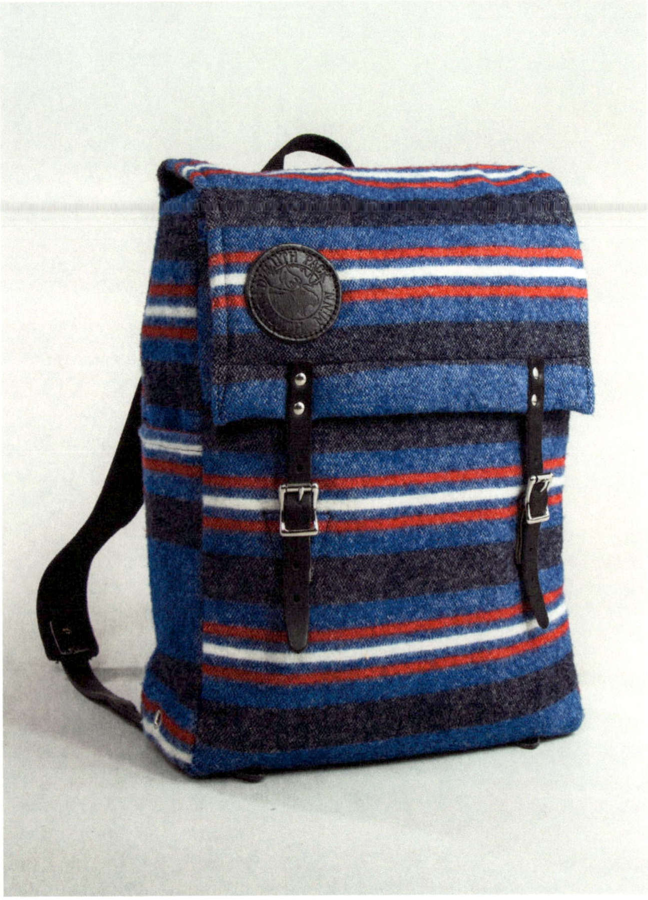
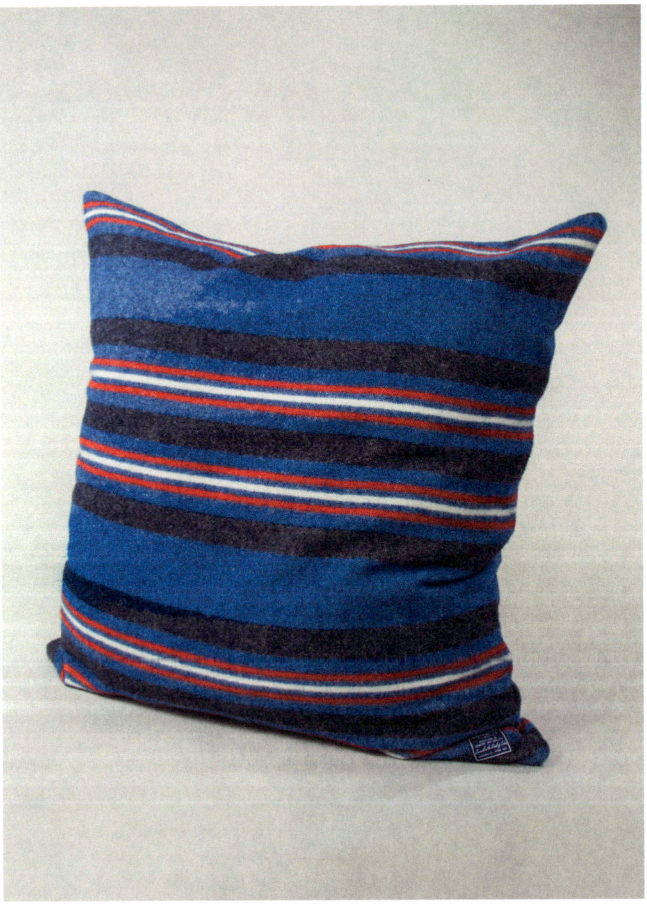
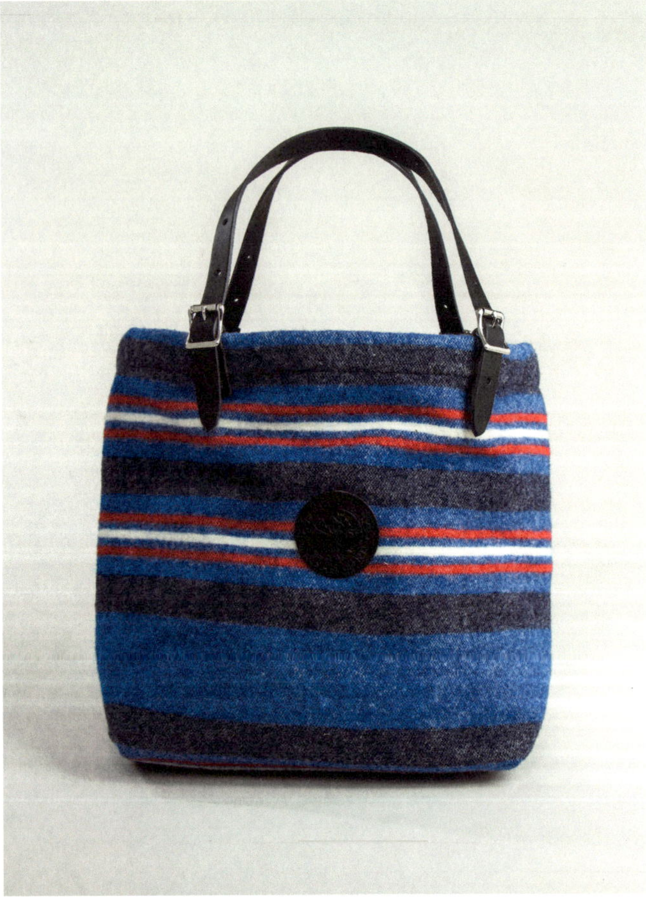

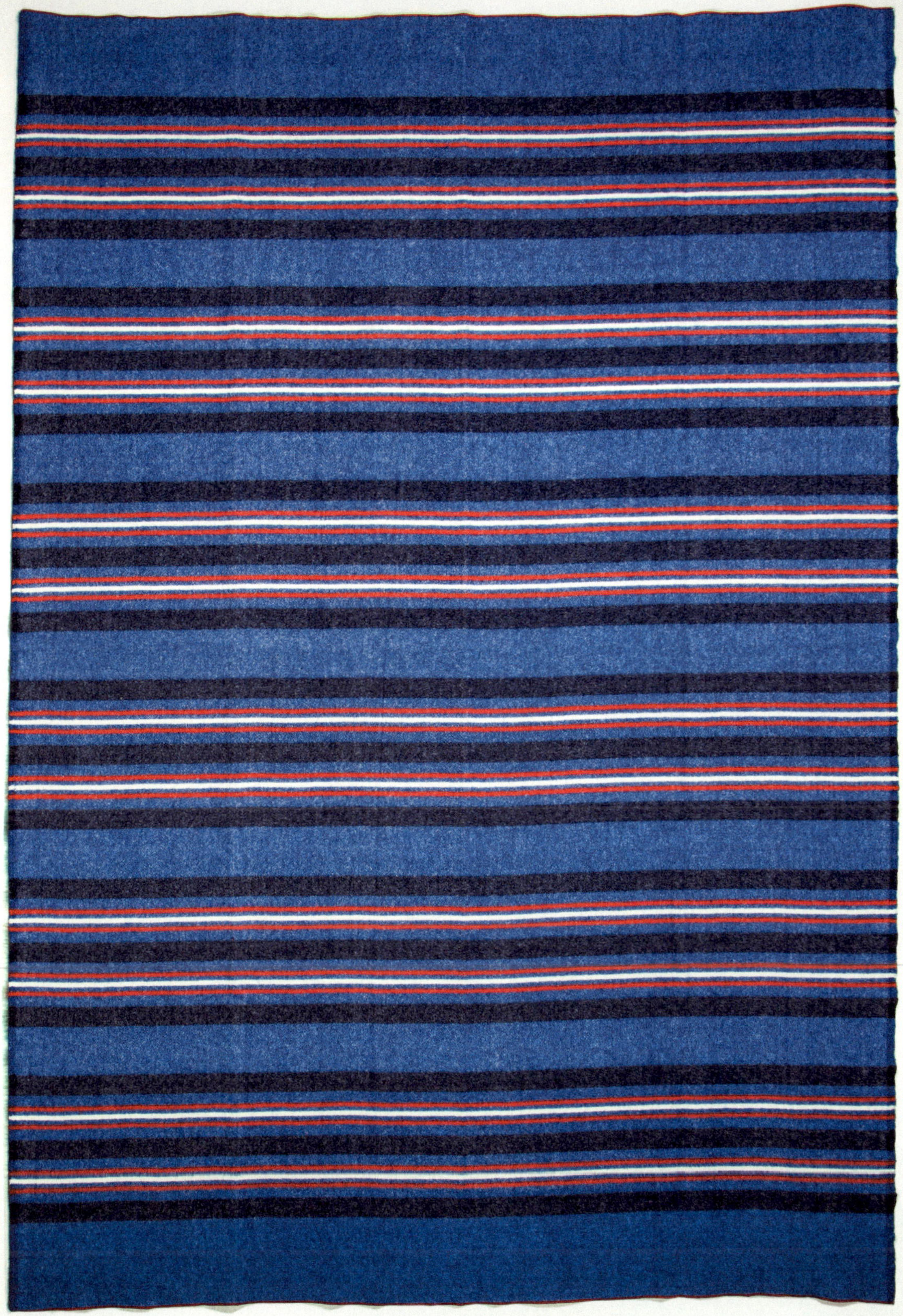

Ø

CREDITS

MARFA

PHOTOGRAPHY

GARRETT CORNELISON
42, 45 *(bottom)*, 48, 56, 70 *(bottom)*, 71

JAY GULLION
10 *(top right)*, 11 *(top right)*, 14, 16, 24, 27, 28, 30, 34, 37 *(middle right)*, 38, 44, 51 *(bottom)*, 52, 54 *(bottom)*, 55, 69, 74, 78, 81, 84, 124, 132, 134, 135, 145, 149, 172, 176, 177, 178, 179, 180, 183 *(middle left / bottom)*, 184, 186, 187, 188, 189 *(bottom)*, 190 *(top left / bottom)*, 191, 192, 193 *(top)*

JESSE LENZ
Cover, 2, 3, 5, 6, 8, 10 *(top right / bottom)*, 11 *(bottom)*, 12, 18, 26, 32, 33, 37 *(top right and left / bottom)*, 39, 40, 45 *(top)*, 50, 51 *(top)*, 53, 62, 64, 65, 66, 67, 72, 75, 79, 80, 86, 88, 89 *(bottom)*, 90, 91 *(top left and right / middle left and right / bottom left)*, 92, 93 *(bottom)*, 94 *(top right / middle right)*, 95, 96, 100, 102, 103, 105, 110, 130, 148, 160, 162, 163, 164, 166, 167, 171, 175, 183 *(top left)*, 189 *(top)*, 191 *(background)*, 192 *(background)*, 193 *(bottom)*

CHRIS MANTZ
54 *(top)*, 94 *(middle left / bottom right)*, 106, 107

ALEX MARKS
118, 121, 122, 123

JOHN MOOTY
183 *(top left)*, 190 *(top right)*

SETH PUTNAM
11 *(top left)*

KEVIN RUSS
20, 89 *(top)*, 91 *(bottom right)*, 94 *(top left / bottom left)*, 108, 113, 115, 117, 126, 150 152, 155 *(top left / bottom left)*, 156, 157, 158 *(bottom left)*

NEAL WARREN
109, 194, 195

MAX WASTLER
58, 60, 61, 68, 70 *(top)*, 128

DUNCAN WOLFE
22, 85, 93 *(top)*, 154, 155 *(top right / bottom right)*, 158, 159, 174

SPONSORS

THE BEAUTY SHOP
www.thebeauty-shop.com

BILLYKIRK
www.billykirk.com

BUCKSHOT SONNY'S
www.buckshotsonnys.com

CLARKS
www.clarksoriginals.com

DULUTH PACK
www.duluthpack.com

GARRETT LEIGHT
www.garrettleight.com

GITMAN BROS.
www.gitmanvintage.com

THE HILL-SIDE
www.thehill-side.com

HOMESPUN KNITWEAR
www.homespunknitwear.com

REPUBLIC TEQUILA
www.republictequila.com

ROGUE TERRITORY
www.rogueterritory.com

SHINER BEER
www.shiner.com

SHINOLA
www.shinola.com

STOCKSY UNITED
www.stocksy.com

TORRANS MANUFACTURING CO.
www.torransmfgco.com

UNIONMADE
www.unionmadegoods.com